OUTSPANSBERG
SPELONKEN
PIETERSBURG
MARABASTAD
BLOEMHOF
KRUGER
NATIONAL
PARK
Limpopo River
Olifant's River
Steelpoort River
Spekboom R
OHRIGSTAD
KRUGER'S POST
MORGENZON
PILGRIM'S REST
BURGHER'S PASS
MAUCHBERG
SABI R
RIETFNTN
LYDENBURG
WITKLIP
SPITZKOP
SPITZ KOP
ZWAGERSHOEK
PALMIETFNTN
DULLSTROOM
WITPOORT
BADFNTN
SCHOENGEZICHT
KROKODIL RIVER
KOMATI PT
Komati River
ZWARTKOPJES
HELVETIA
ALKMAAR
KAAPMUIDEN
MALELANE
HECTOR SPR
BELFAST
MACHADODORP
DALMANUTHA
BERGENDAL
AVOCA
BARBERTON
Kaap
IPRONG
PAN
WONDERFNTN
GELUK
WITKLOOF
VAN WYK'S VLEI
TWYFELAAR
FRISCHGEWAGD
D Komati River
WITKLOOF
WITBANK
CAROLINA
KLIPSTAFEL
ERMELO
KLIPFNTN
SWAZI
LAND
Vaal River
BEGIN DER LYN
MEERZICHT
AMERSFOORT
ROOI KOPS
GRAS KOP
Zand R
VOLKSRUST
WAKKERSTROOM
ALLEMAN'S NEK
CHARLESTOWN
MAJUBA
POUGWANA MT
LAING'S NEK
BOTHA'S PASS
UTRECHT
VRYHEID
BIGGARSBERG MTS
GLENCOE
DUNDEE
ELAND'S LAAGTE
ARCADIA
LADYSMITH
COLENSO
Tugela River
ESTCOURT
DURBAN
ZULULAND
PORTUGUESE EAST AFRICA
LOURENCO MARQUES
LEBOMBO
DR = DRIFT
FNTN = FONTEIN
PT = POORT
MT = MOUNTAIN
R = RIVER
SPT = SPRUIT
& OF TRANSVAAL

Thomas Gordon-Duff and Lachlan Gordon-Duff
at Drummuir Castle. 1911.

WITH THE GORDON HIGHLANDERS
to the Boer War and beyond

The story of
Captain Lachlan Gordon-Duff
1880-1914

by

Lt.-Col. Lachlan Gordon-Duff

SPELLMOUNT
Staplehurst

British Library Cataloguing in Publication Data:
A catalogue record for this book is available
from the British Library

ISBN 1-86227-095-3

First published in Great Britain 1997
by Travis Books UK, SK11 ODG

This edition published in the UK in 2000 by
Spellmount Limited
The Old Rectory
Staplehurst
Kent TN12 0AZ

135798642

Set in Monotype Imprint by
Alex Dufort, Presteigne
Printed in Great Britain by
T J International Ltd.
Padstow, Cornwall, UK

To Bee in gratitude
and for the Gordon Highlanders,
a fine Regiment, that is no more.

Contents

Acknowledgments

I am most grateful to my friends Bob Carter, Bill Neish, and Alan Campbell, who encouraged me at an early stage to make this book as a tribute to my father. June Jones, and Monica Anton were most helpful on the historical side, and Caroline Gordon-Duff helped greatly in drawing up the family tree.

I would also like to thank David Henshall, Ken Wilson, Julie Smith, and Mary-Anne Martin for their invaluable help,

Above all I must thank three members of the Dufort family; Bee, for her constant encouragement and help with the text, Alex, who designed and produced the book, and Antony, who drew the portrait of the author and designed the dust-jacket. I am also indebted to the artists Payne ('Snaffles') & Ivester Lloyd whose contemporary drawings bring much of the text alive, and to Leo Cooper for his advice.

LACHLAN GORDON-DUFF.

Langley, October 1997.

List of Illustrations

Introduction

I never saw my father. He was killed in action at Festubert in Flanders on 24 October 1914 just a few short weeks into the war. I was born, almost a month later, on 23 November 1914, my birth being described, according to Burke's Landed Gentry, as 'posthumous'. As a child I did not know what the word meant and thought I had some terrible disease.

I was the youngest of three. My sister Pauline (Posie), was the eldest by six years. Next came my brother, Robin, three years older, then me, tail-end Charlie! At my father's death Robin had inherited the estates of Park and Drummuir, to be held in trust for him until his twenty-first birthday.

PARK HOUSE

Both Posie and Robin had the advantage over me for they had actually seen and spoken to Lachlan. They had felt his caress, had heard the sound of his voice, and been held in his arms. I never felt that emotion because he simply was not there, but I did feel a sense of hurt whenever they talked about him in their superior way. I was jealous .

My mother Lydia Pike came from an Irish Ascendancy family and, being both undemonstrative by nature and too upset over his death, said little to me about my father. Anything I did discover I had to ferret out for myself, and two people who knew and were more than willing to tell me about him were, William Murray, our head game keeper at Park who had been in France with my father before he was killed, and Susan Macdonald, our Gaelic speaking Nanny from Crieff. They both loved him, saying what a hero he was, lamenting the tragedy of his sudden death. They made me realise that I must, sometime or other, find out all about him. They were in some respects surrogate parents when I was young and lonely with Posie and Robin away at school, and later when an unsympathetic stepfather had moved in.

The game larder was Murray's fiefdom. He taught me how to gut rabbits and other such matters not discussed in the nursery or drawing room. He told stories about Lachlan, how much he liked him and how brave he was in the Great War. When I was eight my mother decided that the time had come for me to learn to shoot. She gave me a 410 single-barrel folding shotgun, the smallest of the shotgun sizes. Though it had small cartridges it had a long range and if held in the right direction could outdistance larger guns. I was taught by Murray to use this weapon and to be safe. I was heavily chaperoned, quite rightly, in case I shot anyone.

I became rather accurate with it and managed to shoot a snipe which all the other guns had missed, which did not increase my popularity! My stepfather said it was fluke, which of course it was, but he needn't have said so!

I learnt a lot about life from William Murray and the people of the North East of Scotland. At one time I could get by in the Doric. This was frowned upon in the nursery.

To get round the estate, Murray had a motor cycle and side-car into which I was squeezed when we went on fishing expeditions. It was very exciting. Off we went to the Deveron a few miles away. Those were great occasions and it meant a day out with packed lunch and so much wonderful talk, while I learned to fish. He used to smoke the strongest black shag tobacco called 'Bogy Roll', powerful stuff which he cut from an evil-looking lump. After a good deal of preparation it was packed into the pipe, a tubby affair, seldom cleaned, with a silver band around its middle. It was known as a 'Steenhein' (Stonehaven), popular in those parts. When it was lit it emitted a cloud of the strongest smoke in which no midge could live!

Murray was no saint and could drink with the best of them, and fight if necessary. He was always loyal to the family and a true friend. He was devoted to Lachlan and to Lydia and the family. After Lachlan's death he was a great help to her. He never got on with my stepfather. He was out of a John Buchan novel, probably 'Mr Standfast'.

It was a happy area around the Gas House and the game larder, safe from interfering grown-ups, peopled by my allies! The Park Burn ran in between

DRUMMUIR

with a bridge over it to the road leading to the laundry drying green and to the Rampart Field. I later discovered that it was in this field that the English troops camped during the 1745 Jacobite rebellion. They were sent by Cumberland from Banff to capture my Jacobite forebear Sir William Gordon and loot the house. Both missions failed, the Laird had been warned and went into hiding, and the valuables in the house taken to a place of safety.

Sometimes in the night I used to think I heard the clink of tethered horses, the sound of trumpets and men talking, and maybe the pipes skirling defiantly on the Brown Hill behind.

I was lucky to know those lovely people who taught me so much about life. They don't exist now.

In 1924 I was, so my mother informed me, 'growing up' and had to be educated. I was sent five hundred miles away to a preparatory school at

Broadstairs on the Kent coast. The headmaster was a clergyman who smelt of chalk and ruled by fear. Most of the masters there were shell-shock cases from the First World War. I hated the place and was glad to get to Eton, where I was happy and where I learnt how to keep out of trouble. I wasn't good at games except Rugby football which was considered rather non-U in those days!

In 1925 my widowed mother had married a penniless army officer, the son of a dignitary of the Church of Ireland. He had his eye on the family estate of Park and kept calling it his 'little place in Scotland'. Fortunately it was entailed and he couldn't get hold of it. He tried to sack Murray which enraged me. Luckily my mother would not allow that, but did allow one of my father's portraits to be removed from the house.

From Eton I went to Sandhurst and eventually into my father's regiment, the Gordon Highlanders, I recall that it was around this time I made the startling discovery that girls were extraordinarily good fun and far nicer to be with than boys! Young and variously occupied as I was, there was not much time or opportunity to explore Lachlan's life; there were too many interesting things going on. Then, of course, in 1939 came the start of World War II.

I had always been under the impression that all my father's letters and papers had at some time been destroyed, and it came as a wonderful surprise to find after the war, that a large cardboard box of papers had been bequeathed to my sister Posie by Joan Lindsay, my aunt, the beloved sister of my father. It was full of the correspondence between Lachlan and Joan, together with many letters to his father and grandmother.

The letters date mainly from when the two of them were very young to when Lachlan eventually married in 1908, with some correspondence and papers beyond that date up to the time of his death in 1914. Posie died before she could get around to dealing with them. She left them to her son, Andrew Palmer, Ambassador to the Vatican, who had no time for such temporal matters and passed them on to me in 1990. It was tremendously exciting!

I have transcribed and linked together the 179 letters covering the Boer War from 1899 to 1902 to tell the story of Lachlan and the Gordon Highlanders during the three year campaign. I have also made an effort to paint a broad picture of the political and strategical backdrop to the war and its effect on the day to day life of the regiment.

The correspondence covers a wide range of friends and relations, some of whom will crop up throughout this history, displaying their foibles, their idiosyncrasies, and, in some cases, daftness! Their identities are explained under "Biographical Notes".

The last section of this book has been compiled from Lachlan's diaries between the wars and concludes with the last few letters he wrote home from France until his death on 24 October 1914. Through these records I have learnt to admire and love this lively character who was the father I never knew.

Langley June 1997.

William Murray,
head-keeper and
best of friends

Susan Macdonald,
'Nana', to whom I
owe so much

Grandparents

Jane Gordon-Duff née Butterfield
circa 1844

Major Lachlan Duff Gordon-Duff
circa 1848

Lady Tennant née Emma Winsloe
1852

Sir Charles Tennnant
1860

Biographical Notes

Part 1. The Family Circle

My Great-grandfather Lachlan Duff Gordon Duff, while a Captain in the 20th Regiment of Foot, was posted to the garrison of Bermuda in 1841, arriving there in HMS Cornwall. Previously he had been stationed in India and, as ensign had carried the Regimental Colours at Queen Victoria's Coronation. In 1847 he married Jane Butterfield (referred to in these pages as Grandmama). She was the daughter of the Chief Justice of Bermuda. The Butterfields, as a family, still exist and are successful bankers.

Grandmama was fair, lovely and seventeen at the time of her marriage and had the most beautiful auburn hair. There is a portrait of her at Drummuir, the castle built by Admiral Duff in 1850. In the picture Jane looks very sweet and beguiling but, at the same time, very determined! Jane and Great-grandfather were married in 1842 in Bermuda, spending their honeymoon at Park, which must have been a terribly cold and forbidding place after the warmth and sun of Bermuda. Their income at the time was £250 per annum, more than ample for a young family starting out in life. Their first son, my grandfather, Tom, was born in Bermuda on 11 August in 1848.

Great-grandfather's tour of duty in Bermuda ended in 1850 and he was posted home. The return journey across the Atlantic was made by sailing vessel, the only method of transport available at the time, and it took many weeks. Despite what must have been an arduous crossing at a difficult time in her life, Grandmama would not entertain the idea of a nanny but insisted on looking after Tom herself except for the odd little bit of maternal advice and practical help from one or two of the sailors' wives who travelled back with them on the ship. Once home, they settled into the house at Park. In due course, when the Admiral died they moved to Drummuir. Great-grandfather was elected Liberal member of Parliament for Banffshire in 1857.

Drummuir was one of the coldest houses in Scotland, which may be a reason for the oddness of its various inhabitants. For instance, the Admiral's wife is noted for once having torn out of a priceless edition of the works of Voltaire, pages liable to corrupt the morals of the Presbyterian staff! I remember my Aunt Katherine Torrens, at the age of 90, telling me that she was terrified of Grandmama whenever she stayed with her as a child. The old lady looked rather like Queen Victoria. She used to sit by the fire, dressed in black and crowned with a white mutch cap dispensing tiny pink and white comfits to visiting children.

Grandmama died in 1915. She had had three children, Tom, Archie born 17 years later and Helen. The latter who had inherited her mother's lovely red hair, died of tuberculosis shortly after marrying Jack Tennant. They had one daughter also called Helen who died young.

In 1875 Tom married Pauline Emma,'Posie',eldest surviving daughter of Sir Charles Tennant, the multi-millionaire with a self-made fortune from the invention of chemical bleach. A shrewd financier, he was a rich and powerful man. All his daughters married well. Margot married Herbert Asquith, later Prime Minister. Charlotte (the Aunt Charty of these letters) married Lord Ribblesdale and Laura married Alfred Lyttleton.

Pauline, my grandmother, contracted tuberculosis and, in the faint hope that the right sort of climate would help her condition, a small party consisting of Tom, Posie, my father Lachlan, his sister Joan and Nanny from Elgin, travelled to Hyeres, Pietermaritzburg, and later Davos, in what proved to be a vain search for a cure. Pauline died in 1888, leaving her disconsolate husband Tom with my father, then aged eight and Joan aged six. Pauline had loved Park, especially the garden from which she was exiled by her illness and about which she left a touching poem (see Appendix I). Her letters that survive display her deep Christian faith and compassion. She was possibly the nicest of the Tennant sisters and was loved and missed by all who knew her.

In 1893, after five years of lonely widowerhood, Tom married Mildred Walker of Chester. Coming from an entirely different background, she was the complete opposite to the gentle, intelligent Pauline. Mildred and Tom had seven children together, making the grand total of Tom's immediate dependants nine; and he was not a rich man. At about this time Grandmama moved to Braemoriston in Elgin, taking Nanny with her. Joan in her book 'My Recollections' describes Nanny as being wren-like and tiny, with bright brown eyes and quick, neat ways and mannerisms. Joan loved her dearly.

Mildred was jealous of her two step-children, and not all that kind to them. My father was natural heir to the estates, but it must have occurred to Mildred that should anything happen to him, her eldest son Geordie would take his place. However, by the time disaster struck in 1914 Lachlan had married and had two sons so that situation never arose.

BIOGRAPHICAL NOTES

Early Childhood

Thomas and Posie Gordon-Duff on honeymoon
Montreal 1875

Posie and Lachlan aged two months
1880

Lachlan Gordon-Duff aged two years
1882

Posie with Joan and Lachlan
1884

The Search for a cure

1884 The family at Pietermaritzburg, South Africa.

Lachlan with Margot Asquith
Davos 1886

Lachlan and Joan at Davos
Posie in invalid chair. 1886

AT DAVOS, OCTOBER, 1885

Scents from an old Scotch garden
Come floating across the snow,
Of roses and musk and heliotrope
And old fashioned flowers all aglow.

And I stand once more in that garden
And I see with my " inward eye "
The grass walks, the hedge of holly,
With its arches deep and high.

And trails of red tropæolum
Fling their arms round it every year ;
They whisper, " The summer is coming;
They sigh out, "Autumn is here."

And in front the tall white foxgloves
Like stately ladies stand.
And by the gray wall are dahlias,
A gorgeous glowing band.

And further up by the beehives
Are great hedges of sweet-peas
And mignonette and phloxes,
All musical with bees.

And, oh, how I love that garden,
Each flower has roots in my heart,
But God has willed that my garden
And I must be far apart.

O God, wilt Thou once more let me
See that garden fair and bright
Ere Thou takest my hand to lead me
To thy fields of golden light ?

P G-D

Posie and Laura 1888
Last photograph

Lachlan at Torquay 1891

Joan and 'Grandmama' 1892

Poor Joan was used as an unpaid nursemaid to the ever increasing flow of step-brothers and -sisters. She and Lachlan developed a deep affection for one another which is very much in evidence in their correspondence. Joan had a sad life with her husband Jamie Lindsay severely wounded in World War I and losing both her sons in the Mediterranean in World War II.

My father, Lachlan Gordon-Duff, born in Edinburgh on 11 January 1880, was educated in the traditional manner of the time, firstly at a preparatory school on the south coast of England and then at Eton. Later, he attended a crammer at Buxton, and finished his education at the Royal Military College, Sandhurst, passing out 31st in his year. He was posted to the 1st Battalion, The Gordon Highlanders, at Edinburgh Castle in October 1899 before sailing for South Africa, which is where, more or less, this story begins.

Biographical Notes

Part 2. Some people mentioned in this book.

ASQUITH. Herbert. 1st Earl of Oxford & Asquith 1852-1928. Liberal Prime Minister (1908-1916). Second marriage (1894) to Margot Tennant. See Tennant.

BUTTERFIELD. Jane "Grandmama" (1831-1915), daughter of Hon Thomas, Chief Justice of Bermuda. Married 1847 Thomas Gordon-Duff of Drummuir and Park. See Gordon-Duff.

DUFF. Patrick of Hatton (1655-1731) "The great progenitor". See Chapter 7.

DUFF. Admiral Archibald of Park (1777-1858). Built Drummuir Castle (1848) and Hopeman Lodge and Harbour. Succeeded by Major Lachlan Gordon of Park. See Gordon-Duff.

DUFF. General Sir Beauchamp Duff (1855-) At siege of Ladysmith and later in South Africa on Ld Robert's staff. Father of 'Beechie'.

DUFF. Garden of Hatton (1853-). Father of 'Gardie'. m. Annie Urquhart of Meldrum.

DUFF. Garden (b1879).'Gardie' Captain Cameron Highlanders. At Sandhurst with Lachlan. Served in Malta. A great friend of Lachlan's.

DUFF. Beauchamp (b1880). 'Beechie'. 1st Gurkhas.

ELLIOT. Baroness of Harwood (b1903) 'Great Aunt Kay'. 9th daughter of Sir Charles Tennant. Married Rt Hon Walter Elliot.

FORBES. Bill of Rothiemay. 'Kissing Willie'.

GORDON. Sir William of Park (1712-1751) m. Janet Duff 2nd daughter of Ld Braco (who built Duff House). Jacobite ancestor, fought at Culloden, was attainted and forced to live abroad.

GORDON. Col Thomas (1790-1855) succeeded to Park aged 18. Fought at Trafalgar where his brother died in his arms. Served in the Crimea. Died of smallpox. Buried at Fort George. His memorial is in the chapel.

GORDON-DUFF.Major Lachlan of Park 'Great grandfather' (1817-1892) reassumed the name of Duff. m. Jane Butterfield. See Biographical Notes.

GORDON-DUFF. Capt. Lachlan (1880-1914), Gordon Highlanders m. Lydia Pike (see Pike). Fought in S. Africa. Killed in action at Bethune 1914. The author's father.

GORDON-DUFF. Joan (1881-1961). Sister of Lachlan. m. James Lindsay.

GLENNCONNER. Lady Pamela (1871-1928) nee Wyndham m. Edward Tennant 'Eddy'. Eldest son of 'The Bart'. One of three beautiful sisters painted by Sargeant. Known in society as 'The Three Graces'. See Chapter 11, ref. 'Beauty and the Beast'.

GRAHAM-SMITH. Lucy (1860-1942). See Tennant.

GRAHAM-SMITH. Thomas 'irascible fox-hunting husband' of Lucy Tennant.

LINDSAY. James of Carnousie (1871-1940). London Scottish Regt. Husband of Joan Gordon-Duff. Severely wounded in World War I. Two sons killed in action in World War II.

LISTER. Hon. Barbara. Daughter of Lord and Lady Ribblesdale. m. Sir M. Wilson.

LISTER. Hon. Laura. Daughter of Lord and Lady Ribblesdale. m. Lord Lovat.

MANNERS. Violet, (1856 - 1937) Lady Rutland neé Crawford. First cousin of James Lindsay. Portraitist . Her best known work is the marble memorial to her nine year old son in the chapel at Haddon Hall, Derbyshire.

MILES. Marguerite m. 1898 Sir Charles Tennant. His second wife, 45 years his junior. See Chapter 11.

PIKE. Joseph of Dunsland, Glanmire, Co Cork. m. Frances Critchley of Stapleton Towers, Dumfriesshire. Shipping magnate. Father-in-law of Lachlan.

RIBBLESDALE. Thomas 4th baron. (1854 - 1926) 'Uncle Tommy'. m. Charlotte Tennant.

RIBBLESDALE. Lady Charlotte 'Charty'. See Tennant.

TENNANT. Sir Charles (1823-1906) 'The Bart'. m. Emma Winsloe. Father of Pauline and 15 others over a span of 54 years. Millionaire founder of a chemical empire. A genius in finance and commerce and a shrewd collector of works of art. Built baronial castle 'The Glen' near Peebles.

TENNANT. Pauline I 'Posie' (1855-1888) m. Thomas Gordon-Duff of Park and Drummuir. Beloved mother of Lachlan and Joan. Eldest of the Tennant sisters. Died of Tuberculosis at Davos.

TENNANT. Charlotte 'Charty' (1858-1911) m. Lord Ribblesdale. 'She had the Tennant wit and vivacity, tempered by sunny serenity and gentleness'. The closest of the sisters to Lachlan's mother.

BIOGRAPHICAL NOTES

TENNANT. Lucy (1860-1942) m. Thomas Graham-Smith. A gifted artist regarded by some as the most talented of the Tennant sisters.

TENNANT. Margot (1864-1945) m. Herbert Asquith. Perhaps the most vital and enthusiastic member of 'The Souls'. Energetic society hostess. Renowned for her candid and acerbic comments. Nursed her sisters at Davos where they sought a cure for Tuberculosis.

TENNANT. Edward 'Eddy' (1859-1920) m. Pamela Wyndham. Later Ld Glenconner. Peerage given by Asquith in recognition of financial contributions to himself and the Liberal Party.

TENNANT. Harold John 'Jack' (1865-1935) m. Helen Gordon-Duff, sister of Grandfather Thomas Gordon-Duff. Created Under Secretary of State for War by his brother-in-law, Herbert Asquith. See 'The Family Circle'.

TENNANT. Hercules. See Chapter 15.

TENNANT. Nan, daughter of John Tennant (brother of 'The Bart'), a great friend of Joan's.

RUSSELL. Charles. Cousin of Lachlan's descended from Col. Thomas Gordon-Duff of Park.

WYNDHAM. Pamela. (1871 - 1928). See TENNANT. E.

FAMILY TREES

Some Gordon-Duff, Tennant Family & Pike Connections

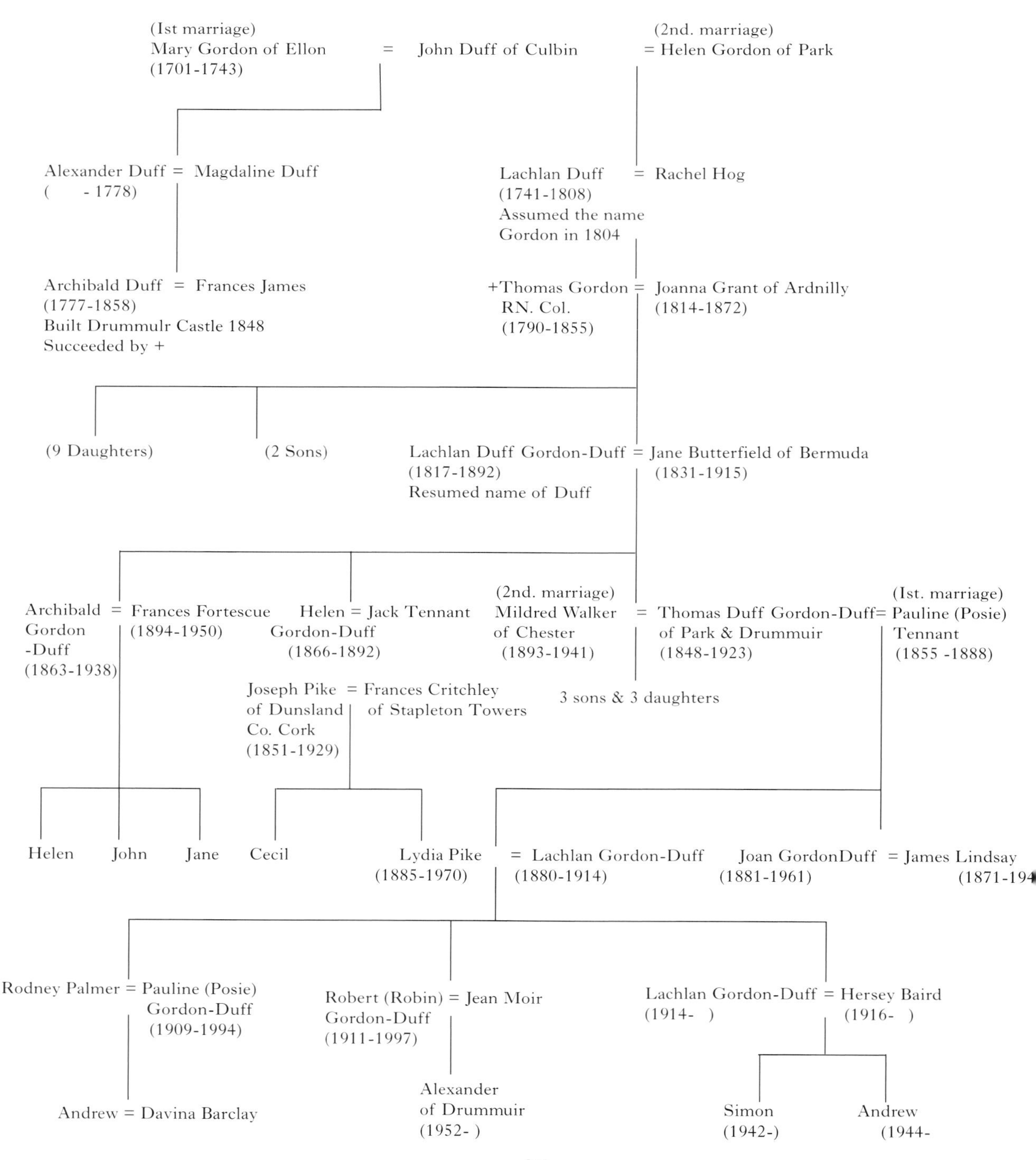

(Ist marriage)
Mary Gordon of Ellon
(1701-1743)
=
John Duff of Culbin
(2nd. marriage)
= Helen Gordon of Park
Alexander Duff = Magdaline Duff
(- 1778)
Lachlan Duff = Rachel Hog
(1741-1808)
Assumed the name
Gordon in 1804
Archibald Duff = Frances James
(1777-1858)
Built Drummulr Castle 1848
Succeeded by +
+Thomas Gordon = Joanna Grant of Ardnilly
RN. Col.
(1790-1855)
(1814-1872)
(9 Daughters)
(2 Sons)
Lachlan Duff Gordon-Duff = Jane Butterfield of Bermuda
(1817-1892)
Resumed name of Duff
(1831-1915)
Archibald Gordon -Duff (1863-1938)
= Frances Fortescue
(1894-1950)
Helen = Jack Tennant
Gordon-Duff
(1866-1892)
(2nd. marriage)
Mildred Walker
of Chester
(1893-1941)
= Thomas Duff Gordon-Duff=
of Park & Drummuir
(1848-1923)
(Ist. marriage)
Pauline (Posie)
Tennant
(1855 -1888)
Joseph Pike = Frances Critchley
of Dunsland
Co. Cork
(1851-1929)
of Stapleton Towers
3 sons & 3 daughters
Helen
John
Jane
Cecil
Lydia Pike
(1885-1970)
= Lachlan Gordon-Duff
(1880-1914)
Joan GordonDuff = James Lindsay
(1881-1961)
(1871-194
Rodney Palmer = Pauline (Posie)
Gordon-Duff
(1909-1994)
Robert (Robin) = Jean Moir
Gordon-Duff
(1911-1997)
Lachlan Gordon-Duff = Hersey Baird
(1914-)
(1916-)
Andrew = Davina Barclay
Alexander
of Drummuir
(1952-)
Simon
(1942-)
Andrew
(1944-

BIOGRAPHICAL NOTES

The Tennant Family

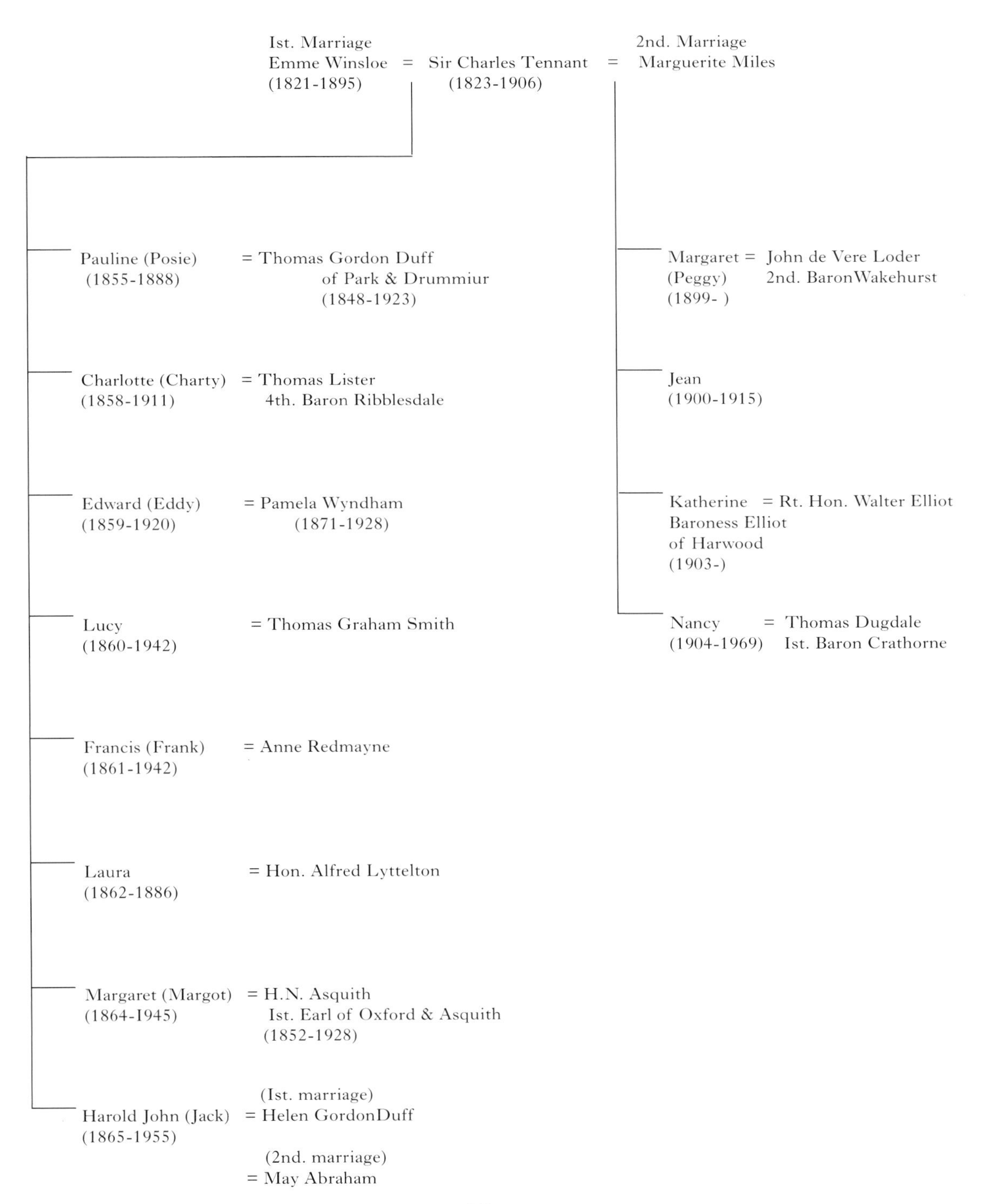

Ist. Marriage
Emme Winsloe = Sir Charles Tennant = 2nd. Marriage Marguerite Miles
(1821-1895)
(1823-1906)
Pauline (Posie) (1855-1888) = Thomas Gordon Duff of Park & Drummiur (1848-1923)
Charlotte (Charty) (1858-1911) = Thomas Lister 4th. Baron Ribblesdale
Edward (Eddy) (1859-1920) = Pamela Wyndham (1871-1928)
Lucy (1860-1942) = Thomas Graham Smith
Francis (Frank) (1861-1942) = Anne Redmayne
Laura (1862-1886) = Hon. Alfred Lyttelton
Margaret (Margot) (1864-1945) = H.N. Asquith Ist. Earl of Oxford & Asquith (1852-1928)
Harold John (Jack) (1865-1955) (Ist. marriage) = Helen GordonDuff
(2nd. marriage) = May Abraham
Margaret (Peggy) (1899-) = John de Vere Loder 2nd. BaronWakehurst
Jean (1900-1915)
Katherine Baroness Elliot of Harwood (1903-) = Rt. Hon. Walter Elliot
Nancy (1904-1969) = Thomas Dugdale Ist. Baron Crathorne

Glossary

Boer words and military abbreviations

berg	mountain
burg	town, literally a borough
burgher	male inhabitant of the Boer Republics possessing full political rights
bush	country covered in a varying degree with trees and undergrowth
C.I.V.	City Imperial Volunteers
donga	cutting made on the surface of the ground by the action of water, sometimes filled, often dry
dorp	village
drift	ford
fontein	spring, literally a fountain
I.L.H.	Imperial Light Horse
inspan	to harness up
kop	hill, literally head
kopje	small hill
kraal	native village, or collection of huts, an enclosure for cattle
kranz	cliff
laager	camp, bivouac
M.I.	Mounted Infantry
nek	pass between two hills of any height
outspan	unharness
pan	pond, full or empty; a saucer-like depression, usually dry in winter
poort	gap, breaking a range of hills, literally gate
R.A.	Royal Artillery
S.A.C.	South African Constabulary
S.A.L.H.	South African Light Horse
sangar	defended position above ground too hard to be dug. Protected by stones.
spruit	watercourse, sometimes dry
veld	the country as opposed to the town; the open country
vrou	wife, woman

CHAPTER ONE

Edinburgh to Capetown 1899

11 August 1899. The War Office to L. Gordon-Duff Esq.

Sir, I am directed by the Secretary of State for War to acquaint you that Her Majesty has approved of your appointment to a Second Lieutenant in The Gordon Highlanders which will appear in the Gazette of this evening.

Further instructions will be communicated to you by the Adjutant General in due course. Your Obedient Servant etc.

1st Gordon Highlanders. Edinburgh Castle
November 3rd 1899

Lachlan joined the regiment on 1 October 1899, which was stationed at Edinburgh Castle. Two days later, on 3 October 1899, Mobilisation Orders were received to prepare to go to South Africa where the political situation had become dangerously unstable.

3 October 1899. Lachlan to Joan. Edinburgh -The Castle.

Yesterday was fine enough. So far I have had no work to do, except appear in Orderly Room at 9.45. I had an exciting time counting coppers with Capt. Macnab! They were from the canteen, coffee room, etc., and were numerous and dirty. Beyond that there was nothing to do, but one has to stay in uniform till after lunch.

I have not yet got my things arranged, but shall get into a room today, as the Battalion returns tonight from Balmoral. There are only recruits here who know nothing, but we are getting out about 500 reserves to take to the Cape.

This is another appalling day, a great wind and driving rain. I live in the Rookery, five or six stories up. There is a splendid view, and plenty of air, though on a day like this it is not extra inviting, and noisy from the wind.

1st. GORDON HIGHLANDERS.
BEFORE THEIR DEPARTURE FOR SOUTH AFRICA
NOVEMBER 1899

3 October 1899. Lachlan to Grandmama

We expect to sail for the Cape in about a fortnight, so there is a fearful lot to do. Everyone is being worked to death. All our Reserves are being called out and their clothing, kits, necessaries etc. have to be got, as well as our own. There are also lots of recruits to be looked after and 101 little things to be settled. Today we are to be medically inspected and sometime to be inoculated against enteric. Father was up here seeing about it. I shall only get away for 24 hours I expect before we set out, as all leave is stopped, but everyone is given a chance to say good bye.

6 October 1899. Lachlan to Grandmama

We are preparing for departure as fast as possible. It is a great business. We leave here late at night on Wednesday. I shall be very glad indeed to be started, and have done with all the worry and fuss. Joan and father are here now. I am afraid Joan's foot is not so well on as I thought it would be. I expected to find her walking on it. I only hope it is not serious. There is a good Doctor coming tomorrow.

The weather has not been very nice; cold and a lot of rain, and a very high wind that makes all the doors and windows rattle and shake like anything. The Provost gave the Grays and us a dinner the other night. Rosebery was there and spoke, as well as other people. It was fairly interesting. I wonder what sort of a passage we shall have? I hope the gales will have blown themselves out before then.

6 October 1899. Lachlan to Joan

Yesterday we were all medically examined, and the men had a little lecture on inoculation.

I am pretty busy today. I am supernumerary orderly officer, for the purposes of instruction. It means getting up before 7.30 and going around to inspect rations of bread and meat before they are served up, then go around breakfast and ask if there are any complaints. I attend two Church Parades and turn out and inspect various guards. I inspect prisoners, canteens, hospitals, go around lunches, and do lots of little duties which keep one on the perpetual hop with no quitting barracks or getting out of uniform for the day.

Will you have a look and see if the little silver match box Macbean gave me is any where about, as I never brought it here? Tell Father the boots turned up all right yesterday. Will you tell me how much I owe you as I am settling up and there are many heavy bills to pay. Ornaments alone cost over £38 with false jewels and sword £10. 16s. 6d., boxes £11 odd, bedding £6. 8s., boots £17 odd, bonnet £14. 14s. In fact, about £100 without tailors, and £50 for furniture, as well as lots of odds and ends, and a heavy bill for camp equipment.

1 November 1899. Post Office Telegram addressed "Duff Drummuir" and

handed in at Edinburgh

"Sail on the 9th in S.S. Cheshire. Lachlan."

The SS Cheshire was to set sail from Liverpool and cousin Nan Tennant visited the Docks to see Lachlan and the Regiment off.

9 November 1899. Nan Tennant to Joan. Liverpool

I have so much to tell you. I feel I could write pages and hardly know where to begin. Do you know, I saw Lachlan off this morning and I'm simply longing to tell you all about it and how it came about that I had this unexpected good luck.

I only arrived in Liverpool from Edinburgh very late last night and, as I was very tired this morning, I had breakfast in bed when in rushed my friend Chris Sharp excitedly waving a letter above her head. She told me her cousin, who is consulting engineer at the Docks, had managed, as a great favour, to get a pass for three people to go on board the S.S. Cheshire to see the Gordon Highlanders embark. You can imagine my delight. I hadn't even known they were going to sail from Liverpool.

I simply threw my clothes on and then we started off. When we got to the Docks we found a dense crowd of people, but we managed to push our way through and find Mr Ramsay who piloted us on board. The whole place was a scene of wild excitement. The lower deck seemed alive with redcoats all busy stowing away stores, kits ammunition etc. On the upper deck were groups of young officers and their relations talking together - but no Lachlan.

I thought I would never find him in such a crowd and at last I went up to a very nice young officer and I said, "Would you mind telling me if Lieutenant Gordon-Duff is on board, and where can I find him?" He said "I know he's somewhere, I'll go and find him for you." And off he went in search of the missing relative, returning after some time with the person in tow, who looked just a trifle surprised at seeing us as you can imagine. He did look so handsome and wore his kilt better than anyone else. I should like to have hugged him but thought his new dignity might be somewhat ruffled at such a proceeding.

He was Orderly for the day and fearfully important, continually in request, running hither and thither at the bidding of his superior officer, standing by when the men had their breakfasts served out, inspecting the food, and ready to attend to any complaint. It amused me to stand on the upper deck and watch him do the "Officer on duty", as if he had been in the service for years. Every now and then, when he had a minute to spare, he gave a hand wave in my direction, and once, I was sorry to say, he winked, which I don't consider at all military! In spite of all he had to do, we managed to get in scraps of conversation during the intervals, and I sat with him while he had his breakfast.

I felt very proud of my cousin. I saw his cabin which looked quite a fair size for two. He is sharing it with a Lt. Lumsden. Then he took me to see the four horses in their narrow stalls, and by that time it was getting late. The bell rang and there was just time for a warm hand clasp, a God speed, and we were hurried off.

We asked when the boat would start, but they said not for an hour and a half. We did not feel we could wait all that time in the crowd, so we rather reluctantly retraced our footsteps homewards. Then a brilliant idea struck us, at least it was more Chris's suggestion than mine. I remembered suddenly that Lachlan said he hadn't seen a paper and he didn't think there was one on board. All the officers had been busy since early morning, so Chris and I took the first tram into town rushed into a newsagents, seized a few papers and things to read, had them tied up and addressed, scrawled a note, put it inside, rushed out again down to the electric railway and got down to the Docks again in no time, very out of breath.

The Police made a feeble effort to bar our passage but we paid no attention. Across the gangway and on board, they were ready to start, and we only had time to hand the parcel to a soldier and get off again. Then we stood at the Dock Pier while the big vessel slowly edged away from the side. Chris and I scanned the upper deck but no Lachlan was to be seen, so we called up to a young officer, who was leaning over the side, to ask if Lieut. Duff was anywhere near. He shouted back, "On duty, can I give a message?" We told him that we had left a few papers with a soldier and would he see that Lachlan got them? He waved to show he understood, and of course we waved by way of thanks. The Band struck up, and the crowd shouted "Hurrah, for the Gordons!" while the women waved their handkerchiefs till the boat disappeared through the Dock Gates.

It was a wonderful sight and one I shall never forget. I should have enjoyed it even if I had not been the proud possessor of a Lieut. Cousin, and that of course made all the difference, and I assure you I have bristled with importance ever since whenever the Gordon Highlanders have been mentioned. I am going to send you a Liverpool paper with a full account of the embarkation, but I am so glad to have been able to write to you about it all, and hope I have left nothing out.

9 November 1899. Post Office Telegrams . Lachlan to Miss Gordon-Duff. Drummuir Station

Just starting. Bright sunshine. Orderly Officer for the day. Three ladies to see me off. Nan being one of them. Lachlan.

13 November 1899. Lachlan to Joan. S.S. Cheshire, South Lat. 36. 30

I hope you are getting on well and are able to run about again. It is not a week since we left Edinbro, but in its way has contained more variety than the usual run.

As I write, we are in a beautiful calm blue sea and sky, a delicious air just right, and a lazy gentle roll of the big ship which is very soothing It is a pleasant contrast after the last few days of turmoil and cold, for we have had a rocky time of it. Not geometrically rocky, as we should probably not be here now, but in the other sense of the word.

To begin at the beginning! After an exhilarating march to Waverly through a wonderful and wildly enthusiastic crowd we had a beastly cold and uncomfortable journey to Liverpool. At 1.30 there was a shouting crowd at Carlisle, where we paraded, shivering up and down the platform, and at 5.30 had a small and very insufficient breakfast at Blackburn. Liverpool at 7.30 and a tedious wait, dark, wet, and cold, then another triumphant march of about 1 mile to the Docks.

I never saw such a crowd. They were waving their arms off, and were full of blessings, and every one wanted a bit of Kruger, usually his whiskers, so he must have very big ones.

At the Docks it was a great job getting arms, ammunition and baggage of all sorts. I was after all Orderly and had a lot to do, though generally did not know what. About 11, to my astonishment, Nan and two friends turned up! I could not look after them as well as I ought, owing to the calls of a devoted country, but I think they were amused. It was such a wonderful sight, every available spot filled with dense cheering crowds.

At 2 p.m. we started. It was a never to be forgotten scene, a lovely afternoon, lots of great ships, a vast crowd, all for us, and indescribable enthusiasm. All down the Mersey we were escorted by pleasure-boats packed with crowds of people, right out to sea. They yelled and played patriotic tunes, and we answered back with a vengeance. They all left at New Brighton, some feeling rather squeamish I expect from the antics of their boats. We all cheered, the foghorn blew, and every hooter of any description tooted away from far and near at us. It was certainly a record send off. Once away, we began to settle down. You can imagine what a lot had to be done.

Luckily it was absolutely calm, but about midnight it began to blow, and by morning we were in a gale of wind and heavy sea, (even the ship's officers called it a gale. This for father who is a sceptic!). Strange to say I have turned into a very good sailor, and was one of the select body who disposed of meals and rather enjoyed it.

I never saw such pitching. The ship is much too light, having practically no cargo so she fairly danced, with huge great waves and clouds of spray coming right over the Bridge. We had to slow down to avoid shipping too much water and for fear of smashing up the temporary structures for troops. We did not roll too much but pitched heavily.

I got soaked by a huge wave right up on the very highest deck by the bridge, and anywhere to windward except the very stern was swimming. It was most exhilarating watching the big white-topped waves that seemed as if they must come over but always with a great swoop sank into a mighty hollow. The very

EMBARKING FOR SOUTH AFRICA. NOVEMBER 1899

stern was the place to watch. It was dry and one had a glorious view of the big boat, her bows one moment miles beneath and next soaring above my head, descending with a great splash which sent up a vast column of white spray. A magnificent sight, but a bit damp! Later we began to roll as well, and the ship showed us what she could do.

Everything movable such as boxes, crockery etc. led us a rare dance, crashing about from side to side. In fact we had a boat stove in, a horse rather badly cut, and breakages to crockery innumerable. A teapot during tea hopped across the table and emptied itself on my lap. The poor stewards were in despair, and nearly everyone driven frantic.

This was a bit too strong, so we turned round and steamed north-west for some hours to ease the ship and give the horses a chance of being secured properly, but about 11 we resumed the course as much as possible and kept up the rolling all night and next day.

The cabins were pandemonium till everything that was moveable was secured, and there was some difficulty in staying in bed, a good many people being chucked out. I managed to sleep very well in spite of it. The men had a fearfully bad time of it, all crowded together, and nearly all very sick. My servant, who said he was never ill, was as bad as the rest of them, not turning up for a long time. Lots of officers were very bad, but on the whole we did pretty credibly. The only mitigating points were a fine sunny day, and being quite well when I never expected to be. Saturday was very rough, but gradually improved, yesterday continuing the improvement and everybody pretty well recovered. Now it is simply perfect, though it is a marvel how this ship can roll on a calm looking sea. They say she is usually very steady, but this trip has about 2000 tons stowed in her very bottom, too low down as she gets a swing like a pendulum and never stops. I think we would miss it if she did.

We have not sighted many ships, but there was great excitement yesterday morning when we overhauled "The Columbia" with the 10th Hussars on board. We were very close and had a long signalling conversation. They were all very well but going pretty slow, and will not arrive till 3 or 4 days after us, which is satisfactory. There have been the usual minor excitements, such as a porpoise, seagulls and stormy petrels. Meals are much looked forward to just now. We had no service yesterday for some reason, though the men had two extempore ones of their own.

Today the band and pipes have been going, and everything is very pleasant. The men are very good and give no trouble. We have about 300 Army Service Corps on board, also Royal Army Medical Corps and their officers. The 2nd Lieutenants have physical exercises from 8-9 a.m. and arms drill 3.30 to 4 p.m., besides an infernal exam daily from 11 to 12 on various subjects set by the Adjutant, which is beastly. They will persist in bullying us.

The ship's 3rd officer is a very nice chap. He took me round to his cabin yesterday and gave me some awfully good cigars, which he gets in Burma by the thousand. We are just caught up in our turn by "The Bavarian" with the Connaught Rangers and the Dublin Fusiliers on board. She will pass us in a few hours I expect, but is still some way behind. Later she passed within 150 yards. I never saw such a pack, she has 2300 troops aboard, and looked Red with them. We both cheered and played tunes as usual. With glasses it would have been possible to recognise a friend on board. The men on her poop tied a lot of handkerchiefs and trailed them aft, offering us a tow.

Tuesday. Another lovely day. Cricket is being started on the Hurricane deck. Tomorrow we reach Las Palmas, and I hope will get ashore. It is distinctly hotter every day, though there is a sea breeze. My information is about exhausted, and you will hear no more until Capetown. We are expecting to overhaul several more troopers on the way. This is a sort of family epistle, so give my Love to all. I hope Uncle Jack has done well with the pheasants.

It is extraordinary to think that, in 1899, a part of the British Army was actually going to war dressed in 1854 Crimean Red! This time the enemy was not the Russian but the Boer; a sharp shooting farmer, equipped with the latest Mauser rifle and Krupp artillery. On arrival at Capetown the units were in fact issued with Khaki.

At this time Joan was staying with her grandfather, Charles Tennant at his Haddington home, Amisfield. She wrote to Lachlan at sea.

16 November 1899. Joan to Lachlan. Amisfield

I see this morning that the Cheshire has passed Las Palmas; it gave me a thrill of joy to read even this dry newspaper news of you, dear brother. No words can say how I loved getting your note sent off I suppose by a pilot. Thank you for it, and for your telegram from Liverpool. The latter went to Drummuir and John stupidly sent it on by post instead of wiring it so I only got it with your note.

I am always thinking of you. I do hope it has been fine, and that you are well and happy. Nan sent me a splendid account of her seeing you at Liverpool. Lucky girl, I envied her horribly. We are still here as you see. Tomorrow or Saturday Barbara and I go to Gisburn.

There have been some nice people staying here, Uncle Frank and Aunt Annie, Sir John Maxwell who was very amusing and delightful (though he never threw me a bone, as Barbara would say), a charming Mrs Whitbread and now an extraordinary Mr Crum-Ewing, who looks exactly like the Elgin grocer. I cannot realise he is a Gentleman.

May is a very poor hostess. She goes and plays Bridge with the men in the billiard room immediately they come in from shooting, till bed time, which is not amusing for us. However the last two evenings we have persuaded the men to play innocent games with us. Mrs Whitbread introduced us to a charming game yesterday with matches in a wine glass. You each extract one in turn and pile it up on the top, so that it gets more and more difficult and if you upset the pile, your adversary gets it.

Granpapa Tennant came yesterday. He is very proud of his new daughter, 'The finest baby I ever saw.' She must be if she takes after her mama! I wonder if you are thinking of our mother who died 11 years ago today? I am sure she is watching over you.

Oh! If only this war would hurry up and be done with. I had a delightful letter from Cousin Annie. Beauchamp Duff was only 22 when he was first in action at Tel-el-Kebir. Such beautiful weather here, I hope you have it fine too. We have seen nothing of the meteors, so I suppose they must come into orbit in the daytime. If you saw them you must have had a glorious view.

We lunch with the shooters every day nearly. We had a lovely drive yesterday to get to them. It is not really pretty country, but the colouring was so beautiful yesterday. Barbara is rather jealous of your ship being ahead of the Isinore. I suppose you will get there a good deal sooner. I wish I could keep you back.

'John' who encountered Joan's wrath for not forwarding the telegram, was the butler at Drummuir. Uncle Frank was Sir Charles' second son. married to Ann Redmayne. Aunt Annie, was the wife of cousin Beauchamp Duff, who fought at the battle of Tel-el-Kebir. Their only son, Gardie, was a great friend of Lachlan's.

Barbara was the daughter of Charlotte Ribblesdale and married Sir M. Wilson. After the Boer War, Lachlan was to spend much time at Gisburn hunting.

Lachlan's father Tom, was in many ways a sad man made so by grieving for his beloved Pauline dying so young. As a child I remember him, a small man with a grey pointed beard, dressed in a knickerbocker suit. He was reputed to be very intelligent.

Social activities in the north-east of Scotland in winter were few and far between. Because of the snow, the lairds could not get out and about much. They spent much of the time staying at each other's castles or houses for shooting parties. There was a great deal of social interaction, and many families intermarried.

EDINBURGH TO CAPETOWN 1899

Ladies' maids, gamekeepers and valets all had to accompany the lairds and their parties as they travelled from castle to castle. They had their own good time in the servants hall.

27 November 1899. Lachlan to Father. S.S. Cheshire at Sea off Las Palmas.

You will think it odd no doubt not hearing before, but though we looked in at Las Palmas, there was no post. We arrived there between 1 and 2 a.m. I was on deck for a few minutes before we dropped anchor, but did not stay, as we were to go ashore next day. Apparently, as soon as we were anchored, a boat from the man-of-war in the harbour put off and gave us orders to go straight to sea again. They refused to take any letters or anything else, so we turned round and were miles away by morning. They did us out of a run on shore, which was rather annoying.

28th - We had pretty hot weather for a few days. Afterwards it was puckish going and people were sleeping on deck. A whole crowd of us were inoculated. It was quite a simple job. We were done at about 12, and by 2 o'clock I felt as cold and as wretched as it is possible to be, and a short time later was in a high fever of about 104, which lasted about 36 hours. Lots of people had terrific headaches and severe vomiting, so it was not a very pleasant operation, but after two days all were well. We passed very close in to Cape Verde on a lovely day. It is rather a pretty place, a round hill to the north with a lighthouse on it and long undulating hills south of it, with a white house in a sort of park [with] trees and grapes etc.

There were great games crossing the line. Neptune and his wife (two of the biggest men), with a doctor and with two barbers came on board, and a big sail was rigged. Crowds of people were had up and were shaved with a horrible made-up soap and wooden razor. After taking some delightful medicine and pills they were tipped over backwards into the bath and a big hose turned on them. Several officers were done, and numbers of men. The ship's chief officer, a jolly little chap who was superintending things, was unofficially hoisted in by the bystanders! The hose was turned on anyone and everyone in the neighbourhood, and eventually Neptune and his crew and victim were tipped off his platform into the bath. They were beautifully got up, and altogether it was very funny.

The moment we got across the line it turned very cold, and we were very glad to get out of Khaki into Serge, and sleeping below again. It was just like being in the Channel. There were squalls of drenching rain at intervals lasting about half an hour. The cold weather has lasted to the present moment. The ship's people say they have never seen anything like it. I have been sleeping in two blankets and a rug and have been none too warm.

There have been a lot of sports for the men. The best of all is the blindfold boxing. It is the funniest thing I have almost ever seen. There are one or two very good concerts as well. Your favourite song, "It's a fine quiet place where I am lodging now", being given great effect by a comic man, with verses made to suit the ship. It was wonderfully clever, and quite brought the house down.

Macbean also got a concert up in which all the 2nd Lts. had to sing. I luckily got hold of "The Campdown Races", a nice simple tune and eventually everybody present from the Colonel downwards had to sing.

It seems incredible that we arrive at Capetown tomorrow, when we shall hear what is to become of us after we disembark. It is a lovely evening, though cool, and with a swell that makes us pitch till the screws come out of the water. There is a fearful bustle and fuss on board, getting out kits and arms etc. There are numberless deficiencies of all sorts, and everyone seems to be thieving from his neighbours! The days have got so long and bright, it seems as if it could not be near Xmas. I wonder where we shall be when it arrives? Perhaps you will be skating on the loch, and we shall be entering Pretoria.

10.45 p.m. - We have had a tremendous night of it. A great dinner with champagne and tons of speeches from all the ship's officers and the Colonel and crowds of others. Later there was a sweepstake on the time of arrival at Capetown morrow, in which I drew a number that sold for 14 shillings. The first I've ever made, as I generally draw blank.

I wonder where we shall be this time tomorrow, on the train, at Capetown, elsewhere, or still on board, on the way to Durban or Port Elizabeth? In some ways I shall be sorry to leave the ship, as we have had a very good time, and not too much to do.

The 1st Battalion The Gordon Highlanders had arrived in Capetown to fight a formidable enemy who was not only flexible and mobile, but armed with the latest German artillery, ironically all supplied by the German Emperor, Queen Victoria's grandson.

The Boer was a dangerous foe and had to be taken seriously. He knew the veldt and was an accurate shot on horseback, and each man owned his own horse. The Boer's main weakness was his lack of skill in static battle warfare.

EDINBURGH TO CAPETOWN 1899

The British Government failed to take the Boers seriously to begin with and generally assumed that the war would be over in a matter of months. Since the Crimean War in 1854 against the Russians, the only wars fought by the British were small tribal affairs; battles fought defending outposts of the Empire. At the start of the Boer war some of the generals were definitely out of practice. Their bravery and courage were beyond question, but such vital matters as hospitals and hygiene did not seem to have high priority in their thinking.

16 November 1899. Joan to Lachlan at sea. Drummuir

We have not yet got any letters from Las Palmas. I suppose there have been no mails from there lately. We are wondering so much where you are. I hope (don't be angry with me, dear) that you are still a long way from Capetown. I can't bear to think of the time when you will be landed there and actually "On active service". You will take care of yourself, won't you?

I left Gisburne last Friday and went to Edinburgh to see the Doctor that evening. He seemed quite surprised at the beautiful way in which I walked, and said it was not necessary to take any of the pellets out but that I was to behave in my usual and ordinary way now, so I can no longer ever pretend to be interesting. I rather enjoyed my invalid time. I got so much attention, and I love that, as I suppose does every human being. The Doctor was quite charming. I quite wished I could go and see him again.

I stayed with the Aunts for 3 nights. It was very nice seeing them. Aunt Isabella was much better and getting up again. It is extraordinarily warm but fine here. We went to Buchromb yesterday and were nearly blown out of the carriage. The Lumsdens are leaving this week. Next week the Auchlunkart people and the Sheriff and Lady Mary are coming here.

I have not begun this letter with Xmas or New Year wishes; I can't realise that you are so many weeks away from us. But you know that I am always praying for Xmas and New Year blessings for you all the year round especially now. I can't bear to think of Xmas without you. It will be a sad Xmas all through the land.

Everyone asks tenderly after you. They collected £ and £'s here and the same at Park for the War Fund, wasn't it wonderful? So much money has been collected all through the county that people are wondering what is to be done with it. There is nothing exciting to tell you, and my paper is finished, so farewell, my beloved; it feels like years since you left; if only it were time for you coming back!

With more good wishes and love and blessings than I can express or even think of for your Xmas and New Year.

While Lachlan and the regiment were on the last leg of their sea voyage and preparing to enter port, Methuen had already fought the Battle of Modder River gaining a victory over retreating Boers.

CHAPTER TWO

Capetown to Enslin 1899

LACHLAN GORDON-DUFF
SOUTH AFRICA 1899

7 December 1899. Lachlan to Joan. Orange River

It is nearly a week since we landed and as you see we have got this far. We started for De Aar in two trains on Thursday, 3 weeks from starting. We entered Table Bay on a glorious morning, anchoring about 12. It was the most lovely place imaginable. We nearly ran over a great black fish, a kind of whale, who jumped right out of the water then raced with a shoal of dolphins and played with the seals. The sea was beautifully calm but we rolled tremendously, very sedate and dignified, but it was if we were going upside down.

The Bay was packed with empty transports of every size and description, but more were still pouring in. We passed the Canadian contingent as we entered and the Hussars came in next day. I got ashore to shop, one hour to go and come back in, and did marvels in the time; stylos, housewives, dubbin, tobacco, papers, etc. by the ton. The first train with all the officers but 11, and 5 Coys, left about 11 a.m. on a 40 hour journey. B Company had to clean the ship so we were the last to go. We were quite sorry as the voyage was very comfortable and the ship's officers were awfully nice chaps.

Our train left at 2.30, amid great cheering. We had a big corridor carriage and were very comfortable. Dingwall and I shared a compartment and as we had no Col. or Adjutant to worry us, we were very well off, especially as the Mess President was with us with the eatables and 2 servants! We had regular meals of excellent quality. We were to have breakfasted at a certain station on Friday but were two hours late and, on arriving at a station called Magersfontein in the Great Karoo (you will see it on the map), a delightful man called Mr Logan, to whom all the surrounding country belongs, met us, gave the men breakfast with tea, and to the officers a magnificent feed and fresh milk included.

We were lucky being late. Logan is very wealthy and a member of the Upper House; in fact the swell of the country. Soon after leaving Capetown the country became rather barren, with beautiful hills the whole way, and a tufty growth over the ground very like the hills at Glen. There was a fair amount of cultivation of sorts, rarely a village to be seen, but lots of little stations where we often stopped, and terrific gradients like a switch-back up which we went often at a walking pace, and once stuck having to go down and get up speed for a charge. We barely managed it, and thought we should have to get out and push. We were timed to get to De Aar at 1.45 on Saturday morning, but only got there at 5. We were at once ordered to go straight on to Orange River, where we still are, being shot out into a sandy desert at about 11 o'clock on a real South African summer's day!

For about 3 hours we loafed in the sun. While a camp was being marked out and tents pitched, we lunched in the station, the water khaki-coloured. Then we relieved the Seaforths on Outpost duty. B Company was among those detailed, and at 5 p.m. we paraded and marched across a sandy waste to some low-lying hills about a mile off.

It was hot, and the road was deep and sandy. My new Edinburgh shoes played me false, raising a big blister on each heel, so I barely struggled up, and to improve matters, at the top, my nose bled ferociously refusing to stop. I had a slight touch of sun, and they said it was lucky I bled as it relieves matters. I felt very stupid and did not enjoy going round 5 pickets on a rough stony path which was difficult to find and marked by white-washed stones at intervals.

I had to sleep out with Number 3 picket, and keep alternate watches of 2 hours with a corporal. It was very tiring and cold. I had a rug and great-coat, and did not enjoy it a bit, especially visiting sentries with sore feet, over invisible rocks. The whole picket got under arms from 4 to 5 a.m., the likely time of attack, and being only a night picket we marched into Number 6 picket where we spent the day. It was blowing a dust storm, simply horrible, a terrific sun, no shelter but what we could rig up with the blankets, stones and stunted shrubs. And the dust! I again bled that night, when luckily we got a tent up by mule transport, and I stayed in it till 1.30 a.m. when I watched till 5 a. m. Next day was a bit better, less dust and a tent.

We also bathed in the Orange River, which was refreshing, though it was full of sand. It is not unlike parts of the Spey, but dirty brown and deeper and not so swift. There is a magnificent railway bridge across it. All our drinking water is from it, pumped up, and brought over a mile. One would hesitate before washing in it at home. It is often tepid, no ice of course!

We were three days on the hill, and relieved by the Shropshires who had just arrived. That was Tuesday. We were then to march to Belmont at 4 a.m. on Wednesday, but it was countermanded, and we go by train today, Thursday, to Modder River, at 4 p.m. This is the most vile place on earth. It is blowing today and the dust penetrates everything. Meals are awful; we eat tons of dust, and drink more. For the last four days I have had a trying headache, chiefly from indigestion and the sun.

The men keep wonderfully well, and play football when it is cool in the evening and mornings. It is all the exercise they get and need. Officers' and men's kilts are covered across the apron with khaki. Officers all carry rifle and bayonet, like the men with no badges or rank differences. They say it has greatly reduced mortality in them.

So far we have not suffered from fleas, but flies are beastly. We only saw one snake on the hill, it was a Puff Adder. It was just the place for them. I shall be thankful to get out of this; the dust is unbearable. They say it is worse than India. Modder River is I believe higher and cooler. I have had a nasty cold in my head ever since we landed, which I believe the dust keeps going.

Clowes, our latest-joined, came up yesterday from Capetown, where he was Base Officer. He saw Gill the astronomer, who had father's letter, and he says he is a dear old boy, and sent me all sorts of messages.

We have not yet had any letters, and I have not heard how you are getting on. By the time you read this, all sorts of things will have happened and I hope we are to have a big fight shortly soon. I have no more news, so love to all till next week.

THE BATTLE OF BELMONT. DECEMBER 1899.

The Battalion was off to Belmont at once to turn out the Boers who had blown up a culvert and who were holding the line. Belmont was one of the small stations on the way north to Modder River. It had been held by a small force of Boers who retreated to their main positions at Magersfontein after a minor confrontation with the British. The Modder River would feature prominently in this war.

There were three main railway lines that ran north from the main ports through South Africa; Capetown to Kimberly, 647 miles and thence on to Mafeking, via the all important De Aar junction. Port Elizabeth to Bloemfontein, 450 miles, branching off at Naaupoort junction for De Aar and the north: and Durban to Johannesburg, 483 miles, via Ladysmith. This latter line remained in Boer hands until it was retaken in February of the following year. Even then it was not fully operational for some time.

There were approximately 10,000 British troops in South Africa, all of whom were some 600 miles away from the main ports. All the provisions for these men had to be carried along the single track railways. These were also the only real lines of communication between the front and the ports, and thence the rest of the world. They had to be kept open.

The only other forms of transport were horse, mule, or ox-drawn wagons and, of course, foot. The roads were almost non-existent and, for all practical purposes, impassable in bad weather. Movement was slow and only averaged about 15 miles a day. If there was not enough grazing for the oxen, they had to be abandoned.

The Boers on the other hand had no such problems. They were fighting in their own country; food was plentiful locally and the population friendly. As long as they could retain their high mobility they had some chance of success.

The altitude varied between Johannesburg at 5600 ft to Ladysmith at 3284 ft and this, together with the heat and the lack of water, took the men some time to get used to. There should have been a period of acclimatisation but Lachlan and his regiment went straight from the boat to the train, and a few days later were on picket duty on the hills around Orange River station. The men had little or no training, were in a strange land and up against an enemy who was expert in mobile warfare.

Lachlan was on escort duty at Modder River.

10 December 1899. Lachlan to Father

The right half Battalion left Orange River 3 days ago for Belmont, arriving late that evening. Next morning half B Company were sent out to repair the line which the Boers had destroyed. It was a longish job, in spite of engineers and native plate layers, but we finished without being attacked. I will give details later. Yesterday at 3.30 a.m. B Company were ordered to escort a Battery of Howitzers here. There were endless delays and we didn't get off till 8 a.m. nor arrive till 5 p.m. 30 miles! The other 3 Companies were supposed to arrive that evening and wretched Dingwall and self spent the night rushing about expecting them. They came at 5 this morning and it rather knocked me up today, but I have been much fitter lately.

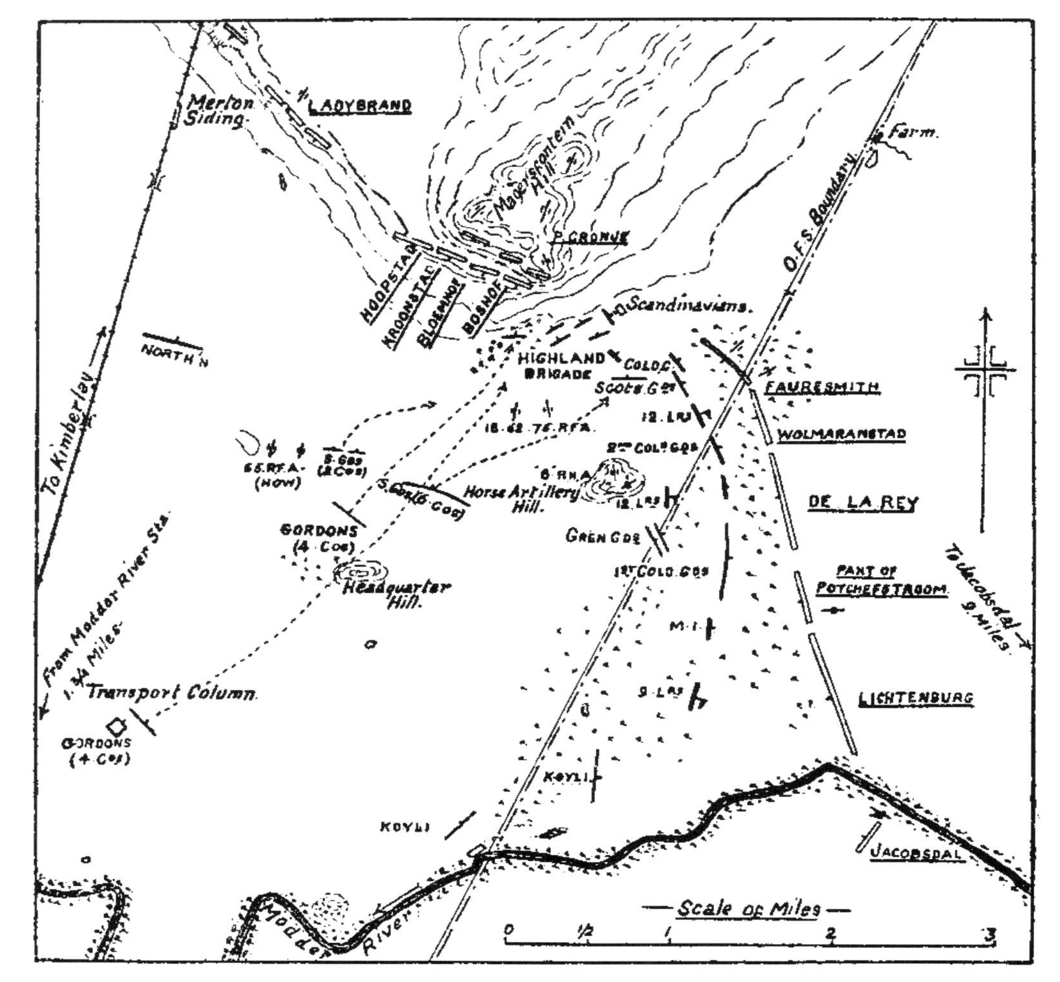

MAGERSFONTEIN, 11TH DECEMBER, 1899

The rest of B Company came this afternoon and we are attached to the Highland Brigade. There was an artillery duel this afternoon at long range, in which we saw shells bursting, some close to the camp, but no danger to us. I do not know if it hurt the Boers, but we have a lovely naval gun which gives them socks up to 10000 yds. Possibly tomorrow the big fight begins, and no one knows what will happen, but we will do our best. There was rain here today for which I was very grateful, and I hope the weather will keep cool. The post is just going, give my love to all, it may be the last time.

13 December 1899. Lachlan to Joan. Modder River near Grasfontein

I got your's and father's letters this morning. It was a great pleasure as you can imagine, the others never found me. I suppose they are still in Capetown. Since I wrote the other day, there has been an awful time here but I will return to the time we left Orange River, the 8th I think. The first four Companies were suddenly ordered off Belmont way to turn an indefinite number of Boers from a culvert somewhere, to hold it until reinforcements came; very vague. However, we started in the expectation of an immediate fight, but after a great delay starting at 5 o'clock we weighed anchor, the men in open trucks and the officers in a cattle truck. We did not go fast, and reached Belmont after dark, having seen no enemy, but we heard that morning they had blown up a considerable portion of the railway a few miles further on.

It was a great job pitching camp in the dark etc. but about 10 p.m. the officers were given dinner by the Munster Fusiliers in the Station Hotel, owned by a captive Boer, and run by his wife and daughter. The house had many shell holes. Belmont was where we turned the Boers from a strong position last month, with hard fighting on both sides. At 3.30 a.m. the camp had to rouse and stand to arms for an hour, as this is the likely time of attack. After that B Company started in trucks with a few engineers and line directors to repair the Cape Government railway.

We ran for about 10 miles to Grasfontein, a lovely veldt station, where the wily Boer had been operating with some success. The first thing we saw were the lines standing up in the air in a very peculiar way, beautifully twisted, so for a few yards we stopped and started. Luckily it was a cool cloudy day, and we got along comfortably enough. We hauled up the repaired line, mended the permanent way and, with the assistance of the native plate layer, put down fresh sleepers and rails. It was very hard work and Dingwall and self were slave drivers because unless we kept the men at it, they would gradually drop away and sit down to look on. It was great fun for all but the few who stuck to it.

We had rations with us; Bully Beef and biscuits, with tolerably clean water. Dingwall and I even had some rain water. In some places the Boers had just taken the rails and turned them bodily over, sleepers and all, so they had only to be put back again, which did not take very long. I had bad back ache, the last of the series, and did not enjoy it, but we did so well that we were particularly mentioned by the Ordinance Corps Engineers.

We met the Armoured Train with a Company of Seaforths in it, who were further up, and we each started the last bit at opposite ends. We all went about 4 p.m. in trucks, though Dingwall and myself went in the engine. It went backwards and we ran into a sharp shower, which cut you up if you tried to look into it.

We were all armed in case of attack, but the 12th Lancers, Australians and Rimington Scouts were scouring the country in all directions, and there were pickets on lots of hills, so we saw nothing. The wires along the line were all destroyed and were being temporarily repaired, and they had a drunken look. The country is quite treeless with very little water, and heathy scant grass and scrubby prickly plants on mostly horrid red sand and boulder-covered hills. It gave fine cover to the Boers, and was difficult to climb, very hot by day, and horribly cold by night. We had by no means too much water. It is very unmistakably Africa, in every way.

That same evening Dingwall and I climbed a hill a mile from camp, where we had attacked the Boers. There were all sorts of relics. Old bullets, cartridge cases, shells etc. also a partially buried Boer, old saddles, helmets - every blessed thing in fact.

Next morning B Company were told to be ready by 6.30 a.m. to act as escort to a battery of Howitzers. We were under arms as usual before sunrise but the infernal battery were ages entraining and we only got off by 8.15, this time in a saloon as it is called here and most of the men in open trucks. It ought to have been a 2 hour journey even in this place, being about 30 miles, but for some reason the traffic got blocked, and we did not get to Modder River Bridge until 5 p.m. The bridge had been wrecked by the Boers, and a wonderfully ingenious substitute put up by our Royal Engineers. The original bridge being very high, the temporary one was approached through steep and deep cuttings to the river.

We pitched our tents by the Seaforth and Highland Brigade Lines. Numbers of them were absolutely crippled owing to the effect of the battle, when they were on their faces for hours with the backs of their knees being burnt off. They could hardly hobble with great bandages. The Black Watch were the worst of all. That night Dingwall and self spent a wretched time. We dined off very hot tinned curried chicken which we had bought at a wretched store, though some quince jam was a slight improvement. Then we had to go and meet the rest of our half Battalion, who were to come from Belmont that night at 8, but of course they were late, eventually arriving at 3.30 a.m.

Next morning, the 11th, we were all up at 2.30 a.m. in inky dark and pelting rain, which luckily stopped. The Battalion fell in and marched off to go as escort to a huge convoy of supplies for the attackers. We went about 2 miles and then waited. We could hear the big guns on both sides, and the infantry fire, but could not tell how the horrible massacre of the Highland Brigade was going - I will not give details now. The position we attacked was 4 miles or so further on and, I suppose, at about 8 a.m. 1st. Gordons were sent for, all but one Company, and that was B. At the time it was maddening. We could do nothing but eventually it was not such a loss. We and the convoy moved up and up. There were all sorts of rumours about, but as you know for about 2 hours our Battalion was under cross-fire, lying down with no cover and unable to move, for the slightest movement brought a hail of lead.

The Colonel was killed immediately. He would not wear a kilt, and stood up to wave the Battalion on with his stick. Then poor Wingate, one of the nicest and best of chaps was killed. Then Willie Gordon, the Adjutant, was shot through the chest, I am thankful to say not mortally. He is now at Winburg and said to be doing well; Campbell was also shot in the spine and liver and died next day, never regaining consciousness. It is too horrible, and seems impossible that they are dead. Campbell was an awfully good chap too, and what made it worse was his having a brother in command of the big Naval gun here, who he had brought into our mess often. Macnab insisted on shooting at the Boers, or where he imagined they were, though he carefully advised us not to, but after the 3rd shot was hit in the left hand. I do not know how bad it is, but of course he had to go and may take 6 months to recover.

We had 42 casualties, about 4 men died. That day there were 80 casualties, many of the wounded being hit at 5 a.m. or thereabouts on Monday and not picked up until late on Tuesday afternoon. It was the coldest night we have had, no food, or water, except the little we had on us. All this time Dingwall and I were keeping with the convoy, and at night we formed a picket. We were in easy range of the Boers, but they never noticed us. At midnight we got word that the convoy had retired, so we got up and followed their tracks by moonlight for about 3 miles. I took half the Company and Dingwall took the other and we formed a picket on each side of the convoy. We experienced an appalling cold night with nothing but a rug, and the men with only one blanket between two.

We stood to arms from 3.30 to 4.30, but nothing happened. Then we lit a great fire, got some rations of Bully Beef and biscuits, and were much happier. Then we were finished, and were off to the front with the convoy and rejoined the Regt. Later we marched off very slowly as a flank guard to the ambulances, which were coming in and out in a never ending melancholic procession. The Boers fired at them, a few shells for us, but luckily did no damage. One went over my head, making a great whirring noise, pitching down in the very place we had just left.

Wauchope, the General, was buried that afternoon, Wingate in the morning, Colonel Dowman the next day.

On Wednesday afternoon we got secret orders to go back to Enslin, where the Northants were fighting. We struck camp about 8 and started to entrain in the dark so as not to let the Boers know we were leaving, as they were supposed to be mining along the line and we did not wish to be blown up. We had an awful time entraining carts, mules, transports etc., and did not start till about midnight, taking 2 hours to do 18 miles. One Company could not be entrained as there was no room. Eventually they got another truck and an engine followed. B Company as usual was on fatigues and unloaded the train, then for 2 or 3 hours lay down in their clothes and got a little sleep.

Camp was pitched on the first grassy slope we've struck, on the east side of the railway close to some Australians, Rimington Scouts, and Engineers. It is a pretty enough place. There are four little kopjes; horrible rocky, bouldered things. We keep pickets on all but Sharp Picket, where there is a detached post of 10 men and one NCO and a look-out by day. The reliefs start at 3.30 a.m. every morning, 20 men and one officer, and at night they are reinforced by 20 more. We have some rough defences of boulders etc. erected with much labour and a rough path cleared up the side.

From these hills in a north easterly direction, Modder River Camp and Magersfontein, or what ever the place is called where we fought, is plainly to be seen; in other directions the ground is broken up with scattered kopjes and deserted farm houses, and occupational small Boer parties which never attack us. The rest of the line, forward and back for miles, is patrolled closely by the Rimington Scouts.

Since we have been here, we have been employed on all sorts of fatigues, fortifications on kopjes and others for defences etc. There are perpetual rumours of Boer parties about, and no one knows how much to believe. This is a wonderful country for what are called "shaves".

I am beginning to think that there is no decent general in Britain. Even Buller has taken a knock, and Gatacre a bad one, but you get far more news at home than we do, though well cooked. We are possibly to stay here a month or two, but 3 Coys are starting tomorrow for Graspan down the line, to hold the place and to protect communications.

I am off at 3 a.m. on picket to Big Kopje, Dingwall on the South. Our food is cooked here and carried up to us. Water is the great difficulty; it has to be brought mostly in tanks by rail from Modder, though there is one well of poorish quality and they are sinking another. The men do not get much washing, but yesterday they managed an impromptu bathe by scooping holes in the ground and then with a water proof sheet made some sort of a bath. It was very primitive! There is also a shortage of firewood. Some passed in the train for the Modder camp the other day, and the Australians promptly boarded the train and carried off some of it before they could be stopped. They are a rough lot!

Big Kopje, 20 December - Came on picket this morning, got up at 2.30 a.m., and after a steep but short climb found myself with 25 men on the top of this kopje. There was a bright moon, but it was awfully cold. We relieved the Australians. Soon after sunrise it gets quite hot, and the flies are horrible. I would like to see every one killed. I live in a little stone hut supported with brushwood, just room enough to lie down out of the sun, but with rugs and an air cushion. Very comfortable! I walked around the kopje with Sgt. Martin, an awfully good chap, to see if the sangas or the defence walls were very visible from below. We came across 3 wild donkeys and some strange birds and flowers, and decided that the sangas must be disguised, as they make good marks for the enemy. This was done by stuffing grass and green branches into chinks, so it looked quite natural.

The Australians are very piggy, and left quantities of refuse, such as old bones, bits of meat, half empty tins of sardines, bully beef, bread, biscuits, etc. which went bad of course, and bred innumerable flies everywhere. So we collected as much as possible and buried it. I saw the most gorgeous lizard, bight blue in front with an orange and red back and spotted and brown tail. He sat on a rock and looked at me, but he was not to be caught. There is also a funny little bird in this place, who every morning flies up about 8 yards perpendicularly, and comes spinning down with a melancholy pipe. He flies worse than any bird I have ever seen. His wings hit very hard across his body, and make a clacking that can be heard a very long way off.

21 December - We came off picket at 4.30 a.m. There was a rumour that we had captured 200 Boers at Modder but the 200 has since been found to be two! We do little when off-duty but eat and sleep; the latter has to be got when it can. I was sent off in charge of the water guard till tomorrow night. There is a well for drinking and cooking purposes, with certain hours allotted to the different units. We sleep in a dirty compound by the line with a lot of stones and swarms of flies. There is a station house occupied by the telegra-

phists and natives who keep everyone supplied with flies by chucking out the refuse!

22 December - Orderly duties are combined with the guard so there is plenty to do, we have just got a paper from Capetown with news of the Colenso fight. Things look pretty bad all round. Methuen is not a man one feels much confidence in, but I hear Hector Macdonald is coming out. They ought to send Kitchener. I have not thanked you for the last letters. I got one yesterday from you and father written on Nov. 10th. It must have got to Capetown before we did. Will you please order me a pair of shoes from Wright in Elgin exactly the same as the last he made me. This is a scorching day not like Xmas at all. I feel as if it ought to be August. No presents this year. This is an unconscionably long letter, but I missed the last post by being on picket, so it is two very confused and rambling instalments.

Please tell Father that the "Banffshire" arrived and was most interesting. Much love to yourself. Wishing you all a Happy New Year, and a successful Bonspiel, if it comes off. I hope to be home for the 1900 one, however there is no saying. I hope this will reach you some day as it would be a terrific waste of energy otherwise. It is now midday and a blazing sun overhead that casts no shadow.

What a miserable Christmas it was going to be!

How right Lachlan was to comment that there seemed to be no decent generals in South Africa at that time. Buller, the Commander- in-Chief, was particularly incompetent, and had a tendency to favour ill-reconnoitred dawn attacks, usually after a long night approach march when everyone was tired and hungry on their start line. This was what happened to the Highland Brigade at the Battle of Magersfontein. The Brigade marched in close column right up to the Boers' positions and only then shook out into extended order. But by that time it was too late as the Boers, in their well camouflaged positions, had discovered the British presence. They had previously erected some agricultural barbed wire to hamper the advance and, using this to their advantage, then poured in such a hail of bullets that the troops were forced to retreat as the position was untenable. It was a black day for the Highland Brigade and for Scotland.

Methuen, the general in command of the attack, had failed to properly reconnoitre the Boers' position, which he thought was on high ground. This was not the case; they were on the flat at the foot of the hill, well dug in, well camouflaged and protected by barbed wire. General Wauchope, formerly of the Black Watch, was commanding the Highland Brigade, and did not agree with Methuen's plan of attack, as this form of night/dawn attack had been tried before without success, but he reluctantly agreed to carry out the operation. The result was 902 British dead - of which Wauchope was one - to 236 Boer.

Methuen, after the battle, made what could only be described as an ill-advised speech insinuating that they had not done as well as they should and that there must be no surrender. This created immense ill-feeling and a row in the Scottish Press. The Highland Brigade never served under Methuen's command again.

Many of the generals, at the start of this war had what has been described as a "Crimean Mentality", though of course later on very fine leaders appeared, men such as French and Kitchener, but this was only after Roberts replaced Buller as Commander-in-Chief.

Magersfontein was Lachlan's first big battle. The 1st Gordons were not engaged in the initial phase of the battle as they were guarding the convoy, but when things began to go wrong they were called forward, leaving B Company guarding the convoy, much to Lachlan's chagrin.

14 December 1899. To Duff, Drummuir. Telegram handed in at Modder River 13.12.

"Safe. Lachlan"

Prime Ministers Office, 10 Downing St. Telegram to Mrs Gordon-Duff, Braemoriston, Elgin

"Your boy safe and untouched. Five officers Gordon Highlanders killed or wounded. Asquith".

21 December 1899. Hatton Castle. Cousin Pat Duff (Gardie's younger brother, aged 8 years) to Lachlan.

Dear Lachlan, Will you write and tell me all about the Battles and all the places you have been to in South Africa? I wonder what you will be doing on Xmas Day? I wish you a Happy New Year. Kenneth is here just now but he is going away today. My holidays begin tomorrow, I wish you and Gardie could spend them with me. We all send love and hugs and kisses, Your Loving Pat.

28 December 1899. Father to Lachlan. Drummuir .

Another mail day. I wonder if they come around so quickly to you as they do to us! You will not be very unhappy if so. But it is strange how the minutes go quicker every year. Glad to have yours of 27 November. I wonder if you got the pair of shoes I sent off by mail on the 26 October. Wright has made a pair of shoes for me that did not fit (too big) and they seemed just right for you, so I make you a present of them. It is sad to think that De Wet is still at large and Boers raiding in Cape Colony still. However the Cape folk should have made up their minds 12 months ago. They could have swept the board with them. The Almighty has not been on the side of brother Boer, but on ours.

This is a prayer from Joan for her brother, written from Gisburn whilst she was staying with Aunt Charty Ribblesdale.

"I pray often for you that the Spirit of God may blow on your soul, and keep it fresh and pure from the hot fever bed of the world, and that the Peace of God rest on your heart, and keep it from the cruel fret of life, safe and blessed."

CHAPTER THREE

Enslin to Ramdam Farm 1900

12 January 1900. Lachlan to Joan. Near South Kopje

There is no news to speak of this week. There are repeated cries of 'wolf' but nothing ever happens.

Last Saturday C Company was ordered to double off and reinforce South Kopje, all because six Australian grooms took their masters' horses out to exercise, and thought they might as well combine a little amusement with duty. They took their rifles, and went out several miles in front of the pickets to the east and advanced on them in skirmishing order, stalking buck or anything else they chanced upon. As they looked exactly like Boers with their squash hats, the pickets thought they were scouts, and signalled down to that effect. However the mistake was discovered, and didn't those Australians catch it!

That same evening we had a magnificent concert. It was a glorious night and the stage was a wagon at the foot of Camp Kopje, the audience being seated on the slope. The performers were all men, ours and the Australians. Some of the items were wonderfully clever. There were all sorts of songs and duets, and recitations and violin solos etc., and an exhibition reel to finish up.

On Sunday we had the usual service, and in the afternoon Mitford and I rode over to Graspan along the line, when about half way we saw 2 miles to our south-west a party of what we thought were Boers heading south-east. They looked about 50 to 100 strong with perhaps 5 to 10 wagons. We went and warned the picket, but nothing but dust could be seen. They signalled here and two lots of Australians went off to find them, but had no luck. Graspan is a vile place, it was blowing rather hard, and the dust was terrific. You could hardly breathe and had to keep eyes and mouth tight shut. We all went into the veldt for a bit until it subsided somewhat, and it was possible to get tea. On the way back we found 3 ponies about 2 miles from camp, and drove them in with some trouble. They were not up to much, two having very sore backs.

Monday - There was another false alarm. B Company were just going out on arms drill at 6.30 a.m. when we were suddenly ordered off to reinforce Big and South Kopjes. I doubled up to the top of Big Kopje with one half Coy, and when I got there they wanted to know what on earth was up. I thought they were being attacked by the Boer Cavalry, but they were quite unaware of the fact. It eventually turned out that some of our people from Modder had been amusing themselves all night, and we nearly fired at them from one of the pickets.

It began to rain that evening and continued most of Tuesday, which was refreshing, though every bug in the place came out for a walk. One of the Australian officers found a snake in his bed and my servant caught a lovely tarantula in my kit bag among my clothes, but called it a Scorpion Spider. I am keeping it until another is found.

Wednesday - The rain all went. I played football for the Company against D Company. There was too much wind for a good game, but we won by 2 to nil. Late that night a draft of 182 men and Wedderburn turned up from home. They consist of 4th class reserve, militia, recruits etc.

Thursday - I took 90 of them to Graspan by truck and intended to walk back with the accompanying Sgt, but just as we were going a stray train came along, so we got in. While there, a fawn was brought in, a wood-gathering party having caught it. It was very frightened of course, and was put in an oven and given some milk! All the companies have built beautiful ovens of bricks from a neighbouring farm house. They afford amusement and are very useful; the mess has one rather like a pyramid.

Yesterday, that is, Friday, everyone rushed off to a big kopje about 4 miles to the west to try and establish Helio communication with Kimberly, but it was no go. At night we can 'hear' what they are saying by their searchlights in the air, but as they only talk in cipher, it is not very satisfactory. Two 4.7 guns, a powerful patent pump, and other articles went past us to Modder yesterday.

SIGNALLING TO KIMBERLEY

The poor Marconies (wireless operators) have had a bad time. Their big pole was broken by the wind, and a kite they had does not seem to work. They then tried a balloon, which went up very nicely, but a dust-devil scampered into it, whisked it off from its mooring and carried it to heaven where it burst. Yesterday afternoon I went for a long walk with Tytler and 3 of my NCOs; the latter with rifles and after buck or something else. We were extraordinarily unlucky. I got a shot at one, which came down, but I could not find it. The others never got a shot. I found 2 tortoises, which are now in a Laager of bricks and boxes.

The Mail came today with never a word from any of you. I had a letter from Mrs C. Turner, and a card from Duke Montauro. I got Grandmama's parcel, which is being kept for emergencies. We are not starving in the least, living on fresh meat, milk and even butter, when it is not oil.

2 February 1900. Lachlan to Father. Enslin

I got your last lot of letters this morning and was surprised to hear you had not heard from me after Magersfontein. I do not think I forgot to post my letter, in fact I know it went, and I told you all about it, at least my own experiences that day which were very disappointing, though I avoided getting made a target of, which might easily have happened otherwise, so perhaps it did not matter much. But it was very disappointing to miss everything with all our people up at the firing line. In case anything may have happened to my letter, I may as well say that B Company were left to guard a wretched convoy and spent a beastly day hearing a lot but out of fire, a long ridge hiding us from view, though if they had tried they might have given us a bad time with shells. We watched them all day and night, the coldest night I've ever been out in; it was vile. We had wild reports through the day that we were beaten and every one killed, so I was very jolly indeed.

But to return to the present times, we are just off to Modder River. Troops are pouring in by every train and we expect to go away soon, though we have no definite orders yet.

3 February - We are still here, but have packed all our heavy baggage ready to send to Orange River, and may march off tomorrow. I suppose another attempt to relieve Kimberly is contemplated, but by the time you read this it will probably be over. We have a lot of guns gone up, so I suppose they mean business this time. We have had a hot week, with plenty of dust storms, much the same as usual.

Sunday - We had a service and several of the Graspan people visited. Monday I was Orderly officer.

Tuesday morning - The Australians left us for Belmont and Naaupoort in great state. They were marching, the band and pipes accompanying them out of the camp, amid enthusiastic cheers. They are a good lot of men, though their officers, with few exceptions, are very odd, practically the same class as the men, so discipline is rather slack. They were not out of camp before there was a wild rush of our chaps to collect and loot anything they could lay hands on. My servant picked up a chair for me from a man for sixpence, and the mess acquired some very fine property, which was originally got by their mounted infantry from Boer farms. That afternoon I went with an escort of four men on a shooting expedition We went around some kopjes and I got 6 partridges, losing several others and missing a lot. One of the men said he hit a buck, but lost it. There are also a lot of partridges to be found, but they are very scattered.

Wednesday and Thursday - I went to get some more partridges, walked about 9 miles, but found only one covey and got none. Yesterday we prepared to go and tomorrow A Company march to Knockfontein, a few miles from Modder, by themselves. Last Monday a huge supply of pipes and tobacco were sent to us, every man and officer getting a pipe and 2 ozs of tobacco. My servant, Whitaker, then told me everyone was going to be given 10!

I enclose two sketches of this place, one is the camp as seen from the station with the four kopjes we have pickets on. The other was from the very top of South Kopje, and Big Kopje in the foreground with Camp Kopje north of the camp and the railway from south to north, with the flat kopje dotted country west of it. You must put the two halves together by the lines drawn. I have sent Joan the Queen's chocolate-box with various designs on it. I hope it will arrive as the box is very interesting.

9 February 1900. Lachlan to Ettie. Maple Leaf Camp

All our transport was taken from us the other day, so our baggage came here by rail. As there is no one to get it out here (we are 9 miles from Enslin and 4 from Brigade) it went on to Belmont, where the mess furniture is; among which is a very fine rocking chair, enviously eyed by a distinguished sapper and his staff. All of it was originally looted from Boer farms by your fellow countrymen who on leaving Enslin handed it over to us. We have a big mess tent and do ourselves pretty well, getting fruit and vegetables from Capetown, though they have a knack of going to other than the destined tummies.

We picked up stray cows at Enslin, and formed a herd so that we always get fresh milk, which still continues as they were marched over here. We have also some miscellaneous ponies picked up on the veldt, very useful, tho' not much to look at. I hope we shall soon leave this place, as it is very slow. There is only one picket to do. I do hope something will have happened by the time you get this letter if you ever do get it. I am sure the Censor couldn't stop this, I haven't even mentioned Methuen.

Ettie was, I assume, an Australian who was with the troops at Enslin. They were very good at 'finding' things!

10 February 1900. Lachlan to Joan. Maple Leaf Camp

I forgot who I wrote to last week, but it is probably your turn. Since last week we have made a move as you see by the name. We left Enslin, a place I have come to look upon as a second home on Friday the 6th. We got orders to go to well 591 on the west of the railway. It is about 7 miles down the line, and a very deserted spot.

A few Canadians were in occupation but they went at once, and the North Staffordshires and the South Wales Borderers came in their place, but they went yesterday for Graspan, and the Duke of Cornwall's Light Infantry came instead. You will be glad to hear that we are brigaded under Smith-Dorrien, with the DCLI, Royal Canadians and the Shropshire Light Infantry.

We started from Enslin at about 8, sending our baggage by rail, except for some mess stores, which went in some commandeered old dogcarts, patched up for the occasion and drawn by two of the Boer ponies picked up on the veldt, and two mules. It was an extra specially hot day of course. At Graspan we had a drink and picked up the 3 Companies there. Strangely enough there was a train with some cavalry drawn up as we passed the station and who should be looking out of the window but cousin Tommy. He saw me in time to get out and say a few words as we passed, but we had no time for more. He was very well, and on the way to Modder, and seemed very enormous.

John Ingleby had been to De Aar seeing about our Mounted Infantry equipment, and came back saying that the horses were Indian ponies, on their way out. However, two days later he marched off to Belmont with over 100 of our best NCOs and men to be trained. We were very sorry to see them go. I only hope they will not get into a mess anywhere. As the Colonel says, 'they are very good on foot and wasted on a horse'.

One advantage of this place is that the flies are not nearly as bad as they were at Enslin, though on the increase. It is very flat here, no near kopjes. We have only one picket out by day and an officer by night, and various posts of observation of three men and an NCO dotted. I am for picket tonight. It has been blowing with dust storms at intervals, the worst at lunch; it is always the way. The tent nearly came down, as the soil is three inches thick on solid limestone, so it is nearly impossible to get a peg to stick tight. We all cleared out for a bit to let it blow over. There has been a little rain that has caused as much fuss as a deluge would have.

The Hampshires and the Norfolks came in the same day, poor brutes, leaving a man behind at every ant heap. It was rather trying weather for troops, just newly out, and just made to march with soft feet, and no condition. Please thank Mildred and Father for their letter. The shoes arrived today. I am trying to get them stretched as they are too short, so I am afraid they will not be much use, but she says the others are coming soon, and those two brown pairs I had last summer will last a long time longer, but it is as well to be on the safe side.

12 February 1900. Lachlan to Father. Maple Leaf Camp

In case I do not get a chance of catching the mail this week, I will write a note now. We are off in an hour to Graspan for the night, and then for a little trip from Graspan to Bloemfontein and do not expect to see our luggage for a bit. We leave here with all our tents with poor Clowes and a few men to look after them. We are supposed to take 35 lbs a piece thanks to Kitchener, including blankets, but mine I am sorry to say is considerably more. It is still very hot. I hope we shall be successful. I have absolutely no ideas of our plans and there is no news.

Troops had been pouring into South Africa from the UK, India, and all over the Empire for the past month and assembling around Orange River Station. The Field Force consisted of over 25,000 infantry, 8,000 Cavalry and Mounted Infantry, over 100 guns and thousands of wagons. Behind them were 7,000 men, under Methuen, to confront the Magersfontein defences. Finally there were 18,000 men to guard the railway down to Orange River Station.

Lord Roberts' plan was to advance on Bloemfontein, which at that time was the Boers' seat of Government. He hoped to bluff the Boers into thinking that he would attack north up the Western Railway, but in reality use the Central Line for his communications.

Besides organising and planning a major campaign with such long supply lines about 600 miles from Capetown, there was the question of relieving Kimberly, which needed to be done as soon as possible. The hugely profitable gold and diamond mines were at risk. The army was organised into Divisions and Brigades but it was being done in a great hurry and sometimes on the move.

New generals were now arriving; younger men who believed in attacking in open order, in camouflage, and in 'man management'! Lachlan was lucky in his Brigadier, General Smith-Dorrien, then in his early forties. He was young, enthusiastic and energetic and, moreover, had not been exclusively trained on the North-West frontier of India.

Major-General H. L. SMITH-DORRIEN, D.S.O.

Major-General IAN S. M. HAMILTON, C.B., D.S.O.

To counter the lack of mobility of the British Army, Lord Roberts decided to form the Mounted Infantry by taking one Company from each Infantry Battalion. There were certain logistical difficulties at first; a shortage of horses, saddlery, and trained riders. The Mounted Infantry were to be armed with Carbines, unlike the cavalry who rode heavier horses and were armed with either a sabre or a lance. Once the new infantry had learnt to ride they did extremely well.

The Gordons M.I. had difficulty in finding the appropriate riding breeches. It would not have been very comfortable or decent wearing the kilt! The saddlery was brand new and very slippery, which did not help the budding equestrians. Eyewitnesses said that they had never seen such an amusing sight.

3 February 1900. Mrs E. Findlay to Joan.

I went to pay a farewell visit to one of my Gordon wives to day, as her husband has just come home, and I had a most interesting talk with the man. I asked him if he knew your brother, as he is in his Battalion, and he beamed all over and said he knew him well and that he was a "little hero". He said he was a boy when he went out and that now he was a "fine big man", and that he was most popular with the men, and was most enthusiastic about him.

He was such a nice looking superior man that I thought it would please you to hear what he said of your brother. I always think that the devotion of their men counts for more than anything else.

21 February 1900. Lachlan to Joan. Between Graspan and Ramdam Farm

I sent home a note on Monday the 12th and have crammed more events into the subsequent period than ever before. We left Graspan early on the 13th, and had a terribly hot and trying march with our Brigade to Ramdam farm in the Free State; only 10 miles, but heavy going. A lot of men took sick, and some went back. There was no ambulance or conveyance for them. We drank from a filthy pan, where men and animals all bathed and, strange to say, no one is dead yet from it. Macdonald and the Highland Brigade came too from Enslin.

We went on the next day and another hot march to the River Riet, crossed it, bathed in the evening - it was delicious - and camped the night. At 5 a.m. on the 15th we moved off with all the troops in the place, and left B Company to protect and bring on a huge Convoy at night. All the neighbouring pickets were withdrawn. I posted a section of the Company about a mile from the camp towards the kopje, and went back to breakfast about 9 a.m.

Soon we heard shots and the Boers attacked us from the kopje, about 800 to a 1000 yards in front of the picket. We had a great fight all day, assisted by a few volunteers, and Kitchener's Horse and had many marvellous escapes. I will send details later, there is no time now. We fought all day till 9 p.m. by moonlight, luckily a few Coys of K.O.S.B. came after marching a very long way and held our flanks, and a few guns turned the Boers from the kopje, but did very little good. We held over 1000 Boers until 3 o'clock without help and with about 150 men all told, in the open, and only lost 5 men - one killed - and four wounded, all of whom I hope will recover.

Roberts then wired that we were to leave the convoy and come out at night. We cleared out at 2 a.m. with everyone, including the sick and wounded. The Convoy was left to the Boers, except for a few wagons. Several volunteers, Mounted Infantry and Kitchener's Horse were wounded. We buried the dead man on the march, and did 12 miles into Wegdrai on the Modder River in over 3 hours by night, with many of the men with fearful blisters on their legs and practically no food or water since 3 a.m. on the 15th (this at 5.30 a.m. on 16th) when they filled their water bottles on starting our march and got a bit of biscuit.

The Regiment had gone to Jacobsdal and we were attached to the Highland Brigade. We washed in the river and rested a bit on that day, but were ordered to march till 7 a.m. on 17th with a few halts, covering about 18 miles to Modder Spruit. Many of the men were incapable almost of marching when we started, but struggled through. Dingwall could not walk. His legs were worse than most; the back sinews of the knee were affected. Macdonald himself lent him a horse to come on.

We left at 5 that evening, expecting to do only 5 miles, we were so done up. I was about the best in the Company as I remembered to pull up my hose during the fight, and was not so tired as the others. We went on till 11.30 p.m. and got here just after a big lot of Boers. We were on the Modder about 55 miles from Bloemfontein. The Regiment came in that morning and we fought all day. B Company were sent to look after the baggage and got home. The Boers were hemmed in and matters are much the same still.

This is the first chance of writing I have had. It goes with some of the wounded, who are many. I will send a further account when I can. Much love to all. I am very well indeed. Dingwall is still hors de combat.

A short undated note after the battle, from Dingwall to Joan.

"The cub did very well."

Ramdam Farm was a filthy white-washed, iron-roofed, single storey building, with half a dozen rooms. But it had water. Some people said it tasted a bit strong, but the doctors said it was excellent and quite safe to drink and that the flavour of the well water was from salt and lime, which was a very healthy combination of chemicals. On this recommendation it was drunk dry. Late-comers using the well fell sick and the corpse of a black man was found in it which no doubt imparted to the water its unique flavour.

As Dingwall's note shows, Lachlan had by that time been nicknamed 'the Cub', probably because he was the youngest officer in the Battalion. Dingwall was his Company Commander in B Coy, which had been detailed to stay behind to guard this enormous convoy, while the rest of the Battalion went on to Jacobsdal.

They left Ramdam on 14 February and marched to Waterval on the Riet River, a tributary of the Modder. It was here that they fought the Boers, from 5 a.m. to 9 p.m. and it was in this battle that Lachlan found himself in sole command of the Company, Dingwall having been incapacitated by the effects of the sun on the back of his legs, like so many others in the Company.

In the Regimental History, Vol. 3, 'Life of a Regiment' there is the following comment that runs; 'Senior Officers spoke very highly of the behaviour of Capt. Dingwall, Lieut. L. Gordon-Duff, and their men, whose small losses they attributed to the clever manner in which they used or made cover'.

Meanwhile the convoy was to be abandoned. It consisted of wagons belonging to two different formations going in different directions which became inextricably mixed while trying to cross the Riet River, whose banks were very high.

By now Kimberly had fallen and there was precious little time to waste, even on organising such things as food, medicines and clothing for the troops. Amongst all these stores were the riding breeches for the Gordon Highlanders Mounted Infantry Company! Some 176 wagons were abandoned which spelled half-rations for the men. Roberts was reported to have said that the troops would understand!

30 January 1900. A. G. Duff to Father

Your boy is much liked in his Regiment. This I heard while in Hospital at Winburg from the Adjutant and others, and I know you will like to hear it. He is in a nice healthy place now at Enslin. It is on the Lines of Communication, so out of danger while there.

The fatal 11 December * is a day one will never forget. The finest Brigade any commander could wish to have under him was sacrificed for no object. But this of course is strictly 'entre nous' and I hope to tell you all details some day.

* *(This refers to the Battle of Magersfontein)*

CHAPTER FOUR

Paardeberg to Bloemfontein 1900

The regiment was to have a tough start to the campaign, as all movement was done on foot. Lachlan's father kept a record of the mileage covered that week taken from the letters.

On the 13 February they left Graspan for Ramdam, a journey of 10 miles in about 3 hours, to join the Highland Bde. On the 14th they moved on to Riet River, a distance of approximately 16 miles. The following day the men of B Company were left behind with the Convoy while the rest of the Regiment went on to Jacobsdal. They started at 5 a.m. and four hours later the Boers attacked and the battle went for 12 hours. On the 16th at 2 a.m. they abandoned the convoy as ordered and marched 12 miles in 3 hours to Modder River. There they rested a short while before marching for another 8 hours. On the 17th they left Modder River at 7 a.m. and covered 18 miles in 8 hours. After a short halt they marched another 10 miles until 11. 30 p.m. On the 18th the Company rejoined the regiment at Paarderberg and were assigned to baggage guard duties. They were utterly exhausted and had 12 hours rest before moving on with the Highland Brigade under Macdonald. They had covered, after their fight, over 40 miles in 46 hours.

Kimberly had been relieved by General French on 15 February. The Boers had escaped and were at large, and no one knew their position. Roberts' plan was to advance on Bloemfontein, 55 miles to the east, leaving the Western Railway behind.

However, the Boers still occupied Magersfontein and, to counter this, the back up force under Methuen was to saturate the enemy's position with artillery fire, while the main force executed a flank march.

Cronje, the Boers' Commander, was described as a 'broken man' by Rayne Kruger in 'Good Bye Dolly Gray'. Whilst enduring Methuen's fire, the news of Kimberly's fall had reached him and he was gripped by a 'paralysis of will', and did not know which way to go.

CRONJE

Eventually he decided to move east. His army had a huge administrative tail of 4000 wives and families and a convoy of 400 wagons with several thousand horses. There was a brilliant moon that night with excellent visibility and the target was moving at an ox's pace and could so easily have been destroyed. It presented a sitting target to any British sharp-shooter. Incredibly though, no one spotted this huge, monolithic creature snaking its way across the veldt and it passed

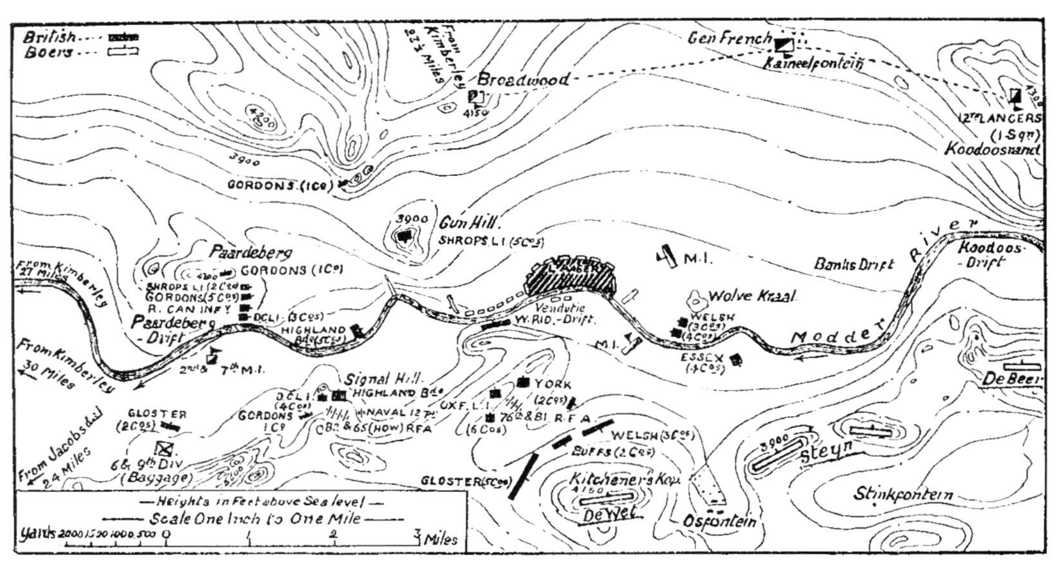

PAARDEBERG—EARLY PART OF THE NIGHT OF 18–19TH FEBRUARY 1900

unharmed. Cronje and his huge convoy halted near the Modder river at Paarderberg Drift.

26 February 1900. Lachlan to Father. Paarderberg on the Modder River

I had just time to send you a line a few days ago by the wounded, which may or may not arrive. This is meant to be a rather fuller account up to date, beginning from Tuesday 13 February. I told you we got to Graspan the day before, and at daylight on Thursday we left with our Brigade for Ramdam Farm. It was very hot and dusty. After going five miles or so we had to wait for some broken down baggage for two or three hours, while the Brigade went on. It was very trying. Lots of men were affected by the sun. My Company did advanced guard and could get no water. However, we struggled along arriving about 1 p.m. at Ramdam, a big Boer farm in the Free State. The boundary from Capetown was a barbed wire fence and there was a well with a dead native at the bottom (this we only discovered as we left). There was a shallow pan with mules and men bathing in it. We bivouacked near it, the Highland Brigade finding us there, under Macdonald, who visited us. We were very glad of an afternoon's rest. I and a lot of others bathed in the pan; very muddy and shallow, but refreshing. We drank some of the water, made tea of it, but it was very nasty; smelly, even after being boiled.

We left early Wednesday morning with two big naval guns which came from Enslin with the Highland Brigade. They are drawn by 32 oxen apiece on great carriages. B Company marched in the rear that day and were told to guard them if they ever got behind owing to rocks etc. They were a great nuisance at first, and we were always running after them, but after we had a halt they got ahead and ceased from troubling us. It was another very hot day, any number of men falling out from heat and lack of water. We halted at Waterfall Drift, near Kaffirfontein on the Riet River, at about 12 and got water from the river, which was very low but shady with trees and grass-grown banks. This time there was nothing but a dead mule in it, so it was very superior! We crossed at a drift, and bivouacked above the river and caught the convoy there to take it on next day. The Battalion left last of all on Thursday 15th at 5 a.m.

B Company were left behind however to bring on the convoy that night, as it was to wait for a few of its wagons not yet across the Drift. All the surrounding pickets were withdrawn, but the Cavalry reported all clear 10 miles round. We had only 80 men and so we started to put out outposts. The ground rose in slopes from the river line to a line of kopjes about a mile from the camp.

I took one section out nearly 1 mile up the hill and found a bit of broken ground with stones lying about which afford good cover if you lie flat, so they sent four men to look around the kopjes. They returned shortly seeing nothing. We were just starting breakfast about 8.30 in camp. Luckily we had had a little at 3 a.m. with the Battalion. The men were about to slaughter two lambs they had caught when we heard shots firing in front. I doubled up with the other section to reinforce the picket. We got up safely and lay down behind a few stones and found that there were Boers in the kopjes in front shooting at us. We did not see any for some time, but heard a great deal of shooting to our left, where Dingwall and half the Company were.

We could do nothing so, after a little, I started with a corporal and two men to crawl away to the left to see what was up. We got 50 yards but the ground showed no sign of improving and was absolutely bare with a lot of bullets flying about, so there was no object in going back to the picket. We were determined to join the half Company Dingwall had.

Two men were sent first, singly. They got about 150 yards with a lot of bullets after them, and lay down flat, and then not knowing quite what to do or where to go and also not liking the sound of the bullets, they stayed there all day. Cpl.

Britain went next, crossed about 700 or 800 yards of open ground in about 3 rushes, throwing himself flat after each, with a regular hail of bullets after him cutting up the ground all around, whistling through the air. He arrived safely. I started, then ran along stooping and after each run threw myself flat. There was a hail of bullets which struck all around. I lay still for a minute. They thought I

'I dodged behind a little ant heap'

was bagged, so I got a chance of going some way before they were on to me again. Everyone who saw our run thought we must be killed. One place I dodged behind was a little ant-heap when a bullet shot the top of it over my back.

I found the rest of us lying along a very slightly defined crest line of the slope shooting away at the Boers who rarely showed themselves. We were rather afraid of a flank attack, but a few Mounted Infantry prevented the Boers a bit. We tried to signal through to the Regiment, but it was found impossible, tho' luckily they got a wire through to Roberts. Some of Kitchener's Horse and some of the London Volunteers came out with us, as well as a few men left behind that morning as sick.

They all did very well though two of the former were the first to get hit. Drummer Nicholson and I tied them up as best we could as there were no doctors or ambulances, then they had to lie there until night. About 3 p.m. we got reinforcements of a few absolutely exhausted Coys of K.O.S.B. who shot away on either flank, preventing the Boer from getting around but otherwise they were unable to do much. Also a battery of artillery shelled the Boers out of the left hand kopje, but where they were really thick they left them, firing a few shots on the right.

The Boers had several guns firing at us, one a pom-pom, which was disconcerting, though it failed to hit us. They also had a small field gun and plugged away vigorously. We could hear the report before the shell arrived and flopped down whenever it went off, so only one man was touched by them. He was bruised in the arm, very severely. I watched them bursting near me till one nearly got me and with my next door neighbour cleared out to another place out of their line. The first thing they did was to was to plant a shell bang into an old ambulance wagon, luckily deserted. It was marvellous how we escaped. I went down from the line to send a wire.

It was very warm work; bullets were as thick in the laager as on the hill and several were hit right down by the river, which has very steep banks but where bullets were still going. A lot of Mounted Infantry sheltering down there were hit. We began to run out of ammunition, but the A.S.C. and some of ours got more up. I started with two North Staffordshire Mounted Infantry to take some up, but I never saw if they arrived.

We went on like this all day till dark when the Boers shut up and we went to see how the advanced picket had fared. They had been all alone without food and water all day, but being closer up managed to bag more Boers than I think the rest did. Strange to say they all escaped, except a mule conductor who volunteered with them and was hit in the shoulder, but they were very much exhausted from the sun and want of food and water. Some had shots through their haversacks which showed what sort of fire it was. The stones in front saved them. I went and shouted for them in the dark and, as they were coming back, the Boers evidently heard a row and fired a volley at us. No harm.

We then retired to where our firing line had been. Everyone got food and set to work to dig himself a kind of little grave for use next day. The moon was very bright, so the Boers had one last blaze at 9 p.m. Our casualties were one killed and four wounded; marvellously low. It was a tremendous fire for nearly 12 hours.

About 1.45 a.m. that night the order came from Roberts to retire leaving the convoy, so silently and quickly as we could we cleared out and marched to Wecht Wey on the Modder, 12 miles off, burying our poor dead man on the way and covering the whole distance in 3 hours, not bad by night and after such a day. Nearly all the convoy was lost, about £60,000 worth. It was impossible to get it away as we had lost numbers of mules and oxen. We very nearly lost our kits. The Company mule cart was driven by a very good Cape boy who, deserted by his assistant and having a mule shot, inspanned and cleared out, saving all our possessions after the enemy had recommenced shelling the laager. If they had sent us more reinforcements we should have saved it, and captured 1400 Boers, but Roberts was anxious to waste no time but to catch this lot, which he has - but this is anticipating.

We found on Friday that our Regiment had gone to Jacobsdal as we came in. Macdonald was very pleased to see us, and attached us to the Highland Bde. The men, and especially Dingwall, had their legs terribly burnt in the sinews behind, and many could only walk with great pain We were rather objects of interest, which was a novel situation.

We bathed and rested as well as we could, receiving orders to march with the Brigade to Jacobsdal next day, only 4 miles away. However, that night we were hauled out of bed and marched off in the opposite direction. We got away by 11.30 p.m. and marched with a few halts till 7 a.m. arriving on Saturday with many of the men including Dingwall unable to move another step. This was at Modder Spruit. Nearly 18 miles that night. Our poor mules were almost dead, chiefly from want of food. I went and saw Macdonald (Dingwall being unable to go) and told of our plight. He was very kind and lent Dingwall his pony to ride, but said that we were going at 5 p.m. This was rather a stagger, a 20 mile march, but we started, and the Company kept going marvellously. We only did about 10 miles luckily when we got in here about 11 p.m. and lay down and slept where we were till daylight and woke to the sound of guns and musketry fire. This was Sunday. Our Regiment then arrived and we returned, very thankful to see them again.

Cronje had abandoned some 78 loaded supply wagons which were very acceptable to the British troops. He was pursued by the 6th Infantry Division, and they were catching up fast. They and French's cavalry made contact on 16th and 17th February. He was almost trapped.

4 March 1900. Lachlan to Father. Paarderberg

When I wrote the other day, we had got as far as Paarderberg about midnight on Sunday 18 February, very tired and many of the Company unable to move. The Battalion came in about 7 after we had managed to beg some forage for our valiant mules who, poor beasts, were done up from want of food and overwork. No rations were issued to mules because they were supposed to live by grazing, which is miserably insufficient. We also got an issue of rum and a few hours of sleep so feel much refreshed. It was a great relief getting back to friends again after being wanderers on the face of the earth, tho like us they were on half-rations and pretty tired. We had not reformed half an hour before we were turned out to go and fight. Nobody quite knew what was up, but we heard firing at intervals. B Company was sent out as baggage guard, which was just as well, for they were not fit for much else. Dingwall managed to hobble after us, but was unable to command. We went across to some kopjes on the south side of the river. About 2 miles from it were all the staff and the D.C.L.I. We had a splendid view of the battle. The latter were called away later to reinforce and, as you know, lost heavily through attempting an impossible feat.

Towards midday we discovered 2 or 3 kopjes in the neighbourhood which we were told were occupied, but were not. We sent out what men we could spare to do outpost duty. It was lucky we did, as next morning about half a dozen staff officers, full of their own importance, came fussing around explaining it was a most important post, for we were guarding the supplies of the whole British Force!

That shows how careless we are, if the Boers had attacked these kopjes with only one weak Company holding them, it would have been most unpleasant for us, and also the baggage. We spent an unpleasant night, no great-coats or anything. Every hour I divided between walking about and, when warm enough, trying to sleep. In the early morning the men found an old bullock, so we fired bits and ate them They were very like old India rubber. That evening poor Mitford came in with a splinter in his eye. He has since gone to Jacobsdal, where I hope he will recover. We had three killed and ten wounded that day. On Monday we were relieved by two companies of the DCLI, and told to rejoin the Battalion.

We marched back to where Dingwall and the baggage were, about a mile off. We got some lunch and about 4 p.m. set off to find the Regiment. We had to cross the river at the drift. Luckily it was down a bit. The day before it was nearly up to one's neck, and a rather dangerous current, so we all crossed with the aid of a rope without getting wet. The night we arrived we could have crossed nearly dry and within a few hours it was 5 ft. deep. Luckily we fell in with a guide and after going 3 miles or so found the Battalion extended in attack formation. We did not advance that night, holding instead 2 miles of ground, being extended at intervals of 4 to 5 yards between individuals, with a section of each Company in support 100 yards in the rear.

We got into position by dusk and every man entrenched himself with his bayonet. This was to prevent the Boers from breaking out. The Canadians and the Shropshires were doing the same on either side. A few did try firing into the darkness, but hit no one and, as a volley was fired into space after them, they evidently retired. Next day we did a general advance towards the laager and river but did nothing. We scarcely fired a shot, and had no casualties, but suffered a good deal owing to our getting no food and water for 24 hours, and having a blazing hot day. It was an extraordinary piece of mismanagement. We played the same game as the night before. This time the Canadians had some shooting, as the 30 of them went out after dark to rescue some meat which a pom-pom forced them to abandon by day. They met some Boers, whom they drove back with lots of noise and no loss, without finding the object of their search.

Next morning after some coffee (nothing more for the men) half my Company were sent with me to do a picket on a high hill by the drift. There was a wonderful view, but somehow our rations again went wrong and, in spite of repeated signals, no food came. We expected to have to stay all night and were in a very bad temper being starved, (I was better off having a private store). About 7.30 p.m. in pitch darkness, we were relieved by our other half Coy, and with great danger to our necks, as it is a stony and precipitous descent. We then got back to camp and some food.

At 8 a.m. we started to relieve the Shropshires in the trenches down the river. It was quite interesting as no one knew what was going to happen and we all went into file, scrambling along very rough places, full of thorn trees and bushes, and a most horrible stench from dead mules, cattle and the occasional corpses. We were trying to keep under cover of the banks, as bullets came pretty thick just over our heads, sticking in the trees and making a great noise! The Shropshires came out, looking very hot and uncomfortable and saying that once in the trenches it was all right, but a bit warm getting there, which we quite realised! As only two Companies at a time could get in, we had to wait a long time and rescued the ammunition off our mule, which had tumbled in and drowned. We were lucky as it was 5 ft. deep and very muddy.

Dingwall returned to duty that day. B Company were sent off to guard the Howitzer Battery overlooking the enemy's position to the north, about 2000 yds off and 3500 from the laager. It was interesting watching the shelling, but it rained heavily in the afternoon, drenching us and stopping by nightfall. We were cold and miserable, and had no coats, but after it stopped a few blankets were sent up, which was better than nothing, and we dined off cold, tasteless and unchewable bullock, killed that day.

The naval guns were on our left, and I got a cup of tea and an excellent bit of mealie bread from Campbell, brother of our Campbell killed at Magersfontein which, after Ration Biscuit, was a great treat. Next day we sat there. It passed like the one before but drier. It rained heavily during the night but the blankets kept us fairly comfortable. On Saturday about 5 p.m. the DCLI relieved our people on the river and we slept in a stony enclosure behind the guns. I was sleeping by the river on picket. We had an awful night of rain and I woke up about 2 a.m. to find myself sopping wet in a beastly bog. It was horribly cold and miserable. We dried out that day, Sunday, and had a fine night. Monday we did nothing, when two Companies were sent to reinforce the Canadians in the river; the rest of us being formed in the open to prevent the Boers from trying to break away. It was done with great difficulty by night. My Company was next to the river, and about 600 yds. from the Boer trenches.

We had orders to fix bayonets, but not to fire as we might hit our own people. At about 2 a.m. on Tuesday the Canadian Sappers did this gallant advance. We were all lying flat. Those with bayonets dug trenches and the bullets whistled over our heads, within a few inches of many of them. Smith-Dorrien was with the forward troops all through the battle. It was a marvel that no one was hit. This lasted at intervals till morning and when all was quiet we retired to our previous positions.

About 8 a.m. on the 27th we were told that Cronje and the Boers had surrendered.

It was hard to believe at first! Post just off.

What a wonderful relief that it is all over and one is still alive and in one piece! That is the normal feeling of all who have been through such a gruelling time.

The British force was around 15,000 supported by French's cavalry, but they were weak in numbers. There were strong infantry reinforcements on the way, but by forced march which meant that everyone arrived exhausted.

The Boers in the laager were surrounded and Kitchener thought that it could be captured in one day. He was wrong. They were extremely well protected by their clever camouflage and well designed groups of trenches which also contained, wives and families living a strange sort of troglodytic existence.

The battle lasted from 18 to 27 February. Lord Roberts had gone sick at Jacobsdal the day before it started so the command of the army fell to Kitchener as Chief of Staff. There were two alternative plans for defeating Cronje. The first was to completely cut off supplies and force him to surrender; the second was to overwhelm him by an attack up both sides of the Modder. The first was favoured by Roberts as it would be cheaper in casualties though it would take longer. Kitchener's plan, swamping the Boers with numbers on both sides of the river, would be quicker but expensive in casualties.

Owing to Roberts' illness, Kitchener's plan was adopted, but failed after an advance of only 1000 yards, mainly because the troops were utterly exhausted. Some had not even eaten that day.

Inside the laager, the Boers were in a bad way. They had 300 casualties, had lost many horses and were thus no longer mobile. There were no doctors and the lack of hygiene was appalling. There were dead animals, screaming children and a terrible stench. A sort of miasma hung over the camp.

The river was so full of carcasses that it was known to the British soldier as 'Dead Horse Soup'. Rayne Kruger records that in the middle of all this, Cronje sat patting the hand of his semi-hysterical wife. He had been urged to break out by De Wet and other commanders who were hovering around to help, but refused to do so.

Lord Roberts returned after having been informed of Kitchener's reckless behaviour as Commander-in-Chief. He was very popular with the troops who loved him. He despatched Kitchener to organise bridge and railway repairs as the Boers retreated and turned his attention to winning the battle.

Lachlan and B Coy had left Graspan on 13 February and fought on and off until the surrender on 27 February. They had marched 79 miles besides being involved in many battles en route. The Regiment was fortunate, it had a very low number of casualties, only 21 in all, including two killed. 4000 Boers eventually surrendered, including 50 women and 150 wounded.

British casualties totalled 1270. 24 officers and 279 men killed, 59 officers and 847 men wounded.

This was the first great British victory.

9 March 1900. Lachlan to Joan. Poplar Grove on the Modder River

I have to thank you for three letters in three days, also thank Father and Mildred for theirs, which came at the same time. We got no mail for three weeks after leaving Maple Leaf, then they all came in a bunch from Kimberly. We have, as I suppose you know, been fairly busy lately. In my last letter to Mildred, I got as far as the surrender of Cronje, which appeared to have made a great stir at home, and which, with the clearance of Boers from Natal, should help us along a bit.

But to resume from where I left off on Tuesday 27th. After the surrender at about 8 a.m. our Brigade was marched down to take possession of the laager. There were white flags flying, but in spite of them we fully expected to be fired on by brother Boer, so we moved up - or rather down - the two mile slope where the Naval guns and Howitzers were. We were in attack formation, that is extended 4 paces intervals, and in many lines 200 or 300 yards apart. I was in the front line with one section of B Coy, so had a good view of things before they were disturbed.

Smith-Dorrien and his staff rode in advance with a white flag, and strange to say we got down without a shot. No one was allowed to enter the laager, and we all sat down for two to three hours while arrangements were made. We were then ordered to camp close to the river amongst numerous and offensive dead beasts. Six men and one officer were then allowed to go from each Company to collect from the trenches and laager any articles that would be useful, but dire warnings were issued against private looting. We collected a lot of flour, salt and sugar, pots and pans, some old clothing and sundry minor articles.

The trenches were marvellous, narrow at the top and so deep that only a man's head and shoulder were visible standing upright. They must have been practically shell-proof, and were situated in extraordinary little odd corners and places along the river for miles, as well as in the big trenches outside the laager. There was the most extraordinary collection of rubbish and useful articles imaginable. Everything apparently was left at a moment's notice, half-cooked meals being found in the pots, and every description of clothing lying around, besides huge quantities of ammunition of every kind and vast stores of arms from Sweden to beautiful Mauser rifles, and innumerable empty tins of provisions.

The damage in the laager was considerable, hundreds of wagons having been burnt up until nothing but a heap of old iron remained and many others properly smashed. The ground all around the laager was littered with shrapnel bullets and old shells, many of which never exploded owing to the soft soil, and were consequently very dangerous to play with. There were also a lot of dead and mangled beasts all around which made sweet incense. The Provost Marshal then set parties to clean up, all the ammunition and arms being put in heaps, and the clothing and blankets etc. which the dirty old Boer loves to cart around, were burnt. I forgot to mention the huge quantity of stationery and old letters which littered the ground, lots of it labelled in Dutch, and also the books, including many Bibles, I even picked up a 'Pilgrims Progress' in Dutch! By the way, for 2 or 3 hours before they sent word of surrender, we heard them singing for all they were worth very weird and melancholy hymns.

You will know better than I do that their casualties were heavier than we imagined, many of their dead and wounded being found for days after. Cronje, the old ruffian was given a Guard of Honour. If it had not been for him, they would not have given in when they did. They were all in a horrid funk of him and hated having to fight; this we learnt from prisoners. We guarded the laager to prevent any one getting in and looting that night. The smell was highly odiferous, and the camp was little better.

On Wednesday we continued cleaning the laager and on Thursday I was in charge of a picket down by the river to prevent anyone bathing and regulate traffic at the drift. The Regiment was moving at 9 a.m. to a place about a mile up the river, so we followed and squatted down higher up. Nobody came to bathe and the traffic at the other place was practically nil. It also rained with great violence for a space of three or more hours. Luckily we had greatcoats, but it was depressing. Under my able supervision we made a road down a steep place into the river for water carts to fill, and an old Colonel of R.E.s deigned to approve of it, so I felt quite an engineer!

I picked up a sturdy Bull terrier down by the river and took her back, a very nice dog. On Friday 9 March I went and surveyed the scene of our recent battles where the Canadians made their fine but costly charge. Ogston has been sent to Capetown. On the night of this attack, his Company was supporting the Canadians in the trenches by the river with orders not to fire. When the Canadians were retiring under terrific fire, one of them, just as he was climbing, was shot in the neck and killed. His body tumbled over Ogston knocking him down, then another live Canadian came over on the top of him, and Ogston thinking that this must be a Boer tried to stick his bayonet in to him. Luckily he was unsuccessful but got his ankle badly sprained.

We pulled some lovely pink and white lilies on the way back growing close to the laager. Clara, the bulldog was out with us. She is a wonderful swimmer and thoroughly enjoys the water and tows you round by the tail. She was not very obedient, as might be expected of a reclaimed waif accustomed to leading a roving independent life. As long as there are no Regiments cooking she follows pretty well. She slept with me taking most of the bed. There were heavy thunderstorms and heavy rain.

On Saturday we did nothing. Dingwall took over the Mess Presidency from Tytler and is now an important personage. We are the only Regiment that has a reasonable mess going, but we have to be very careful of stores. We got our first mail for three weeks. It was very welcome and the toffee very good.

We had our Sunday service and there was more rain. Sgt. Duncan, our mess Sgt., came to relieve the 1st Gordon Highlanders with a little wagon that he procured for £40 in Kimberly and 6 oxen which were given to us by Rhodes himself. He also bought a lot of stores and the last mail. This was splendid, as our poor mules were quite unequal to their task of drawing the Regimental baggage.

We were under orders to move next morning, and Tuesday 6th at 8.30 we started. We did rear guard, with half the Battalion to the Brigade; and had to assist wagons that had got in the mud. We only went 6 miles up the river, but the wagons seemed to find it very hard, and we had to leave a lot of stuff and then go back for it. Grant (Monymusk) passed us on the way.

Wednesday morning we got up at 2.45 a.m., breakfasted at 3 and off by 4. We were going out to have a battle, our Brigade with 3 guns this side of the river and a little Mounted Infantry, and all the rest with 120 guns. We were to march on a big table shaped kopje, Leuk-Kop, and if no Artillery were there, to capture it. There were supposed to be 1400 Boers with 40 guns. We marched in quarter column until 4 p.m. doing 6 or 7 miles and when we were within 2 miles of our kopje, we deployed and advanced around the kopje keeping it 2 miles on our right. We advanced by Coys 300 yards. 4 of our Coys had been out on picket and caught us up here, the Shropshires leading, and we next and the Canadians in the rear.

The DCLI were sent across the river to help the Black Watch. I believe there was a big gun on the kopje, a Krupp. I am glad to say it did not fire on us, but on the guns that were shelling it, doing no harm to anyone. Our guns made it very unpleasant for the Boer on the hill, and there and then when they saw us marching around to outflank them they got into the devil of a fright, leaving the gun to its fate, so the Shropshires occupied the kopje. We marched on steadily over rather rough ground. The Shropshires had a little shooting and some skirmishing amongst some stones but they cleared out pretty quickly; otherwise nothing happened. The plan I have drawn gives a rough idea of the way we went and where we halted before the advance. The shelling continued about 2 miles from the big kopje and we then wheeled around it, keeping much the same distance from them all the way. We went without opposition until about 3 p.m. when, on our left flank, infantry began to shoot at us. It was a surprise as our left flank was supposed to be guarded by our own M.I.

The first we knew about it was 'bang-bang-bang' and three or four bullets whistled past our ears, and hit the ground close to our toes. We extended to 4 pace intervals and were the leading Company but one. We went stolidly on, their fire enfilading us. We imagined the M.I. would tackle the Boers, but the bullets still continued to narrowly miss us, and we were allowed to do nothing. I never felt so uncomfortable before. It was a great wonder no one was hurt, but after a minute of this Dingwall ordered one section to form and fire at them, and the Companies in the rear did the same. It was a great relief. We fired volleys at 1800 and 2000 yards, and the Boers got on their horses and galloped away. The whole thing lasted about 10 minutes. I think we got one or two of them, but it was hard to judge the range, and at that distance galloping men were a poor target, but anyway they cleared and we continued without interruption.

We had a short rest, and luckily there was a good well which was much appreciated. We then went straight ahead again until we reached the river at a place called Poplar Grove. We were pretty tired having been on the go since 4 a.m. and marched with nothing but biscuits some 20 miles. We were glad to learn that we had turned the Boers out of a strong position with little fighting.

The 19th Brigade were complimented on the way they performed a long and trying flank march which did more than anything to make the enemy clear out. The mosquitoes were very troublesome that night and the transport did not turn up until 2 a.m., when there was great confusion in getting our kits etc., which were all mixed up in the dark. We got to bed at 3 a.m. Next day we rested and bathed.

Tuesday, we crossed the river on pontoons, the drift being too deep to wade. We only got over by 7.30, the Highland Brigade taking a long time to cross at Leuberg on the line near Bloemfontein..

Saturday 10 March, we started on a four day march for this place. Breakfast at 4 a.m., parade at 5. We marched with halts of 15 minutes after each hour. At 10.15 we reached a big farm with a German and white flag. It had nice trees and flowers about it and looked comfortable. We stayed until 1 p.m. and got plenty of beautiful water from wells.

Roberts and Kitchener with Colville, our Divisional Commander (an awful brute!) and Macdonald etc. were all with us, we being the centre column with Kelly-Kenny, with the cavalry on the north or river road. Tucker was on the southern route, but I imagine the papers had all this in them. We were told we had only 6 more miles to go, but we went on interminably, until we had completed 18 miles. We got to Driefontein, where we stayed the night. We were pretty tired. Many of the men had new boots that day from a supply column, so their feet were very sore and they could hardly move. One carries, counting clothes, 50 lbs including a rifle which, combined with rough tussocky ground and a hot sun, is no joke. The baggage got in about dark, and the poor mules were in an awful state. They get very little food, brutal treatment from the drivers and fearfully hard work. It is piteous to hear them at night crying for food like children.

Next morning we paraded at 5.30, but were told we did not march until 10 as the naval guns were not in. We then heard rumours that Kilberry had had a reverse and dead and wounded were being brought in all night, but after we had started we heard that 102 Boers had been found, so we thought it must have been a victory after all. So far that is all I know.

We started over a huge ploughed field with mealies and melons which were very unripe, and it was great difficulty preventing the men from eating them. It was a very hot day and, though only 12 miles, it was the most trying march of any. I had on the shoes sent out and of course after a few miles got a large blister on my heel which was very painful (they are not the same as he made me last time and rather tight all over, so I feel very angry with Mr Mitchell). We got to Arvugal Kop and camped there. The mules had to be grazed and watered on the way or they would never have got in and it was very late. We started next morning at 5 a.m. and marched steadily for 16 miles, to Ventura Vieri I think.

There was the usual farm house and dirty dam. I went to wash in a filthy puddle with Tytler and Craufurd and we saw Macdonald with his wounded leg done up in a kind of case. He was very cheerful and came and talked to us. My heel was very sore, and coming here yesterday made me think evil of Mr Mitchell!

The last march to this place was only 11 or 12 miles. We got in by transport and all quite early. The water is good, but what we got at lunch upset several people. Nothing has had any effect on me which is lucky. Our camp is close to the railway, and it is quite strange to see anything so civilised again. In a neighbouring farm lived Steyn, a brother of the President. All the various H.Q.s (Staff etc.) have taken up their abode with him.

Wednesday 14 March, we sat there and rested. I climbed the Leuberg Kopje across the railway. It is very high as kopjes go and tremendously steep with huge boulders and bushes, but with the most glorious view imaginable. Bloemfontein looks quite near.

Bloemfontein, 15 March - We are camped about a mile outside the town which looks very inviting. Dingwall as the mess president went in yesterday morning but as yet I cannot go in, one officer per Company being obliged to remain in camp. I am Orderly officer tomorrow which is annoying. Prices are very high, and everything edible is at once bought up. We expect to stay here a month. Poor Willie Gordon was taken very ill today from the effects of overwork on an improperly healed wound, and I don't suppose he will be fit again for a long time.

PRESIDENT KRUGER

There are weird rumours that Buller is in Harrismith having taken many prisoners and having many casualties himself, but no one believes it. I think the Free State is done for and hope the Transvaal will not take long.

I sympathise with Gardie, but am not sorry he can't get out as I am sure if he didn't get shot he would get ill! We would like more toffee and anything in the way of biscuits which are far more appreciated than at home, though when the line is opened there will be plenty of things here.

There were an estimated 4000 Boers, under De Wet, at Poplar Grove which was the only resistance Roberts was likely to meet on the road to Bloemfontein. De Wet was a very different type of commander to Cronje, and had no intention of being caught in the same manner.

The British plan was to surround the Boers at Poplar Grove with the three Infantry Divisions, attacking their defensive line of kopjes. Simultaneously, the cavalry under General French would do a flank march around the back of the Boers, cut off their line of retreat and mop them all up.

At the same time President Kruger was visiting his troops and only just managed to escape in a four-horse Cape Cart. It would have been an great boost for morale to capture a real live President!

It was a good plan but, as usual, there are things that go wrong caused by the human element. The cavalry were late in starting. Their horses were exhausted and half starved as a direct result of Roberts' supply staff miscalculating the horse rations. They had overestimated the amount of forage that the horses were actually getting and consequently supplied them with far less than they needed. Ill feeling crept in between Roberts and French.

The infantry were very slow in advancing, further delaying the planned 'coup de grace' from the cavalry which, in the event, never took place. The Boers cleared out with very few casualties and lived to fight another day, though badly shaken and demoralised. The defeat and retreat from Paarderberg had eroded their will to fight. French reached Bloemfontein after capturing the high ground above the town, threatening to turn the Boers' flank, so they decided to leave lock, stock and barrel, much to the surprise of Roberts, who expected a fight for the town. The first to enter Bloemfontein were three British journalists. Purely by chance President Steyn was in Bloemfontein at that time and could have been captured, much as Kruger might have been at Poplar Grove. Two Presidents in the 'bag' in one day would surely have been a record. President Steyn went by train to Kroonstadt, further north on the Johannesburg line, a town which was to be the new seat of government. The rest of the retreating Boers travelled by ox-wagon. The combined Boer force on the long trek north was close on 7000 men, with 800 wagons and 10,000 oxen. A convoy 25 miles long.

This huge and unwieldy procession could have been attacked by Roberts but he left them alone. Some Boers had already gone home to their farms and, after the two defeats they had suffered, he thought the rest would follow suit.

A far more important consideration in Roberts' decision not to press further with an attack on the convoy was the fact that his army now consisted of 34000 tired and battered men who had been on half-rations for the past few weeks and who were in no fit state to continue without a rest and refit. It was all a question of logistics. Only 5 days' supply of food and forage remained and, even though there were captured supplies in the town that might last for a few weeks more, the situation was serious.

The lines of communication with Capetown stretched 500 miles and were dependant upon a single track railway whose bridges had in some places been destroyed. There were only eight trains available to ferry up stores; two to carry up the army's daily maintenance requirements and the other six for the much wanted supplies of medicine and clothing.

There was now a plague of enteric fever sweeping the army and a widespread shortage of medicines and hospital equipment. Before Paarderberg the troops were on half-rations and not strong enough to resist disease. Drinking polluted water was the main cause of the infections, which spread rapidly. There were more casualties from this disease than from bullets.

There was also a chronic shortage of horses with only a third of the required number available. The Remount Department responsible for their supply was poorly run and was looked upon as a sinecure. Roberts had expected to stay only a short time at Bloemfontein but with these problems, he was obliged to stay on for longer.

To cheer everyone up the Queen had ordered the introduction of a new decoration, The Distinguished Service Order, for bravery of a high degree. The first to receive this highly meritorious decoration were three sons of the Dukes on Roberts' staff. The order was christened 'Dukes' Sons Only'! One wonders what decoration, if any, the long-suffering soldiers got.

20 March 1900. Joan to Lachlan. 20 Cavendish Square

My Own Heart's Dearest. We got your long letter this week about the dreadful day with the convoy. Thank God that you were so wonderfully preserved and that you kept strong and well through all the marching afterwards with so little food and such bad water. It is too terrible to read of all the hardships you went through. But God is merciful. Don't think me a hypocrite or a Pharisee, but do you know that the Sunday before that Thursday was especially set aside for intercession for the army, and I was at Elgin and went to the Holy Communion and prayed so hard and I do think God listened to me.

This week has passed very quickly for me and there has been so much to do and to think about. I had my first piano lesson Saturday from a very charming little Miss Jerningham. Then on Sunday, Margot and I went to St Paul's Cathedral. It was too glorious. The music is the best in the world, and so simple. They sang your favourite hymn, "And now O Father." while we were receiving the Holy Communion. It made me cry...

In the afternoon Barbara and I went to the Abbey to hear Canon Gore. He wasn't as splendid as the first time. Wednesday evening was the dress rehearsal of the play Margot is acting in. I went to sell programmes.

I seem to roam the streets and spend my money. I was horrified this afternoon to find I had nothing left in my purse out of about £4 I had when I arrived and really nothing to show for it. Everyone is so generous I hardly ever pay for a cab myself. But you may want to know what I have been doing. Well, on Friday evening we all went to a most killing entertainment, a performance of Greek dancing, music and reading! The dancing was good but the music was too weak for words and the reading! An old woman, who looked like a vulgar governess, read very dull idylls and odes by Theocritus and others in a most melancholy voice, while the music jumped around in the background. One could hardly hear a word she said. The whole audience rippled and shook with laughter, but the elderly female (who was a senior wrangler) went on calmly and sadly. At last Margot and I had such hysterics that we left.

Saturday I went down to the Boltons and had a delightful evening. On Sunday Barbara and I went to the Abbey. We had the most glorious sermon I have ever heard in my life from Canon Gore. It was perfectly beautiful, and I am sure he is a Saint. On Monday I went to the play "She Stoops to Conquer", Goldsmith's masterpiece. I enjoyed it enormously. Tuesday I dined with Uncle Jack. A Captain Stirling, and our old friend Sir John Maxwell were there. Sir John was nicer than ever, but after a short and pleasant talk May collared him and they talked factories for hours much to my boredom, especially as Margot forgot me and I wasn't sent for till after 11. Wednesday, Margot had a dinner party, quite nice. Thursday, Barbara had a dinner party for me, or it was supposed to be. She had entrapped three young men into coming, but she sat between two of them and only left me the least of them, Mr Hart Davies, for whom I have a feeling of loathing, I don't know why. He plays the piano divinely, but he has such a horrid look in his eye and he is so superior in his ways.

It has been bitterly cold here ever since we came. Everyone has colds or influenza and I am terrified of it and drug myself with Quinine. I am sending you another parcel this week, a Cardigan jacket and some special lozenges. If you want anything in a hurry, you can always telegraph me now that wires are cheaper. If you wire me the name of the thing you want, I would understand. I hope you have your warm uniform now. I must stop and dress as it is getting late.

CHAPTER FIVE

Bloemfontein to Germiston 1900

30 March 1900. Grandmama to Lachlan. Drummuir

Yours of 28 February, the long one, was most interesting though not pleasant reading to hear of you making yourself into a kind of running deer to those Dutch men. I thank God there were some ant-heaps and that you were spared to see another day. It is splendid to hear of you standing the marches so well. The only disappointing thing was that you wrote on the 28th just when your story ended, which started on the 18th. Ten exciting days. You give no hint of the part you played. Don't make a target of yourself if you can help it.

Best wishes from Grandmama.

March 22nd 1900.
This is a dear little town, very pretty and nice, it has a links, cricket ground, race course and many charming houses with lovely gardens and flowers.

22 March 1900. Lachlan to Father. Bloemfontein

This letter will go with the one I wrote Joan. We have been here about a week, very uneventful. We take no exercise and eat too much. The town is a pretty little place, quite English. Practically all the shops are English, as are most of the people. Most of the Boers are away fighting. They did not want to, but were commandeered, as were lots of articles. They are at ruinous prices, especially eatables which are all bought up. Whisky is a guinea a bottle but we got some first at 11 shillings a bottle.

There is a club of which we are all honorary members, and a very nice little swimming bath which I went down to with Cameron the other day. We also went over the museum, which is nothing very great. The town is quite small, the chief street being Maitland Street, running into Market Square. A daily market is held there in the early morning where butter and vegetables etc. can be got with luck at exorbitant rates. Eggs and poultry are absolutely unprocurable, the generals and the staff having a monopoly of what there is.

Graham Tennant is here. He belongs to the Grahamstown Mounted Infantry, and is very well. They have not seen much fighting, but have a good chance of being sniped. We dined at the Phoenix Hotel last night and played billiards afterwards at the club.

A lot of us went to church last Sunday at the Cathedral, which is quite a fine building, like a good sized church at home, and very well got up, with a good organ. There were hundreds of officers and quite a big civilian congregation. It was the first church service since leaving home.

There has been a lot of heavy rain, and the weather is getting much cooler, the nights being very cold. In about a month's time the frosts begin, which will be very unpleasant.

Colville inspected our Brigade yesterday morning. It is the first time he has vouchsafed to show us his noble person. He is singularly ugly, and this time appearances do not belie, for he is the most awful rotter. However he complimented us and said we were the best Brigade out here, which nobody denies, and Smith- Dorrien said we did the best Brigade march past he had ever seen, even in Malta the land of ceremonial, so we were quite pleased.

The men are all very well and cheerful. We get no news but rumours, but the last is that Kitchener is hanging everyone he can catch at Prieska or some place. I hope it is true. It will do more good than any amount of proclamations and talking to the pious Dutch.

We have had no mail since Paarderberg, 3 lots are due. It is very annoying, as the papers come with great regularity. No one seems to know anything about letters and parcels. I have sent a picture of the market place, evidently in more prosperous times. The flies have developed in a most remarkable way since we have been here They are a horrid nuisance and rival a month's growth at Enslin.

When Roberts entered Bloemfontein, which was the seat of Government for the Transvaal, he issued a proclamation saying that if any Boer who had been fighting the British laid down his arms and signed an affidavit of neutrality and return home, he would have immunity.

He was under the impression that the war was nearly over, and he was convinced that the Boers would accept his terms, but they were in no mood to surrender. General Joubert, one of their most senior generals and a moderate, died at this time. He was the last of the old guard and was succeeded by the so called 'hard men', Christian De Wet, De la Rey, Smuts and other younger and more able leaders.

Meanwhile the Boers who signed the neutrality declaration did bury their arms as ordered. But they were not operational weapons such as Mausers. To meet their obligations they buried old and obsolete Blunderbusses and out-of-date Lee-Enfields, and in due course slipped away from their farms and rejoined the laagers.

Lachlan's remarks about the hangings that Kitchener ordered refer to the execution of spies who, as enemy agents, were indirectly responsible for the deaths of British troops, and should pay the price. At the start of the occupation, the policy was to be nice to the Boers. Now the country was awash with spies and increased and tightened security was the watchword.

The army was at Bloemfontein for six weeks. Besides refitting they had to contend with the enteric outbreak. Unlike Scutari there were no 'ladies with lamps', at Bloemfontein.

After the battle of Magersfontein there was a shortage of nurses and 40 had to come out from the United Kingdom, but these were not enough to cope with the much more serious outbreak of disease at Bloemfontein, when an urgent request for an extra 300 medical orderlies and 30 extra doctors was made.

30 March 1900. Lachlan to Joan. Bloemfontein

We have suddenly had orders tonight to move to Thabanchu. It is 40 miles away I believe. Tomorrow we go to another place, Waterfall Drift 20 miles off, so we have our work cut out. No one knows what is going to happen when we arrive, but I suppose we will try to kill Boers, and hope we will succeed. Please thank Grandmama for a parcel of things she sent, and say I will write when I get the chance. We move at 5 a.m., reveille at 3.30! How would you enjoy that? There was a great medical inspection today and we were the only Company with nobody unfit to move, which is good.

14 April 1900. Lachlan to Mildred. Bloemfontein

I have only time for a line as, when I intended to write, sudden duties arose which they always do when not wanted. We have passed a quiet week with none of war's alarms. A Company of volunteers has arrived with a draft of 60 men, Col Burney in command. Hay and Sworder who seem good fellows came with them. Ogston is also back. Murray, one of our reserve of officers, is here, Allan too, and Marshall.

Col. Burney's son, George would later be my commanding officer with the 2nd Gordons in Gibraltar in 1936. He was a fine soldier and a great leader of men as, no doubt, his father was before him. As a Brigadier he was taken prisoner at St Valery in 1940 and died shortly afterwards of cancer of the throat.

5 April 1900. Lachlan to Father. Rietfontein

Many thanks for your last letter, and the parcel of dates. The latter is much appreciated, especially the raisins, which are very good on a long march; they are easily carried. A week ago tomorrow we got an order at 5 a.m. next morning, so at that hour we were off and marched east, and after doing 8 miles, we heard a big gun going in the distance. After another 8, we got close up and prepared for an attack. The Shropshires were in front and the enemy retired across the Modder without doing any harm. There was a good deal of firing, and I believe some Mounted Infantry came in for it, pretty warm. We did a circuitous course and crossed the river getting to our destination at about 6, just as it was getting dark. We had done about 24 miles, our longest, at it the whole day and pretty tired. It was wonderful how the men stuck it out with worn shoes and rough ground.

We heard all sorts of rumours of Broadwood having a great smash up of artillery, owing to sending them without escort, and Boers shooting their prisoners, though the latter is not true. Next morning we fell in early, but did not move until 11. We crossed the river and marched 5 or 6 miles along the south bank, until the flank guard across the river became engaged. We expected to fight, but were ordered to retire; the enemy was too strong. So we turned round and went off at a great pace, marching towards Bloemfontein as far as Bush Kop. Where the water pipe reaches its highest point, the enemy had captured and smashed the works. We got in some time after dark, and B went out on picket. We had been out all day doing about 14 miles and were very tired.

There were several showers, but we kept dry enough. We cleaned ourselves next day, and were nearly massacred by a Shropshire gent who loosed off his gun, wounding three of his men and just missing several of us. At 2 a.m. we marched to Springfield, a kopje 6 miles off and about 8 miles from Bloemfontein. We were plagued with locusts which came and clustered in the bivouacs and mess tent. They flop in your face, food and drink and cover the floor and worry everyone. I fully sympathise with Pharaoh!.

DE WET

Next morning we went back to Bloemfontein by a circuitous route, owing to nullahs, and marched through. Little Bobs looked at us, and was much pleased with the smart way the men stepped out, as if they were only just out of camp instead of at the end of a long march. We got our mail, a clean up, kits from Orange river and some tents, and were very happy.

On Wednesday we were suddenly ordered off again at 2 a.m. to this place. So we packed up and went, and arrived, at about 8, by the light of the moon. It is 12 miles east by south. Next morning, we and all our Division went forth to do battle, but somehow, though we searched diligently, there was no enemy and we had to go back to camp. We were none too soon, as we had to get bivouacs etc. arranged and lunched while it rained in torrents.

9 April Bloemfontein - We were not very uncomfortable, but Dingwall and myself in my bivouac found it rather leaky. We ate your dates, and smoked some good cigars of D's and were quite happy. This morning we came back here about 1 p.m. D and I have a tent, as have all the officers and a proportion of the men. Everybody is quite comfortable. You asked who the 3rd officer in the Company was. Till a week ago we never had one. Now Clowes belongs to us. He is a very good chap. We have just had a week of tramping and covered at least 100 miles or thereabouts and are all very fit as a result. The ground was heavy going today, very muddy. And the weather is still thundery and unsettled. We have a deep trench round our tent as without it the ground we occupy would be a morass. The Camerons are here with sword and sporran.

At the end of March 1900 the Boer generals and the two State Presidents had a top level conference at Kroonstadt, their new seat of government after being forced to leave Bloemfontein. Their situation was not at all good. De Wet, Louis Botha, De la Rey and others decided on a change of strategy. The commandos were to be divided into flying columns and they could now do what they were good at, moving fast and sending out raiding parties, such as that at Sanna's Post.

General Broadwood was in charge of the British force at Sanna's Post and had not thought it necessary to post sentries or even reconnoitre the ground. People just slept without sentries. 7 guns, 117 wagons and 428 prisoners were captured and sent back northwards.

The army was ready to advance on the 3 May for the next move to Pretoria. General Hamilton was in command and had been at Ladysmith. His orders were to do a left flank movement and capture Pretoria. Winston Churchill was one of the war correspondents with the column.

Hamilton's first task was to retake the town's water supply.

21 April 1900. Lachlan to Joan. Bloemfontein

I thank you for your letter. I have a horrid pen and cannot write legibly. We are in a horrible fuss subsequent to a sudden order to march just as suddenly countermanded. Hence from order, 'disorder.' It is really too bad, and what is more we do not know whether we are off tonight, tomorrow, or not at all. The order came last night about 7, and I was dining with Graham Tennant about 2 miles off. I knew nothing of it until after 9 o'clock. We were to be fallen in, ready to march off at 7 a.m., which we were. We waited until 8, when we were informed that we were to stay a bit longer. It is now 8.30 and nothing more is known. We were only destined to Springfield, about 9 miles march, to relieve the 18th Brigade at present sitting there, and we were to come back Monday or Tuesday.

We have had an awful week of rain, I've seen nothing like it before. Easter day was dull and showery. We had the usual Presbyterian service at 9 a.m., and most of us afterwards went to the Cathedral as it is called. They had a very nice service, and crowds of people, mostly military. The singing is very good, and the church was decorated with chrysanthemums. It started to rain that night.

Monday was beastly, Tuesday ditto; the camp was like a pond. We have any amount of drains made but the ground is so flat they could not run off much water, though they had regular rivers in them. Of course all the tents are moated, with the earth baulked inside, so they kept dry, except for leakage, which was sometimes considerable. We indulged in tropical showers of several hours duration, with steady drizzle in between. I had my rubber boots to my great delight, as heretofore, whenever they might have been useful, they were always with my heavy kit. I felt compelled to wade through every pool in the way to get some money's worth out of them.

Wedderburn's brother turned up the other night. He was supposed to be safely in Pretoria, so it was very astonishing. He slept in my tent, as Dingwall was on picket, and told me his adventures when he was a trooper in some colonial horse, helping to guard a little convoy not many miles from us, and also on the Riet. They were surprised by Boers and rushed, the officer in charge being killed with several others. They gave in, for resistance would have entailed them all being shot. The old commandant was all for shooting the prisoners at once, but after a long argument, decided not to, but he pressed a revolver at Wedderburn's head, and made faces at him. Luckily one of them could talk English, and explained he only wanted his bandolier! They were only taken to Jacobsdal after an unpleasant journey, where he developed pneumonia, but was well looked after by an English woman, to whom some of the mine belonged. When the Boers evacuated he was left, coming here as soon as he was well.

Monday was fine and we were out all the morning digging trenches on St. Andrew's Hill in case of attack. Wednesday was a terrible day of wet. Yesterday I got the transport pony and rode over to see Graham, but found them all out to be photographed tho' the man never turned up, so their CO seized on the opportunity to give them an extra drill and inspected them. I was given tea and introduced to several fair damsels.

Thursday - We were photographed! The wretched man kept the whole Battalion waiting an hour, then took one. The woollen clothing so far has been very useful, but the cardigan jacket has not arrived yet. Please do not send any more meat lozenges - I never eat them - but chocolate is always good. I am sending this to Drummuir as they will read it on the way. If not, tell father I got his letter.

2 May 1900. Lachlan to Joan. 10 miles north of Thaba Incline

I think it is some time since I wrote to you, and we have had plenty of experience. We left Bloemfontein on 21 April at 2 p.m. after falling in at 5 a.m. marched 8 miles to Springfield, where we passed once before. We were told we were only taking the place of the Brigade until Monday, when we were to return, so didn't take much baggage as tents would be provided. That was nearly 14 days ago! We bivouacked that night without tents, started off for picket at 4.30 a.m. in pitch dark until about 9 a.m. by a little kaffir village we got breakfast, and shifted to another occupied camp. As there was available only one quarter of the number of tents required, and I was on duty, I had to hunt around for hours with two wagons and a party and got 40 shifted. Sunday was anything but a day of rest! We heard Rundle fighting in the distance, but stayed quiet.

Monday 23 April - Off about 10, past Bushman's kopje to Sanna's Post, near the Modder, arriving at dark, about 12 miles. We were for picket and had a cold tiresome night along a river and up a nullah. The enemy were across the river; in fact some pickets heard Boer scouts talking.

Tuesday 24 April - Next day we forded the river, ankle-deep, and marched to the waterworks from which the enemy had cleared leaving them in pretty good condition though bits of machinery were gone and windows smashed. We killed a very fine cobra near by and then crossed the river, again fording, deployed and advanced. We were in the reserve line but nothing happened. We crossed a lot of beastly little streams, and after some firing and a few shells, the enemy cleared. We had no casualties, the position was strong and we expected a big fight, but by 1 p.m. it was all over, and we camped in a pretty place by some shady bushes.

Wednesday 25 April - We were off early via Weel for Thaba Incline a lovely mountain, which looks huge, 33 miles off Bloemfontein. There was a good deal of firing. Mounted Infantry and about two Companies were in advance and attacked the kopje. The Boers were in a long line, on a very strong kopje. B Company were in support, and advanced but hardly fired a shot. The Canadians were on the right. The Boers bolted, leaving a few dead and wounded and some prisoners. 1st Gordon Highlanders were as usual very lucky, no casualties, the total in the 3 Battalions was 13. The Shropshires were left at Bloemfontein. One Canadian killed, their CO wounded. Graham Tennant's regiment lost heavily, five officers were hit. Lucky for him he was absent with fever. We too were attacked that night, and on 26th marched into Thaba unopposed. It is a long straggling village, very picturesquely situated under the mountain. It was the old capital of Basutoland, and the kaffir town is still uninhabited. I also believe they worship the mountain. B Company were at once sent to do policeman in the town.

It was a very tiring job, rushing about and turning out all soldiers and putting sentries over shops and stores, and generally protecting property from the brutal and licentious soldiery, and seeing the town beauties, who all came to have a look. One house was broken into and we enquired at a neighbour who told us which it was, and expressed a wish that the soldiers had pulled the whole thing down, which showed us that neighbourly feelings were as amicable here as elsewhere. We were told 2000 Boers passed through the town, looting and commandeering the property of Britishers, of whom there were plenty. We bivouacked below a kopje north of the town. The weather at night is cold, with very heavy dew and as we have to sleep in the open without bivouacs, it is singularly unpleasant. Strange to say there is no dew on the kopje, which is lucky or picket would be a terror.

Friday 27 April - Quiet, but several Boer guns opposite shelled our M.I. when they got the chance. They were in range of our camp, but did not molest us as kopjes sheltered us from view, and they did not attempt to shell us. We were for picket with A Company that night, going into a big stony kopje in pitch dark. Next morning we found the Regiment gone. They went by night marching about 18 miles, to relieve some of Kitchener's Horse in a tight place, but lost their way. We were not relieved for hours, and captured a little kaffir boy trying to break through the line. We gave him back to his Mama and Grandma who rushed to claim him, and they showered benedictions on us when we returned him alive.

Sunday 29 April - The Boers shelled our guns on the picket hill vigorously, killing and wounding four men. We replied. I went with several fellows up a kopje behind our camp and watched it, then the Boers had a shot at us, which whistled over our heads, and landed amongst a number of horses right below our camp but did no damage. The range was about 6000 yards. They did not try any more at us. There was a voluntary service at which many attended. Our little Padre preached very nicely, much better than one would expect. The Guards climbed Thaba hill that evening and we watched the Boers shell them. A few days before, six of our signallers had a private fight up there. They were signalling by night to Bloemfontein and were surprised at dawn by a party of Boers, but they kept them off and escaped unhurt with all their apparatus, a very plucky performance.

Monday 30 April - Marched to Probia. Finding a Boer laager and a big kopje, we shelled the laager, and then began the hardest fight I have ever seen. Kitchener's Horse attacked first and the Boers, after a few shots, retired from the front edge. We deployed and got up to the kopje safely with a few stray shots at us. We then came under very heavy fire and crawled behind stones returning equally heavy fire.

B Company with some others were sitting up, half way up the hill, under a terrific fire. Two Boer guns captured from us at the Tugela, were enfilading us, and they were wonderfully accurate, but luckily the shells burst on impact, and we had many marvellous escapes. One shell burst only burst 4 yards away from me, showering me and others etc. but no harm done. The two Coys below had to retire and take shelter. We all had extraordinary escapes, a few being slightly hurt and one of A Company killed. Murray had a big rock hurled against his back and is on the sick list, but will shortly rejoin us. Here we climb up, crawling under a hail of bullets.

6 May 1900. Lachlan to Father. Winburg

We are fairly started for Pretoria, the house of Oom Paul, and the goal of our endeavours (that is not a quotation)! So far our progress has been pretty satisfactory, but I will begin from Thabanchu. We left that enjoyable spot on Monday 30 April, early, and marched 8 or 9 miles northwards in our usual style. Then, as we were mounting a long slope to a ridge, our own pom-poms and guns started banging away at a Boer laager, and it was found that a big kopje to our left was held. The M.I. and K's Horse advanced first and the Boers, after a few shots, retired from the front slope, up which they followed and we advanced next, in three extended lines. B Company were in the 2nd, supporting K's Horse. They got up the hill and half K's Horse with Towse, were suddenly confronted by a large body of Boers a few yards off, at the top of the kopje, who told him to hold up his hands. However he gave them a volley, but he was shot through the eyes and will, we fear, lose both. He is to be recommended for a V.C., but it can in no way compensate for such an injury. It is frightfully sad, and he is such a good chap.

We got to the bottom of the hill over about 2,000 yards of open ground, with only an occasional shot at us and sat there for a bit. The Boers then opened on us from the right with 2 guns making marvellously accurate rapid shooting, shells bursting all over the face of the kopje, enfilading us, wherever they could see a few men. One burst 2 or 3 yards in front of me, showering us with small stones etc., and cutting two men under the eye, but hurting no one. This happened constantly for hours, our guns being outranged and ineffectual against theirs, which by the way, they had captured from us at the Tugela! Luckily they used home made percussion shells. Shrapnel would have had, I should think, terrible effects.

All the time the Boers had from the front crest to the rear, which was higher and commanded it. Several of our Companies had gained the front ridge, which we also did, a few men at a time going up and taking cover behind stones under heavy cross rifle fire from the front at about 600 yards, and the left front at 1,200 yards, and shell fire from the right. We had only one man slightly wounded, and all got into position and returned their fire as well as we could. The noise was considerably the worst, bullets and shells, whining and screaming, guns roaring and small arms spitting angrily everywhere. The Coys behind us were forced by shell fire to retire, though of course they were out of rifle fire. They were very lucky, and of course extended, but we saw shells put beautifully into their ranks, wherever they went. A Company lost one man from a shell that passed clean through him.

Soon after dark firing dropped, though the Boers fired every few minutes at us gaily, on spec, doing no harm. We occupied the time by building stone sangas in the dark, filling water bottles and resting. I always carry bundles of warm garments, and the men each a blanket, and as dew does not seem to fall on kopjes, we spent a passable night.

Before 6 next morning firing began on our right and we noticed that the big kopje in front seemed unoccupied. As this would make a very commanding position Dingwall, without orders, cautiously advanced with two or three men and crossed safely. I then reinforced directly with all but 1 section of the Company. We kept well extended, but when we were 100 yards from Dingwall, a heavy fire opened on us from the right, wounding L/Cpl. Simpson in the stom-

CROSSING THE ZAND RIVER
May 1900

ach. He died soon after. We thought our own troops were shooting by mistake, and shouted to them to stop, one man even being allowed close up and getting the answer; "All right!". They missed the rest of us, and we got out under cover of stones etc., hardly daring to move.

We began to realise then that it must be Boers. I was close to Younger, of F Company who followed Dingwall with a few men. We'd apparently been seen without seeing. So it seemed advisable that the Colonel should be informed of our whereabouts. I started to go back. I was hardly up before 3 bullets just shaved me, so thought better of it and wriggled on my stomach down the hill, a tedious process, and at the bottom got up and ran across the open until a ridge hid me. After I'd seen Col. Burney, the two Boer guns started again. I sat behind a fine big stone and in the intervals of shells, packed up the warm clothing etc., and when I heard one coming lay flat behind the stone, several passing just overhead, patterning. For some reason it soon stopped, and I got back to B Company with some water carriers.

They had now detected some Boers about 600 yds. off along the ridge of the hill and in the bushes and stones a little way down the sides. Several of our men got to the very top and much astonished some Boers on the plain below the hill, by shooting several men and horses below them, also accounting for some six Boer snipers out in the bushes, and a negro. We had meantime four more of us wounded, only one dangerously, Cpl. Patterson. I was with two men lower down shooting hard at some bushes they were among. I just missed a fine grey buck who clambered across between us and the Boers. 2 others were fired at and missed. The sniping was a bit too much, so I crossed again under cover of a hot fire.

22 May 1900. Lachlan to Father. Heilbron

It is some time since I wrote after Zand River. We have been quite peaceful since we plodded over many miles of dreary country, arriving here about midday today. After Zand River we marched next day, only to go 8 miles. However about 5.30, when it was pitch dark they discovered it was not a suitable place and said we must go on another 6 miles, which we had already done. We were off next day at 8.30, and after 10 a.m. had a 3 hour halt in a blazing sun, which was supposed to be a rest, but with no shelter was not much good. We went on another 6 or 7 miles getting in as usual over very rough ground after dark, horribly tired. The nights are very cold, and until the baggage and greatcoats get in, it is pretty miserable, though we have a mess tent and usually get a pretty good dinner soon after arriving in camp, and a fire. We expected a great fight at Kroonstadt but the Boers, after a little fighting, cleared and we camped 5 miles from the town in a rather pretty place, but bad water.

Sunday we had a service and stayed quietly where we were. We managed to get some stores from the town which were very valuable. Monday. I got a pony and rode in with Craufurd and Younger to shop. It was beastly dusty, the road crossing two bad drifts, and a squalid ugly town; all the shops shut except about two stores. We had to get out lists of purchases signed by the controller of supplies, and then got very little, though we got a good deal of Boer tobacco for the men and matches, soap etc. Roberts inspected us this morning and we were to go to Lindley next day where Steyn was reported to be disguised as a labourer. We marched on Tuesday at 8.30 a.m. to a place called Meriba, 5 miles taking about 5 hours. We were rear guard.

Next day we went on at 2 p.m. and did 10 miles very rapid marching, passing 3 or 4 big veldt fires, which looked very fine by night. It was very cold. We were off early next day, the 11th, and after doing 11 miles had a long halt by a spruit for lunch among thick thorn bushes. We then went 4 miles further getting into Doornkop at dusk, 15 miles from Lindley. The baggage only got to us by 11 p.m. through the incompetence of the chief transport officer who outspanned in the dark on the wrong side of a very difficult drift. There was some skirmishing at a neighbouring farm by some misguided Boers resenting our intrusion, but they were soon kicked out, and the farms looted. The country there is very hilly, big billowing, undulating ones. We did not move that day. It was one of the first nights that we have had frosts, ice being formed on the buckets.

Next morning instead of proceeding to Lindley, we crossed the drift, and waited the whole day for two convoys, only one of which turned up. We were rear guard and started at 9 a.m. and only did 8 miles by 8 p.m. Another frosty night at Quaggersfontein. We were off next Sunday by 6 a.m., and marched steadily for 12 miles and had lunch, then on another 6 miles to Vaal Bank, near the Rhinoceros River, a long march. We rejoined the other Brigade from Lindley, who apparently had a jumpy time of it owing to the attentions of some 1200 Boers, 60 M.I. being captured. We had a miserable windy night which has given me a cold in my head.

Monday morning was frightfully cold; we were apparently to march at 7 only to get off at 9.30. It was terribly dusty and I had a very sore foot, so hated it. We arrived at Veclet Kop with the baggage, getting in before sundown. Today we have come on 10 miles here. It is a pretty little town. We saw some shelling going on some miles away off to our left front this morning, but have not heard what was up. We may stay here for a day or two, then either to Mt. Prospect or straight to the Vaal. We have not had a mail since leaving Bloemfontein, and are on half-rations, which is very hard on the men. who have to march and work like mules for far too little food and of course they grouse like blazes. We have some flour and make some very bad scones, which keep us going and occasionally get a few fowls or butter, but the Cavalry generally take everything, about all they can do. They are a positive disgrace, and let opportunity after opportunity go, and do nothing when they might do so much.

Mafeking is rumoured relieved, I hope it is true, but we never hear anything. The men seem to think the war will be over in a month, though I can't see why. They keep wonderfully well and cheerful considering all things.

31 May 1900. Lachlan to Joan. Florida, 12 miles west of Johannesburg

I am honouring you with my first epistle from the land of Oom Paul. We are having our first halt for 12 days, and are sitting down about 12 miles west of Johannesburg. We are reduced now to 14 officers, a very small mess, compared to what we left Bloemfontein with, and the whole Battalion is sadly reduced in NCOs. I wrote to Father when we reached Heilbron on the 22nd but have been unable to post it, so it is still in my desk, likewise I know not how or when this will depart, but it will be with his. But to continue our tortuous and sometimes tortured progress from here ....

23rd - A bitterly cold morning, high up and freezing cold overhead. We are rear guard, and loaf about from 7 to 11, infernal! Christian De Wet and his commando are waiting to swoop into the town as soon as we are clear of it. At about 12 the last of the baggage gets off and we start cold as ever, with the possibility of a rear-guard fight. We march steadily over hilly bleak looking country, a grey sky, cold wind and the colouring and general appearance of the country being curiously like a Scotch moor in the highlands. Expecting to do 12 miles and get in about dark, we were agreeably surprised, after 8 hours to suddenly get over a hill to find our camp, luggage in, lunch ready, and time for a wash down before sundown, at a place called Elandspruit.

24th - Off early intending to go to Mount Prospect on the railway. After 10 miles we arrived but could find no water so we turned to the right and went 4 miles over burning veldt, and got very filthy from black ashes.

25th - Start about 7 a.m. Go 1 mile, sit down to wait supplies till 3 p.m. Very sickening. On again, get in 6 miles on over rough ground in pitch darkness, very cold and beastly.

26th - A great day. We started early, and marched over flat country some 10 or 12 miles and got the first glimpse of the long desired Vaal river. Halted and lunched about 2 p.m. on very sandy ground and had to empty out my shoes several times. Had to wade the river, the banks very rocky, bottom shingly, water cold and knee-deep, but very clear and good. A good few crossed bare-footed including myself and it burnt horribly. At a drift called Boschbank, several miles west of where Roberts crossed, we encountered no opposition.

Dingwall and self were for picket, and walked another 6 miles having fearful difficulties in picking up the line through the darned stupidity of old Inglefield, the Brigade Major, and the slackness of 21 Brigade who omitted to send out pickets, while we hunted for people who were not there, and a kaffir kraal somewhere in the veldt. It was too dark to see 50 yards but by luck we tumbled across it. My temper was sorely tried, but dinner and blankets came to the rescue. Luckily it was a very cloudy night, and neither wind nor frost, so we were quite warm. The Canadians relieved us in the morning, and we had time for a good bath before marching. We did 14 miles that day through not very interesting

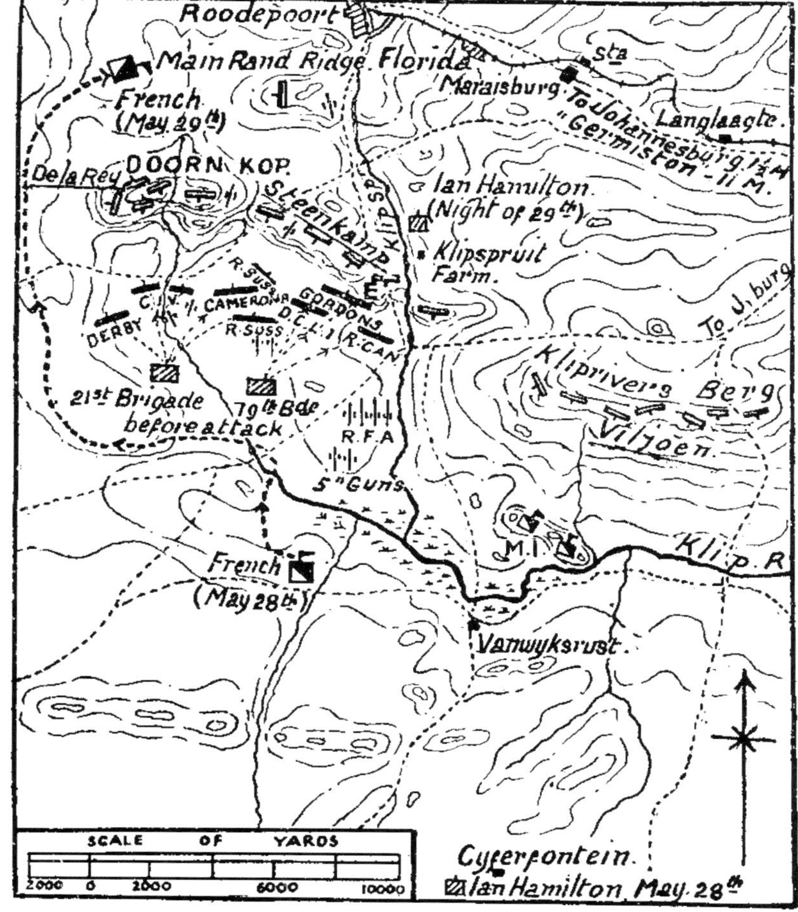

DOORNKOP 29 MAY 1900.

country, even for these lands of monotony, and had a very cold night with hard frost.

28th - Off early marching north to Swyfontein about 9 miles. Heard French's pom-poms a few miles ahead shooting away. The Boers' original plan was to hold the hills we camped under. They were fortified and all cover burnt from their faces. We caught two American Scouts asleep!

29th - A sad but a memorable day for the Regiment. We marched early, the grass long and swampy, thick with hoar-frost. After going 10 or 11 miles with a running Cavalry and M.I. fight on our ridge to our right, we were told to prepare for attack, as they were compelled to retire. We could see the chimneys and buildings of the Great Rand scattered all about in front. We halted behind a ridge, about 3500 yards from the Boer positions while our guns shelled them vigorously. The 21st Brigade were on our left. The enemy shelled us, but most burst too far back to do harm. H and K Companies were in the front line, G and M (the Volunteer Coy) in 2nd, then half B and half A supported their other halves in the third line. I was with the front half Coy. The two front lines were extended to 30 paces interval, we were 10 paces, but opened to more as we advanced. The different lines started 200 yards ahead of each other. C and D followed us, F were in reserve. The whole ground was absolutely bare and much of it burnt, sloping gently to a rocky crown held by the Boers. We very soon came under a scattered fire which hit few.

We did not reply and some shells came uncomfortably close. Originally we were to have advanced to 1800 yards range to lie down and fire, but a bugle sounded the "Advance" and an order was passed down our line to advance rapidly, which we did and then were catching up with M Coy, who caught up the front line, so we got mixed up. Anyhow we arrived within 400 yards of the tops, where the Boers were behind a lot of rocks and had burnt away all the grass where we had to advance. The fire was now very heavy and many men were falling and the only thing to do was to charge, which we did, fixing bayonets as we ran, and raising an almighty yell. I never felt so blown in my life, chiefly from the weight of kit.

The Boers cleared to rocks further back not wishing to be pigsticked, so we gained the first rocks under a most terrific fire actually within about 50 yards of some Boers, tho' the greater lot got to cover about 500 yards back, before we got right up and kept up, literally, a hail of bullets. Buchanan (Capt. of the Volunteers), and our Doctor Benson, a very plucky chap, were both hit a little to my left, as well as many men all around. I got behind a very small stone at first, and fired away most of my cartridges at some very objectionable Boers, but could not say if I hit any.

About 40 yards in front was a much bigger rock and, as they had very nearly got me a good many times, I got up as quickly as I could and raced across, being missed by a shower of bullets they favoured me with, tho' I did not give them much chance, throwing myself flat as I got behind 2 Volunteers, who were behind some other rocks about 30 yards to my left. By shouting at the top of my voice, I got them to throw some cartridges and we shot away like blazes. Several other Coys came up in the meantime, or a portion of them. White on my right hand with a wounded man handing him cartridges, was also lucky not being hit. After we had been there about 10 minutes the Boers seemed to make a final effort to dislodge us pouring in a tremendous fire which lasted several minutes. Evidently they were using magazine fire as hard as they could loose off, my rock and everyone else's being plastered with bullets. Many were hit who incautiously showed a foot or a hand. At the time I did not think we were suffering as heavily as we did, being amongst the first Coys up and no one in front of me.

I was fully occupied shooting at half a dozen or so Boers among some rocks close to a solitary tree. They were very sporting. One got up once and stood upright on a rock to get a view of us as he shot. I had a steady shot at him but missed I think from over-sighting, but he got down pretty quick, and did not try again. We hit a good few of them, but they were very plucky getting their wounded away. They had ponies a few yards behind them under cover and when one had enough he got on his gee and galloped off. Luckily they were not first class shots, otherwise not so many of us would have come off Scot free, having to cross such a lot of black burnt grass under such heavy fire. Corporal Mackay, the Doctor's assistant, has been recommended for the VC which I hope he will get. He several times brought in wounded men under cover and tied them up, himself exposed, and did wonderful work all along the line under the heaviest fire. Many men died under the same. After an hour of this the enemy, finding that the expected reinforcements did not turn up and that we would not be shifted, began to clear out. They did it very cleverly, getting a long start by all being mounted. As soon as it was noticed that they were giving way, everyone got up and rushed across as before, this time without being fired at. We got a few prisoners and some dead and wounded, and fired long range volleys at those riding off, by which time it was getting dark and it was all over.

Parties were sent out to look for our own dead and wounded. As the papers will have told you, they numbered 97 including poor Meyrick killed and seven wounded officers and Benson, the doctor. In B Company we had four men killed. Later 15 or 16 died of wounds, another four or five died of wounds in hospital, and many were badly wounded. The Boers nearly always use soft nosed bullets. At Houtnek on 1 May we found some with their bandoliers filled with bullets covered with verdigris, a suspected poison for the wounded. Don't let this get out as it has been reported to the General, who is investigating it. Later, the green bullets were proved after analysis to be harmless.

After we got collected and fallen in, the rolls were called, a melancholy business with so many good men missing. We waited a long time in the cold and the dark before getting into camp. There was no water to be got so the men had no tea that night and we got no breakfast in the morning. We spent a long time burying the dead on a very cold morning, and then continued to march to Florida.

It got very hot and dusty, and our thirst was considerable, the country very hilly. We got to the great Witwatersrand (rand means ridge), that is the great gold reef. Mines were plentiful, huge buildings with great iron chimneys, like the brick factory chimney at home. Very few were working. At length we found a well, and bottles were filled at about 1 p.m. Camp was quite close, and we only did 5 or 6 miles and camped about 8 miles west of Johannesburg, and were very ready for lunch. We sat down 14 officers. I am in command of M Coy, the Volunteers, and a fine lot they are. It was their first chance of distinguishing themselves and they took it, though unfortunately they suffered heavily, losing three officers and a lot of men. Today we were ordered to move nearer Johannesburg between 1 and 2 p.m., but it was countermanded, and we marched to a little cemetery close to Maraisburg station (on the Potchefstroom railway) and buried Meyrick and two men who died.

After it was over I went with Lumsden to see the wounded who were accommodated in a building belonging to one of the mines, half a mile away. They were all very cheerful. Col. Burney expects to be back soon. Forbes asked me to send a line to Donald the keeper, a friend of his. He is severely wounded in the leg, so please give the enclosed to Donald.

We were very short of food, no rations being given to us, but we got some mealie flour issued, and Roberts promised a train-load from Johannesburg, which did not arrive till next morning. The men halfstarved.

We moved then from Johannesburg to Brandfontein, 5 or 6 miles. The country was very pretty and interesting, many woods of young gum scattered about, which a little way off look exactly like fir woods, and countless huge mines. There was also a certain amount of cultivation to be seen. Johannesburg is 5600 ft above the sea, so it is very breezy and healthy, no enteric which is from bad water. Our new camp was in very long thick grass, like a hay field, and one had to be very careful not to set it on fire, as there had been no rain for about six weeks and a strong breeze was blowing. Several fires started and in spite of many men with blankets, they were difficult to master, so rapid and fierce were the flames.

On all the hills great veldt fires could be seen burning leaving stretches of land burnt and lifeless. About 2 p.m. permission was given to go into Johannesburg. However it was so late that few availed themselves of it. I started to walk in with Murray. The road was very dirty, but there were plenty of gum-tree woods and nice houses all along it. Instead of only 2 miles as we expected, it turned out to be 5 or 6, and though we walked over 4 miles an hour, owing to delays in getting off it was dusk before we got in, the suburbs being very big.

Most of the shops were shutting, many being permanently shut as their owners were disporting themselves elsewhere under compulsion. We shopped hard, getting some warm underclothing and small luxuries. We had tea and dinner combined at a very good restaurant: "eggs and beef steaks" with very good coffee and cakes to fill up, drinks and a real table and chairs. The town is very

Johannesburg 1900

big and fine and marvellous, considering its age, but prices are terrific. It is the most extortionate place we have ever been to. The streets shops, houses etc. are all lighted by electricity, and many of the shops rival Bond St, giving the latter points in the prices they put. We had frightful difficulty in getting a cab out, but eventually we did so, our trip back cost us 25 shillings.

2nd June - I was on duty. We did not move. A lot of fellows went into town. About 40 men taken to work on the railway.

3rd - Off again. Long march, about 15 miles, very hilly and pretty country woods, and a little cultivation visible. We walk through the stream and camp at Deepsluit.

4th - Off early, march 9 or 10 miles to Crocodile River. Heard fighting all day, crossed river by stepping stones. Pretoria is in view about 6 miles to the north east, nestling in hills. Glorious 4th of June! The promised town in sight, and our last fight up to date. Have no desire for more. We returned at dusk, but baggage could not find us, and we could not find the baggage. After another 3 hours waiting about in the cold and the dark, we get in, and get dinner about 10 p.m. very thankful not to be shivering in a kopje waiting for dawn to shoot more Boers!

5th - We started at 6 a.m. to march to Pretoria, the road is hilly and wild (we were coming from the south-west) and the morning as usual was cold, but light and sunny. After going some 5 miles we found the road lined with troops of all sorts, the King's Own Scottish Borderers cheered us as we passed, they are old friends, and we also left the road and were halted on an eminence on the left. There we were to wait for some time until 9.30. a.m.. The meaning of it all was that Roberts wanted all his available troops to be present at a pow-wow between himself and Mr Botha. However Mr B thought better of it, and departed secretly beforehand.

I hope this is correct, at least we heard so then, and were left rejoicing at reaching Pretoria. All this time we were only a mile to the west of the town, which looked very enticing, what with shady roads, steeples and big buildings showing above the trees, practically surrounded by hills with clustering villas nestling against them.

About 12.30 we camped outside by the race-course, where the wire entanglement is still to be seen. We had lunch and started on a march through the town at 2.30 p.m. It was very filthy and dusty getting in, but they actually watered the street outside. All the troops in the place marched with fixed bayonets through the big square up Kerk Street, the main street of the place. Roberts and all the bigwigs and crowds of spectators were on the hotel verandah. The band played "The Old Brigade" as we passed. Just when we were expecting to return to camp we were told that Roberts had made us his bodyguard, apparently as a reward for past services, and to give us a rest. We were sent to the side of a hill overlooking the camp, very stony and uncomfortable. Of course it was ages before the baggage turned up, and we had no coats or anything, but lit fires by pulling down fences (our usual way of getting wood on the march). We were overlooking the town, our camp being just south of the Delagoa Bay Railway. It was a very pretty place but rather un-get-at-able.

6th June - I was on picket and could not go into town. We heard of the release of the prisoners at Bloemfontein. 80 men and 7 officers died of enteric and were buried there that day.

7th - Went into the town, bought photos etc., and bread for the mess, things much cheaper than Johannesburg. A fine town, lovely flowers and gardens, pretty houses, many deserted, as the large British population was kicked out at the beginning of the war. Got in to lunch, storm carried off plates from table (made of gate off its hinges and water proof sheeting). We heard we were off to fight Botha. SORROW AND INDIGNATION! So much so for being Roberts' body-guard!! We marched that afternoon. It thundered, lightened and blew, and the dust all but choked me. The men's shoes are all worn out nearly, some have no soles left and have to tear a bit off their blankets and wrap their feet in it to get along. Of course most of them are terribly footsore under such conditions, but they show great pluck and determination, very few falling out, in marked contrast to the Cornwalls, Shropshires and other Regiments.

That was a vile march, we did 10 miles almost without a halt, most of it stumbling along in the dark (we did not start till 4 p.m.) but owing to a bad guide we only got 5 miles from Pretoria. Next morning as we were starting to go and join the 21st Brigade, we were told that the enemy was off, and we were not wanted, but to go back to Johannesburg instead to be a reserve Battalion, ready to dash up and down the line as required. So we marched down the rail-way to Oliphantsfontein, dropping the DCLI, who are scattered along the rail-way as lines of communication.

9th - To Riefontein. 16 miles.

10th - Riefontein. We are to go to Germiston Station, Elandsfontein, 3 miles away, however as usual we go the roundabout way through Driefontein and make it 7 miles. Marched through Germiston, 8 miles from Johannesburg, re-ally a mining suburb. Our camp is just east of town, close to the station. Very bleak and windy and ugly. Mines many and hideous.

11th - Today began a rumour. Alas, it was too soon verified. 'De Wet cap-tures all the mails'. It was confirmed or contradicted by everyone we met. Nei-ther Roberts nor our General knew anything about it, so it was concluded true for some time. I have bought some fine canvas for a bivouac.

12th - De Wet's camp is captured by Methuen and Shropshires. Three of us are allowed into Johannesburg. Our wounded are doing well.

13th - Ordered off to Irene to help Bobs, distance 20 miles. Start about 12, arrive 4.30. Ordered to wait there, our baggage all left behind. Very cold night, but made fires. We slept at intervals, though the minister thought he was going to die, it was his first night on the veldt without blankets and kit. He was really killing; he would not care for pickets where no fires are allowed, and it is often just as cold and wet. Next morning ordered to return, enemy retired. Hear wild stories of Boers charging guns and cutting up and capturing whole militia regiments and I can easily believe the latter part. The loss of mail confirmed. Very sad. I have not heard a word of news since leaving Bloemfontein. We have an awful long journey back, having to fill the engine with buckets of water, breakdowns etc.

19th June - This letter is almost up to date. We are still in Germiston by Elandsfontein Station. It has been impossible to get letters off as there have been no opportunities, thanks to De Wet, but I think this might get through. I wonder when I will hear from anyone; it is two months since the last letter.

Roberts' plan was to advance on Pretoria with a force of 38,000 men and over 100 guns in three columns. One of these, the central column, was under Roberts' direct command. The Cavalry made up the left column, while the third, on the right, commanded by Ian Hamilton, was a mixed force of the Mounted Infantry and the 19th Infantry Brigade, which included the 1st Gordons and Artillery.

The expedition which was drawn from all parts of the Empire, set off from Karee Junction on 3 May 1900 with the object of making a triumphant entry into Pretoria. Roberts had a personal staff of 70, mostly untrained members of the aristocracy and described by Rayne Kruger as "useless"! Roberts took complete control of all movements but did not always inform his Chief-of-Staff, Kitchener, of what was going on. Rayne Kruger commented that although this particular system of unilateral command had worked so far, because of the now increasingly complicated nature of the campaign, it could not be expected to work well for much longer.

Roberts' advance was slow. After reaching Kronstadt on 8 May, the Boers cleared off to Heilbron. He had to halt for 10 days in order to allow the railway behind him to be repaired, the Boer's Irish Brigade having made a very thorough job of blowing up every single bridge and culvert on the track from Bloemfontein to the Vaal River.

The main reason for the ten days' delay was the appallingly inadequate state of the Field Medical Services. The hospitals in Bloemfontein were described as scandalous. Typhoid caused more casualties than all the battles of Black Week. Roberts and Buller did not appear to understand that soldiers have to be fed and have proper medical back-up.

Winston Churchill accompanied Hamilton's column as a war correspondent.. The day after the battle he visited the spot where the worst slaughter took place, between the false and true crest lines. There he met a Gordon soldier who described the action and how they were trapped between the crests. When asked by Churchill what they could have done next, he replied that they just had to go on. Like all patriotic Englishmen, Churchill had refused to believe the connection between this war and the control of the gold mines. But faced with the sad sight of 18 dead Highlanders awaiting burial only a few miles from The Great Gold Reef, he saw the evidence for himself, and found himself scowling at the tall chimneys of the Rand.

The Boers were having their own limited successes. At one stage they captured a vital convoy of many weeks' mail, which included the long awaited breeches for the Gordon Highlanders Mounted Infantry!

There were a lot of irregular cavalry units. Some were extremely efficient; others not so. One of the most interesting was the 13th Imperial Yeomanry, otherwise known as the Irish Hunt Contingent. It was the social and political show piece of the new volunteer army and consisted of Irish MFHs, including the Earl of Longford, Viscount Ennismore, two Companies of Ulster Protestant Unionists, including Lord Leitrim, Sir John Power (the whisky baronet and the future Lord Craigavon), and a Company of English and Irish men-about-town, raised by Lord Donoughmore, who insisted on paying the men's passages. This splendid Regiment was commanded by a regular officer called Spraggs, who was not bright. Under his dynamic command he managed to get these valiant warriors lost and then captured by the Boers, much to the disgust of Roberts and the alarm of the public at home.

22 June 1900. Joan to Lachlan. 32 Green St Park Lane

No letter from you this week. I suppose you were marching hard. I had not seen anything about your Brigade for ages until today when I see a correspondent says Smith-Dorrien has charge of the communications between Pretoria and Kroonstadt. This is probably untrue, but if it is true, I hope it means a little rest.

I feel rather miserable and I hate uprooting myself when I have settled down anywhere. But I have been away three months and it is high time to get home. If only this war was over. I can't see any end to it. God Bless you and keep you, my dearest Lachlan.

2 July 1900. Lachlan to Father. Germiston

I have today received three letters from you and Mildred, three from Joan, one each from Uncles Archie and Jack, chocolate from Mildred, ditto plus handkerchief, 1 pair of socks and writing paper from Joan; and all very satisfactory. Your last was written on the 1st of last month and we have our mails pretty well up to date. It is a great joy getting letters out here, though we still swear at De Wet for getting 5 weeks of them, all in fact that you posted during April and the 1st week in May. I often wonder if he secured any valuables destined for myself?

It is now three weeks since we arrived here, and in spite of minor numerous alarms the time passes quietly enough. The chief complaint is 'how little there is to do', tho' with very little trouble one can find plenty, it is easy to get books. The men have just cause for complaint in various ways, especially the want of warm clothing, which went with the mails to form a little bonfire.

The weather is detestably cold. It freezes nearly every night, often quite hard, and tho' the days are usually sunny there is always a beastly cold wind from the north. They have absolutely no shelter except little bivouacs made with 2 blankets. Two men combine, but that only leaves them one blanket apiece, which is insufficient, tho' somehow they manage to keep warm with the aid of a greatcoat and bits of sacking. In fact the health of the Battalion is wonderful and we take tremendous precautions to keep the camp and everything in it scrupulously clean, as the majority of the men are old campaigners from Tirah, Chitral, or Egypt.

We lunched at the Goldfields Hotel, played billiards and wrote letters at the Rand Club, which is magnificent, and dined with Dingwall and Southwell, the clergyman of our Brigade, an awfully good fellow, and caught the 7.45 back. It is a very fine town in its way and I imagine will be the principal town in Africa, if it is not already.

We are 8 miles outside and shall be safe enough. Concerning the alarms I mentioned. Firstly the Irene one I told you about resulted in nothing; secondly, nearly a fortnight ago, just as we were comfortably gone to bed, a telegram arrived ordering 300 men to be sent off at once to go and relieve a place near Kronstadt, about 90 miles off which was attacked. We got ready in a great hurry and marched to the station. It was infernally cold, a hard frost, and arriving at the platform soon after midnight, the train was not ready to go. The poor General was furious. Eventually we all got away, the men packed 40 in a truck. It helped to keep them warm I suppose.

We crossed the river at Vereeniging by the deviation, a great dip to a temporary bridge, 300 or 400 yards below the old one, of which one span is bust. We stopped at Viljoens Drift about 6 miles on. After waiting an hour or so, we were told, 'Oh, you are not required. Go home like good boys'. A few days ago it was attacked by our old friend De Wet, who succeeded in cutting the line in several places and walking off unharmed. We started about 12 for here, nearly sticking on the hill up from the bridge. With fearful efforts from two wretched little engines at each end of the train, we crawled to the top. The railway gradients out here easily beat the old Highland line. The next alarm was when 300 men were ordered to entrain at once for Springs, a big coal place on a little branch line, 10 miles out east from here. The following night just as I was going to bed, an orderly galloped up with an order to send 200 men to Springs, with 2 field guns and a 6 inch gun on the armoured train, which has 2 pom-poms and a Maxim of its own.

To my intense joy I heard my Company was not included. It does not sound as if I was very keen, which is just the case, as these shows are infernally uncomfortable and never result in anything. Besides, I shall be quite happy if we get no more fighting in this country, as in fact everyone else will be. We have had what is vulgarly known as, 'our belly full' long ago, though generally on pretty empty stomachs!

Miller and Davis are the two keenest soldiers, as they only joined at Pretoria, and have not been baptised and are longing for a fight. I suggested to them to go and shoot at each other a safe distance from camp! There is an expedition to Heidleberg in which I was to have gone, but K Company started first, only got to Aausluiting, the next station, and came back. My Company is on permanent picket south of the railway, 15 men and an NCO every night, so I never go on picket, a great advantage. We have 1 Company on every night with 2 big heaps dug out of mines quite close to camp. The manager of one of them showed me specimens of gold bearing rock which he'd picked up. Younger and Lockley are in the armoured train. It looks just like an ordinary one except there is a gun of sorts at each end, and the engine is in the middle.

They and 12 gunners live in a 2nd class carriage with most of the seats out and have made themselves very comfortable. The men are in trucks and they sleep at night under tarpaulins, so are very well off. All the train is armoured with big plates inside, so that though it looks quite innocent it is really pretty formidable. We found the other day they had defeated the Boers with great loss. However, when a day or so afterwards they turned up here, they said the only foundation for this story was that they fired a few rounds from their guns at a carcass lying in the veldt, and sure enough some Boers did appear in the distance evidently thinking they were to make an easy capture of the train, but seeing the guns going off took fright and cleared. The firing was just to see how the guns fired on a truck. The result was very satisfactory.

We are to be moved to Pretoria very soon, where the old Brigade will be reformed and we shall start on a little trip. I should hardly be surprised if we finished up some day in Cairo. Sgt. Duncan, our Mess Sergeant, arrived the other day with the old bullock cart and stores from Bloemfontein. It took him 6 weeks to march here. He was most of the way alone, and managed to escape being captured which was very clever, as there was a lot of fighting going on about the districts he passed through.

FIGHTING FOR JOHANNESBURG.

FROM WINSTON SPENCER CHURCHILL,
OUR WAR CORRESPONDENT.*

DOORNKOP, MAY 31.

On May 29 General French, advancing northward on the western side of Johannesburg, found himself confronted by about seven thousand Boers with fifteen guns, occupying strong positions in advance of the main ridge or reef of Witwaters Rand.

After an artillery duel which lasted all day, and was at times very loud, but was fortunately not accompanied by heavy losses, he withdrew further to the west.

On the 30th General Ian Hamilton advanced, according to orders, and found General French still obstructed by a part of the enemy's advanced position.

General Hamilton, being unable to move further owing to the scarcity of supplies, resolved to attack forthwith.

General French, with the Cavalry Division and Broadwood's command, lent by General Bruce Hamilton, co-operated on the left.

During the morning the artillery on both sides fired heavily, but at midday, while the Infantry were getting into positions for attack, there was a strange lull.

At two o'clock General Hamilton launched his whole force on the enemy.

General Smith-Dorrien, commanding the Infantry Division, directed the actual attack, the 21st Brigade being on the left and the 19th on the right.

The ground favoured the enemy, and the bare grass slopes terminating in rocky kopjes seemed to threaten heavy loss; but the attack was well conceived, and the advance of General Bruce Hamilton on the left and of General French beyond him materially weakened the Boers opposed to the British right.

The City Imperial Volunteers, who were the leading battalion of the left attack, were sharply engaged, but moving forward with great dash and vigour they pressed the enemy hard, and drove him from all his positions in advance of the main ridge.

On the right the fighting was more severe.

The Gordon Highlanders strongly attacked a kopje, and in spite of the terrible fire, which caused heavy losses, carried it at the point of the bayonet with their customary devotion.

The Cornwalls supported them.

The Boers fought stoutly, and managed to save their gun, but the whole of their position fell into the hands of the British, and the enemy were driven back towards the main ridge of the range.

Night closed in while the musketry and cannonade continued, and the stubborn combatants fought on for nearly an hour by the glare of the burning veldt, which shells had set on fire.

The Boers suffered heavily in their retreat, and our troops bivouacked on the captured ground.

General Hamilton spoke a few words to the Gordon Highlanders, "the regiment my father commanded and I was born in;" and told them that all Scotland would ring with the tale of their deeds.

There is no doubt that they are the finest regiment in the world.

Their unfaltering advance across the naked plain on a concealed enemy in spite of frontal and enfilading fire, which spotted the ground on all sides with bullets, their machine-like change of direction as the attack closed, and their fine charge with the bayonet constitute their latest feat of arms the equal of Elandslaagte or Dargai.

CHAPTER SIX

Krugersdorp to Welverdiend 1900

10 July 1900. Lachlan to Father. Krugersdorp

I have been writing this on picket by moonlight. Since writing last we have been fussing around the country. Last Thursday we paraded at 5 p.m. to go to Springs. We got on the armoured train, but did not get away until 7. The train soon stuck up a hill and Davis and a gunner, who got out to see what was wrong, were left behind as the train started suddenly without warning. Luckily they attracted our attention by their yells, and after going a mile or so, we stopped the train. They had been running nearly as fast as us, and were very blown and hot. We arrived about 10.30. The Canadians were comfortably installed in the Station Hotel. I had relieved one of their pickets on a coal mine, some 2 miles out. We spent a quiet day with only one false alarm, and on the Canadians' returning, entrained. The Boers evidently fell in with Hunter, as we heard his guns going a long way off. We were unfortunately delayed 2 hours after entraining, as a sergeant and 17 men, who had gone to the wrong place for a picket, could not be found to be recalled, so we did not get back to Elandsfontein till about 1 a.m.

Sunday, we moved at 10 a.m. and entrained for Irene, getting there about 4 p.m. The Brigade was to concentrate and march to Middleburg. Monday we sat quiet, but about 11 p.m. an order came to entrain at 6.30 am. This was a staggerer. We were up for some unknown reason at 3, breakfast at 4, after which we shivered around a fire until daybreak. All the mules and baggage had to be entrained, so we did not get off until after 8. The men were packed 40 in a truck and we were in the luggage van. We got here at 2.30 via Elandsfontein and Johannesburg. It looks a pretty little village, well built in a hilly country. Any amount of gold mines of course. The Shropshires and our General came here just after us.

Tomorrow we set off on a little tour to clear the country of some obstreperous Doppers and someday we hope to get back to Irene, then march to Middleburg. After that I hope to get a transport to Delagoa Bay. I have seen no friends for a long time, nor have I heard of any. Yesterday we got your letter of the 15th, and you say I only tell of our doings, not what I think. The latter is easily remedied. Like everyone else I shall be very thankful to get out of the country with a whole skin, if that is to be. Also I am heartily sick of being shot at. War is very like the Dead Sea Apples, tho' it has its redeeming feature. Also it forcibly brings home to one's mind how we are in the hands of a higher power than any, especially, when you do not know whether you may be alive or not 24 hours from now, as we shall probably tomorrow be fighting. All one can hope is to do one's duty and avoid any mistake which may make you responsible for other peoples lives.

It is no joke taking a Company into action by oneself, especially when they are mostly boys like my Volunteers with NCOs as young and inexperienced as themselves. However they showed what they were made of at Doornkop after losing

OUTPOSTS. JULY 1900

all their officers, so I shall have no fear of them, but hope we shall not be tried again.

The Regiment's operational role at this time was the guarding of the lines of communication, which were under Kitchener of Khartoum's command.

At this time the Army Service Corps was formed It was accepted initially in the same reluctant and unenthusiastic manner as was the wearing of khaki. The Service Corps became famous for its devotion to duty, and eventually became the Royal Army Service Corps with many battle honours.

The capture of Pretoria changed the war considerably. The Boers suffered a further defeat with considerable loss of men and equipment in the Brandwater Basin, 65 miles due south of Lindley. The Basin is in a mountainous spot and the

Boers had hoped to rest and regroup there under De Wet, now Commander-in-Chief of the Boer army. However, the terrain assisted General Hunter to box them in. Hunter was one of the new generals, a competent Scot who was well liked by his men, and his victory cost the Boers more men and equipment than at Paarderberg. It was a disaster partly of De Wet's own making though not entirely his own fault, for his main concern at the time was the safety of the Presidents Steyn and Kruger, who were at Brandwater at the time and who had to be got away to Middleburg, some 70 miles east of Pretoria and thence by rail to Delagoa Bay.

Christian de Wet

Lord Roberts

On 15 July 1900 he broke out taking 3000 of his men with him. De Wet was a military genius who always managed to evade the pursuing British, desperate to capture him. There was a certain romance about his exploits and he earned the same sort of respect from the British public as Rommel in the Second World War. He was efficient and had trained his men. The secret was that everyone lent a hand and knew exactly what to do, men and kaffirs alike. In the British Army only the latter performed menial tasks and took much longer over them. He was a strict disciplinarian. The punishment for sleeping on sentry duty was a sojourn on an ant-hill and the penalty for moving off it was to be shot.

At De Wet's break out, three British columns were despatched in pursuit. He, taking advantage of the unco-ordinated British, eluded them and escaped across the plains to the hills of the Vaal at Reitzberg, south east of Lindley. Despite the sluggish speed of his ox-drawn wagons and the clouds of dust they created he still managed a rear-guard action outside Reitzberg.

Roberts' aim was not only to catch De Wet but also to sever the Boers' supply link with Delagoa Bay. In the meantime they had speedily reorganised their remaining forces by grouping commandos as near to their own districts as possible to rest and re-provision as well as to restore morale.

In early August Roberts sent Queen Victoria an optimistic despatch saying that the War was 'practically over'. Amongst other things he asked her if he could erect a bronze statue of her in the main square in Pretoria on the site reserved for President Kruger. The Queen was most definitely 'not amused' at the thought of stepping into President Kruger's shoes in this fashion, nor was she pleased at Roberts' wife, Nora, and their two daughters being in Pretoria at all. She disapproved of camp followers of any kind, especially women. Roberts pleaded the excuse that she was helping to organise and administer the hospitals, the deplorable conditions of which were provoking a scandal in Britain. This brought the charge of 'petticoat government' and the accusation that she was 'carrying the Field Marshal's baton in her knapsack'.

They must have seemed an incongruous couple for she was tall and imposing and Roberts was small and wiry. Up until Nora's arrival, Roberts' attitude to the Boer women and children had been one of leniency and tolerance. Now, his attitude hardened and for 'reasons of security' he felt it necessary to remove them from Pretoria, forcing them to trek considerable distances to the nearest Boer commando.

As far as Roberts' staff were concerned, Pretoria was an idyllic place. One Indian Army Officer compared it to Simla and wrote enthusiastically of the officers 'playing polo and taking part in mounted paper chases and sitting in the garden at Mimosa cottage'.

11 July 1900. Joan to Lachlan. Drummuir

Another week and no letter. It is hard, and I am very anxious, but I hear from different people that they have not heard for just as long! I suppose it really is the tremendous accumulation of letters. Oh! my Lachlan when will it be over? I always feel depressed; it is always raining. Until yesterday morning it rained incessantly since I last wrote to you, then yesterday we had one of the most perfect days imaginable, very hot and so lovely, and this morning the same, and now this afternoon it is raining as bad as ever.

What have I done since I last wrote last week? Very little it strikes me. Thursday and Friday, it poured steadily. Saturday was bright cold and windy. We drove into Keith to see father off by the train to catch the boat to London. Yesterday, as it was at least fine, I rode over to Buchromb, which I enjoy. Thursday, today, there is no news at all, no message from Bobs or anyone; only a long list of deaths from enteric, and a list of people coming home. God knows, I don't want you to be ill, but oh what joy it would be to see that you were coming home.

16 July 1900. Lachlan to Joan. Krugersdorp

I hope we shall not be here to receive any more mail, after this reaches you, tho' things do not look very well now. I told Father how we got here, by a letter that will go by this mail, in which I said we expected to be fighting, and sure enough we did, and in many ways it was the nastiest and most exciting little battle I've ever taken part in, as with a little less luck half the Battalion might have been wiped out.

I came off picket that morning, and had just time to get breakfast, when we started, ourselves, the poor Shropshires, who had been travelling in trucks till 4 that morning, some Yeomanry, and 2 field guns of the 78th Battery under Turner. It is a tiring country, as soon as we were up one long low hill, we had to climb another on a road such as only a S. African road has the face to be. My Company were told off to be escort to the guns, so we marched with them. Turner was a very nice chap, and had been through the relief of Ladysmith, and with Barton around Kimberly nearly to Mafeking, and across to here. After about 9 miles, when we were getting rather tired, firing was heard, and the guns ordered up. Of course we went with them, passing the advanced guard and everyone else.

We had to climb a low grass hill. There was a valley and the Boers position was on 2 kopjes overlooking ours. The guns went too fast for us making for a gap 80 yards wide between 2 rocky heads on our kopje. Luckily before they halted and unlimbered I got the Company extended with one half in support under C. Sgt. Campbell. The two guns were unlimbered and had fired about 2 shots when a very heavy rifle fire was opened on them and us. We were still 100 yds. behind, but doubled up occupying the rocky heads and ant-heaps near the guns, everyone getting into a position from whence he could shoot back. The guns were still firing very pluckily at the two hills opposite, the nearest only 850 yards off, and the other about 1700 yds.

About 10 minutes after my Company got up we were reinforced by B C A F and D in succession, ridiculously close range for guns, the result was that nearly all the gunners were hit in a few minutes and very soon the whole lot, but then an attempt was made to bring up a team of horses to get them away, but before they could be harnessed several of the horses were killed and the remaining men and horses were luckily escaping, with their lives. It was a terrible sight to see.

Poor Turner was wounded in three places, having continued to serve the guns to the last. Luckily none of them are dangerous. All the Gunners and drivers showed splendid pluck, firing away until every man was wounded. Strange to say none were killed outright tho one of two I'm afraid will die. Things were looking rather bad. One of 2 guns out of action and an unknown force of Boers opposite. The latter then managed to occupy a hill to our right where they got a nasty flank fire on us hitting several chaps. Firing was next heard in the rear, where the Shropshires were attacked, but luckily they kept them off or we should have been taken in the rear as well and pretty well wiped. Next they attacked our baggage pretty hotly, killing a mule or two and firing into the wagons. However it was repulsed without much loss chiefly through our servants' efforts. The poor little padre had to take refuge behind our ant-heaps where they shot at him, according to his own account.

Next, Roberts sent an order to chuck up the show, not knowing we had found the enemy, and the general signalled to retire and abandon the guns. The Col signalled back that if we stayed on till evening we could save them, so we did not go, which was very lucky, as if we had retired the Boers in a few minutes would have got into the place where we were, and had great sport, besides getting the precious guns.

The whole thing only began at 12 a.m. and about 1 p.m. a very fine attempt was made to save the guns. I did not know anything of it till I happening to look around. I saw about a dozen of our fellows trying to haul out the guns lead by Younger and Gordon. However, it was absolutely impossible under such a fire and lots of them were hit, poor Younger first in the head, which apparently was not very bad, then in the thigh, and badly in the stomach. He was now most gallantly rescued by Cpl Mackay, who was recommended for the VC at Doornkop, so he is certain to get it now, but unfortunately could not save Younger's life. He was conscious for some hours, but suffered terribly. It is a most ghastly thing, as there was no need for such an attempt which was practically impossible.

Another sad thing about it was that he was out once and came back unhurt, but went out immediately after and was shot. At the same time an attempt to save the limber was made, but equally futile. A good many of us were going to try and help them, but it was just as well we were stopped as we could have done no good, and there would have been many casualties, but it was a bad thing to see and do nothing. Poor old Younger. It is terribly sad; he was one of the kindest and best chaps I've ever met, and his loss is very much felt by everyone, men and officers alike. The general says that if he had lived he would have recommended him for the VC.

After this, for the whole afternoon we lay shooting at each other. We could see the Boers plain enough looking over the kopje opposite, but neither side did much damage to the other. We had our Maxim up. At length, to our joy, the sun began to sink and the moon, which was full, began to rise

Then began the most exciting period of the whole day. The moon was rising just behind us, and the sun had just set behind the Boers, and when it was fairly dark we could see the outline of the of the hill against the red glow. All firing had ceased for a few minutes, and Tytler and self, with some of our men of our respective coys, had been lying out in the grass in front of the little kopje we occupied. I was looking for a pair of gloves I dropped early in the day and, not finding them, went across and talked to Dingwall, who had built himself a nice little sangar. We noticed a lot of figures against the skyline, and I remarked they looked as though they were coming down our way, but we did not think anything of it.

However a few minutes later they began to fire at us again, and we noticed by the sound that the shots were much nearer. We had hardly realised this when a tumultuous fire at close range was opened on us, and we heard a yelling and whooping and a variety of strange noises advancing, and saw shadowy forms here and there, and many flashes in the darkness. The stones around us were spurting fire and sparks where their bullets hit them, throwing stones and splinters in all directions. By Jove, you should have seen our fellows out in front come tumbling back to the kopje. It would have been ludicrous under different circumstances. Luckily none were hit.

We all began shooting back recklessly at the flashes and the figures still growing closer. You can hardly imagine such a pandemonium. We could hear them calling "Vorwarts" to each other, and personally I expected we should be rushed every second, as it was impossible to see how many of them were there. We all fixed bayonets, and found we were very short of ammunition, many of us having but 10 rounds left or so. We told no one to fire unless he saw something. Dingwall then got a skelp on the head from a stone and for a few seconds I thought he was killed. The man on my right was lying motionless and I imagined he was dead too, but strange to say he also got a severe blow which temporarily incapacitated him.

Things looked pretty black, and still the Boers kept coming on and the bullets whizzing just past one's head and hitting the stones all around in a most obnoxious way. Luckily just then more ammunition was brought up and the Boers seemed to think they could not get closer. Many must have been only about 100 yards off, and could plainly be seen when they moved, but as a score of missiles came whenever they did, they contented themselves by shouting "Vorwarts" to each other and not moving. By degrees, all firing ceased and for about half an hour we strained every nerve to see if they were crawling closer, momentarily expecting them to try and rush us, but nothing stirred. Then we were warned to be ready to shoot as the guns were to be removed. This was the crucial moment, for of course the aim and object of the Boer's attack was to rout us by a sudden and desperate charge and collar the guns, before we had a chance of saving them.

I noticed they fired towards the guns to prevent our going to them as they advanced. Of course they were very obvious as they advanced in the moonlight, and when a great team of 6 horses was brought up and hooked on without a shot from the enemy, we knew they must have sneaked off, or had too much respect for our rifles to disclose themselves, as they must have suffered heavily in this attempt. The former is the most likely, as they would also have been afraid of our making a counter attack on them.

To our intense relief, both guns and a limber were taken away without a shot being fired. After another interval of anxious watching, for we did not know what tricks they might be up to, many of them being German, we got an order from the General to retire at 8, which we did, a Company at a time without a sound, joining the baggage about 2 miles off, very thankful to have escaped so easily. We halted there until 9.30 and called the roll. We had only 16 casualties, none killed and none dangerously hurt. My Company had three; two trying to save the guns and one from the flank fire from the right. The whole Company behaved admirably under trying circumstances. After falling in we started back for here doing a fiendish night march for another 10 miles or so, coming back on a hillier and rougher road than we came out by.

We reached camp exhausted at a quarter to 3 in the morning after a most eventful day and went to sleep on the spot till my servant, good man, after putting up my bivy and getting out my things found me and woke me up at 4 a.m. Next day we rested. I looked around the town with Murray. It is a pretty little place with nice gum-tree avenues but a hot bed of boredom. I got a lovely hot bath at a French barbers the following afternoon for 2 shillings. In the evening I visited the Yeomanry with Murray and we saw poor Towse's brother. Towse himself is doing wonderfully well.

Saturday was uneventful, tho' the garrison of this place was rather nervous expecting to be jumped. We have 4 Companies out on picket together, and one as town guard at night. Nobody at night is allowed through the lines and, if they appear suspicious, are shot at. The pickets bring in numbers of prisoners every morning, mostly natives. All bicycles and horses are commandeered here and in Johannesburg, and lots of people arrested. Dogs around the picket lines are shot to prevent them getting messages out that way. Miller tried to shoot one the

other night but shot a pig instead. I dined that evening with Tytler, Dingwall, Craufurd and Maclaren at the Grand Hotel. We got a good dinner and enjoyed ourselves.

Tuesday 19, Sunday - We had a service at 10 o'clock. Had a headache and fever and went to bed, and did not go on picket that night. Yesterday remained in my bivouac and got well. Methuen and troops arrived. We expect to go and hunt Boers tomorrow in 2 columns. We have 18 guns, 4 Howitzers and 2 pom-poms between us, so we ought to do something.

We have heard since our fight that we inflicted some damage on them, wounding Oosterhuizen, their leader, severely, which is good. Also that there were 1200 other Boers with Artillery, trying hard to get up that day in time. If they had, there is no knowing what might have happened to us.

The commando we fought was largely German, and has a bad reputation among other Boers, however they were good fighters. What fools these chaps are going on like this, causing useless misery on both sides. I have enclosed a photo done by Gregson at Bloemfontein, including Meyrick, Towse and Younger, and many others, sick and wounded. Scarcely half are with us now.

The action last described by Lachlan took place at Leekoehoek, a few miles due north of Krugersdorp, on the Johannesburg-Klerksdorp railway. De Wet, after his escape from the Brandwater Basin, took his few thousand strong army of Boers and joined up with De la Rey's forces around Krugersdorp, and kept the British on the hop. Methuen had arrived with a large well equipped army, much stronger than that of De Wet.

Roberts wanted to trap the Boers in the mountains around the pass of Oliphants Nek, capture De Wet, and press on east to Komati Poort on the Portuguese East African border and cut off their supplies coming in from the outside world.

Led by De Wet at Krugersdorp, the Boers wanted to escape south into the Transvaal. They were scared of being caught in the mountains around Oliphant's Nek, 50 miles north-west. This was roughly the state of play before the start of the next phase of the war, the advance from Pretoria to Komati Poort.

Younger was awarded the VC. At the time of his bravery it was a decoration only for those who survived but shortly afterwards that rule was changed and he became the first to get the award posthumously.

Lachlan was very tired from all the fighting and nervous strain. He must have dreamed of strawberries and happier times, sun-kissed lawns and lovely girls in summer dresses, this was the sort of image most soldiers see, only to be shattered by

KRUGERSDORP TO WELVERIEND 1900

the harsh realities of battle; feelings reflected 14 years later in the war poems of Rupert Brook, Siegfried Sassoon and others

26 July 1900. Lachlan to Father. Near Banks Railway Station

We have just regained the Potchefstroom railway after a tedious, uncomfortable, little tour. Last Wednesday we left Krugersdorp at 2 p.m. and marched about 6 miles by one road, while Methuen went by another, our object being to annihilate the brutes we were previously at on the 11th.

Smith-Dorrien had ourselves, the Shropshires, a battery and some Yeomanry. I had a slight go of fever, I think from a chill, and was nearly left, but it cleared just in time. We started early Thursday morning to attack the Boers' right flank, but apparently they did not appreciate our looks and cleared. We went on a good way. It is very hilly country, some of it rather like Natal, but there was only a little sniping at the Yeomanry. We got a hasty lunch after about 10 miles of tramping, then climbed a great range of kopjes, and the pom-poms opened fire rigorously at some Boers at the bottom who did not stay longer than they could help. We puffed up to the top and hastened their departure by 3000 yard volleys which seemed to amuse some. Personally I saw nothing else, but we shot where we saw shells burst, and I believe one Boer was killed.

The view was lovely. We looked down into a green fertile little valley with the great Mahaliesberg Mountains opposite looking very fine. However we went down when there was nothing more to shoot at, and as it was nearly 5 p.m. expected we should camp, but they made us walk a tremendous way on over a rough road, and a very bad drift. We had been tramping all day and were pretty tired, but we did not get in till after dark, about 6 o'clock, across some ploughed fields, another burn, and up a sort of precipice. My feet were soft and had blisters, and another mile would have about finished me, at least I thought so. The moment we got in we were sent off, up a great rough kopje, pitch dark and frightfully steep. We got up somehow, and then had a frightful time finding what the ground was like for sentries, defence, etc. The enemy were supposed to be very close, however it was done at last. Of course none of us got any food or blankets except what we carried, as all the transport stuck at the drift, but we were too tired to mind that much.

We must have done about 18 miles and luckily it was not a very cold night. We descended the opposite way to that we came up and started our march. My feet were horribly sore and some of the men were worse, so it was a sort of penance to move. We did about 5 miles arriving through a thorn jungle into camp about 7, got dinner and went off to bed.

Reveille was at 3.30 next morning, marching at 5 a.m. We expected to catch the enemy about 6 miles west. We and the Shropshires were in the rear with the idea that if everything went off well, we were to do a forced march south to the Rand and then come to Potchefstroom or Krugersdorp, while Methuen went to Rustenberg. The Yeomanry started fighting about 10. We were marching in a narrow valley, the Mahaliesberg range of great precipitous hills on our right, and south there were lower irregular hills which were weakly held by the enemy. Our guns shelled them and they retired. A running fight went on for a long time, while the column gradually pushed on. We never came under fire though the Yeomanry had some casualties. After a bit the valley widened and a pass in the Mahaliesbergs appeared in front, which the enemy was making for. They had 3 pom-poms and a tremendously strong position, so I can't think why they made such a poor show.

This was Oliphants Nek. We got the batteries up at the gallop and as they went through gave them a terrific dose of shrapnel, every gun blazing away for dear life. Baden Powell, the great advertisement, was on the other side, and if he had not played the fool we should have collared the lot, but they escaped with a lot of casualties and a bad fight. We then crossed the pass and camped 2 miles on about 8 from Rustenberg in a lovely bit of country. We were in a big plain, covered with scattered trees like an orchard, beautiful grass and streams and splendid orange plantations covered with fruit - the best I've ever tasted - with the great range of mountains towering behind, a perfect day and place. We lunched, and washed in a stream. It was the first wash for 3 days. Afterwards a lot of us crossed the burn and visited a deserted farm, the owner out fighting. We got sacks of beautiful oranges and lemons. I got a pink pig and the Doctor a black one. We also pursued and captured several fowls and a fine turkey. The mess waiters assisted in carrying the spoil home, so we did not do so badly.

STANDING CAMP—DINNERS

22nd - We had a service and rested, Monday after expecting to go to Lichtenburg, we all started back the way we came. I was advance guard and we had a rough walk crossing a lovely little burn, and fighting the way through thickets, thorns etc. I put up a brace of fine wild duck, partridges, hares and wood pigeons. We did about 12 miles and were very tired. After getting lunch

White and I got leave. We started off with carbines to try and get a buck. We went some way but only missed a hare.

We then visited some very quaint kraals, and bought 2 chickens from the Kaffirs, and were on our way back as it was getting late when to our horror there was a great roar and a shell burst about 200 yards from us. First we thought we were attacked by Boers, then we saw that it was our own guns in camp as another great shell hurtled over our heads, then another. We were exactly in the line of fire but could not discover what was up. We made tracks for camp, thinking they had gone mad. Before we got back we met a troop of Yeomanry going out, who explained that Boers had been seen in the bushes and 2 wagons were being cleared out full of stuff from a farm house quite near. We got into camp as it was getting dark, having just missed the Boers and escaped our own shells.

24th - We were off early in a southerly direction, ourselves, the Shropshires, 2 guns and some Yeomanry. Methuen kept more to the east of us. We spent some time filling in a drift with stones to help the wagons over as they stuck in the mud. We only did 9 or 10 miles, camping near a nice farm, where we got large quantities of oranges, each man getting about 1 each. Next day we did about 15 miles starting at 7, with one halt to let the animals be outspanned and watered; as we were rear-guard we got in at 3 p.m. It was very cold and beginning to rain. Luckily it gave us time to put bivouacs up. Then a great circular thunderstorm started and the rain came down in torrents. My tent kept it out beautifully, but many others leaked like sieves and the men were very uncomfortable, but with mackintosh sheets etc. they kept alive. About daybreak it cleared but was still cold and cloudy.

26th - We started at 7 a.m. and marched here, about 5 miles. The line has been broken and a train wrecked by De la Rey, who is sitting on some low hills south of the railway about 5 miles from here. We nearly went on to attack him this morning; however, as everyone was cold and damp and the men very foot-sore with rotten shoes, and absolutely worn out, we halted, got out everything to dry, and bivouacked. We are in a farm yard, calves, goats, poultry etc. running about in all directions, also pigs. It was rather funny at lunch. Buchanan, a militia Capt. of the Scots Fusiliers, who is attached to us for the expedition for what he calls "to see the fun", announced slowly and solemnly that he had 8 beautiful ducks, so Dingwall as Mess President had to investigate.

They were in the possession of a horrid looking old Jew with very little English. We assumed he was a Pole. So Murray the ex Warsaw Consul was summoned. He is very deaf but at once took in the situation and knowing the proper style to treat this class, as the fellow was rather cheeky, he swore at him in choice Russian, and kicked him out saying that 1/6 for the eight was rather little, so he would give him 2/-, however we got them for 1/6 each and also 50 eggs.

We had a great foot and shoe inspection this afternoon. The wonder is how we managed to get here. Many men had frightfully bad feet and shoes with no soles on them. The Col has made a list of the bad feet and bad shoes in the Battalion.

Krugersdorp - We left Banks Station for here at 4.30 p.m. on 27 July, packed in trucks and the remainder on the roofs of cattle trucks. We took hours over the journey of 20 miles, getting in about 8 p.m.; we went to our former camp. We have meals at the Grand Hotel, sending our rations there and get awfully well done for 5/- a day, excellent cooking. On Sunday, we had a service and on the 30th a draft of 130 men arrived, including about 22 volunteers under Duncan, who is a volunteer officer.

31st - Duncan has taken over M Company from me. I have had them just 2 months and liked them very much, tho' of course they are not as smart as regulars, which annoys the adjutant very much. I have transferred to G Company under Allan. That catch of 5000 Boers by Hunter is the first success we have had since Pretoria almost. I am glad you enjoyed the Links so much, my golf will be rather poor when I get home, but I hope not all forgotten.

De Wet's escape through Oliphants Nek from the mountains was most unfortunate. By the time Hamilton, who was making slow progress, arrived at the pass it was too late to stop De Wet slipping through to safety. Baden-Powell was in command of Rustenberg, about two miles away.

7 August 1900. Lachlan to Joan. Krugersdorp

We are still here. The times uneventful. The weather is appallingly cold. Last night and today a horrible south wind has been blowing half a gale, it cuts like knives. There was also a frost and as in-lying picket I had to parade at 4 a.m. this morning and sit outside till after daylight. I find I can wear more clothes than ever I have at home and yet still be cold. Luckily I managed to get a good serge jacket instead of the wretched khaki one which was torn to ribbons. The latter has been cut up to patch my spats and haversack which are also shocking.

We get up at 5 a.m! I don't think I told you, we have a room for messing in a tin hotel that was deserted. It has a billiard room; the table is a good one, so we have great games and tables are rigged up around the sides for meals. The Welsh Fusiliers occupy the remainder consisting of another big room and a piano. One of them is a beautiful musician. One or two other little rooms are used as orderly rooms and Colonel's room etc., so it's very convenient.

I got your last letter of 7 July, but none from anyone else. I was much interested in the Gobbo performance. I saw it done previously and it was very clever. I am glad Drummuir is let. I am afraid tho' there is no chance of our being home for pheasants unless by January; tho' we shall probably be in China by then! I envy you being at Park again. It is a long time since I have been there. When you get this it will be almost a year. I had a little ride this morning on a rough fiery pony of Maclaren's that nearly put me off, but it was great fun. I will write a better letter next week. But it is late now and there is no news.

The Battalion was at Krugersdorp until 12 August, (the day Grouse shooting starts!) refitting, getting shoes with proper soles, warm clothing and so on, all very important for morale. In the meantime, Roberts had arrived at Middleburg, further east along the railway, with a very strong army.

14 August 1900. Lachlan to Joan.Welverdiend

We left Krugersdorp on the 12th at one hour's notice and came here to assist in the capture of De Wet, who as usual escaped, crossing the line here before we arrived, tho' he lost a gun and was very hard pressed.

De Wet we heard, was about 17 miles off pursued by 5 different Divisions. He is a most wonderful chap, but ought to have been taken a long time ago. I hope the whole thing will collapse when he is. English mails get here all right, which is a good thing for us. I have not had a line from anyone but you for a long time now. I suppose I am bad at writing, and the post worse, so people do not think it worth while. Yesterday was the first day of the season and it was pretty sickening being out here still. A year ago today we were out on the White Cow [the name of a moor on the estate, it had a large white rock in the shape of a cow.] It seems a long time ago.

Today I suppose you are at Park, while out here we are doing nothing but wait for orders. I suppose we are off somewhere, which is a good thing, as this is a vile hole, only a station in the veldt, nothing to do at all, I and every one else are frightfully sick of it all. I scarcely know which is worse, trekking or doing nothing. The days are getting warmer, but the nights are still very cold, and when the south wind blows it is appalling, a regular biting gale, accompanied by a frost. We did a few days digging at the fort at Krugersdorp, and in the wind the sand and the dust was horrible.

The line was bust up 6 miles from here but is now working again. We are only about 15 miles from Potchefstroom, which we evacuated in our efforts to catch De Wet. The country is flat and uninteresting with low hills in the distance. If you have a pair ready you might send me same socks, as the many pairs I spoke of were left in my heavy kit at Bloemfontein.

We have given up most hopes of returning before the year is up. We shall be very lucky if we get back before Xmas. I think the people in this country are pretty sick of the war, but as we cannot protect them even after their Oath of Allegiance, they are forced go out and fight again by the first passing Commando, and are then afraid of coming in, which is a bad state of affairs.

A chance mail is just going out so I will end, there is nothing more to say, and I've no idea where we shall be in a week's time. Unless I get hit there is no fear of my coming home, as my health could not be better, and am still very fat.

CHAPTER SEVEN

Welverdiend to Komati Poort 1900

16 August 1900. Joan to Lachlan. Hatton Castle

The shooting began on Monday of course. They got 10 plus brace which was very good; we were not allowed to have lunch on the moor which I thought was very bad treatment, as it was a perfect day, not quite so hot as last year.

We are really having very lovely weather now, beautiful Autumn days. On Tuesday they went duck shooting. Cousin Beechie asked me to go with him, which I did, much to poor Cousin Garden's annoyance, as he can't bear women out shooting. It was very nice sitting among the trees and there were plenty of duck. In the afternoon we drove over to tea at Fyvie. We met them in their four in hand, all very smart in Paris clothes. We went around the garden which is pretty and the lake which is lovely.

I have just heard that Margot has a daughter and that she is doing well though the child is feeble which sounds sad, but the great thing is for her to be well. I am staying here until Monday or Tuesday, Jessie has got a most beloved little dog, a young fox terrier called Bobs. He is perfectly fascinating. He has slept with me for the last two nights and is perfectly delicious.

22 August 1900. Joan to Lachlan. Park House, Banffshire

Another week passed and apparently no nearer the end of the war. De Wet and De la Ray comfortably joined under Lord Roberts' and Kitchener's noses. It is very maddening and it makes one admire De Wet enormously. I see that one Gordon was killed at Elandsfontein with Hamilton, but I hope it was only Mounted Infantry and not you that have been fighting again.

I left Hatton today. Cousin Annie and I sat up last night very late talking; she was so happy at the idea of Gardie, her son, perhaps coming home on leave in October. Of course she did not mean it, but it made me so terribly jealous; I did long for you so. I went to my room and cried with Bobs. It has been delightful having Bobs to look after. Cousin Jessie, his owner, went away and he was entirely my charge for 5 days. He was more than fascinating, so good, so playful and so pretty and so soft. I hated leaving him, but his mistress was to be back tonight and his master, who worships him comes in a few days, so he will be quite happy but I am sure he will miss me tonight.

If Hatton could ever be dull it would have been so these last few days. Cousin Jessie left on Saturday and two old maids called Blackburn arrived. One of them is very nice but dull and sat upon by the other sister, who is rowdy and athletic and contradictory and disagreeable and vulgar. They are very heavy, metaphorically, and someone has to be detailed to entertain them, which is very trying work. Yesterday we were just starting to go visiting when some callers came, so I was sent off alone with the Miss Blackburns. Luckily they knew Marguerite quite well, so we discussed her and all her affairs which kept the conversation going. We did a lot of driving while we were at Hatton. We went to Forglen on Thursday and saw a lot of lovely paintings done by a Mr Severn and by Lady Baring.

On Friday we were going to have a most exciting afternoon. We were going to start by visiting the Duke and Duchess of Wellington at Byth, then on to Craigston where there was a Lord Abbot staying, a very magnificent person to whom you kneel and kiss his hand if you are a Roman Catholic; and we were to finish with the Crown Prince of Siam at Inverichnie. However our entertainment fell through as the Duke and Duchess were out and it was too far to go to Inverichnie, so we only did Craigston.

I was not to have gone into the house, but luckily we met Francis in the avenue going out shooting so it was all right and I got some tea. The Lord Abbot had not arrived, but Francis's brother, who is a priest, was there. He is called Father Jerome, and is a most delightful person. It was the first time for years that he has been out of the monastery. He is most cultivated and interesting. He took me over the house which I had not seen for years; it is so lovely. Father Jerome also played the piano most beautifully.

On Sunday I had to escort the Miss Blackburns and Pat and Dolly to the Episcopal church in Turriff. The children were angelic in church but having been good for so long made them extra naughty coming back. They were most boisterous, and Mackenzie at last had to reprove them from the box! The day before that Bobs and I went for a lovely walk along the "moor". I actually found a scrap of white heather which rejoiced my heart as I have a great belief in it. I gave a quarter of it to Cousin Annie and the rest I send to you. I forgot to put any in last week. Bobs did not at all like jumping over the long heather and he was very much surprised when he put up a very noisy brace of grouse.

There is a very funny old Colonel there, aged 87 and very blind. He was much taken by the elder Miss Blackburn, whom we all dislike so, and he told long stories about "the thin texture of his trousers" which amused us very much. We repeated them to Cousin Nelly Duff who is always terribly shocked by Miss Blackburn (who smokes) and was horrified, but she saw her chance of annoying Miss B. and said "He must have thought you very motherly, my dear". Miss B. who poses as being very youthful was furious.

We played a violent game of rounders that evening with the children. Bobs added vastly to the general amusement running after the ball. He got it once and wouldn't let us have it. We all laughed so much so we couldn't catch him. Col. Pollard Urquhart's sister and her husband came to lunch. Very tiresome people. Bill Forbes bicycled over. He has grown extraordinarily good looking but has a fearful amount of "side", but for all that is much the best of the Forbes family.

Yesterday I came back here. The wagonette met us in Turriff and we drove here. The last 8 miles of the way it rained in sheets. I haven't seen so much heavy rain for ages, but we were well covered up and did not mind. I miss little Bobs dreadfully at night. Father is at Buxton where he has already met some friends.

There is not much news; poor Margot's little baby died which is terribly sad. Tibby Russell is going to be married which is I suppose a good thing. I am going to Glen next week. Aunt Charty will be there but Uncle Archie is still yachting. I don't know when I shall see him.

The Duffs were great progenitors and formed a sizeable portion of the population of Aberdeenshire and Banffshire in those days. In the 17th century Patrick Duff of Hatton sired 36 children: 13 by Ann Innes of Edingight, who then died, and 23 more by his hapless second wife Mary Urquhart. He is said to have been complimented by George II on the addition he had made to His Majesty's subjects in Scotland! How many of this vast family survived is not known, but it is on record that Patrick was carried to his grave by 12 of his sons, and there are records of 17 out of the 36 surviving into adult life. Towards the end of his life, this one-man population explosion had great difficulty in recognising many of his offspring and would often ask them who their father was. It did not enhance his popularity.

The big houses or castles mentioned by Joan are all quite close to each other, within calling distance. Their large estates march with each other, surrounding the 'douce' market town of Turriff with its red sandstone buildings, occupied mostly these days, by banks and law-firms, and the Episcopalian church where the Lairds, their families, as well as all their retainers, worshipped. It was a peaceful town and had no truck with Stuart Pretenders, though the dreaded Montrose did once pay a visit. The river Deveron flows serenely through the town and is shared by the various estates on its way to Banff and the sea.

Hatton Castle was owned by Gorden Duff who married Annie Urquhart. Annie was a local girl from Craigston, the castle down the road, and came from a family of scholars, a rarity in those days. Delgaty Castle was owned by the Grant Duffs who had just changed the name to Ainslie. Forglen is the last and richest of this clutch of castles. It was owned by the Abercromby family, descended from the famous General. One of them married a Baring. The line is extinct now, more's the pity, they were a great family. William Forbes, who cycled over from another castle, Rothiemay some miles up the river from Turriff, later joined the Navy. The good looks and ''side", which struck Joan enough to comment upon, earned him the title of "Kissing Willie"!

27 August 1900. Lachlan to Father. Belfast

We have got here for a change, and it promises excitement of a doubtful sort as just now a great Boer shell whizzed through the air and burst outside the camp. I believe it was aimed at a 4.7 which has been expressing itself just outside the camp at intervals. Outside a little way beyond us up the hill, guns seem to be going off all around us with occasionally a little musketry around a picket not far off. But I will go on with our doings from when I last wrote which I think was at Welverdiend on the 17th.

We stayed there quietly enough till the 22nd. Miller and I got a rather good English mare brought in by a kaffir, a lost remount, a bit knocked about, but in good condition and sound. We also picked up a good saddle and bridle at Frederikstadt for 7/6 and found a sack of oats that had been formerly forgotten by someone, so we did pretty well. She was a ripper to go and jumped awfully well. Miller knew the O.C. of remounts so we had no difficulty in borrowing animals, and there were hundreds of poor beasts worn out and cast away that were wandering about and dying all over the place. White caught one of these ponies - not a bad one - but he got bucked off (another shell just passed) and skinned his nose and face so that next morning he could not march. That night orders arrived: half the Battalion was to escort an empty convoy to Krugersdorp, and the rest to come on later by train, bringing on large quantities of rations and forage to be stored here.

We marched early on the 22nd with the convoy. The beasts had to be outspanned at about 12 a.m. for 3 hours, as oxen will not graze at night. We camped about 3 miles beyond Banks station and were told to stay there. It was so cold that, with the help of a very kind Lt. of mining police, Col. Burney got the use of a long row of tin buildings used for mining employees in ordinary times which were most comfortable after perishing in the gale. Allan and I got a furnished room, but it was too good to last. We were ordered off that evening! G Company marched in to Krugersdorp, the remainder training.

We got a good room for mess that evening, and 2 mails which were very welcome. The last was the one after you heard from me. I am glad they were not lost after all. I am sorry to hear about the gout. We had a very cold wind and hard frost that night, and next morning we got orders to entrain at 1 p.m. for Pretoria, which we did, being packed in open filthy coal trucks, so tight one could hardly turn round.

'packed in open filthy cattle trucks.'

'Kitchener turned up.'

We had a very slow journey arriving about 10.30. The Battalion lay down in the square behind the station and got tea; the officers slept on any part of the platform that took their fancy. Alexander and I made a kind of joint bed. We got some very nasty tepid coffee and ate cold tongue and sardines. As we were entraining at 4.30 we had reveille at 3; however, as is usual on these occasions, the train was not ready owing to one or more lazy Railway Staff Officers, and we loafed about the platform till after 8.

Kitchener turned up, a horrid bloated-looking man, with the vaguest resemblance to his popular photos. Buchanan stalked him with a Kodak around the corner. We got off about 9 in the same trucks, only 3 men succeeded in getting drunk! As the Colonel and Adjutant were absent we managed very comfortably. The run out of Pretoria was very pretty and interesting for a considerable way. I noticed the paths that we cleared for our camp on the Muckleneuk were still undisturbed. We made ourselves very comfortable in a van with forage and got a much-needed sleep. We stayed 6 hours at Wonderfontein, only getting in here at 7 a.m. on a bitterly cold bleak cloudy morning. This place is 6550 ft above sea level, so you can imagine what it is like. There is a small village north of the station.

Bobs met us on the platform. We were the most grimy disreputable looking set imaginable, and we camped here just south of the station. The Royal Scots gave us a good breakfast, for which we were most grateful.

29th - Shortly after breakfast as I began this epistle 3 or 4 shells burst at intervals very close to the camp, and I began to wish my tent was bomb-proof. At a neighbouring picket a brisk musketry fire was going on, with our guns bellowing all round, while we pursued our ordinary avocations in camp as if it was all quite quiet. We saw Buller's column advancing along a ridge some miles east of us, and the Boers clearing off in front. About this time all shooting around here ceased. Bobs rode by in the evening and said things were going very well and that we had punished the Boers that day, and that we would see our friends soon! The men all shouted, but we have been much exercised to know whether he meant friends at home or referred to the 2nd Battalion which is only a few miles off with Buller.

Mr Jaffrey, our minister, was very angry at his beastly pony being left and kicked up a great fuss. He is a silly ass and annoys everyone, as he did not get the sympathy he desired at the prospect of having to foot it for a time.

I would like a good waterproof cape if it is worth sending. I should have thought of it before, as the rains are due any time now. There was thunder and a little rain on picket this morning.

There is to be a big show at Machadodorp I believe, and Bobs is said to have determined not to come in until Botha is smashed. De Wet is continuing his sporting career in the Free State I believe.

Things were not looking at all good for the Boers. To add to Botha's problems he had the responsibility of escorting the aged President, Paul Kruger, to Portuguese East Africa. As part of his luggage he had all the gold from the South African Republic, £2 million worth, which must not fall into the hands of the British. The railway carriage was his mobile seat of government, an engine attached with steam permanently up. He was now at Belfast but he had to move later to Machadodorp and Nelspruit as his army withdrew before the advancing British. The plan was for him to cross over the border into Portuguese territory where a Dutch cruiser would be waiting at Lourenco Marques to take him to Holland and the safety of Europe. He hoped to get assistance from sympathetic European powers. His capture by the British would be a terrible blow to the Boers' national pride.

With only 5,000 Boers, Botha had to contend with two enemies. The first was the British and their 30,000 troops almost knocking on the door of the railway carriage. The second was the President's age and poor health. Belfast was situated in the low veldt, swampy ground, riddled with Tsetse flies, and extremely unhealthy. He had to get his frail old President out of the low veldt and take him to Lydenburg, right up in the Drakensberg mountains, 6,600 ft. high. This would be suitable for his health and difficult country for pursuers.

On 27 August 1900, the day when the final leg of advance on Komati Poort started and the Boers lost the battle of Belfast, things were very much in favour of the British. The Boers had escaped into the mountains with their President, protected by a tiny force, and presented no threat to the British. Roberts was so elated that he telegraphed the British Government that the war was over. He had done the same thing after the fall of Pretoria! How wrong he was. Though he had won the battle of Belfast, which was the last set-piece battle of the war, he had not destroyed the Boer army. Because of its mobility it was still relatively intact, even after the Belfast defeat. The war went on until May 1902.

30 August 1900. Joan to Lachlan. The Glen, Innerleithen

We got your delightful long letter all about your expedition into the Mahaliesberg. I was very sorry to hear that you had fever, but I suppose it is hardly to be avoided and that you were lucky to get well so quickly and hope you have not had any more, and that you are having a nice time at Krugersdorp.

Everybody has been very much excited by the battles with Botha. It really seems that Buller was going to have a big victory, but apparently just as we got close, they dispersed as usual. However we have got into Machadodorp (you would laugh if you heard all the different efforts at pronouncing this).

There is a delightful family party, Aunt Charty, Uncle Tommy and all three Uncles, Eddy, Frank and Jack, and May and Marguerite. The three uncles are worth anything. Grandpapa is not very well; Marguerite is so vast that she can only waddle with the greatest difficulty in the most absurd way, but it must be horribly uncomfortable. She is bigger than Mildred ever was!

The Glen. Peebles

Shooting with the Tennants

They have been grouse shooting the last few days and got 60 brace yesterday. Aunt Charty, May and I went up to lunch with them, and May and I went up the hill and saw one drive. Sunday, at Park, was a bitterly cold day, almost freezing. I went for a long walk in the afternoon over the Gallows hill and up the Culvie Hill, where I had never been. I looked down on the Druid circle but I did not go to it as it was in the middle of a field of barley. I did not find any white heather.

On Monday Geordie had his birthday party and the house was creeping with babies.

Staying at the Glen must have been quite an experience. Joan took the whole thing in her stride. Like all her Tennant relations she was very intelligent and also highly critical.

The Tennants had plenty of money and made some very successful marriages, thus joining the aristocracy of the day and becoming well established in Edwardian Society. They were witty and amusing intellectuals. All this took place at the end of the nineteenth century. Years later things were very different and the Glen was sold.

Marguerite Miles was Sir Charles' second wife. His first, Emma Winsloe died in 1896, after presenting him with 12 children. Marguerite, forty five years younger than her husband, added three more children to the family. One of her children, my great-aunt Kay - the only member of the family that I personally met - married Walter Elliot. He later became Secretary of State for Scotland and, following his death, great-aunt Kay became a life peeress.

The grouse shooting ritual was, and still is, celebrated on many a Scottish moor in August. It was a gentleman's sport; there were certain strict rules which had to be observed; ladies were not allowed to join the guns until lunch time; it was bad form to shoot a fellow gun but not to hit a beater; you must not load your own gun, this would be done by a loader. The head keeper was more important than the host and had to be tipped. To be correctly dressed you had to wear sober heather-coloured knickerbockers (to confuse the grouse), have two guns, dogs to pick up the game, and of course masses of cartridges!

Those ladies that wanted to, came out with the lunch, which was carried in panniers on ponies. Conversation was limited to the activities of the morning; who had shot what, whose dog had behaved badly and other technical shooting matters. After lunch the ladies were permitted to sit in the butt of any gentleman who would have them and watch him shoot and mark the fall of his birds and not talk. (A butt is a fortresses of heather built to protect the guns from the attacking grouse!)

I share Joan's love for Park and the bleak countryside around, steeped in history. The walk she made up the Gallows Hill and on to the Culvie was the same as that made by the Jacobite William Gordon as he escaped to France. The Romans had an outpost there, one of their farthest north.

6 September 1900. Lachlan to Father. Kwag's Hoek

We left Belfast on Monday morning last, ourselves, the Royal Irish and the Royal Scots under Ian Hamilton and Smith-Dorrien, exactly a week after our arrival. It was spent quietly, only enlivened by occasional games of football, all with the Royal Scots and half of us doing rear guard to a great convoy. Bobs watched us march out. He was looking very fit. We were bound for the relief of Buller, who had trapped 2000 Boers on the way to Lydenburg. Buller said he wanted reinforcements to turn them out, as their position was very strong; I believe 2 Boers would hold him up.

We had with us our two old cow guns for which I have a great affection. They are so very business-like and reassuring. Our wretched cattle are in very poor condition, dropping out and dying all along the road. We had a long halt to get them fed and, as the road was hilly, only got in about 6 p.m. having done only 12 or 13 miles. We found that our half Battalion in front, who got in a good bit

General Smith-Dorrien and Colonel Macbean

before us, had been shelled a little by a Boer Howitzer or Long Tom, but no harm was done. The Boers retired.

Next morning we had barely got under way before "whizzle, whizzle, bong" and a succession of great fat shells burst 2 or 3 hundred yards off us. We halted a few minutes and watched them, while a cow gun came up, and having located the enemy, planted a shell so close to their gun, that they promptly decamped; the range was, I believe, 4 or 5 miles. We then proceeded to Dullstroom, a funny little place snugly hidden, consisting of a church, about 10 little houses and gardens with lovely Mimosa trees in bloom under a sugar loaf kopje with a little river or burn at the foot; quite pretty. After a halt to feed the beasts we pushed on 4 or 5 miles over very hilly wild country that reminded me of the West Highlands, a terrible road for the transport.

The 18th Hussars or "Kruger's Own" came from Buller to assist us and were sniped a bit. I was on picket with half G Company and Maclaren with F. Next morning it was very foggy indeed and we could not march until it lifted. However, about 8 the sun appeared as usual and we did advanced guard without opposition over a magnificently rugged country of huge hills and little burns

'Our two old cow guns'

and occasional waterfalls with, here and there a farm house nestling in a grove of green willows and pink peach blossoms. The whole appearance of the country was very like the Highlands; the burnt grass being just the same as heather out of

Dulstroom. September 1900 Woodside Tytler
Col. Macbean Padré Jaffray
Maclaren. Ogston Cameron Craufurd

bloom. There was a little breeze, and altogether it was delightful walking. I only wish I could transfer it into a genuine moor with necessary accessories.

We only came about 7 miles when we got here, a most picturesque spot, situated in a "Hoek" with good grass and lots of water. We are only a few miles from the Boers' position and will probably fight tomorrow, tho' as a rule when expected a fight does not come off; it is now rather late so I will continue another day.

Lydenburg 8 September - A convoy just off, got here today. It had a devil of a time. The enemy shelled us all afternoon, Long Toms etc. We did nothing, absolutely damnable. Luckily very few casualties. Enemy supposed to be off. They have exact range of our camp!! (92nd are up here).

18 September 1900. Sir Charles Tennant to Father. The Glen, Innerleithen

Dear Tom,
You will like to read the enclosed, received today from a young fellow whom I got to the front.

20 August 1900. David Millar to Sir Charles Tennant. 1st Gordon Highlanders, Welverdiend

A grandson of yours, young Gordon-Duff is one of my brother officers. He is a splendid young fellow and every one is very fond of him, a good soldier and as plucky as possible. Curiously enough we both belong to the same Company, although at present we are serving in different ones. You must excuse this scrawl but I am lying on the ground in a small bivouac with the dust blowing all over the place.

27 September 1900. Lachlan to Father. Komati Poort

We are now in a region very different to the old high veldt, crawling with noxious bugs and reptiles, facing a hill which the wily Portugoose has bedecked with flags.

We left Lydenburg on Sunday 9th and marched 10 miles towards Machadodorp, camping in a big basin where Buller was held up just before. We heard his guns going as he attacked the great Mauchberg, of which Paardeplats is a portion. We half expected to be sent off to his assistance. Our camp had a good many holes where the big Boer shells entered the ground, some up to 5 to 8 ft deep, showing the rifling marks as the shell screwed. Dingwall dug one out, and was luckily prevented by the Colonel from trying another which was unexploded.

10th - Off again. We did about 12 miles, finishing with a long and frightfully dusty hill of some 3 or 4 miles.

11th - We trekked to Helvetia. It is only a district, no town.

12th - Had a day's rest, and got a mail in. Your letters arrived safe.

13th - Marched to Waterfall Onder, a fall of 1000 feet in about 8 miles. It is a pretty little place which bursts upon you around the corner of a great mountain lying far down below in a hollow, and the Crocodile River running past it. The road down is frightfully steep, twisty and dusty. The difference in temperature below was considerable tho' it was not very warm. We crossed the river which is

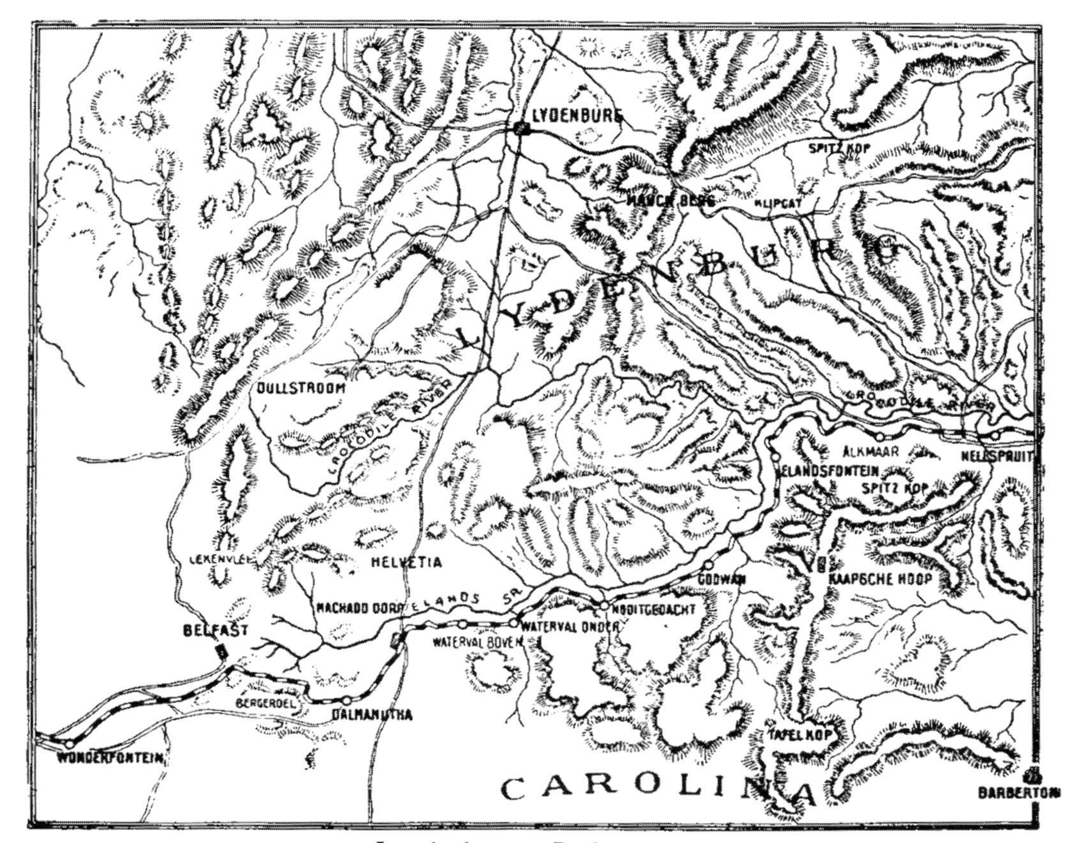

Lyndenburg to Barberton

as big as the Fiddich near Craigellachie and we camped by a little burn between big hills by some Swazie Kraals.

We got a lot of Claret and tinned butter which the Boers had been unable to get away, and made ourselves comfortable in an uncompleted kaffir hut; not the round kraal. It was airy and shady. We also bathed in the burn.

14th - To Nooitgedacht, marched along the railway. Very hot. G Company pulled the wagons up a bit of rough, steep road. The oxen did not do so badly, but the unfortunate mules needed a lot of assistance. We did not know then that this was a joke compared to what we should experience in a short time.

On our way into camp we passed the place where the British prisoners of war had been confined, a huge enclosure of barbed wire entanglement, with rough bivouacs of galvanised iron looking very dirty and uncomfortable. I had a ripping bathe in the Crocodile river, which was very shallow but swift and clear.

15th - We passed Godwaan Station, where we climbed a mile or so up the hill on our right and made 12 or 13 miles, very hot. Since leaving Waterfall Onder we had followed the railway, which was little hurt, down a long narrow valley with high hills on both sides, and valleys at intervals running into the main one. It was all along very pretty and well-watered country. We all had a good swim that afternoon, tho' a high mule rather marred the pleasure.

16th Sunday - Started at 3 a.m., bright moon. Men all carried an extra blanket to lighten wagons. Ascent of Devil's Kantoor, very well named. The road leaves the railway here. We reached the top just as the sun rose and put down our arms and started pulling up the wagons ourselves with drag ropes - a frightful job. We got into a pretty little miners' village called Kaaps Hoops about 1 p.m., having only done 6 miles in a very breezy cool place on the hills.

17th Monday - Off again; foggy, drizzly morning, this time worse hills than we came up the day before. Never saw such a glorious view as we got in one place from the road downhills to the valley running away from us for miles. Saw Barberton in distance. Short march again. I did picket on a hill, a fine view, and covered with grass instead of stones, most unusual. Gullies up sides thick with vegetation; saw some fine ferns.

18th - A 12 mile march towards Barberton; did a good deal of pulling at a bad drift. Craufurd got enraged with a native who beat his mules, and rushed through the water and knocked him down. The native thought he was mad I believe. Dingwall is thoroughly in his element beseeching mules to pull, and worrying himself, natives and all concerned; very ludicrous. We did a pretty long march, camping near the Roos Sisters, 3 odd hills in a row. There were two heavy showers soon after we got in, but the rain held off though clouds very threatening for some days.

19th - We were advance guard and picketed the kopjes on either side of the road, very pretty country, plenty of brick and gold and copper about. We passed near Barberton and waded in the Kraar river coming into camp by the railway about 6 miles from Barberton. We bathed in the river, and some engineers killed fish by bursting bombs in the pools.

20th - Hot dusty march, hilly road, crossed the railway at Avocca; many engines left there by the Boers. The country here is bushveldt, very thorny. There are mines all over the hills, but now deserted. We crossed the Kraar River 3 times, twice wading and once by a railway bridge.

21st - Temperature 105°, frightful dust, bad road, nearly choked. We camped at Lows Creek, 9 miles from Kaap Muiden. Got to Kaap Muiden by 9 o'clock, a better road. Big game country, three lions killed here last year, and two leopards seen the other day eating a dead horse. Bathed in Crocodile River. Sick men and those with bad boots were left behind.

Help for the Cowguns: September 1900

23rd - Sunday - Marched 12 miles to Melane Station, very hot. Bush veldt in places has fine big trees. Rode on mule with Alexander and Maclaren to bathe, the river nice.

24th - To Hectors Spruit 13 miles, much the same march, the line being replaced as we go. Bathed and saw the remains of Boer guns blown up by river and scattered all over the place.

25th - Very hot, we leave at 1.30 p.m. to go 20 miles to Komati Poort and march along the railway, one rank either side of rails. Very thankful when the sun goes down, in shirt sleeves all night, trying march. We arrive at last at 10.30. Got some food and slept where we were. Very cold towards morning. The transport arrived late.

26th - Bathed early in Komati River, one dead crocodile seen! The rest were frightened away below the bridge. The hill on the other side with the Portuguese

sitting on top dotted with flags. No one allowed to cross. There are supposed to be 10,000 disarmed Boers in laager opposite.

Disabled Long Tom on far side of the bridge. Want to go into the Port territory but no one allowed to. Stores etc. come up from Delagoa Bay. Quantities of engines and some trucks here, many of the latter burnt. We have been steadily exploding Boer ammunition. Very hot, nothing done. This is a small place and we have a small shanty as mess-house. There are very peculiar trees around here. One with yellow powder on the trunks called the Fever Tree. I got a scorpion, about 5 inches long.

Our ancient allies - The Frontier Guard

CHAPTER EIGHT

Komati Poort to Belfast 1900

9 October 1900. Lachlan to Mildred. Komati Poort

We are gradually returning to Pretoria. The Volunteers left yesterday morning for home; they were frightfully pleased and I should think most people envied them. We shall miss them as they were good chaps. This is really a nice place, tho' I would not like to live here. About 3 days after arriving on the 28th, there was a grand review of the British troops by a Portugoose from Lourenco Marques. It was a very interesting performance, as we are not likely to see such a sight again. They arrived by train early in the morning and rode up with Pole Carew , the general commanding British troops, to where we were paraded. The ground was too thickly interspersed with thorn bushes and trees to allow of a march past, so we did Royal Salutes, with the Portuguese national anthem and our own played by the Royal Scots Band while the procession inspected us. They were very smart, wearing white tunics and pale blue breeks with a broad red stripe, and good-looking horses. There must have been over 20 officers and about as many of their troopers. They expressed much approval, and were particularly impressed by our kilts and the Battery.

DERAILMENT.

The funniest part of the whole performance was a very fat and fierce looking little German, who toddled past as fast as he could go immediately in rear of the procession. The sight nearly made us collapse. There were a lot of civilians of a mixed kind, Johannesburg refugees etc., who were very smart in cool white costumes, while their womenkind sported coloured parasols. It was pretty warm, tho' all was over before 9 a.m. We had breakfast, and then strolled over to the station and talked to some of the chaps. They gave us iced drinks in the railway carriage. I have never tasted anything so good; ice has been unobtainable and the heat considerable even for the Transvaal.

The train left about 12 p.m. for the coast, but unluckily the engine was in the rear and, running down the incline to the bridge, a misfortunate bullock strolled in front of the train which ended him, but in return a truck and 2 big carriages full of people were hurled off the track and upset, the latter one on each side of the line. The passengers were shot out of the windows, or crawled from the wreck. It was only about 400 yards from the platform, so a crowd at once assembled, including K of K. No one was really hurt, except the engine driver, who had his jaw broken, but they were a bit bruised and shaken. Symptoms of hysterics were not wanting; one lady considered it necessary to rest her head on a Jock's shoulder, while another fanned her.

We took several over to the shanty doing duty as mess house and restored their nerves with whisky and port, which they seemed to appreciate. Among them was the barman from Resino Garcia, the station just over the border, and his relations! However at the second start they got safely off. Next day a lot of us crossed over the bridge and hunted for relics along the railway, where the Boers were encamped. The Komati runs along the left of the line, and the Lebombo mountains on the right. The Boers just bivouacked where they pleased on both sides. They left enormous quantities of stuff, such as every sort of ammunition and explosive, flour, beds, tents, tarpaulins, empty tins, old guns and rifles etc.

The best rifles were loosely buried, but I got a very nice Mauser Carbine from a man who found it, with the name P.J.J. Smit carved on it. The Doctor was with me and we went to see how Portuguese territory was getting on; however, as there were sentries on the line we climbed the kopje, and had a look at Resino Garcia where a lot of Portugooses were playing a kind of quoits. We were just moving off, when I was pursued by one with a gun, very excited. Woodside had disappeared, but saw me led off and imagined I was going to see the barmaid! I was wearing an old pair of bags minus a coat, and very hot so was rather disreputable. A crowd of jabbering fellows, none of whom knew a word of English, took away the carbine in spite of all protests.

Then an officer appeared and took me to a kind of barracks, where I was shown in to the Commandant who was very comfortable in bed. He knew a few words, but it was not until I tried French that he understood what was up. Then he gave me a bottle of beer and we had a long conversation. He got up and with another Portuguese fellow, I was shown over the border, with a beer bottle for Woodside, who appeared. I introduced him, and we all went along to hunt for curios and try the carbine.

The river is clear and rocky, but they say it is full of crocodiles, (a few have been seen lately) and a hippopotamus close to the bridge. However everyone bathes and nothing happens, tho' it is safer with plenty of people.

That same day Gardyne and Craufurd went with 40 of Steinacker's Scouts on a trip up the Selati railway for 4 days. They had plenty of adventures. They were all mounted of course. They came on a Boer convoy trekking with supplies for Botha about 60 miles off, and attacked them, 32 men covering about one half mile of firing line. The Boers numbering about 400 men were quite surprised and demoralised, and if 20 M.I. who ought to have turned up had arrived, the whole lot would have probably surrendered or abandoned the wagons on being taken in the flank. They soon recovered, and the Scouts had to retire, tho' without any casualties. They knocked over a good many Boers, ponies and oxen, but were bitterly disappointed at the non-arrival of the M.I.

What proved to be much worse than Boers was a lion. The second night he took a horse from the lines within the circle of fires, and next morning it was found a wretched Kaffir was gone, his half-eaten remains being found a little way off. The lion was followed and actually fired at in the night, but it was too dark to hit him. Next night a trooper had just gone on sentry-go, and was standing inside the circle of fire when he was seized and carried off. A second lion seized his leg. The wretched fellow yelled to shoot, a volley was fired, when the beasts dropped him, and he walked into camp, very badly scratched, but apparently not badly injured. However, he died a day or so after from blood-poisoning.

Gardyne and Craufurd each shot an Impala. They came across a herd of zebras, and the spoor of giraffe, but had no opportunity of following. While they were away a serious accident occurred. A fatigue party of 100 men, including Davis, were working under the engineers blowing up Boer ammunition, when somehow a premature explosion took place and about 24 men were hurt. Two died soon after of wounds and several were pretty badly hurt. Davis was hit on the back of the head, and several knocked about besides. It was a marvel how he and any others escaped as they did; he has gone to Pretoria.

We had a frightful 24 hours. It poured steadily and was very depressing; my bivouac kept quite dry, but some people's houses leaked considerably. The fearful and wonderful crawly beasts here are a terror, scorpions and hundreds of centipedes. I had a scorpion 4 inches long. Alexander got stung by one but it did not hurt much as ammonia was close at hand. Lots of men have been in hospital with bites of some sort. Snakes are also very plentiful. There are all sorts of wonderful birds to be seen, of all sizes and colours, and a very pretty little blue-breasted sparrow. I rode out the other day to get a buck. I saw 3 but did not get a shot. I also saw a baboon for the 1st time. A man was clawed by a leopard which another man shot. After the rain we moved up from the railway to a house above the Crocodile River which belonged to some boss here. It is on a stray knoll and, tho' destitute of furniture, very cool and pleasant for meals etc. It is an ordinary bungalow on piles ; our own tents are all around. There is a lovely bathing place just below. Some of us were moving down to Pretoria, but news of the railway bridge at Kaap Muiden has broken, so of course that means some days' delay. I sincerely hope the time will soon come when we shall sail. The war seems to be drawing to an end, tho' spasmodic outbursts still occur.

Lord Roberts, as Commander-in-Chief, after the capture of Komati Poort had told the British that the war was over and the Boers defeated. The Boers thought differently and continued to resist for another 18 months. Roberts went home shortly after making this misleading statement. He was promoted to the top post in the army.

The big question Lachlan and his colleagues were to ask, after hearing Roberts' statement was 'when are we going home?' After all, the Brigade of Guards were on their way and so was the Volunteer Company of the 1st Battalion The Gordon Highlanders and other Regiments.

But the Boers, who were based near their homes and families continued, their guerrilla warfare. British Intelligence in the Boer War was totally inadequate. One gets the feeling that it was thought 'not cricket' to spy. It was 'not done'. This was Victorian Britain, in the days of Newbolt's 'Play up and play the game' and 'Keep a straight bat'.

As usual Roberts informed his generals in September that the numbers of the enemy were steadily decreasing in the Orange Free State and were now down to 3000. In fact they had risen to 8000.

During the first months of this phase of the war, the Boers attacked the main Central Capetown Railway 40 times, and all night movement had to be suspended. Some unfortunates on their way home had their passages cancelled. To counter this and other enemy incursions, the British formed 'Flying Columns'. This was a misnomer! They consisted mainly of Infantry who were heavily equipped, supported by artillery, field ambulances and overloaded ox-wagons.

But everything was not going the Boers' way. A new and efficient hero emerged, General Knox, who headed a scratch column formed by Roberts to attack the Boers. De Wet was very nearly trapped in the Transvaal but managed to escape in a thunder storm.

After their defeat at Komati Poort, the Boer leaders made their way north to Pietersburg in the Drakensberg mountains to a summit conference. This was a safe area as Roberts had not penetrated that far north. The terrain was inhospitable in the extreme. The conference was attended by all top Boers, including Presidents Steyn and Botha, De Wet and other leaders. The invasion of Cape Colony was on the agenda.

In the meanwhile, the British had built a line of fortified posts between Bloemfontein and Basutoland, each garrisoned by about 50 men, sited 2 miles apart. The idea was to control the movement of the Boers but it was breached by De Wet and 500 British were captured.

At midnight 28/29 November 1900 Lord Roberts laid down his command in favour of Kitchener, saying once again that the war was over. At this moment the Boers were at the peak of their operational strength and were poised to invade the Cape from two directions. They had a government which functioned, though with no fixed seat, and were acting upon a common plan in defence of their own beloved country. They were united.

To quote Rayne Kruger again: 'What Roberts had won was a shadow. He left Kitchener to grapple with reality'.

4 October 1900. Joan to Lachlan. Hatton

As you see I am again at this beloved place, and missing you more than ever. We had news of you this week through Nanny who was overjoyed at getting your letter. You implied you were writing to me too, but that will come next week.

I left Park, very sadly, on Thursday evening. It was looking so lovely. I did want so badly to stay there. Hopeman was looking lovely too. I have never seen the opposite hills so clear; it is a far prettier place than Lossiemouth.

Yesterday morning I shopped violently in Elgin and started for here after lunch by the Express. It started half an hour late, so they had to go at a terrific pace to make up. Between Huntly and Inveramsay we must have been going 70 miles an hour. It rocked and I thought it would leave the rails.

Tonight we dine at Delgaty to dance afterwards. Do you remember last year when Nina carried her ball dress on her bicycle for the same entertainment and how dreary it was?

Hopeman Lodge was the dower house for the family and when Father Tom died in 1923, his widow Mildred moved in. Eventually it was bought by Gordonstoun School.

There were several houses at the family's disposal. Drummuir was built in 1854 and was the largest, the least attractive and the coldest, so it naturally housed the head of the family, the patriarch. Then came Park, which was a Gordon stronghold, which had parts dating back to the 15th century. It was full of charm and a ghost or two. After the 1745 rebellion William Gordon, the Laird and a staunch Jacobite, was attainted for his part in the uprising and was exiled.

The girl who carried her ball dress on the handle bars of her bicycle was Nina Duff, daughter of Folliot Duff. Her father was somewhat eccentric in that he used to write his name in blue chalk on the pavement outside his house and on neighbouring walls.

12 October 1900. Mrs Roberta Turner to Father. Saddlewood, Camberley, Surrey

My sister went to Southampton to meet her husband, who has been invalided home, and while waiting on board where he was getting his things together, she began talking to a Private in the Gordon Highlanders who was loud in his praises of Lachlan, and he mentioned one engagement in which Capt Younger was killed. Lachlan took command of the Company and led them splendidly. This of course is only a Private's opinion, but I think they are as a rule the best judges of a good officer and their views on these occasions are not to be despised. I am sure the above remarks will be of interest to you, especially as this man also added that Lachlan was a splendid soldier and the Regiment was very proud of him.

KOMATI POORT TO BELFAST 1900

16 October 1900. Lachlan to Father. Belfast

The Volunteers left us on the 8th. It was a great surprise to everyone as it was totally unexpected. They have done a lot of hard work and were cheered by the Battalion. Old 'Granny Duncan' [an Aberdeen advocate of 3 Bon Accord Crescent] is an awfully good old chap. The Antique, as he was called from his aged appearance, came out at the same time as Alexander. Forbes is a rattling good chap, a farmer from near Alford, who has invited us all to go and have scones and cream with him. He was badly wounded at Doornkop, but got back again. The men were all very glad it was over, as many of them have been wanting to get back for a long time, tho' about 40 are going to stay in the country. They will have to be careful for the next few years or they will be shot.

We changed camp after the rains to higher ground a mile or so to the north. The mess occupied a bungalow in excellent condition. The Col. and Adjutant had rooms; pantry and dining room, ante-room and orderly room took up the rest. There was big a verandah right round, and a piano also turned up, so we were very well off. The Crocodile River ran about 100 feet below, where there was a lovely place to bathe. You could dive from a rock in the middle into a deep swift stream. It was clear and rocky and beautifully warm. A little way off, by the bridge, a hippopotamus lived. He was seen sometimes, and preserved. Crocodiles were common, tho' I never saw one myself.

The General and his staff, consisting of Col. Inglefield (nicknamed by the men 'Old Trouble'), Capt Weldon and his two ADCs dined with us one night, and had a musical evening. The General sings very well.

11th - Cameron and self with 20 men each entrained as escort to 2 five inch Cow guns. A frightful pack, there were of course no carriages or even covered van. Men, natives and ourselves packed anywhere on trucks, under guns, wagons etc. Cameron and I got a place under an ammunition wagon with our servants, and two natives at the other end of the truck; we had four days of it and were fairly comfortable. We were stopped, as a gun train had gone over a temporary bridge at Kaapmuiden. Our train stayed all night. The oxen had then to be watered. Poor brutes, they suffered very much travelling, two or three dying every day. This is a long job occupying about 6 hours, as they are so difficult to entrain.

While this was on Dingwall and I went on a buck hunt. There were plenty of small buck and hares about, which would be easy shooting with a shot gun, and cartridges, but a Mauser carbine with nickel bullets is useless. However in a rather thick bit of bush, I came suddenly on a herd of 7 to 9 Impalas, 2 with fair heads, about 100 yards off. I had to shoot standing, and they started off before I could get the first shot off. I got two shots off at one of the buck, and undoubtedly hit him, as he went off by himself sharp to the left while the rest went on. The bush was very thick, so it was useless following. I would have given anything then for a few soft nosed bullets. It was a tremendously hot day, and we were very glad to get to the station, which is in a pretty cool place. We were then told that our train would not go at all that day, so Cameron and I went out in the evening across the river. We got nothing, but had a nice bathe and a frightfully thorny scramble in the dark to strike the railway about a mile from the station. We heard bugles tooting away like mad and found orders had come for us to proceed. Dingwall thought we had been eaten by wild beasts.

I got your letter of 14 September. Our train was diverted from there to Nelspruit as bridges etc. were dangerous. Luckily we escaped accidents. This was our third day and we got as far as Waterfall Onder; the line was very picturesque all the way. We left after dark for Waterfall Boven, only 4 miles. I was awfully disappointed at missing that bit of the line. It is a cogwheel section, and very fine indeed. We went through the only tunnel in S. Africa, and nearly choked. We spent a cold night at Waterfall Boven, and next morning impromptu sports took place between the men and a lot of New Zealanders in the station. There was much excitement. The line from there to Belfast is a bit Boery, as trains are only run by day.

21 October - We are still here, the trek being postponed, tho' the General says we may be ordered anywhere any time. We have had rather fun the last few days. On the 17th we started to get up some races for the troops here. There were to be Steeple chases and flat races; so of course there was great competition in trying to raise animals to ride.

I borrowed two grey ponies to try, but they were wanted the next day by the General's staff; we were rather fixed. However we knew a vet called Dixon, so we applied to him. He is a very good chap and said he would do the best he could for us. He had just got 2 or 3 horses from Pretoria, one a rather nice looking grey, which he let me try; he had never been on it and knew nothing of it, but it jumped over some small shelter trenches and bales of hay we put up, so I entered it for the Belfast Steeplechase and Welter Flat-Race, one mile long, with 4 jumps, none of them big. They were built of earth and sods, with a ditch on either the near or far side. The wings were made by transport wagons being shoved against the jumps, one at each side. All sorts of ponies and horses were raised, but most of them would not jump. It was rather amusing watching everyone practising the night before.

I kept my horses dark, not jumping them near the course, beforehand. The first race started at 2 p.m. on the 19th, a fine warm afternoon; there were 9 entries for it. Willie Gordon was riding his big English horse which he brought out with him. There was also White, Ogston and our friend Dixon, who entered at the last. Out of the 9 starters there were five out of the same Regt.

We got away well together, my old grey spurting beautifully, so when we reached the first jump there was only one horse just ahead and another about level. We got over without difficulty and went a good pace. The second jump one or two horses refused, and one came down going into the wagon - no one was hurt. After the 2nd it became a race between me and the Adjutant who was just leading or about level. The last bit of the course twisted about to avoid rocky ground, so the pace was slower and rather uphill. I led by a few feet at the last obstacle, and to my great surprise won easily.

There was a mule race for boys, chiefly black. It was very funny. There were any amount of entries. My costume was raised from 10 different people, including the Padre's breeks, which were an extraordinary fit, a green shirt of Alexander's and a red flash pinned over one shoulder.

22nd - We have got tents at last! They were useful last night as it poured steadily for hours, but it has laid the dust and flies which were getting rather nasty. We had a tremendous thunderstorm before the rain. It is nearly a year since we sailed now, and a pretty long one too. I hope we shall not see 1901 arrive in this country, tho' I suppose it is not improbable. We know more of the Transvaal and Free State than the average Boer I imagine, and have no desire to learn more.

25th - In train to Pretoria. Yesterday I started for Bloemfontein to get up the kits etc. left by the Battalion. I am going 1st class with Smith-Dorrien, Hood, his ADC, and a Major Rouse of the Gunners, so it is very pleasant. The General supplies the food. The General is up for a big review. Bloemfontein will be a civilised place by this time. The line from here swarms with Boers, who attempt to wreck trains, snipe and generally play the fool. There are lots of little commandos, very hard to catch. They have lots of supplies and ammunition apparently, and it is unsafe for small parties. The song the General sang at the dinner was "The old grey mare"!

23 October 1900. Lachlan to Joan. On the train to Pretoria

You will be surprised to see that I am writing from here on the 23 October. When we were having our sports I was asked by the Adjutant if I would like to take a trip to Bloemfontein to get up men's and officer's kits. So that morning off I went. The only thing I was sorry about was that I missed riding the grey horse in some races which the General was getting up, and he is such a ripper. I went down with the General as far as Pretoria. He has two 1st class coaches for himself and staff. We were very comfortable, cooking etc. done on board. We got as far as Balmoral by dark; no trains run out here after dark, it is unsafe. We reached Pretoria at 10 a.m. on 25th and had to get a pass, so I saw Walter Campbell, who is a big bug on the staff now. He was frightfully busy arranging for the review. Old Col. Ewart as usual asked tenderly after my health, he always does, starting when we first met at Modder river. I don't know who he is, tho' he was in the Camerons.

Campbell said there was not the remotest chance of the Regiment going home for at least 6 months, and from what I see of the country round here I think he is right, tho' it is disappointing when we expected to sail before the year is out. I went and saw poor Dingwall who was in hospital with fever tho' he is nearly well again. He had a formidable nurse. I was afraid to ask for a whisky and soda for him in case she saw me drink it. I met a few of the 92nd in the streets. They had come up from Middleburg for the review.

At 12.30 Bray, the ever faithful servant, and myself with Pom-Pom (Macneal's little dog, who I was to deliver to a certain Miss Rose Innes on No. 3 Hospital train) barely got on the south train in time. It was full of every sort of person including women and babies, so I got in the mail van, which was very comfortable. At Elandsfontein I made friends with Capt. Nathan RE. Assistant Director of Railways, by observing 'Good Afternoon'! He invited me to his carriage which was fitted up for him, and was most comfortable.

He was awfully kind and insisted on my coming. Luckily he had lots of food, and a well stocked cellar, so we had a very pleasant run. We reached Viljoens Drift that evening in one of the worst thunderstorms I've heard; it was terrific and the lightning appalling. We crossed the proper bridge, which had been repaired. It was a good thing we stopped at night for the Boers as usual tore up a strip of railway, but we had it replaced in half an hour, so the traffic was not delayed. We passed about 2000 Boers at Ventersburg road. The garrison could not have prevented them taking the train if they had wished to, but they caught the train after us and were dispersed with a few shells from the armoured train before any damage could be done. Since then we have been fighting around there, and I believe gave them the 'Knock'. Strange to say I discovered that a certain Miss Ramsay, who lives at Banchory, and has a brother in the Rifle Brigade, was on the train. She knew us in the Engadine, and has been nursing in the hospitals out here for the last six months and is on her way home. She seemed very nice and had of course many friends out here. Bray and I, with infinite trouble put her and her baggage, which was feminine in quantity, into the through-train for Capetown.

We got here about 9 a.m. on the 27th having passed the night at Smildael. I had great difficulty in wading to Nathan's house where I was dining. There are 4 of them sharing a lovely private villa, just like being at home. The table was decorated with red silk, and plate, with a parlour-maid as well as black waiters. I never saw such luxury, however they work very hard. Nathan is in his office 9 a.m. to 7 p.m. every day.

Sunday 28th - I went to church the first time for 6 months. It was impossible to realise what had happened in between. The church and congregation were just the same as ever.

Monday - A lot of worrying around getting a truck, fatigue party etc. from Railway Staff Officer, Baggage Masters, DAAG etc. Had to wire Kitchener of Khartoum about truck. Arranged everything for Tuesday, and got leave from the Remount officer to take a pony whenever I required one, very good of him. He has lent me a good saddle and bridle. The Drum Major is looking after all our baggage, which is stored with vast quantities of other people's in a big warehouse.

That night I got a wire saying 'Permission to bring kits cancelled, return to Headquarters'. On Tuesday another wire arrived saying, 'Await further orders'. So I have been waiting for the past 3 days, and don't mind how much longer I have to wait. Of course I have got at all my kit, have a real bed to sleep in for the first time for about a year, and am very comfortable. This is a pretty civilised town again; you can get anything you want. There is a very jolly swimming bath, and last night I went to the Vaudeville Theatre. I am glad to see the Drum Major has erected a cross to each of our men's graves. They were in endless rows with nothing to mark them but a tiny tin placard with name and Regt. At one time they were burying men in huge great pits, the only possible way. I wonder what we are going to do?

It looks as if the Battalion was coming to the Free State for a bit. Troops are wanted very badly down here - witness all the attacks on the little garrisons around the country. One of the Guards passed through here last night for home, together with our Volunteer Company. By the way, remember to send me out a plum pudding for the mess. How extraordinary it seems talking about another Xmas here. Last one we made sure of being home for the next. How about 1901? Shall we be back for the 12 August, or for Xmas only?

8 November 1900. Joan to Lachlan. Mountblairy
(This letter was delivered late owing to enemy action)

You have been fighting again and my heart aches for you. It must be too terrible, in the cold and wind and rain, and it seems to have been without much result. I only hope it has not given you a cold. I long to send a cable to find out. Why do they always choose the Gordons to fight?

And Oh! my dear, my dear, it is the 8 November, the day on which I parted from you last year. Are you ashamed of me if I say my eyes are full of tears? That terrible day, shall I ever forget it? The last thing I saw of you was your cap waved out of the cab window. May the cab be cursed that took you from me! And then we thought that in a few months you would be back. And Mrs Elliot was so sweet and kind and helpful but so sleepy, and I was so terribly wide awake. I could not understand how anyone could be sleepy, and she assured me that you would be back; and everyone said that you would not see any fighting; but I knew you would. I am sure you are thinking of that day too and I know we cannot wish that you were back any more ardently than you wish it yourself. But will the war ever be over? Lord Bobs has again put off coming back.

But I must try and tell you all the news if there is any. I went to see a friend of mine, the wife of a Seaforth, and found her husband too, such a nice man. He was looking very ill still, but he had so much to tell; and he said he was sure he had seen you, as one evening at Bloemfontein, two young Gordon officers had asked the way somewhere and he said he was sure you were one. He had a most interesting collection of things. He had guarded Cronje at Paarderberg and got the strap off his rifle and a bit of leather off his saddle, and a varied lot of things that he had picked up. He was so nice. I was late for lunch as I stayed such a long time talking to him. The next day we went to Keith again, (don't laugh) to a service at the church to consecrate a window put up to the memory of a Capt. Thorburn, of the Royal Fusiliers, who was killed at Pieters hill. It was a very beautiful little service.

In the afternoon Mildred and I drove to Dufftown to see a poor woman whose husband was a soldier and had died this year of consumption. It is such a sad world; she is left with three children and not a penny to support her and without a friend up here as she is English. I hope we will get something for her from the Association.

Sunday was a horrible day, a sort of fog. We didn't go to church as it was their Communion service. I went for a little walk; it was very nasty and brought on a cold.

On Monday Father went early to Edinburgh, and I came here. They have stopped half the trains so I had to go round by Banff, and have lunch with Mrs Mackintosh where I found two other ladies.

It was a lovely day, the one fine day of the month, so it was very nice. Tuesday, the two Frenchmen, le Comte de St Ferrol and M. de Tallance arrived. It is heavenly to hear really beautiful French again and I am glad to say I have not forgotten my French yet. The weather is so terrible, I have hardly been out at all. Today at last is fine, but I am afraid it will not last.

There is no more to tell: in fact I doubt if you will read all this! God bless you my Lachlan, and bring you back very soon.

12 November 1900. Lachlan to Joan. Belfast

I got back with a truck load of kits, arriving here yesterday. At Ventersburg Station we thought we were to be attacked. The Boers came pretty close, and after catching a native thought better of it. There was a terrific storm, thunder and lightning and rain. I noticed how beautifully green the country was all the way up after some rain. Marvellous to say I got here yesterday from Pretoria in one day. I passed some of our wounded men going down in the train, and heard a description of a little expedition I missed.

1 November, in pelting rain, we went out south, and marched till we met the Boers at 5 a.m. and had a bit of a skirmish. Then, owing to the weather which still poured, it was necessary to retire. The Boers pressed us hard, coming to within 50 yards occasionally. 15 men and Gardyne were wounded and one man killed. The only wonder is that many more were not. The men were in sodden greatcoats, and badly handicapped. The pom-poms eventually stopped them and the column returned. It was a poor sort of time. The Boers had the laugh entirely. That is the worst of trying to destroy farms in wet weather. Another column went out a few days later and came more to grief, six killed, many wounded. The Canadians lost a bit, 30 taken prisoner. A certain number of Boers were knocked over, but that sort of thing does little good.

However we are off again tomorrow at 6 a.m. for 6 days away, I believe, to burn more farms. It is awful country and no one looks forward to it. If we avoid a mess we shall do well. I shall feel far happier when we get back. I think Smith-Dorrien is off his chump.

It is cold and wet here, the rainy season well set in apparently, it will doubtless be damnable. A lot of our kits were looted in Bloemfontein, bivouacs all gone and any unlocked have been hunted through, the thief taking what he fancied. It is a bit sickening but the average soldier has no conscience whatsoever. I have been lucky and lost nothing but my old bivouac. Please thank Mildred for the waterproof cape. Will you be at Drummuir for Xmas? It will not be like last year after the Magersfontein battle etc. I hope Xmas 1901 we shall be home, tho' with luck we ought to be back by August next.

There was great row in Parliament about the policy of burning Boer farms. It was not an operation any one wanted to have to do. Col. Macbean, Lachlan's Commanding Officer, was particularly averse to the policy. Ventersburg Station is midway between Bloemfontein and Johannesburg in the Orange Free State.

CHAPTER NINE

Belfast 1901

22 November 1900. Nanny to Lachlan

I hope this will reach you in time for Xmas. I wish you were coming home for it. I look at the papers everyday to see who is coming but no mention of the Gordons. What a weary length this war is dragging on. Every day or nearly every day there is an account of some small skirmish in which a few get killed. Will it never end? I am enclosing a letter of Joan's which was in last week's Banffshire Journal. What do you think of your sister writing to the newspapers already?

I thought you might like a cake from Elgin, so I have ordered one to be sent from Austin's which I hope will get you in an early condition and that you will enjoy it. Your Grandmother said she might go to Drummuir next week, but she did not seem certain. She is all alone and I think she is beginning to feel dull.

I do not think I can find anything else to tell you in the way of news; for everything is and will be very quiet here owing to so many men being away at the front. So many that will never come home again. So now I will not stop hoping that you will still keep well and come back to us all very soon. With the very best wishes for Xmas and New Year and much love.

Austin's was the king of Elgin cake-makers and produced the most wonderful goodies with which we were stuffed as children. Like so many past glories, Austin's alas is no more, and the building which housed their premises is now owned by the Hydroelectric Board.

27 November 1900. Lachlan to Father. Belfast

I am very sorry I missed last mail. I was on picket, and it went before I thought it would. Last time I wrote the day before we started on a trek. The first day we marched about 14 miles burning a few farms. There was a little fighting, the Boers sniping most of the way at the Canadian Mounted Infantry, which we returned with guns; no casualties.

The country is now lovely, rich green grass and quantities of flowers. We passed a big farm. Smith-Dorrien gave them 10 minutes to get in the owner from commando or the farm would be burnt; this was unfortunate, as it was found to be a regular depot of the Boers out there belonging to a Mr Gobelaas and is to be burnt in any case.

Then there was a nasty boggy little drift to cross first before camping. Of course the wagons got bogged and while we were unloading them and dragging them out by ropes a terrific storm of rain came on, soaking everyone and making the ground 10 times worse. Luckily it stopped before dark.

2nd day - We did not get far. We blew up and burnt some farms, and the M.I. were outfired by Boers. We watched them riding back under heavy fire but none were hit. Our guns (cow, field, and pom-poms) put in a tremendous fusillade but the Boers walked off somehow from the kopje without signs of injury. G and H companies of ours and 2 Companies of the Royal Irish carried the heights valiantly, tho' as there was no one on them we did not get much credit. The cavalry went on to Witpoort to burn farms and a big mill while we camped.

3rd day - We did about 14 days eastwards, camping where we camped 3 months before on our first trek towards Lydenburg, 7 miles from Dullstroom and 13 from here. Some of the Companies were under fire tho' mine wasn't, again no casualties. We caught two Boers in the act of sniping. We burnt a good deal and collared several mobs of cattle, sheep etc.

4th day - At 3 a.m. half of us and half the Royal Irish, guns, M. I. etc. set out to destroy Dullstroom. We got there, tho' the Boers sat in the hills and sniped all round; one sergt was killed, most of Dullstroom was razed. The church was found full of weeping Belfast ladies. When operations were completed we walked back at a terrific pace. It was a cold dull day so we were glad to get back into camp, which we did by 12 a.m., a pretty good morning's walk. Allan and I were on picket and we slept well in spite of the rain. The fifth day we trekked back here, a fine morning. There were quantities of mushrooms all along the road which we picked and thoroughly enjoyed later. As we got in here an icy wind and dust storm arose to greet us followed by torrents of rain.

Nothing much has been going on here; tomorrow there is to be a gymkhana. A horse and pony steeple-chase of over a mile and a cigar and waterproof are what I've entered for, tho' as yet I have not even seen the pony and know nothing about it. We have a good deal of pickets to do. There used to be 3 Companies on together for 3 days. Boers have been attacking various places and threatening others so one has to be very careful. We stand to arms from 3 a.m. to daylight which is a very poor amusement. I don't think they will come as we have too many troops for their taste. The Canadian M.I. and guns have gone so we gave them a great parting dinner. They are good chaps and beautiful scouters. They lost more killed since they've been here than ever before in the campaign. It's this infernal sniping business, as it is impossible to go even a few miles without a good chance of being shot and they are so difficult to catch.

Dingwall is back from Pretoria with a weird looking coat on his back. He looks more extraordinary than usual, but seems all right. He says that Pretoria is hot and stuffy, which I can well believe. This is a most perfect climate when you don't have to be out in the rain. It is never too hot and, now that it's summer, doesn't freeze. There is always a breeze, and lovely sunny days. We have played a good deal of hockey, it is great fun. Fellows from the Shrops, Royal Irish and many others come, so we get good games and we have the same old sticks we got from Capetown at Enslin.

What a long time ago it is, a year and three days, since we landed on St Andrew's night. This one we are giving a great dinner party to the General and everyone. I shall miss it by being on picket. Lumsden is now transport officer so he has an easy time of it, no pickets etc. While on the march he slopes along on a pony with the second line transport, and draws 2 bob a day extra. We are all doing a signalling class, about 2 hours a day and can read and send messages with a flag fairly well but not very fast.

40 Boers tried to surrender to us the other day and were not allowed to and a fight ensued in which they fought well but were wasted; it is rather extraordinary how they still go on. There are supposed to be one thousand at Carolina which on a clear day we can see at 30 miles off. We had a great scare here a few days ago but nothing happened

As long as we stay here I don't mind, but am not anxious for more trekking. I suppose we shall go home someday - 11th on the list is pretty fair - but when?

I hope our shoot went off well. This ought to arrive about Xmas, so I will wish everyone the usual thing; it will be better than last year after Magersfontein etc., tho' not so good for Johnny Boer. Tell Grandmama that I will write to her next week. Love to all the kids.

This was the first anniversary of the landing at Capetown in 1899. St Andrew's Day, an important occasion honouring the patron saint of Scotland, was to be celebrated by a special dinner with General Smith-Dorrien as chief guest.

30 November 1900. Lachlan to Joan. Pan Station, near Belfast

It is St Andrew's night and exactly a year since we landed in this happy land of Boers, bullets and fever and, strange to say, we were fighting all the morning. Little did we expect to be here this time last year, engaged in the time honoured occupation of killing one's brother.

This is a little trip, plus the Royal Irish, 1 cow gun, pom-poms, 2 field guns, a few 5th Lancers and Mounted Infantry under Col. Macbean. We started on Wednesday, the 28th, the day of the gymkhana, when the grey and myself hoped to win the steeple-chase; it was very sudden. We paraded at 11.15 and marched to Wanderfontein, 12 miles, advance guard.

29th - We did a horrible march to a place 3 miles or so south of this. I was rear guard. It was hot, tiring, and very rapid. Many men fell out, and it was all we could do to keep moving. The Boers worried us a bit, but the pom-poms prevented any real fighting.

Today we started at 7 a.m. and had not gone far when the Cavalry rode helter skelter through us pursued by the Boers, who were much surprised on coming over the rise at being met with a hot fire from B Company and myself. We had just stood up and loosed off at them. Three were seen to fall, and probably more were hit; in fact the ground around them was hopping with our bullets, and they did not wait a second longer than they could help. The Boers were making the Cavalry rather cheap, but in their turn they received a nasty jar when they ran into us at close range.

We were lucky; in spite of shooting all around us we had no casualties, except one cavalryman slightly wounded. It was when Sgt. Allan of B Company mistook one for a Boer and shot his horse under him when he was being closely pursued. The Boers had, I imagine, at least a dozen casualties. The country was long undulating grass ridges. In one farm there was a small plantation which gave them some cover for sniping. Tomorrow night the General and staff dine with us to celebrate St Andrew's Day. We have heard of 5 Coys of the Highland Light Infantry surrendering at De Wet's Dorp, no details but it is very disgraceful.

The Boers here rode boldly up and drove off a few horses the other day, our picket thinking by the way it was done that they were our own people. Pretty cool that.

I am glad the Komati Poort letter arrived - I was afraid it was lost - also that you had a good time at Cullen House. I liked the old lady very much when I lunched there years ago.

BELFAST 1901

With best wishes for a Merry Xmas. (No cards available).

Christmas should be celebrated in one's own home and not in the army, on some foreign field thousands of miles away. A sort of false bonhomie is created and everyone is homesick and tries hard not to show it. The religious service is the highlight of the day and is the nearest thing to home and family. It is always well attended but it is a relief when it is over.

Cullen House was one of the main residences of the Seafield family, part of the Clan Grant. The other house was Castle Grant, at the head of the River Spey. In those days they owned a huge amount of land. You could walk from the coast of the Moray Firth to the headwaters of the Spey at Grantown without stepping off Seafield land.

Sadly those days have gone. The Laird of Seafield was killed, like Lachlan, in the Great War.

4 December 1900. Lachlan to Grandmama. Belfast, Transvaal

I am afraid this letter will be too late for Xmas, but may do for the New Year, which is fast approaching, even out here. I hope to see it out (the new one I mean) at Drummuir. I dare say we may get home before Aug. with luck. The most hopeful people now expect to be here some five or six months more, as in spite of our being the 11th Regiment for home there must really be some 40 before us, including Indian regiments, Militia, Volunteers, Colonials and Guards.

We are very well off here. It is a lovely climate, no hotter than at home, and nearly as much rain. We have our tents though, and have built a fine mess house, and got a lot of lamps, plates, chairs, tables, etc. from deserted Boer habitations in the town. Our kits are up from Bloemfontein, at least those that are left, as many people had a lot of things stolen, so we are quite happy. We have horses to ride, sports of all sorts, dinner parties and sing-songs. The only drawback is having three Companies on picket, and very often going on a little trek round the country, sometimes to murder and to ravish, at others to hunt Boers.

The latter are a confounded nuisance. They worry everyone and spoil entirely an otherwise lovely country. We came back from a little six-day trip to

Capt. Craufurd & L G-D. Belfast

Pan, two stations up the line. Our own Colonel was in command, and we had a pretty little skirmish giving them something to think about and digest. I am afraid the Boers, poor things, will have a rather poor Xmas this year, puddings at a premium, unless they wisely determine to capture a few trains about the right time, which is highly probable.

I hope you will have a good time at home. Joan told me that you were very fit, also everyone else, so am I. My nose peels very persistently. It has never stopped since we came out here and I don't think it ever will. Tomorrow we have a great St Andrew's dinner. It was postponed till we returned from trek.

Wishing you all a happy New Year.

29 November 1900. Joan to Lachlan. Drummuir

We have had such delightful letters from you this week it was joy getting them, the first written on 29 October, and the other finished up on the 25th. They were so much more cheerful than anything we had lately that I was quite happy. Darling I congratulate you a thousand times on winning that steeple chase, it was a glorious victory, and I would have given a good deal to have seen it. And at the end of the last letter when you were going off in state with the General, I felt so proud of you and I envied the General very much. I am sure he enjoyed that journey more than any he has ever made.

I have the honour to inform you that you were on 11 November presented with a new Aunt, number 2 of Marguerite's family.

The bag was not very satisfactory; 148 head the first day of which were 70 pheasants, and yesterday about 40 pheasants. This morning all our guests have departed. It is a fearful day; but we actually had two fine ones for the shoot which was great luck.

I can hardly realise that this is my Xmas letter to you; I had so hoped and trusted that you would have been home for it, my brother. Xmas without you is so sad and dreary; but I do hope you will have a very cheery Xmas out there. Nanny is sending you a parcel from me this week, but I suppose it is quite a chance if you get things. And may you spend many Christmases to come safe at home with us. God Bless you.

4 December 1900. Lachlan to Mildred. Belfast

L G-D writing home

These treks are an infernal nuisance! This one started without any notice on the day of the intended races; however, I dare say they will come off some day. Today it is raining, and is rather cooler than usual which is a good thing as it subdues the flies a trifle. They are a perpetual nuisance, dropping into everything in a most disgusting way.

I got a letter from Father in Edinburgh in which he accuses me of not acknowledging things sent out. I dare say I've forgotten some, but not the waterproof, which is very handy, and I've noticed that whenever I carry it, it does not rain! As for the shoes, do not worry about them as I can get Government shoes in future.

I am sorry the weather has been so bad for the harvest; it seems to have been the same in most places, but by the time this arrives it will be the New Year, and perhaps a Bonspiel coming off, which will be more cheerful. If ever I see ice again I will have forgotten both how to skate and the look of the stone.

By the way I am on the watch for the pudding and the haggis that are promised, especially the latter. There will be ructions if it is not forthcoming. I am afraid there are no Xmas presents to be sent from here as the veldt only produces trek-ox and sheep, though it is delightfully flowery and green still.

This is a dull letter as there is nothing to say but, A happy New Year to all.

5 December 1900. Joan to Lachlan. Drummuir

Thank you more than I can say for your delightful letter of the 2nd. I suppose it will be very near New Year when you get this, so I wish you a Happy Xmas and New Year and many of them. May the New Year and the new century too, be full of joy, and may it be very different from the last dreadful year. I do hope you will have a good time at Xmas. Mildred has ordered you a plum pudding from Buzzard. I have asked before if we ought to send one, but father thought it was no good. I believe that clever little Nanny sent you a small one a fortnight ago. I am sending you my photo this week, you will not like it, hardly anyone does, and I did not send you one before because of that, and also I thought it would be such a bore to carry around. It is so big, but you can cut off the margin. We were very glad to see by your letter that you must have escaped that horrid fight at Belfast in the rain. It must have been quite fun at Bloemfontein, and just like you, you seem to have made dozens of friends.

On Sunday we went twice to church, in the evening to the Free Church, where they have such beautiful music. There was a very young new minister who preached very well. Grandmama was a little shocked by his modern ideas, but he was so in earnest and had such a refined musical voice that on the whole we approved. He certainly touched the right spot with me by insisting on perseverance, that character is not built up in a day, and that it is never too late to improve.

In the evening we have been reading aloud from Lucas Malet, about a very charming ghost who walks and talks and loves everything human and then disappears at dawn. The language is a little high flown and though I skip the longest words Mildred laughs at it all the time. It is a little silly, but I rather like it.

Perhaps it will be quite near your 21st birthday when you get this, my beloved. If it is, it must take you all my love and blessings, my dearest Lachlan, and may you use independence and power rightly and truly and may life be full of happiness and love.

Lachlan's 21st birthday was on 21 January 1900.

5 December 1900. Joan to Lachlan. Drummuir, Keith

Though Lord Bobs said in one of his farewell speeches that the war was over, I wonder if K of K will be effectual. So many of the Generals have come home, one wonders who is commanding you all! If only you could pretend you were a general and come home.

There is remarkably little to tell you this week. I have been very depressed about nothing in particular, but everything in general. On Friday I went to Elgin with a cheap weekend ticket. I was delighted to feel that there at any rate I was wanted as Grandmama, being all alone, wanted me very much, dear person. She bullied me a good deal too, as if I wasn't already the very stupidest and dullest and idioticest person and therefore the most unloved on earth. She tenderly hinted that I couldn't sing or draw or talk Italian or keep up my German, and wasn't even literary! Its all terribly true.

We went to the Poor House on that afternoon, where one has not been for a long time. It strikes one how terribly sad it is that all these old women after working all their lives should come to this. It seems almost a sin to keep them alive. Those that are not too ill to be intelligent, all take a tremendous interest in you.

The brutes of road people have cut out all the grass along the Dufftown road, it is too horrid. One can hardly get a canter at all. It takes half the pleasure away of riding. On Tuesday I rode again and went the Davidson round - the grass is off - where I had a lovely gallop. It is so idiotic of them as no one wants the roads wider. It would be so much better if they would turn their attention to the middle of the road, which is in a shocking state of holes and mud.

We went up to the Walker Hall in Elgin to try the piano which is a very good one. I played the old Carmen march which I am going to play at the concert on the 17th. Mildred and I also practiced our duet, the Tannhauser march, which sounded very grand. The election is practically over now. The Unionists' majority is about 130. Uncle Jack got in, which is a relief, Uncle Eddy did not, which is probably a relief to him. The Unionists won this constituency, East Aberdeenshire, which is a great victory as the Radical majority had been over 1000 for years and years.

10 December 1900. Lachlan to Father. Belfast

We still 'flag wag' very violently for about 3 hours per day and make ordinary progress, but the helio and lamp are not yet begun. From 5 to 6 each evening we have great games of hockey. Usually some of the Royal Irish, Shropshire, and odds and ends turn up and the remainder of our Sgts and men.

Last Friday the gymkhana came off. It was a lovely day and quite a success. Our drivers won the mule driving competition, 10 pair of mules in a cart, driven by 2 natives through a very narrow and twisty course. There was a 'cigar and mackintosh race'. You started bare-backed, mounting when the flag fell, rode to the saddles, saddled up, into the mackintoshes, when you were provided with a cigar and 2 matches, which you lit, put on the mackintosh, of which at least 2 buttons had to be fastened, ride around a post and in. I had a pony in, but did not get anywhere. There was a great crowd, and it was very difficult to hit off the right saddle etc. There were several other events, and men's races.

A small column went out yesterday towards Carolina. They have only gone about 10 miles, and seem to have had some shooting as we have heard lots of guns going, and violent looking cipher messages have been pouring in all day. They reported a big column of Boers advancing from Carolina. The Boers here say they want to stop fighting, but can agree to no terms but independence. They are very down on Kruger, but don't seem very clear as to what will happen, and in the meantime worry us all they can; attacking patrols everywhere. Ours here are constantly having scraps with them a few miles out, and they are all around the pickets, often visible.

Chamberlain will be clever he if brings them to terms and establishes anything like government and order. As Sgt. Martin says: he will not be able to go outside the range of the cow guns. They have again taken to busting the line which is troublesome, and attack trains by climbing up on the rear truck going up a steep hill, disconnecting the vacuum brake, bringing the whole show to a standstill, which they worry at leisure.

The flies here are frightful, in spite of every effort they flourish and multiply appallingly. Will you get some good fly papers and send them out, as here they are nearly impossible to get? The tents are black with them. Burning kills many, tho' it is a very temporary check, as 1000 more wait to come in.

If ever you are in Dufftown, you might go and see Cpl. Watson, who I think works at the Parkmore Distillery, certainly one of the Dufftown ones. He left at the Malelane skirmish (Komati Poort) time-expired, so I did not see him. He is an awfully good little chap and a great friend of mine. He was wounded at Doornkop, but soon recovered.

Lachlan's love of and success with horses was beginning to show in his letters. It reached its peak years later when he won the Army Lightweight Steeplechase in 1908 on Juanita who he owned and trained.

When Roberts relinquished command to Kitchener a grateful Britain voted him £100,000 for his services. Of him it was said that "No returning Caesar ever met with a greater triumph and no General had ever been so overrated in England's history". (Rayne Kruger)

The situation when Kitchener took over in December 1900 seemed simple enough. He had over 200,000 men, and though the Boer numbers had been growing all the time, they still could only muster a force of 60,000, including foreigners and rebels, of which barely a quarter were in the field at any one time. But he had many problems. Half his men were guarding lines of communication while thousands more were either on garrison duties or else in constant movement, supporting threatened posts. Many Companies had become scattered on endless marches and were lost track of for a long time.

The Boers' guerrilla strategies were proving so successful that the only sure way to reply was to play them at their own game. But to do this the players had to be of a very high standard. They had to be mobile, drawn mostly from the Mounted Infantry and the Yeomanry. The Cavalry were of course involved but were less mobile as they carried more equipment.

Upon Roberts' insistence that the war was virtually over, the army was slowly being run down and Regiments from which a British guerrilla force could have been assembled were returning home and the Remount Department was closing, creating a shortage of horses. In the meantime at home there had been a general election, known as the Khaki Election, fought mainly about the conduct of the war. Britain was becoming weary of the muddled way in which the war was being waged and angry at the appalling waste of lives. The election was won by the Unionist Conservatives under Lord Salisbury with the influential Chamberlain as Colonial Secretary responsible for South African affairs.

Something had to be done, and everyone was looking to Kitchener to do it.

'Brother Boer'

19 December 1900. Lachlan to Joan. Belfast

Another mail day around again. The time is going fairly fast, tho' it doesn't usually fly. News out here has been pretty bad of late. Convoys and trains captured as well as occasionally half Battalions. I only hope the old 19th Brigade will preserve its record without any such mishaps. The day before yesterday was Dingaan's day, when the Boers are in the habit of dancing around a small monument about 2 miles north of the town, a most sacred custom, so we were expecting an attack that night, especially as many Boers were seen fooling around quite close. If an attack is expected on a particular night it never comes off; if it is not expected, it does! So whenever we expect an attack, we don't. That sounds rather Irish, but you will guess what I mean. I came off picket last Thursday morning.

The same morning, which was very cold with a fine driving rain, we got up at 3 a.m., had breakfast and with some of the Shrops, 2 guns, and Mounted Infantry set off to cut down a young wood about 5 miles from here, past the colliery. It was a very cold walk but warmed up later. The wood was planted in about 20 long narrow strips of very young tender trees - of the Acacia kind, I imagine - and none more than 2 or 3 inches in diameter. As we had plenty of tools and natives, the whole thing was down by midday. Part of the time my Company was covering party, and we amused ourselves by shooting at some 10 Boers by a farm a long way off. They did not seem to mind much, but did not stay long. The wood was levelled as it afforded the Boers cover rather too close to the pickets. It was there that a few days ago they wounded an M.I. man, rifled him, and retiring 100 yards started firing at him till they wounded him 3 times, and left him for dead. Luckily he was not badly hurt and was found. They are unmitigated blackguards and deserve no quarter.

We have hockey nearly every night. There is another gymkhana on Thursday, but I have heard nothing about it. The poor grey has been lame ever since the last, from a cut by a rope on each side of his hind pastern. I had an invitation from Graham Tennant to stay 2 days at Middleburg for Xmas. He is with the District Commissioner. I don't think I will manage it. I also want to get to Lourenco Marques or Pretoria to see a dentist. As I have been having toothache off and on for a few days it is high time I saw one. It seems a great oversight of the War Office's part in not providing them, as they do doctors and vets. They would get plenty of work on service, and be of inestimable value as many people suffer from teeth out here and have no means of remedying them.

Yours and Father's letters arrived yesterday. The mail is very regular out here, arriving on Monday or Tuesday. Father wants to know what to send for a Xmas present and said I never have a clue, which is very true. I have everything I want in the way of clothes, and can think of nothing else that would not be rather an encumbrance out here where one has to pack up and off at a moment's notice, unless it is a pair of Zeiss glasses, which are just like a telescope. I should like a pair awfully, but they are very expensive, and would need the hat being sent around the family. A good many people have them; they are very handy, and absolutely marvellous.

Dingaan was a Zulu chief whom the Boers defeated at Blood River in 1838 during their trek north through Natal. Attacked by the Zulus, the Boer formed the traditional defensive laager with their wagons and the women augmented the fighting Boers by arming themselves with axes to chop off the hands of any Zulus incautious enough to poke them through the barricade.

25 December 1900. Lachlan to Joan. Belfast

We have had another quiet week. The General has taken over the Middleburg command, and we do not know if he is coming back or not. I have just gone on picket with Allan for 3 days which is not very enlivening. He is an awful grouser. Went out for a stroll with Dingwall's gun at 7 a.m. and returned about 8.30 with 6 snipe, 1 fine wild duck, 2 plover and 1 sandpiper, having had great sport wading about a long boggy strip of ground towards the town. I had luck in picking up everything I hit, as it is very difficult to mark them down. Three little Boer boys were much interested and spotted a snipe I would otherwise have lost so I gave it to them. Their Papa was looking on from a safe distance. The birds were excellent. Maclaren and I are getting up a lot of cartridges from L. Marques, as at present we can raise only 20 or so.

Yesterday we had another gymkhana. It was a grand day for it. First a long jump for the men - two of ours were first and second - then an officers' mule race, bare-backed. It was very funny. There must have been at least 40 entries. Lumsden, our transport officer, provided ours. I had a grand mule, very fast and fat. We got well away, and half-way I was leading by about 10 yards, but unfortunately my moke spied all his comrades happily grazing a little way to his left. The course went around to the right. This was too much for him, as his stables were beyond them again, so in spite of all I did he dashed off among them, and we lost a probable win. I was going to ride a mare of Ogilvie's in a steeplechase, but he scratched as she is only 3 years old and he thought it would be too much for her. She is a little beauty, but would not have won as she has not been trained.

30 December - I did not post this the other day as owing to the Bogeyman pulling up the line, we were told the mails would miss the steamer. Then we heard that a train between Pan and Wonderfontein, the next station to us, was captured and all our mails looted, which was as you may imagine bad news. The Colonel received a gory envelope, supposed to be the sole survivor, but yesterday the remaining ones turned up having been on a later train. I got yours with the photos, which was very interesting; you seem to be a regular

monster now. I should think Mildred has had a bad time. Father seems to have shrunk to about half size.

1 January 1901, New Years Day - Allan and I are on picket again and it is now about 8 a.m. We stand to arms from 3 to 4; since then I've been for a ride for an hour or so and done the enclosed drawing of our tent. It may amuse you. Observe the flowers; the veldt flowers here are lovely and gorgeous, many are like those at home, but there are many kind of orchids, lilies, and wonderful flowers, quite different. There has been a lot of rain as usual, and everything is beautifully green and nice.

The plum pudding arrove too, we are going to have it tonight. Smith-Dorrien came back. The capture of the Helvetia garrison was a bad job and we heard the firing. I hope we shan't get caught too. The Boers are full of brick [sic] and I expect that we shall still be out here for next New Year.

Many thanks to you and Nanny for the wire, which came on Boxing Day. Don't be extravagant!

Tent on picquet (F.W.) Belfast January 1st 1901. Captain Allan is under the great coat on the bed.

Helvetia is near enough to Belfast for the firing to have been heard. There was a small post of some 200 soldiers there which Viljoen surprised and captured. Part of his booty was a 4.7 inch gun.

The British were engaged in a gigantic game of hide-and-seek, with columns of men chasing through the South African veldt in an effort to winkle out and destroy the small pockets of Boers who, despite their occasional losses, were still holding on.

General Clements, the British General was surprised at Nooitgedacht Gorge near Mahaliesberg losing 115 casualties and 138 wagons.

26 December 1900. Emma Winsloe to Lachlan. London

I feel myself very proud in being able to write to an officer at the front, and I thought that you might like to hear that Mother and I are thinking of you always, reading and rereading the papers trying to find some news about your Regiment. We were sad enough when we heard that your Battalion was in that terrible fight at Magersfontein. Oh! Lachlan, how terrible it must have been. It seems to me that an experience such as that has made you years older than I. You will not like that, will you? You do not want to be old. When I lie in my comfortable bed, I think of the hardships you may be having and I don't think it is fair. I would like to share my comforts with you. This was a very sad Xmas in London yesterday; few of the churches were decorated; all the money is being saved and sent to our brave soldiers.

I am sending you just a little pencil case, nothing of any value, for I do not know if the post can be forwarded to you; this might be useful - if it ever reaches its destination.

The American Hospital ship has at last started. Lady Randolph going as secretary or treasurer. Mr. Winston Churchill is said to have escaped from Pretoria dressed as a woman. I hear that you wear khaki aprons to hide the colour of the kilt. It is so wise to do everything to save the splendid Highlanders from harm so that they may be ready (as ready as they always are I mean) to do the work they do so well. All the papers, foreign as well as English, speak of the bravery of the 1st Battalion Gordon Highlanders.

I boast of knowing one of its officers to my friends. Great shouting in the street by the news boys. I rush out, buy a paper and read: "All quiet at the front and everyone enjoying Xmas festivities". I do hope this is true and that you have had some relaxations, but the papers are not very reliable. The other day they published 10,000 Boers captured, and it was all a fraud.

Mother joins me in love to you and being so affectionate I will write again. I give you no address, for I do not wish you to be bothered to answer this.

CHAPTER TEN

Belfast 1901

19 December 1900. Joan to Lachlan. Drummuir, Keith NB.

Wish we knew where you were and what you are doing; but it is better not to know than to know from the papers, as that generally means fighting.

I wonder if you will get this about your birthday? I hope you will. It takes you all my heart and all my love, and all the wishes of my heart and soul for your happiness and success. All my congratulations on reaching the great age of 21 and on being one of the most delightful and dearest people; and above all my prayer that God may bless you and that you may serve him always. You know that it will be impossible for me to long for you any more on that special day than on any other day, as I always long for you.

There is not very much to tell you. We are anxiously waiting for news of the capture of De Wet and his force. General Knox ought surely to get him now, he seems to have got himself into a corner; but I believe he will not be caught. He will disappear mysteriously or, if he can't do that, he will die a glorious death. He certainly is most wonderful, don't you think so?

We have not done much, but I will give you my usual diary. On Thursday afternoon we had a delightful entertainment. The factor came up to practice for the concert with Mildred. Daisy and I listened through the big doors as Mildred would not let us in the room. It really was very funny. He sang "Jack's the Boy". He can hardly sing at all, but he bellows away lustily, and arrives somehow generally at least three notes below the right one! We were in fits behind the door. He was so pleased with himself, Mildred trying to correct him. He then tried another song, "A jovial monk am I". This was lower and easier, and it has been decided that he shall sing it at the concert. He said that if he got a right start he was safe!

On Sunday we went to church, and stayed for Holy Communion. I prayed hard for you and thought of the same Sunday exactly a year before, when we did not know to what part of Africa you had gone, and then the day after that Sunday was Magersfontein, and then came those terrible hours of anxiety before the lists came out, then your telegram. Oh, how can we thank the Almighty enough for having brought you through so far?

Sunday afternoon was not very fine and Grandmama did not go out again, so Nanny and I went for a walk. I paid a call on Mrs Whitton, who was very well and cheerful. She had a letter from a cousin out at Johannesburg called Cathro, an engine driver. He sent her an unused Orange Free State stamp which she was very proud of. She then told me to ask you if you had ever come across him. I told her it was not very likely! On the Monday before I came back here we went to call on the new Sheriff. We found his sister who lives with him, Miss Webster, a most amusing person, who never stopped talking. Another sister is Mrs Steel the authoress. They live in a very nice house near The Pines and do a great deal of gardening, like everyone else nowadays. She was rather funny telling us about herself, her life, and how the very evening before she had with her own hands to administer poison to a very beloved dog. She had another dog, an "Aberdachs", who was the child of a Dachshund and an Aberdeen. He was not beautiful, but rather nice.

Mr Gordon has bet me 3-1 in gloves that you will be back in April; I say not till June, but I hope he may be right, or still more that we both may be wrong and that you may back before that.

2 January 1901. Lachlan to Nanny. Belfast

It was very kind of you to send me the cards and letters and the cake, which is excellent and the joint telegram which came the day after Xmas. I was very pleased to get it as all our mails were said to have been looted by the Boers a few miles off in a train that was captured. Luckily however they escaped as they arrived later on account of Boers somewhere else. Railway travelling here is not quite the same as at home, where it is most monotonous, as no one takes the trouble to wreck, rob and shoot you there.

Things here go on the same as usual, a lot of picket work. The Boers have not thought it worth while to try to capture us here, as we are very much on the look out and well fortified, tho they would be only too pleased to and are always sniffing around us for an opportunity. That was very disgraceful the way we lost the 4.7 and 200 men at Helvetia a few days ago. Kitchener is going to have it back at all costs.

We have had plenty of rain here. The country is like a vast green meadow, tho hilly with bogs, burns and rocks; there are lovely flowers and plenty of small game such as snipe, partridges, quail, wild chick, hares etc. and small buck, tho of course they are scarce round us by now.

It is now about 1.30 p.m., that is 11.30 a.m. with you. I wonder if you are having fine frosty weather. Thank goodness it is not cold here, under one's present conditions cold is most unpleasant, luckily also Belfast is never really hot; at home it would be an ideal climate. I hope we shall not see 1902 begin in Africa, tho many people think it will be a year before we return and I feel none too sure myself. Wishing you a happy new year.

4 January 1901. Col Des Voeux to Father. Buckingham Gate, London

Thank you very much for your nice present of some game which arrived quite safely yesterday. I have since eaten a most excellent woodcock and part of one pheasant. I am alone here as my wife is in Eastbourne. She has been seedy all the autumn and it seems to be suiting her. What a year of anxiety you must have had - a very drawn out year with a daily inspection of the horrid newspapers, and the hopes continually raised and so soon dashed to pieces that the war was over. I think these hopes materially affected Lord Roberts' reception yesterday. I have never seen a London crowd behave as yesterday's did. It was quiet and sober, not caring to laugh or talk, not buying tokens or buttons or flags, not as big as expected, and consisting as far as I could see of a better class than is usual. They took little interest in anything until Bobs came and then gave him one right royal cheer, and it was over. It was a purely personal reception of a favourite personality, not the plaudits of a victorious people; very different from the Ladysmith and Co. mania of last spring. He was evidently pleased, and had full right to be so, and so was her Ladyship.

This must have been a friend of Lachlan's Father. Interesting about Roberts who seemed to be pulling the wool over the eyes of the British public about the war in South Africa.

15 January 1901. Lachlan to Joan. Belfast

You will have got no letters from here last week as just before the mails left the line was broken up. We have had various night attacks here, one very real, and one imagination; the result is that night sentries are apt to loose off at anything or nothing and everyone is rather jumpy. I suppose the bare outlines of events will have got home by now, well glossed over to suit the public palate, which seems to have been tickled by recent news. During the last week there has been a regular mania for fortifying; we have done nothing else. Even the A.S.C. people have their burrows, while gunners and M.I. have walled-in their camps with a terrific bit of work.

However, to take things in order, on Monday 7th, Allan and I went to the S. E. picket while Maclaren and Sworder went to the S.W. where I am writing just now. Mac, Sworder, self and the Royal Engineer man had a tremendous lunch by a tiny burn, intending to shoot a few snipe afterwards. Mac gets wonderful supplies of provisions sent out weekly. I will not say what we had, but it was much more luxurious than the swaggers of picnics at home, including champagne. We did not shoot after lunch!

That night about 12, the Monument Hill, about 4 miles from here and north of the railway, was attacked and after a savage fight the Boers took it and 40 prisoners, including one officer and killing another. It was a terribly foggy night, so thick you could scarcely see 30 yards in spite of a bright moon. The picket was absolutely surprised. The first a lot of them knew of it was shots coming into their tent, followed by Boers. They were some way from their trenches and very badly outnumbered. However, we know they killed a lot of Boers. 17 were taken away on horses and a wagon load also; this from the prisoners who were released within a few days.

Poor Fosberry of the Inniskillings himself was seen to shoot 2 or 3 with his revolver before being killed. The Boers expected to capture one of the cow guns which is often up there but luckily that night was taken away. This made them so savage that they are said to have brained some of our wounded with knobkerries. They had a lot of Kaffirs with them. Luckily they did not go any further, as they apparently had had enough over there, and after carrying off everything they could lay their hands on including all the picket's tents, they departed and the place was soon reoccupied by reinforcements.

All this took place in about 20 mins. We of course stood to arms, but it was not till 1 a.m. that they attacked on this side, coming first at the SW picket. They got through the fence undetected, but luckily one of them let his gun off by mistake in time to warn the garrison, many of whom were asleep in their tents as the firing at Monument Hill was not heard. Maclaren and Sworder just got to the stone fort in time. The latter was nearly shot in his tent, which was riddled with bullets. Then a desperate fight began with about 300 Boers trying to get into our trench.

This is a rough plan of the position. The trench is about 40 yards long without head cover, the stone block house was only completed that very day, and had no overhead cover either, the telephone was only just in. Maclaren tried to work it, but it was broken up by bullets. He had a very narrow escape when three men were killed just beside him, one after the other through the loop-hole by a crawling Boer. Several Boers got within 10 or 15 yards of the position and the defenders only just kept them out by firing as hard as they could (they were about 33 to 300). They had nearly finished their ammunition, having used 5 to 6 thousand rounds before reinforcements approached, by which time they had begun to clear.

It was wonderful how our people got off so cheap, 3 killed and 2 wounded severely, while a few more were slightly wounded and cut and bruised with splinters of stone etc. Meanwhile fighting was going on round the crest of the line. Allan and I were on S.E. main post, with 30-odd men, a very awkward and difficult post to hold. Luckily as it was situated about 130 yards back from the crest of the hill it was not found by the Boers who, I am convinced, if they had attacked it seriously, would have taken it fairly easily; tho of course not without losses. Any minute we expected to have them on the top of us, as one could only see 30 to 40 yards, often not that, and we could hear them quite close. Bullets were flying all over the shop.

While this was going on a sudden terrific fire started on the post on our right. It is a small triangular blockhouse of stone with a few low rows of barbed wire round it, as much good as a sick headache at stopping anyone, with only 11 men. It only lasted about 10 minutes, accompanied by yelling and shouting, when suddenly the firing ceased. But the talking went on, so we knew they were rushed. What rather surprised us was to hear a little later a voice challenging just like we do. This was a blind of the Boers who made some of us think they had not taken the place. It was very sly. Reinforcements from camp were now arriving and the Boers meanwhile retired, leaving all the captured, 30 men and one officer of the Shropshires, at Colliery Hill picket, and a broken Maxim. They saw our man smash it and killed him for it. Of our 10 men, one was shot right through the brain and walked 3 miles afterwards. He is still alive and conscious and may yet recover, and three others slightly wounded.

Mail just off. Have had no time to write this week owing to fatigues etc.

THE WAR.

CONCERTED BOER ATTACKS.

The following telegram from Lord Kitchener has been received at the War Office :—

Pretoria, Jan. 9.

On night of 7th Boers made simultaneous and determined attacks on all our posts at Belfast and at Wonderfontein, Nooitgedacht, Wildfontein, and Pan. A dense fog prevailed, and taking advantage of the cover it afforded the Boers were able to creep up close to our positions. Heavy fire continued until 3 40 a.m., when Boers were driven off. One officer, Captain Fosbery, killed, and three wounded; 20 men killed, 59 wounded. Boers' loss heavy, 24 dead being counted.

(THROUGH LAFFAN'S AGENCY.)

PRETORIA, JAN. 13.

Later details received of the recent fight at Belfast show that 700 Boers rushed an outside position defended by 60 men of the Royal Irish Regiment. The latter fought bravely with knives and bayonets until only 20 of them were left. Eventually the Boers were driven from their positions by our main garrison, consisting of the Gordons and others.

To maintain their mobility while pursuing guerrilla tactics, the Boers did not take prisoners and any men who were captured were handed back minus their arms and items of clothing because they could not feed them.

17 January 1901. Lachlan to Father. Belfast, S.W. Picket

I got yours of 21st just before coming on picket 2 days ago. As you say it is extraordinary the way things drag on. Up here we get very little news, we all sit tight and do nothing except fortify. For over a week we talk and do nothing else, so that it is quite a relief being on picket, where there is more to be done, at least by the outposts themselves.

The people in camp slave like niggers. The Colonel and adjutant may be seen carrying about great stones and turfs etc., putting up barbed wire entanglements, an instructive sight, tho such has been their haste that most of their positions tumble down again in about 3 days time, proving that 'more haste less speed'! This feverish energy arose from the recent Boer attacks, which seemed to have filled the whole place with the jumps, and until our outposts, which should have been completed 2 months ago, are considered fairly impregnable against night attacks of a determined and savage nature, we shall not rest. In a week's time we should be able to defy anything but artillery, which cannot be used at night to any purpose. Enclosed is a very rough plan I've just scrawled which will give you a sort of idea of the hang of Belfast and the surrounding pickets if you can make head or tail of it.

All our picket posts except the main S.W. and S.E. were held by 10 men and one NCO or three men and one NCO. Each picket consisting of 60 men all told; pretty few for such a line. But the insolence displayed by the Boers in coming here as they did was scarcely contemplated till they did come. Several of these small posts on the SW. Picket were only holes made by a few turfs being cut out in which the men lay. Luckily in the fog they were not seriously attacked, or they would have fared badly. The other small posts are stone sangas, more or less fortified, while the picket I am writing from consists of a stone wall about 4 ft 6 high, like a figure of eight with a trench from it to a sunken little house at one end with loop-holes level with the ground, but owing to various mistakes of construction the latter proved a death trap, three men being killed in it and two wounded.

The night of the 8th was very peculiar. I can hardly remember one quite like it. There was thick driving fog and fine rain, but when the moon rose as it did quite early, you could distinguish an object such as a man about 30 yards off very faintly, while about 10 yards off things were pretty clear. This of course favoured the Boers to a certain extent as you could see to ride all right, and follow a well known road quite easily enough while, owing to the fog, a picket could be surprised and rushed at close quarters unless they were all standing to arms. After this it was in our favour, as they could not find the camp with any certainty, tho as you see in the plan, many of them got very close without knowing where they were. Off the road you were bound to lose yourself in the veldt at once. Several lost Boers were caught after the rest retired in fact.

The Boers caught the Royal Irish at Monument Hill by surprise, catching many in their tents which were too far from their works for them to get to, if indeed the sentries managed to alarm them. The remainder made a desperate resistance, but were overwhelmed. 32 men were taken prisoner, and two officers. Poor Fosberry in command was killed after shooting several Boers with his revolver while trying to send a telephone message; 14 men were killed, one was murdered because he broke up the Maxim, just as the Boers were about to seize it; a fine thing to do.

The Boers were very mad at not finding a 5 in. gun as they expected and I believe some of our wounded were knobkerried in consequence. The remainder of the 2 companies retired on reinforcements arriving and the Boers did not pursue them. The latter undoubtedly lost heavily. When the men that were caught were sent back, they said they counted 17 men in a row, and there was a whole cart load besides. During the attack 3 men and an NCO lay doggo on a little trench and were not found. As the Boers were retiring they killed 2 of a party of 3 who passed them, tho' the third escaped and brought back others who took the Boers prisoner, but without harming them. This took place between 12 and 12.30.

All was quiet for half an hour and we were beginning to think that was the end, when at about 1 a.m. firing started on the S.W. picket. Allan and I were in the main S.E. one with 35 men. It was very heavy and quickly worked round to our side, but strange to say, tho' we heard shouting and they must have been very close, they did not see our trench and we escaped what might have been a serious business. We were in a rather weak place with not half enough men to hold it. There were bullets flying about in all directions, and every minute we expected them over our wire fence.

About 1.30 a heavy fusillade and shouting started on post K in the plan. It went on for a very short time then suddenly stopped while a confused babel continued. Of course we guessed they had got our people, which was the case. The post is not very well placed, as there is dead ground near it with 2 gun emplacements which the RA put up before. The Boers in the fog crept up in front and kept the garrison of 10 men engaged, while others got close up behind under the wall, seizing the muzzles of our rifles through the loop-holes and swarmed in upon them.

The Boers were a Commando probably from the Barberton district, about 300 strong, mostly Scottish with English, Irish and some Dutch under a certain Prinsloo, and a Macdonald from Glasgow, or perhaps Macdougal.

They took with them the tent and the possessions of our men and their own dead. Cpl Moir says he thinks there were six or seven and some wounded, as he saw a lot fall while they were fighting and afterwards being carried off, but the Boers said there was only one slightly wounded! They took the prisoners about a mile to their horses and carts, removed their coats and shoes, and sent them back to camp, never attempting to dress the wounded or anything. To deceive us they left a man behind who challenged now and then exactly like our sentries, so that we could not be sure what was up, tho' people do not walk about for amusement on such a night.

Since then we have adopted a new method of challenging. By the time they were going we heard volleys in various directions and knew that reinforcements were up, as John Boer never fires volleys. Shooting still continued all along our posts, but no others were attempted to be rushed, and about 2 a.m. it was all over, tho' the fog was as thick as ever and you could see no further than at night. I took a patrol to see what had become of Cpl Moir. We half expected to find Boers, but it was deserted, showing signs of a hand to hand scuffle, a helmet with a hole in it and other suggestive details, sand bags full of holes and bullet marks all round on the soft stones. One could follow it all, but thought our losses must have been heavier.

I left some of the patrol to garrison the post, and lost my way entirely looking for another one, till we ran up against a stray party from camp and found our road. We then learnt that Maclaren and Sworder with F Company had had a desperate fight at the main SW picket barely succeeding in driving off the Boers, who attacked them in great force, getting unobserved through the fence and almost on them. Mac and Sworder had a narrow escape, their tent being riddled with bullets. The Boers were crawling up to within 15 yards of them, and killed three men at the end of the trench through the loop-holes, wounding a few more, but after a plucky resistance by everyone and having gone near the end of their ammunition, the Boers cleared off hearing the volley of our own reinforcements from camp, leaving five dead behind, many bloody spoors, some rifles, and vast quantities of ammunition, showing plainly that they were very strong.

The fight lasted one hour and we were again very fortunate in losing so few men. The Boers, we think, must have had at least 30 casualties in that one attack, putting it at a low figure, for they were in the open at short range. We fired over 6000, not bad for 32 men, five of whom were out of it early. I saw the place that morning and the dead Boers, genuine ones this time, and recognised one as a deserter from E.P. Horse. It was an instructive, tho not a pretty, sight. We also learnt of the capture of Monument and Colliery hills, and were much disturbed that they were still held by Boers who might attack again at any minute. This of course was a mistake as they had been reoccupied long before, the Boers realising that they would be cut up if they went further.

Colliery Hill was surprised much the same way as Monument Hill, tho' only part of it was captured, including 30 men, one officer wounded, 21 men killed, and six men wounded. The Boers behaved much better there, apparently, to the wounded. Their losses are not known, but are probably considerable as they failed to take all the posts. In camp of course things were very lively. None of our people were hit, but a few others were wounded. Thus ended an eventful night. We have much to be thankful for; if they had attacked us two days earlier than they did, they would almost certainly have got our pickets, as after Helvetia was taken, some very necessary improvements were made. The telephone was only fixed up that very day. It was as well too that the main S.E. post was left alone, or Alan and I would have been on our way to Pietersburg.

13 January - On that night soon after we had gone to bed there was an alarm. One of our sentries round the camp challenged what I think was a riderless horse 3 times; as they did not answer he fired a shot. The sentry next him thinking the Boers really were here gave the alarm signal, three shots in succession, and of course up tumbled the whole of Belfast; various people letting off their rifles in all directions thinking they saw Boers, with the result that one man in the Inniskillings was shot through the head in his tent and killed. Here we lined a railway line, lowered our tents and awaited the Boers. Miller was sent to the telephone at the station to warn the pickets. There was almost a panic and frightful confusion and Miller was nearly shot. Then a terrified individual thinking he must be a Boer threw up his hands, surrendered to him, eyes bulging out of his head.

I was sent with a few men to guard the approach by the colliery railway. First we had to visit A Post, then strike across country. It was very dark and we never knew when we would run into Boers. Eventually after sitting for an hour or so in thick mist we were recalled and found every one had gone to bed again. Strangely enough, at the time, there really were a good many Boers trying to reconnoitre the Outposts. They sniped at some of the pickets and were shown next day to be pretty numerous by their tracks. The result of this has been that everyone dug like rabbits to protect themselves while asleep. The general has put a huge earthwork around his house. The outposts are also strengthened too, so that we can look with equanimity at any attacks and the amount of barbed wire used is terrific. We have heard that the Boers are very dissatisfied with the result of their night's work, repulsed everywhere, and they say they had 100 killed and 400 wounded.

15 January - We went out to the S.W. Picket and escorted a cow gun, as they were going to blow up a farm about 2 miles in front that the Boers were always

making use of. It should have been done before. It is called Weltervreden; its owner is Mr Shalk van Herden, a poor old man with blue goggles. He was brought in on a wagon load of his own furniture, 3 daughters accompanying him on other wagon loads.

19 January - I went with 40 men as escort to Smith-Dorrien to Middleburg. It was very wet when we started, and the general in a horrible temper, swearing at everything and everybody. We left at 9 a.m., reaching Middleburg at 1 p.m. We only stayed 2 hours while S-D interviewed Lyttelton.

The Suffolks came with us to Wonderfontein. They had been hunting De Wet in Cape Colony since we last saw them, and had a very poor time indeed. They said the Essex and Camerons were following, and thought they were for Belfast. However they have concentrated at Wonderfontein and a great trek is coming off under Smith-Dorrien, to Roos Senekal, Carolina, or both. They have a lot of Mounted Infantry and Cavalry, 2 cow guns - everything in fact but the troops necessary to hold this place, so we stay. And very hard work it is, what with pickets, orderly officers etc. When you post sentries round the camp every hour from 9 to 1 a.m., and man-inlying pickets, it is only occasionally one has a night in bed.

We are engaged just now in building a great trench round the camp, the inside of which is being revetted with sods, so it is a very long business. I think it is pretty certain that the Boers will never seriously attack us again. They are supposed to be making peace negotiations. One came into us on picket with letters for Smith-Dorrien, Kitchener of Khartoum and his Adjutant general, all from Botha. The first accused us of using soft-nosed bullets, and sent specimens. It is pretty good cheek, as nearly every Boer we kill or catch has a bandoleer full of them.

Around an hour ago a telegram arrived, sent on the 17th, "Sincere congratulations" from the tenantry. I will answer it as you suggest; it has taken a long time, as the wires are being perpetually cut. It seems strange to think that the other day was my coming of age, but if there are to be any rejoicings etc. when I get back, they will not be for a good while I suspect. Some very courageous people think there is a chance of our sailing in June, but it is impossible to say.

Thank Mildred for her letter and ask her to send out some ginger bread. Alexander is very anxious for some, also a 'bun' if it is not too late? but get John to solder the tin, those sort of things are only to be had by post here.

A dentist has come here, a fighting member of the Imperial Light Horse. I am going to him.

We have just got the wire of the Queen's death, we barely knew she was ill. What a terrible thing. I wish she could have seen the war over. Out here people don't seem to realise what it means.

This is a frightfully long letter, but should have been two.

Ninety years later in the age of the atom bomb and the internal combustion engine it is hard to imagine what it was like to fight a war without modern weapons, tanks and aeroplanes. Even the newly arrived field-telephone was viewed with suspicion by the 'old guard'. The courage of all who took part, including the Boers, was tremendous.

The arrival of the congratulatory telegram in the middle of the battle was dramatic. To be 21 in those days was a great event, especially if one was the heir to a large estate in Scotland! The celebrations would have included a presentation of gifts and testimonials from the tenantry, bonfires, a marquee large enough to seat everyone, plenty of whisky, speeches galore, and energetic Country and Highland dancing. None of this could take place. Lachlan was fighting the Queen's enemies 6000 miles away, making his father's exhortations somewhat superfluous.

The death of Queen Victoria, the Old Queen as she was affectionately known, seems to have come as a great shock to her troops abroad. She had always taken an immense interest in the progress of the war in South Africa. Her funeral must have been a remarkable spectacle with the Crown, Orb and Sceptre carried on her coffin and 4 Kings and 8 Crown Princes following in its wake. There was an alarming moment at Windsor when the horses pulling the gun-carriage bucked and the Blue Jackets had to haul her up the hill to St George's Chapel. She seemed reluctant to go.

By now the war was costing the country a million pounds every week. It had to be brought to an end. It was creating a trade depression, a shortage of manpower, and was sparking off financial scandals in the City.

17 January 1901. Father to Lachlan. Drummuir

Many happy returns of the day for you and everything in life.

First I suppose among them, is a speedy return from South Africa. That means the end of this wretched war - and how much that means to so many far and wide. It is not necessary to remind you that in the midst of life we are in death. That must have come home to you many a time, with all the serious thoughts it must bring to us all of the 'why and wherefore' of this life, and of our duties while we pass through it. There are few things certain, but one thing is certain, viz. happiness is not to be had by seeking for it, and generally not in the way we think we shall get it. When it comes enjoy it and be thankful. As William Blake wrote, 'He who bends to himself a Joy doth the winged life destroy'. The best pleasures come in the course of duty.

It is a glorious sunny warm day, no sign of winter. Peace is over everything, as if your mother was watching over the day. Is she? Perhaps...

At 3 there is the cake and wine banquet in the village hall, to which we all must go, and at 7.30 a bonfire is to be lighted above the castle, similar proceedings at Park. They have sent a telegram. It is from the tenants of both places. I have told them what the chances are of you getting it but, if you do, try and send a few words of thanks to Mr Sidney Smith Esq. He is now being made a JP.

I fear your mails have not been quite so regular since you last wrote. Only two days ago we got the list of your casualties and were relieved by the omission of your name. We look for your next few letters with much interest. They are sending 50,000 more yeomanry and a lot of volunteers. It is a relief to know that every effort is being made.

You shall have the Zeiss glasses by next mail. It is a poor sort of present but you say it is the only thing you really want that will be of use. Joan and Mildred will have told you everything; so good bye.

18 January 1901. Mildred to Lachlan. Drummuir, Keith

Dearest Boy,

Well, the Banquet was unutterably funny, but really very nice for it displayed a wonderful amount of feeling among the tenants. I hope you got their telegram all right.

The Bonfire on the Shians was grand. Joan lit it at 7.30 and it was a perfect night for it. We will of course send you a paper describing it. No time for more, but much love from your loving Mildred G. D.

In the meanwhile Lachlan, far from home, expressed his feelings in this poem sent to Joan.

'A Veldt Want'

I would to God I were
On the deck of a ship once more
With the wild waves playing around,
Mid the genial ocean's roar.

On a ship that is homeward bound
With Table Mount sunk in the sea,
The Southern Cross behind,
And the Pole Star rising for me.

To feel in my face again
The bite of the stinging spray,
The swoop of the bows as she dips
To the surge's boisterous play.

For a weary while I've been,
Parted from home and friends,
But the sea is the road for me
That will some day make amends.

General Smith-Dorrien was promoted to Adjutant General and posted to India and not seen anymore. Usually the removal of one's commanding general can be looked on with relief; with any luck the new one might not be so stupid! The trouble with generals is that they can be too ambitious. Smith-Dorrien, known by the Jocks as 'Doreen', was that rare specimen, a really good general. He looked like a general, brave to a fault, and knew the names of many officers and men and was considered a character. 'Doreen' was described thus by an NCO; 'The general was a great favourite with us. He was decision itself. I never heard any officer swear like him.'!

The Battalion presented him with a banner of his arms worked by the Master Tailor in the fashion of Pipe Banners of Captains. He in turn presented the 19th Brigade flag to the Battalion. On it was inscribed on a silver plate; "XIXth Brigade, South Africa, 1900-01". This flag, named the Half-Ration Flag, marked in the field the position of GOC 19th Brigade (whose racing colours it was) and the 1st Battalion Gordon Highlanders. "

At the time a Pretoria Staff Officer was heard to say: "The 1st Battalion Gordon Highlanders will be home for the grouse shooting"!

What a joke!

CHAPTER ELEVEN

Belfast to Dalmanutha 1901

When Kitchener took over in South Africa, the British troops, who were outnumbered by three to one, were strung out across the 1100 miles between Capetown and the Rhodesian border. Their communication and supply chain depended upon the telegraph and rail systems. The larger towns were held by the British, but the Boers dominated the veldt.

Hertzog and Kritzinger, the Boer leaders, had entered Cape Colony in December with the idea of joining De Wet, who was marching south from the Orange River. He was the 'Eminence Grise' of the Boer army and a thorn in the flesh of the British.

Stopping De Wet and capturing him was seen as a key to the successful outcome of the war and, to this end, Kitchener organised more than 15,000 of his troops into 15 columns stretching along 160 miles of the Western Railway. Operating in relays which helped to preserve the stamina of the men, they pursued De Wet who was nearly captured, but escaped owing to his outstanding ability to think and move quickly. Twisting and turning he slipped away from the exhausted and frustrated British.

Louis Botha.

Mrs. Botha

At this stage the war had somehow become more unpleasant for both sides. The failure to invade the Cape Colony or to capture De Wet, together with the im-

mense cost of the war, was discouraging the British, while the Boers were suffering from the burning of their farms and the introduction of concentration camps. In these latter Boer wives and families were held in poor conditions with non-existent medical facilities.

Kitchener

An attempt was made at this point to end the war through diplomacy between Kitchener and Louis Botha, Commandant General of the Transvaal.

Botha, aged only 38 when the war started, had served under Lucas Meyer at Talana, north of Ladysmith, and succeeded him when Meyer became sick. Botha was a tall, handsome, bright-eyed farmer. Dark-featured with a moustache and small beard, he appeared more French than Dutch. Born a British subject in Natal, he trekked north when young and was granted land in the Transvaal which he farmed with conspicuous success despite having received only three years formal education. His wife was Irish, a descendant of Robert Emmet, the rebel and revolutionary. She was a great asset to her husband, mainly because of her good relations with Roberts following the capture of Pretoria.

By all accounts, Botha was an amiable person, happiest when playing the accordion with friends. He was one of the more moderate members of the Volksraad. He had no doubts about the stupidity and waste of war and abstained from voting in favour of fighting, even though neither he nor his wife had any respect for the British government.

When war was declared in 1899 he joined Meyer's army in Natal, eventually rising to command it, but also developing his skills as a statesman to such a degree that in 1907 he became Prime Minister of the Transvaal and later in 1910 first Leader of a united South Africa.

Mrs Louis Botha was a remarkable woman in her own right, accompanying her husband on the campaigns. She and her husband were forced to part at the fall of Kroonstadt when Botha fled to avoid capture. Following the capture of Pretoria, Roberts was in contact with Samuel Marks, the Russian-Jewish Rand millionaire and friend of Kruger, whose personal view that the war was futile and ought to be quickly ended, prompted Roberts to seek out Botha's own views on the possibility of peace.

To get Botha's views about holding a peace conference Roberts sent Mrs Louis Botha through dangerous army lines but, before any meeting could take place, the Boer Council of War met, and owing to De Wet's success in the Transvaal all talk of surrender vanished. Later the same gallant lady played another leading part in the struggle for peace by carrying a letter from Kitchener to Botha arranging a meeting at Middleburg, on the Delagoa Bay line, on 28 February, expressly to discuss ending the war. Botha accepted under a safe conduct. It was the first serious attempt at peace talks since the war started.

Kitchener knew that no good would come out of the continuation of the war and needed to convince Botha of the undesirability of prolonging the conflict. Though each was respectful of the other, Botha was suspicious of Milner, the British High Commissioner, whom he described as "the tool of alien financiers" and Milner was not present at the negotiations. (Lachlan's Aunt Margot Tennant had considered marrying Milner when he was in Cairo but later changed her mind. She disliked his 'hooded' eyes.)

Kitchener presented to Botha the following peace-package:

An amnesty for Boers and rebels alike, though the rebels would be temporarily disenfranchised.

Speedy return of prisoners of war from abroad.

Self government as soon as possible.

£1,000,000 settlement of debts incurred by the Government during the war.

Assistance to farmers for damage during the war.

No taxes to pay for the cost of the war.

The teaching of both languages in schools.

Non-whites to get limited voting rights as in the Cape, but not until the whites got representative government.

The draft of this document went to Milner and to Chamberlain and, like all politicians they started to tinker with it and alter what might have been acceptable, purely in order to claim the credit for its conception and further their own political careers. The changes were petty and irritating. The amendments ran:

All money for farmers should be loans and not grants.

The Boer nation should swear an oath of allegiance to the Queen.

Boer rebel leaders were to be court martialled.

Dutch in addition to English was only to be taught in schools at the express wish of parents.

Votes for non-whites were to be limited so as not to outnumber the white vote.

Botha was understandably unhappy about the British Government's attitude towards the teaching of Afrikaans and troubled that there was no mention of the independence for which the war was being fought in the first place. The revised peace-package was not what he had expected and he could not agree to it without consulting his fellow generals. Their decision, predictably, was a rejection of the peace proposals. Rayne Kruger summed up the bitterness prevalent at the time; "When all is said, the one solid fact was that the war had to continue, unrelenting and unforgiving, to heap ashes on the heads of future generations".

27 January 1901. Lachlan to Father. Prisoner of war camp, Pretoria.

This is a beastly place in wet weather. There is no news of any consequence since I last wrote. We have 30 more prisoners from the east this evening. I dare say we shall be here for next Xmas, with any luck. Joan is right when she says she has made up her mind not to see us for a long time. As far as that is concerned you had better let Drummuir, if you want. We collected a lot of natives from a village as beaters and retrievers, and got 55 by lunch, walking, most of the time through old mealie corn fields where a kind of asparagrassy-looking grass has grown to a great height, often well above our heads. The birds seemed to like it. We had to stop our beaters trying to kill them as at first, when a bird rose, he went off in a cloud of knobkerries and sticks thrown with great precision. It was rather disconcerting for the guns. The birds were often nearly as big as partridges, the cock birds having lovely dark plumage, quite like a cock grouse. We stopped the evening train to Pretoria, arriving about 8.30 p.m. Bray and I had to get out and pull our cab along, as it stuck in the mud and the wretched horses were unable to pull it out. It is a queer country.

Yesterday we had some good Polo. I have now a 3rd pony which one of the Canadian Scouts got me instead of Peter. It is a little grey mare, but she had both her hind heels badly cut by a rope, and will not be fit to ride for some time. She appears to be very raw and has probably not been ridden, like lots of these off-the-veldt mares. She is very quick with her hind feet and, if you are not careful, she puts in a scientific cow-kick in front or behind, so that dressing her sore heels needs patience

29 January 1901. Lachlan to Joan. Belfast

We are having horrible weather. You never saw such rain, it goes on and on, and falls in regular tropical torrents. At least, it is doing so today, other days it rains as it does at home. The column went to Carolina and returned to Wonderfontein, doing very little as far as we have heard. They cleared out a few inhabitants including a German battery, and found a few wounded. They signalled back to us that they had disabled a Boer pom-pom, but as that same pom-pom then pom-pommed them vigorously back, they were forced to conclude they were mistaken. Miller had a bullet through his horse's tail when delivering a message. He is doing ADC to Spens and times appear to have been lively. The troops suffered great discomfort owing to the rain and, poor things, must be having a perfectly awful time of it now without tents. I have rarely seen such rain, even in tents like ours it is pretty wet. Torrents of water are running everywhere, while the whole ground is one large puddle.

The mornings are normally fine and warm, but big thunderstorms circle round and round. I wish you could see it this very minute; it is a never to be forgotten sight, terrific thunder and lightning and driving volumes of water, such as it would be hard to imagine. There will be tremendous spates down country. I bet a few temporary bridges go if they have weather like this. I have just shut our tent door but it was a forlorn hope, and I risked being drowned.

We are still working on our defences. They were built in such a hurry that they keep tumbling down, which is most vexatious and takes a lot of doing up again! We are fixing up a wonderful contrivance of Tytler's by which a gun is let off if anyone by night walks into a wire stretched round between the pickets. If it ever works, it is sure to be fired by a stray ox or mule and the whole place alarmed.

All the horses in the place have been taken for various jobs, so I am horseless, which is sad, but I hope to get one soon. It is about the only amusement there is. However I can generally borrow one now and again. I have learnt to play Bridge as well as you can; it's a good game.

I have sent back a reply to the servants and employees of Drummuir, Park and Braemoriston estates, who wished me luck and gave a silver bowl; it was very good of them.

19 February 1901. Lachlan to Joan. Belfast

It is just a year or so since I wrote to you from Paarderberg. What a beastly time we were having. It was this morning in 1900 that we cut hunks off a dead ox and grilled them over a fire, and beastly tough they were I remember. The weather for the first few days has been abominable. The column I spoke of in my last letter came back on Thursday 14 February, Kitchener and his people too. They skirmished up to Dullstroom, but the Boers there under Viljoen were too strong and they had to come back here as fast as possible. They had a good many casualties in the Mounted Infantry but the Boers suffered worse, the Australians as usual doing splendidly, and our gunners doing some good shooting.

Matthews, the Royal Irish Doctor, and an ambulance were caught while looking for wounded. Viljoen took him to a concert in Dullstroom that night. A Boer proposed that they sing 'Soldiers of the Queen', but that they said they would not do, then 'Soldiers of the Transvaal', but they said the only appropriate song was 'Soldiers of the Limpopo', which they sang. He said they all live very comfortably in little Laagers and play whist all day; we are going to invite them over to play bridge. They said they enjoyed our little columns as it broke the monotony, and advised us to get in a train and leave the country, as it would do us no good to stay. They gave him Tikkpees and other coins. They live on beef and potatoes, of which there are plenty, but nothing else. That is very little hardship to a Boer.

21 February - During all this rain we do absolutely nothing. Maclaren and I managed to raise a few No 3 and 5 cartridges and shot a dozen snipe. If we had more of the right kind of ammunition we might have killed 50. We wade about the bog in india-rubber boots; it is rather messy but fun. We commandeered 3 little natives who came as beaters, retrievers and gamekeepers, and thoroughly enjoyed it. The snipe were excellent to eat. It seems absolutely impossible to get any cartridges, as they will not let them be brought into the country; the only way is to get someone coming from Capetown to bring them in his kit.

The Colonel has come back from Jo'burg on the 18th and is much better, and quite pleased with himself. We are all going to get a fortnight's leave in turn. I hope the Rome plans will come off, it would be very good for you all. I dare say you will get this letter there. I have just been reading a very good book by Marion Crawford called Saracinesca, about Rome and Romans in the last century.

The papers and parcels mail is not yet in, they always come a day or two after the letters, so the Zeiss glasses and papers spoken of have not yet turned up.

Some lunatic out here has sent up an order that corn is to be planted or rather sown! We have no ploughs or implements but that never occurred to him I suppose. It will be rather funny if we all turn farmers. I shall apply to be Grieve.

Give my Love to Father and Mildred, and tell him the kilt arrived long ago if he did not know, tho I told him; also thank him for paying for it.

1 March 1901. Lachlan to Father. Belfast, Transvaal

I am sorry I did not write by last mail, but I was very seedy with liver of all things and put it off until too late. I do not know how it was, a chill I think, but after 3 or 4 wretched days, I got a touch of jaundice, but am practically well again. It was really nothing, as I never had to go sick, but it was very unpleasant, and I did not know what was wrong. Now, like many other people I have a heavy cold. The weather is still unpleasant; cold and raining on and off. I wonder when it will permanently improve? The rain should be about over by this time.

About a week ago the Adjutant got a wire for three more subalterns and a captain to go to the Mounted Infantry with 30 men. We are very short of officers, so it was not at all welcome. He asked me if I would care to go, but on thinking it over it did not seem much catch. First, they will probably be kept out in the country a very considerable time after we go home. Secondly, I have trekked as much as I want to, and with winter coming on, they will have a very uncomfortable time, pursuing these jokers on worn out nags and little food and no comfort and thirdly, I hope to get home alive, a reason that ought not to be considered I suppose but, having seen a few bullets, there is not much need to want more. These were the opinions of all here who were fit to go, three or four of us. Pickets are out now for four days at a time instead of three, and one fellow is out by himself which is apt to be rather slow, tho of course he gets plenty of visitors.

We have all sorts of stories going about camp; Boers all surrendering, war over, going home etc. Botha and Viljoen had been spending the day with Kitchener. They had all been observed to smile which you must admit is very significant, they were also photo'd together, and Kitchener said to the photographer "Be very careful as this is the last time we shall be taken together as enemies!" I shall not vouch for the accuracy of all this, but there seems to be something up; the Colonel says peace propositions are being considered, but a woman who came in said there was but a small chance of their being accepted. However a buzz from Middleburg is to the effect that the Boers are well enough satisfied, and terms may be accepted. It is, I am afraid, too good to be true; however, we are talking about our return as if it were within definite view. Many people say July. I shall be well content to be back by August.

I had almost forgotten to thank you for the glasses, they are splendid. I made sure that the Boers had got them in that train they bagged at Balmoral as they were so late in arriving, tho' it must have been a near thing. Did my telegram ever reach you? They are very uncertain. Please thank Joan for the parcel, socks and chocolate. I hope before I write again peace may be declared. I have got a pony and am starting to learn Polo. They play a good deal here.

15 March 1901. Joan to Lachlan. 20 Cavendish Square, W 1

I do hope you are resting quietly in Bloemfontein today after your long march. Darling, I am so afraid your dear feet are horribly sore and tired; do take care of them and yourself altogether.

Yesterday morning I spent with Barbara and hairdresser. We lunched here and I spent the afternoon again with Barbara who is looking very well. In the evening I had to try on my dress and we all dined in Green Street. This morning the hairdresser came at 9.15 as he was so busy, and weaved and curled and pulled and made a wonderful creation, which is really not so ugly as I expected. I have made the feathers look quite big enough. I am wearing the dress I had for Inverness last year, done up with an endless train that weighs about 3 tons. I shall have to begin to dress soon.

Fancy - Pamela is going to present Marguerite! They will indeed be beauty and the beast! We all go to Grosvenor Square after the function. I should think Marguerite will be a good sight. I will tell you all about it this evening. I wish it were over.

Friday - It actually is over, and I wasn't very frightened and rather enjoyed it. We sat for about half an hour in a gallery with a few hundred other ladies, not one of whom we knew, then there was a moment's crush. Then we turned a corner, a grey haired nobleman spread out our trains, and we passed into the throne room, where I made my four curtsies successfully, to the Princess, whom I was too nervous to look at, to Princess Beatrice who looked very fat, to the old Prince who smiled in the most delightful way and then to Prince Christian; I then turned my back on them boldly, instead of backing out. The only person that I knew was Lady Baring of Forglen, who refused to recognise me.

Then we went back to Grosvenor Square and exhibited ourselves. Pamela was not looking so lovely as she did at Aberdeen and her dress was not very becoming. Marguerite had a beautiful white dress and looked most imposing. I really think she has improved in looks. Blyth said she thought Lady Tennant looked beautiful! There was quite a crush. Nan came, Fred Lutyens, Godfrey Webb was there and Sir Algy West and Lady Poynder and all the Franks and Uncle Eddie. Grandpapa was away. I had asked Gladys Knox but she did not turn up.

I spent a very quiet evening here as Margot dined out. Fraulein Beaunhart dined with me and I made the most of the occasion and talked German hard. She was slightly more affable than she was at Amisfield.

I saw the baby aunt yesterday, such a pretty thing. She is called Margaret. I hope she was proud of her two nieces in their feathers! Barbara's were so high that they nodded like a hearse and had to be fixed when we got to the Palace.

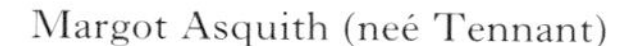

Margot Asquith (neé Tennant)

Joan Gordon-Duff

I feel so horribly ashamed of myself as I meant to send you some meat lozenges etc. this week, but I had no time yesterday and now it is too late for parcels. I am so sorry; they shall come next week.

I am not quite sure that I like being here; I am so accustomed to looking on London as only a place of amusement for a few days that I feel as if I couldn't settle down to any thing serious, and then with Margot I always feel so mad and desperate at my stupidity that I almost wish I hadn't got such clever relations. Tonight I go to an exhibition of dancing with her.

I enclose a "curl" of my hair which was cut off to make me a fringe. I hope you will be properly touched! I hear that I shall breakfast tête-a-tête with Henry which rather alarms me.

My beloved, God bless and keep you, and oh! bring you home soon.

With oh so much love, farewell.

19 March 1901. Lachlan to Joan. Belfast

Our long stay at Belfast is just about over, for a time at any rate, and I do not wish to spend another 6 months here. News came the other day, starting in the usual way, that we were off on the trek again. Belfast is to be garrisoned by 200 men, with the vast accumulation of stores to be shifted and our beautiful forts, which were erected with such heart breaking toil, are to be evacuated or even demolished! I am this minute in the tent in the main S.E. picket, where I have been for the last 4 days in command of C Company with Vivien Gordon. I have been extremely comfortable and get on very well.

After my usual pickets with Allan, the relief is indescribable here, and I positively enjoy it. The weather has been as vile as usual, driving rain, thick fog and cold wind, with few intervals for three days on end. Our tent leaks abominably, being old and very rotten, but that is a trifle. Today has been a little better. It clears up enough to get our bedding and clothes dry in the sun, but the rain has started again, and I suppose we are in for another wet night. The flies find it very depressing, and have little energy to worry us. A very sad thing has just occurred. I put out my three best cigars to dry - they were rather damp - and forgot them till after a beastly shower. I brought them in feeling a bit sick!

We came up here on 6th. Colonel Walter Kitchener is here; he is going to take us trekking with him round Lydenburg way. The Royal Irish come too but the Shropshires stay here as garrison. He is in a desperate hurry to get off, but as there are such quantities of stores and arrangements of all sorts to be settled first, we are not likely to go tomorrow as he wishes. I hope not, as I want to get at my things in camp, and pack up what is not to go. All our surplus baggage will I think go to Middleburg with Jim Gordon, who will stay and look after it.

Walter Kitchener is in an awful funk of big brother, who nags at him by telegrams such as "Haven't heard of you doing much lately, what about that commando?" etc., etc. So Walter gets frantic and dashes off to collect troops and guns for some enterprise.

It does not look as if the peace negotiations were coming to much. We have heard guns going in the distance all this morning, and were watching Lyddite shells bursting on Elandshoek, a hill about 10 miles NNE. We could not see what it was all about. I wonder where we shall be this time next month?

Many thanks for your letter and the chocolate and socks, also thank Grandmama and Nanny. I hope you are enjoying your Rome trip, it ought to be very improving.

18 March 1901. Lachlan to Father. Belfast, Transvaal

I got your letter announcing the arrival of the telegram. It really took 2 days and a few hours, as it left here the evening of the 12th. However, that is very quick. You seem to have been very unlucky with the ice. I wonder if you had any curling since? What would a Boer say if he could see it?

I expect you will have seen my letter to Joan on its way last week, tho as far as I can remember there was nothing in it. Just after I wrote to her I came off picket, where we had spent 4 wet but on the whole comfortable days. It was raining and blowing hard, and as soon as we got into camp news came in that a train was blown up near Wonderfontein. 3 Coys were ordered to entrain immediately, which we did in trucks, 3 in front and 3 behind the engine. I had just taken over command of A Company. We set out accompanied by the Cavalry scouting on our flanks and ahead. They were much bothered by bogs and our progress was slow.

When we reached the scene of the disaster there were of course no Boers in sight. The engine was lying on its side, having been derailed, and had toppled over into the ditch after tearing up several yards of the road and bringing several vans after it, tho' the greater part of the train was all right on the metals. About 70 or 100 Boers had been lying hidden a little way off, and as soon as the burst took place they advanced in skirmishing order and surrounded the train and fired at the 8 armed men, who took what cover they could in the ditch and fired back. They were enfiladed, one was killed and then another, so they surrendered. The fireman was scalded a bit, but the driver escaped. Several horses on board were shot. This took about 20 minutes.

The Boers, a ragged looking crew, were in a great funk of being caught. The train contained a good few of their females with a large amount of furniture, being taken from Belfast. There was also a lot of forage belonging to the Remount Depot, and 29 bags of mails from Lydenburg and the east. Twenty of these they collared, as well as some whisky, food and two of their damsels. They blew up a safe containing £2 and left a receipt for it and departed, taking the Remount Officer, who gave them cheek, along with them. An old Boer vrouw, not liking to be held up so unceremoniously, told them that she could see rooinecks coming with a gun and they had better clear out quick, which they did, only stopping 10 minutes after they took the train.

Another train, a few hundred yards further on was nearly caught, but luckily the explosive did not work properly, and the damage was slight. We spent the day carrying all the Boer furniture across the break to a fresh train, and got back at dusk. The rain had never stopped all day, and we were very wet and cold.

"The train contained a good few of their females"

I saw quantities of mushrooms; this is a wonderful place for them. We eat so many that we are quite tired of them. I have been 4 days alone on the S.W. picket as officers are scarce. It is not really dull as fellows ride up every day some time. We had a great shoot the other day here, but saw nothing, except one cobra which Maclaren shot. It managed to get under a rock. Snakes are very plentiful. Half the Battalion is going out to escort a convoy from Wonderfontein today, so I shall not be relieved till afternoon. I shot rather a fine lizard which I skinned myself yesterday, it was black and red, about 10 inches long. The skinning was not easy when it came to the head and tail. I am afraid it will hardly do to keep, but I am going to try to finish it now, if it is not too high.

Yesterday a wire came from Kitchener to say that Peace negotiations are off. It probably means another year out here but fewer Boers at the end of it. De Wet is being properly hunted. French's operations have been very successful.

Our trek north which was to have started tomorrow is again postponed, how long I do not know. We expect to go by Lydenburg and Steynsdorp to Pietersburg, acting in conjunction with other columns. It is however mere conjecture. This garrison is being reduced and only a few of our lovely forts are to be held, the rest I expect will be blown up. Walter Kitchener is here and we are fortifying the station premises. All inhabitants are gone away, stores, remounts, etc. Robertson, who was with Macdonald, came to be our Padre two days ago. He is a rattling good fellow. A great improvement on the late one. Joan and Grandmama are now at Rome. I hope they are enjoying themselves. You must be rather dull all alone. I should go to Hatton at once. No grouse for me, and no pheasants either this year I am afraid. I have just heard that we start for Machadodorp tomorrow.

Lizard shot at Belfast March 16th 1901
Transvaal
Original 10" long

24 March 1901. Lachlan to Father. Dalmanutha, Transvaal

The day after I last wrote we came here. It was a horrid wet morning, a regular Belfast day. We were to have started at 8 a.m., and had breakfast with the Shropshires, who are staying to garrison the place, but Kitchener put it off till 9. Of course the weather did not improve, and we had a soaking march of about 9 miles in driving rain and fog and long wet grass - not at all pleasant. We were escorting a convoy.

The people here are the Berks and some 19th Hussars with a 12 pounder, quick-fire. They do not seem very well fortified and it is pretty evident that they were not attacked like we were. We are camped in the veldt, with little work for a dog. The Lydenburg trip, if intended, has evidently been put off.

20th - A and B coys, Dingwall and self, with some cavalry, escorted the convoy half way to Machadodorp, which is about 9 miles on, where it was met and brought in. The Battalion went and sat on Elands Kop, a little hill out south, as a guard, tho' only five Boers were seen dancing a hornpipe at the idea of a day's shooting. They did not realise expectations however. There are 18,000 Boers at Carolina with 2 guns, and two pom-poms, and about 400 on outpost between there and here.

21st - We went on a route march! It seemed hardly necessary. We did 4 miles, though. It was a lovely day and quite pleasant. There was a gymkhana at

Machadodorp. We never knew of it till just before. We hear the Boers here have little ammunition but our own, and Martinis, and a fair supply of our gun ammunition, which shows they are running short, but ought to be shorter.

Today it is hot, for this country. Padre Robertson gave us a nice little service this morning. There are all sorts of stories of a night attack this evening, or something very similar. The Colonel, Kitchener and staff, have all been very busy with maps and schemes. Guides have arrived, and preparations seem to have been going on very mysteriously. It is now 2 o'clock, and I shall be surprised if we are not ordered to parade sometime this afternoon in marching order. I think the idea is that we and the Mounted Infantry and several guns, 2 field, 4 Colt and a Howitzer, with Kitchener, are to sally forth, get round the Boers' outposts and cut them off, probably with assistance from Machadodorp, as we are only about 300 strong now when it comes to fighting. This is all surmise, but various things point that way, such as recent reconnaissance, repairing a road for the guns etc.

I suppose the success experienced at Kruger's Post is stimulating Kitchener to try again, tho night work is risky and full of surprises, and the country south of here is very bad, hills and bogs etc. that even by day are very treacherous. Also the Boers know them and we do not. Burney went to Machadodorp yesterday, without knowing anything about the reasons though it was probably something to do with this. I wish he was with us; he is a splendid second in command.

Since so many trains have been caught very few are to be run a week. First a practically empty one goes - three trucks loaded with coal or stones, then two more empty ones, then the engine, then more trucks with goods of little value, then the armoured train, and following it the bona fide mail, passenger and goods train, with its engine preceded by several trucks. If they capture it they will be very clever, tho they I expect they will try with electric wires, choosing the valuable train. Our mails came in this morning. I heard from you and Joan, the latter just arrived at Green Street.

To day is turning showery. I hope it will be a fine night for our expedition. There will be no moon so it will be very dark. I shall be able to give you all the details when I next write; I hope pleasant ones. You may hear of it before this arrives if any thing serious is afoot. There is a rumour of a big advance north within a fortnight, whether for us or not I can't say. All my Boer news is from one who has just surrendered. He says the Boers greatly enjoy surprising our small columns! Troops are coming north again, so I suppose the Cape invasion has nearly fizzled out.

We do not like Walter Kitchener much. He does not seem to know his own mind as a rule. Please send this on to Joan. I am writing her a short note only. Parcels have not yet arrived, hope the gingerbread is all right.

26 March 1901. Lachlan to Joan

Many thanks for your letter from Green Street. This is only a note as I wrote to father and asked him to send it on.

Tomorrow we go to Machadodorp though the tame Carolina Commando seems to worry the people here rather. Not that it does anything, but it is sometimes very active and our movements may depend on it. Since writing two days ago we have had a little trek. A kind of veni, vidi, vici business though not as serious as we anticipated. We left here at 4 a.m. yesterday morning after breakfast at 3 a.m. Various other parties of Mounted Infantry etc. left earlier from here and made for Machadodorp, our objective to worry any Boers who were by a bare chance to be capturable. We went S.W. and by daylight were still a good way from them. A Company and self went to hold a kopje, and signalled away with all sorts of people and had a good view of proceedings. There was a bridge to Komati where they were to be caught retiring but weren't. One man and some cattle went across, the Boers being gone, so after a little fooling about we went off N.W. instead of returning here.

We went a long rough march through pretty country; farms and mealie patches everywhere, as well as plenty of cattle and horses. The M.I. took a few wagons and some cattle, tho not much. Kitchener, who we look upon as an ass, took us to an awful place for the night and we got in pretty tired, having done nearly 17 miles, and many men fell out from heat and want of food. We had some natives up to build sangas and made ourselves pretty safe, tho if we had been attacked as we expected we would have found it difficult to hold as the ground was easy to approach. However nothing happened and at 4 a.m. we advanced about 1000 yards along a ridge in darkness and a thick fog. At 7 a.m. we were relieved by the Mounted Infantry, and the whole column trekked back breakfastless again. The M.I. had a little sniping but no casualties. They say they killed a Boer yesterday.

We had a hot tiring march, getting in here about 11, pretty tired. The Commando is again on the prowl.

Babington has done well. 10 guns of all sorts, ammunition and 150 prisoners as well as casualties from De la Rey.

CHAPTER TWELVE

Witklip to Lydenburg 1901

1 April 1901. Lachlan to Father. Witklip, 9 miles south of Lydenburg

An empty convoy is going back to Machadodorp so there is a chance of getting this posted. We are waiting about till it is time to fall in to escort our own convoy into Lydenburg. This is our 8th consecutive day's trek, more than we have done for a long time. After our two long days fooling around the Komati from Dalmanutha, we left the latter place on the following day and marched to Machadodorp.

With considerable difficulty I managed to get my pack pony exchanged for a big grey one that is very fine, barring it has broken knees and a habit of falling on its nose. Its predecessor was in foal. Maclaren and I had a nice swim in the river and next morning we set out with a great ox convoy for Lydenburg. We reached Helvetia where we camped. We passed a very pretty drift, lined with weeping willows, where a farm once was and now we are cultivating vegetables for the good of the troops there.

29th - We reached Shomans Hock. 8 miles, very hot, rain in the afternoon.

30th - To Badfontein, half way through the big valley. All the horses were sent straight through here as horse sickness is very bad, they must on no account graze. We camped just over the non-coaching bridge over the Crocodile by a funny little kopje in the plain, just like a big ant-heap when seen from a distance.

Yesterday we came on here. I was right flank guard and we had a very rough walk along the river, up and down hills and past some fine kraals.

Kitchener nearly got taken 2 days ago. He started as he always does to ride down the line with two men, a Cape Captain and an ADC, when, half way to Lydenburg, he was held up by Boers who sniped from the long grass by the road side. The men were killed. Kitchener's horse was shot but did not fall until he was a good way back; the rest also escaped. It is a stupid thing for a General to do.

This morning we are loafing about till 1 p.m. to pass an empty convoy through to Lydenburg. When we get there we shall have walked about 100 miles since leaving Belfast. Mails will be irregular here.

The cake was excellent, please thank Mildred for it.

7 April 1901. Lachlan to Joan. Machadodorp.

I have to thank you for a most interesting letter from Rome and another from London. I got both together yesterday. I sent a short note to father by a convoy coming from Lydenburg that we passed en route, but I doubt that it will ever fetch up. After our 2 days in and out from Dalmanutha, we marched here the following day with K.

1 April - We walked to Lydenburg station at 1 p.m., nearly 7 months since our previous visit. We were camped in the market square, a dirty place.

Lydenburg is a pretty little town, bigger than Middleburg, with splendid surrounding scenery. That night some of us dined with the Rifle Brigade, who have sat and done absolutely nothing since the place has been occupied, and some with the Devons. I was with the latter and they have a fine house and gave as good a dinner as you could get at home with sherry, champagne etc., all splendidly served. These sordid details mean much in this country owing to their rarity. It was a pleasant change after dining on tinned stuff on one's hunkers on the veldt. We played Bridge until 1.30 and discussed a gymkhana for tomorrow.

2nd - We pottered around the place and bathed etc. but, heavy rain coming on, the gymkhana could not take place which was sad, as all the fashion and the beauty of the place were disappointed as well as ourselves. We were to have left with the empty convoy to return early next morning, but the rain was so heavy that it was put off till noon when it faired. Luckily we had tents or should have been drowned. Kitchener changed his mind 3 times as usual, and once said we were to wait a day, but to our sorrow this was cancelled.

4th - We went straight through the valley to Shomans Kloof, 18 miles. Showers about all day and terrible mud. We were cold and miserable.

5th - I have at last got the universal veldt sores, beastly things which broke out on my hands and poisoned my arms up to the shoulders. They get better with looking after, but are very difficult to get rid of and are very sore.

A dreadful thing took place yesterday. Jim Botha got kicked by a mule, and had to have his throat cut. In consequence his last act was to thrust his head into an empty Maconochie tin. He is deeply mourned and was interred decently, though we have suspicions that he was dug up and - horrible to relate! - eaten. Jim Botha was our tame pig or piglet, got as we left Belfast. He was small, black and greedy. There is a kitten too, khaki-coloured, who played with him.

J.B. however was rather a nuisance and squealed in a blood-curdling manner when any restraint was imposed, and insisted on sharing your dinner. After all, this regrettable incident may have been a blessing in disguise!

We are to march to Shomans tomorrow with another convoy for Lydenburg. Reveille at 2.15 a.m., march at 3.45 a.m. Since 5 p.m. it has pelted and the whole country seems to have become a raging torrent, with quantities of hail to cool us. The drift four miles out may be impassable, though the streams go down nearly as quickly as they rise, which is saying a good deal as one has no idea how much water has descended in a given time.

From Lydenburg we may go trekking to Leydsdorp or some such place.

16 April 1901. Great Uncle John Tennant to Lachlan. Bay View, Freshwater Bay, Bournemouth

Your letter has filled me with self-reproaches, not so much for forgetting you for indeed you have not been forgotten, but for not realising how welcome letters from any friends in the old country would be to you.

Just now we are spending Easter at Freshwater and can look over from the Downs to distant Bournemouth, where we stayed together many years ago. Barbara was with us as a guest but is now nearly next door. Willie [his son] was here for a few days, but is now back to his work at the School of Music at Cranbourne. Nan spent the winter at Mentone with the Rankines and her visit has had a sad cloud as, just after her return home, Mr Rankine died of a sharp attack of Inflammation of the Lungs.

We have seen very little lately of your father and Joan, as last summer we were not in Scotland but at Arndale near the lake. Barbara was with us a short time and we visited Gisburn. We followed the course of your battalion with great eagerness during the early stage of the war, but have lost sight of you latterly. You must have had many trying experiences, not the least I suspect when you brought your picket in, in the convoy affair just when Lord Roberts' dash on Bloemfontein began.

We are all longing for peace and shall rejoice to welcome you home again. Nan is writing to you and I shall add this to hers. We hope to post this mail but your letter and address have gone with Willie to Cranbourne and he may not respond to our earnest request for it to return in time.

Willie hesitated on leaving Cambridge between the Army and Mining, and indeed he applied for one of those Artillery commissions but did not succeed in getting it. I think he is working and on the whole likes his work.

I have said, dear Lachlan, that in spite of appearances we have not forgotten you and it is true. You have been and you shall be, to use the quaint phrase of an old German friend of mine, now gone to her rest, "enclosed in our daily prayers", and your mother's son will get no warmer welcome outside your immediate family circle than from our own.

The author of this quaint but moving letter, is Lachlan's Uncle John. He was Sir Charles' elder brother and a thoughtful and caring man. Trained as a barrister, he eventually took up philanthropic work in London, and was not all that well off compared to brother Charles. He had three sons, all killed in World War One. Willie was one of them. Nan was one of his three daughters.

12 - 24 April 1901. Lachlan to Father. Bergfontein

I think there will be a convoy going back to Lydenburg today or tomorrow, and I shall take the opportunity of posting this. We are now in the wilds of Spekboom valley, about 30 miles north of Lydenburg and a bit west. We left Lydenburg at 6.30 p.m. on the 12th. They sent us 5 miles in wagons as far as the pickets go, then we marched down a steep hill and across a bridge over a rushing stream. If it had been daylight the view would have been very fine. We marched from 10.30 till about 3.30 a.m. on the 13th. I was so sleepy that I kept falling asleep as we walked and cannoning into people and tumbling all over the place, which was most unpleasant. We slept from 3.30 till 5.30 at Krugers Post, then on again for another 6 miles or so, through a much bushier country than before.

We halted half way down a long hill with thick bush on it. It was beautifully shaded, and we chewed a wild fruit called a Marula. I liked it; it is said to taste like a mango, though some people said it was like turpentine. The baggage got in about 2 p.m., very tired. The place was called Klipkloof, our total mileage, 22 miles.

Four Boers surrendered to us. Our force consisted of ourselves and the Royal Irish, 300 Mounted Infantry, 2 field guns and a pom-pom under a certain Col. Starkey. We were after David Schoeman.

14th - We were off early and had a tremendous climb up a big kopje covered in jungle. We had two guides, though they would not leave the road and their horses. Getting up the hill we had over a mile of jungle to go through. My Company was leading, so I had to find a way through which was not easy. The rest followed in single file and we managed to get into the bed of a water course at last, which led to a nek between our hill and another, and struggled some way up it with a roof of vegetation over our heads; very romantic but not properly appreciated! The hill where we branched off was like a house and we fairly sweated. No Boers there of course, though not far off, one MI was killed and two wounded by snipers. We descended when the baggage was past the foot of the hill and followed it along by this country road, through a narrow pass, very bushy, out to a drift in the Spekboom river which flows north there (we were then going west).

The river was about two ft deep, about 40 yards wide, very swift and strong at the drift. I took off my shoes and stockings and had a terribly uncomfortable passage. Luckily a strong man near kept his shoes on or I would not have kept my feet. Half way across two jibbing ponies in a Cape cart struck at a boulder and made a dash at us, and it was a near thing that no one was hurt. Just across was a row of unripe bananas. We camped a mile on in the Great Boom valley with Koodoo and other game. The view from the aforementioned hill was very striking. This huge valley was at our feet running north and south, covered with sombre bush and enclosed by striking and sinister mountains. Away to the north were range after range of high hills, whose tops looked like great rollers all about to break in the clouds in a north easterly direction, the whole covered with dark bush and scarcely a house visible.

To our south-west, across the valley, were the borders of Sekokerna's country, very mountainous. I saw many tracks of different sizes but no Buck themselves. We were on picket that night as an attack as usual was expected. We could see the Boers' lights to our south, 6 miles or so, and the Jackals and other beasts made strange noises, but nothing happened. I heard a lot of partridges chirping around but we could not shoot for fear of alarming the camp in the early morning. We left at 9 a.m. on the 15th as rear guard. We turned south along the Pietersburg road. There were one or two farms, and lots of oranges, but they were some way off the road and the Mounted Infantry got all the loot as usual. We got a few from more fortunate people. It was very hot indeed, but interesting country. 100 Mounted Infantry were sent off that morning to call on Sekokerna who was acting as a stop. I have since heard that they go about with a big Impi after unfortunate burghers. No Boers were seen and we got into camp in unsurveyed country after crawling about 10 miles. I forgot to mention that the previous day at De Groot's Boom another 5 Boers surrendered, brought in by one of the Klipkloof patrols, also the M I caught a Despatch Rider.

16th - We were off at daylight, advanced guard, a fearfully bad hilly road, frequent rough little drifts, and a long hill up to Bergfontein. We went through a mealie field. They were young and excellent eating. After 13 miles we came on a women's laager, or rather groups of laagers, a marquee tent and two covered wagons, and a little further, a small house and more covered wagons full of women and children and a few sick Boers.

Each day we bagged a certain number of cattle driven by the 'Black Watch' consisting of natives with old Sneiders and Martinis etc. and the invariable assegais. Some were scouts who came up with Buller from Natal and others, I believe, were armed and sent forth by Shoerman to kill Rooineks, but preferred to kill Boers. All of a sudden heavy firing started in the bush near by, and we were sent to reinforce. However, it turned out to be the M.I. burning ammunition. They had about 100,000 rounds of Martini and Steer in boxes. We camped near the laager, where we got sweet potatoes and pumpkins. Our baggage was in before dark, thanks to Sgt Donald, who double-spanned the mule teams up the hill!

The Royal Irish only got theirs up by 4 a.m. They are awful rotters. As our old Quarter master Sgt used to say, "Them Hirish his Hawful"! My veldt sores are pretty bad, one on my left shin and elbow, two or three on my face, both hands covered. I am bandaged in a most absurd and uncomfortable way. They seem to get worse rather than better. It is impossible to look after them properly when trekking. We got in communication with Kitchener that day at Rietfontein, 7 miles S.W.

17th - We went out early with the 'Black Watch' and a guide to snaffle some Boers and cattle in a farm, but they were not taking any. My Company went out about a mile to where the 100,000 rounds were being destroyed by the Royal Irish. They had not been successful, and until we tried we had no idea how difficult it was to do. The Boers had heaved the boxes over the broken edge of the cliff, which went down sheer, 100s of feet, to the valley below - a magnificent piece of scenery. The boxes were hauled up by ropes and violent exertions and broken up and the contents piled in great fires. Unfortunately the fires when lit would not burn properly and after a few had gone off, the fire began to die out, but it was dangerous to approach for some time to stoke it, as at intervals there were little explosions.

We were no more successful than the Royal Irish and a shower dampened everything including our spirits. We had a very steep hill to go down, with a bad drift over the Witvaal River at the foot. A kilt is a good thing for wading deep streams! It was only 8 miles. We were in by 5.30 and got the papers and parcels of our last mail from Lydenburg. Many thanks for the cake and 2 papers, all of which arrived safely.

Early on the 19th, we started off taking wagons laden with Boer surrenders and their families. Nearly 100 Boers have surrendered in this neighbourhood. A Company were for picket on the hill across the river. It was deepish, rough and swift, and with great difficulty we got across fairly dry.

20th - Sekokerna's men are very useful. They do splendid scouting and intelligence work in their own way.

22nd - A quiet day here. The 'Black Watch' had an engagement killing two Boers, and losing 3 killed and 1 severely wounded; the latter did not seem much inconvenienced. They came in singing a new song. They have very fine voices, and keep splendid time. Occasionally one or two would leap out in front and dance, brandishing their assegeis etc. They were very pleased with themselves and everyone ran out to snapshot them.

We have rigged up a hen-house, which is kept well stocked from the neighbouring farms. An old Muskovy Duck is boss and keeps the cocks in tremendous order. Till the last convoy came in we have been for some days on half-rations, which caused the usual grumbling. We hear rumours of surrenders round the country, but no definite news. I would not be a bit surprised if we were soon to join in a Roos Senekal drive. There will probably be Boers there, as no one has been to it yet.

INTELLIGENCERS ("N'KOOS!"—"HAIL, CHIEF!")

Would you please me send out some cigars. 100 of the small Borneos and 100 ordinary sized ones. I will pay for them. Borneos are good and not very expensive. They should be hermetically sealed. I suppose Mildred and the children will have left France before this gets home. Give them all my love.

6 May 1901. Lachlan to Father. Near Lydenburg

There are some of our men, time-expired, who are off to Lydenburg, and thence home this afternoon, so I have just time for a note to say that we are all going on well. We have been knocking about the country for the last week or so.

The other half Battalion are not yet back from Machadodorp; they probably come in two days time. We have been living off the fat of the land, which is very unusual for us, poultry and pigs galore, with a fair number of oranges. We get them from deserted farms, but pay a bob for fowls, and 10/- for turkeys, where the old vrou remains, and rough vegetables for the men occasionally. They have two cows which is a great luxury.

We have collected hundreds of sheep, and trek with about half a Company doing shepherd. A lot of Boers have come in, but those remaining still show a little fight. They sniped one of our companies one afternoon, and yesterday the Mounted Infantry had a little engagement, but no casualties.

My veldt sores are convalescent, but will leave beastly scars. I rather envy the men going home. The Battalion is awfully weak. I will send a detailed account of our doings later. It is just 28 days since our last mail.

By now the Battalion had been divided into two halves to deal better with the small mobile groups of Boers. Despite all they had been through morale was high with letters from home providing a real boost.

Kitchener had now been in command for 6 months and changes were slowly taking place. Hard lessons had been learned in this vast, beautiful and hostile country. He had been using his army as a huge 'beater' (in shooting parlance) hoping to drive the Boer from his lair, much as birds are driven from cover into the sights of the waiting guns. The first of the drives was against De Wet but, as we have seen, there was no tactic that De Wet did not seem always to anticipate and no net wide or strong enough to trap him and his charmed forces.

General French had just completed another such drive through the Transvaal in April 1901. It lasted 10 weeks and employed no less than 21,000 troops an enormous number. The 'Bag' was 400 Boer killed or wounded with 1000 surrendered. Hardware including many field guns, abandoned, due to shortage of ammunition and mobility problems, was also captured. For some time now the Boers had been running out of Mauser bullets and had been rearming with Martini rifles and ammunition captured from the British.

To add to the general confusion on the veldt thousands of untended cattle and sheep were running loose, though this was never a situation that would have lasted for long. Fresh meat was at long last on the menu!

While French's success looked perfectly respectable in a report, real problems were not being addressed. Very few of the hard core of fanatical Boers had been captured, and they were still active in the veldt from which they would emerge to fight and then melt away again.

The British army now comprised 240,000 troops, a third of which were mounted, though mostly only half-trained, on unacclimatised horses. The Boers were reduced to 45,000 men and youths, of which about 13,000 were fanatical veterans with the remainder either too old or too unwilling to fight and on the brink of surrender.

There was also the growing scandal of the concentration camps, those huge secure communities of Boer prisoners of war and their families. By the second quarter of 1901 there were 77,000 white and 21,000 coloured detainees, all being held in appalling conditions and all needing to be fed and cared for. At home a political storm was brewing in Parliament.

But the 'Drives' went on, the next major one planned for the Northern Transvaal beyond Machadodorp into unsurveyed country where, up till now, few of the British had penetrated.

Since Kruger's departure for Holland in 1900, the rudderless Transvaal Government had drifted baseless and was now settled in the mountains East of Lydenburg, (now the Kruger National Park) at Paardeplatz. Here they ran the remnants of Government business, issuing paper money, appointing magistrates, and even maintaining their own postal system. As long as there was a functioning government they reasoned, it ought to be fought for and retained. However, Paardeplatz was not to be the seat of government for long. The newly-arrived and renowned Sir Bindon Blood had his orders to clear Paardeplatz and Pietersburg, including the Delagoa Bay Railway, the latter constantly under attack from the Boers.

It was Blood's first posting outside the Indian sub-continent for 20 years and he was described, rather glamorously by a contemporary, as "possessing a fine head of silver hair with a moustache to match."

He was as successful as French had been. He captured a large number of non-combatants mostly the aged and war-weary, and his men looted and burned many farms; all of it, as usual, having little effect on the fighting Boers who again slipped away into the veldt. Similar 'drives' were taking place in the Orange Free State, employing thousands of troops.

If Kitchener could only have shrunk the vast terrain through which the Boers moved the war might have justified Roberts' claims and ended sooner. The next best thing was to restrict in some way the Boers' movements through the veldt. Barbed wire and the Blockhouses were what Kitchener hoped would do precisely this.

Invented by an anonymous and probably unrewarded major in the Engineers, the Blockhouse looked like a water tower and hundreds were situated along the railway lines at intervals of one and a half miles, each in sight and firing range of its neighbour. Every blockhouse held seven men and all were connected by telephone. Barbed wire plugged the spaces in between.

They were an immediate success. Raids on the line were slashed from thirty a month to virtually nil; convoys travelled unmolested and, most importantly, Boer movements between districts were greatly restricted and hampered.

At the beginning of May 1901, the start of winter in the Southern Hemisphere, Kitchener had at last succeeded in boxing the Boer in.

CHAPTER THIRTEEN

Lydenburg to Cable Hill Pretoria 1901

13 May 1901. Lachlan to Joan. Lydenburg

26 April - We started at 2 a.m, and were taken by Mr Schroder, a surrendered Boer, to Nicks Nek 7 miles off, overlooking a valley where we hope to catch Silverman and Co. We got up as the sun was rising, and cooked our breakfast. We had a lovely view all round and could see our troops moving about. We were 'stops', *(a shooting term referring to a person posted to keep the game within range)*. 72 Boers, 1 pom-pom, 600 cattle, and 1000 sheep were caught and sent in to Lydenburg. I believe there were others besides, but I am not sure if Schoeman escaped. He is an awful brute I believe. We got back to camp at 7.15 p.m., a long day.

28th - To Boschfontein, 8 hours, a very pretty road, little farms along the Watervall river, with the Steelkampf Berg rising on either side, tobacco, oranges, bananas etc. growing. We had lunch. I had just got back from hunting through a house where many novels were rumoured to be (we found Dutch Euclids, Homers etc.) when the familiar sound of bullets whistling past us began. Everyone turned out, and as luck would have it, it began to rain hard. We got on a ridge and began to shoot towards where we thought the sound came from, and in 10 minutes it stopped. No one was hit. It was some of those blackguards sniping to amuse themselves. The worst part was getting wet.

That morning I was advanced guard and a certain Mr Routenbach surrendered to me. He waved a flag. He is a typical Boer and rode a white pony. I have his Mauser with his name carved on it. His home was near our camp, and Col Burney allowed him to get some of his things from it, and then the sniping began, and he returned minus the pony, saying that it was taken by 3 Boers.

29th - To Boschoek at 3.45 a.m., a hilly bad bit of road. I was rear guard and it was an awful job getting started in the dark. We had a flock of sheep that would not be driven and 2 cows and calves that were most obstreperous. There were some Boer families in wagons we were bringing in. They are splendid bullock drivers, far better than natives, even the kids of about 10. They had a frightful shaking up over the stones etc. They ran one of our wagons over a great rock and it took us 1 hour to get it started again, which we did by hitching the oxen onto the back of the wagon. About 10 men hanging on to the pole were jerked in every direction when it kicked over rough ground. Rather dangerous!.

Boshoek is a high bare hill overlooking the Lydenburg valley, very cold. Shoerman's laager was there for a long time; his little turf bivouac still remains.

1 May - We built sangas. The nights are very cold.

2nd - I rode with Tytler to Tante's farm 3 miles out. We took 40 men and the pom-pom. Mrs Tante and 4 or 5 small boys were there. We bought a lot of fowls and vegetables which took a lot of catching.

3rd - Lumsden visited other farms returning with 9 pigs and a cart-load of oranges. V. Gordon took some wagons with stores to Boschfontein which he handed over to the Mounted Infantry. He returned with 1 Boer, surrendered, who lived at Belfast.

5th - As usual we spent trekking. Off at 4.30 by moonlight and occupied a hill overlooking a valley through which the Roos-Senekal road runs. We had breakfast and watched several farms where women and natives were walking about. In one was an immense flock of white geese. There were many sheep and cattle, the latter were miles away. Two Boers, who rode about from farm to farm, were objects of much interest but out of range. C Company, when climbing the hill, put up 2 Boers on horseback just in front who cantered off and they mistook them for their own Mounted Infantry, but then found the place they left, where there was a pair of field glasses, blankets, etc. which they were in too great a hurry to take, showing that it was a Boer outpost.

Later on we heard guns and could see figures riding about the hills opposite, then some shrapnel bursting, and then heard independent rifle fire, which continued till afternoon. Then we saw a lot of mounted men come down into the valley below us and collect horses, sheep, etc. We were not sure if they were Boers or M.I. so Col Burney told the pom-poms to fire at them but wide. They got into a donga, and when they came out we put 2 shells over their heads, but as they came on quite unconcernedly we assumed they were M.I., even though they took no notice of our signal.

They turned out to be Boers escaped to Roos-Senekal, the 'Black Watch' failing to stop them. We heard that they and our own M.I. had a spirited action with luckily no casualties, and then we fired the pom-pom at them, so there was rather a mix up. We got in after dark having walked 14 miles. Smith-Dorrien is off to India and South Africa loses a most competent general.

7th - Lumsden, Scott the pom-pom man, and self got up a little expedition to loot some farms about 4 miles out. We took 8 men, some on mules and some in the cart as escort. We found a lot of pumpkins and some forage, and I managed to shoot 4 guinea fowl and 6 tame pigeons, tho 2 guinea fowl were lost. Scott also shot one. When we got to camp we found four weeks' mail in. Four interesting letters from you. I wish we could fly across to Rome for a bit. Another batch of time-expired men returned to Lydenburg to go home. We are getting weaker and weaker. It is very sad.

8th - I took Harmer (in the Rifle Brigade, doing Brigade transport officer), Spry, ADC to Parkes (an awful ass, and thinks himself a very clever chap and invariably causes great confusion), and another ADC in the R.B. to Broekman's farm to shoot guinea fowl. We got there and after some trouble found a great pack of birds in some mealie fields. We had only got one when Spry gave the alarm that the Boers were on us. He was not shooting, so we had to run for our horses. Mine was a broken-winded old brute and had tied himself up in a knot. We galloped to some rocks and then examined the Boers through glasses. There were about 20 men on ponies with rifles about 2000 yards off and as our escort of 2 mounted signallers had not returned we were afraid they were prisoners. However, there were others much nearer driving cattle etc., who we saw were natives, so we knew they could hardly be Boers, also they had not fired at us. We found out from these that it was a native commando after Boers, so we waited for them.

They were a weird crew, some on foot, others mounted on donkeys or ponies, all with guns, (some our own rifles), also Mausers, Martini's, flintlocks and other strange weapons, and all had knobkerries and assegeis. They had no English hardly. One extraordinary old fellow pointed to himself and said 'Matches', which appeared to be his name! He then illustrated how he had assegeid and shot the luckless Dosh-maan (Dutchman) as he called them. They really had had a skirmish and killed 2 Boers, and captured their cattle and ponies which they were driving into Boschoek. They also explained that they nearly shot us, but recognised we were not Boers in time. It was too late to go on shooting so we returned to camp, the immortal Spry firing with his Mauser at vultures near camp.

The natives gave a great war dance and Mr Jacobus, their leader, sitting on his pony, made speeches, and shook the different heroes by the hand. They performed in turn, firing off guns, dancing, and mimicking a battle, while the rest sang in chorus. Matches I also saw was pulling out the entrails of a sheep with his bare hands and much apparent relish.

9th - We came here 10 miles, all downhill and a good road. We had had quite a pleasant little jaunt. Colonel Burney, who is a ripper, was there. He got a wire to say he was given a C.B. and all the men turned out and cheered him. They did not do the same for Macbean, who also got a C.B. That afternoon a good few of us bathed in the Spekboom river, but it was too cold to be pleasant. There is little to do here. There are some people to call on, but not up to much. The Macintyres are the most respectable. He is a mine owner, and has a lot of daughters from 14 downwards. We go and get tea and play croquet with them, but it is not very exciting.

Yesterday, Sunday, we had a service. A Company goes to Machadodorp in an hour's time, taking the mails. Tomorrow morning we start out at 3 a.m. over to Paardeplatz and the Mauchberg. We will probably end up at Nelspruit on the railway. It is rough country that way.

21 May 1901. Lachlan to Father. Nelspruit

15 May - We started for Nelspruit. Reveille at 1.15 a.m., breakfast at 1.45, parade at 2.15 and we climbed slowly up to Paardeburg as rear guard. There was a very ancient moon which gave a little light, and I was pretty cold. At the top, which we reached after daylight, we halted to let the bullocks graze. There were a dozen or so very strong forts that would hold 2 to 3 hundred men. We climbed right over the top of the Mauchberg, over 8000 ft. above the sea. The road was very bad and the Royal Irish wagons delayed us as usual, tho we got everything in by daylight. The latter were just below the highest point on the road which is the highest in South Africa.

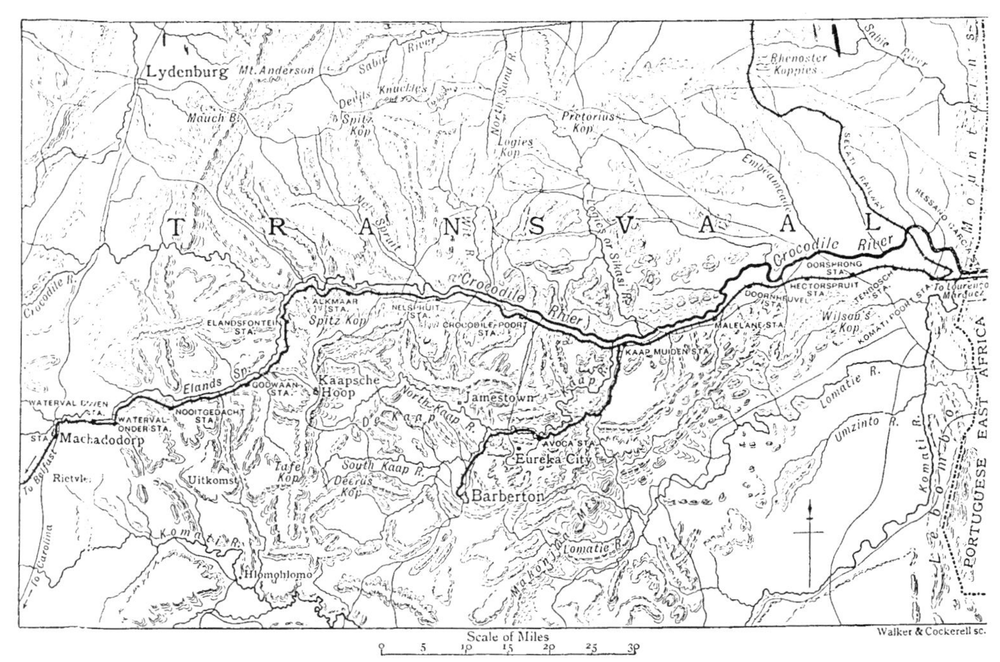

MAP OF THE DISTRICT NORTH AND SOUTH OF THE RAILWAY FROM MACHADODORP TO KOMATI FOORT.

16th - Off by 5.30. Today's march of 12 miles was interesting. We began our descent to the low veldt. The view was magnificent, hill after hill of all shapes and sizes stretching in every direction with the giant Mauchberg and several others about as big to back it, and the sun driving away the mist as it rose. After a mile or so of downhill we came to the Hell's Gates, where the road turns abruptly and goes down a regular staircase in quite the worst bit of road I have ever seen, which is saying a lot. It takes one's breath away, and is about a mile long, with many turns and breaks. About 100 yards of it had a slope of 2 over 1, and all steps and boulders. Strange to say we got all down without accident. We outspanned for two hours at midday and then went over the Devil's Knuckles and camped in a grassy little valley where there was a very pretty waterfall running out, tree ferns, very big ones, and all sorts of plants and bushes growing around it. The place was called Klipgat.

17th - We were rear guard, not starting till 9.30 a.m. Still a hilly road but greatly improved. We passed within 2 or 3 miles of Spitzkop, a very striking hill, conical with a curious top that looks as if it is pointed, but is not, having a rocky precipice like a barrel in shape. The 92nd went by it with Buller; our road branched off south. Three Boers were brought in by the 'Black Watch' from a farm where they were breakfasting. The B.W. said they were fired at with revolvers. I have a good bandolier off one of them who said he was General Viljoen's brother. They are all genuine fighters, not the usual old man who surrenders. We were rear-guard and got into our camp at Tweefontein across a drift in the afternoon, distance 12 miles.

18th - To Boshy Kop, 12 miles, a cold morning. Waded a drift at start. 3 Boers surrendered at a farm we passed; the road as usual hilly and bad now and again. We had accumulated a considerable number of Boer families. They are not attractive. The average that I have seen are dirty, ugly and foul-mouthed, if anything worse than the men, though of course there are exceptions. Their wagons went last, and having few oxen were pretty slow. One wagon with a family on board got left rather behind at a farmhouse and some Boers began sniping the M.I. who were with them. 4 horses were hit but luckily no men.

The Boer women were delighted. They began to revile them and hoped they would be all shot. It seems a pity that they all have to be fed by the Government in laagers, while the families of loyalists and refugees are many of them starving and dependent on private charity while the war goes on.

Sunday 19th - We started about 8 a.m. and should have got to our destination but the drift at Crocodile river was not very easy and, owing to one wagon sticking nearly the whole afternoon, by dark 17 wagons of Boer women and children were left on the wrong side. We were rear guard, and it was considered advisable that we should stay till daylight. Our baggage was gone into Nelspruit, 4 miles east and it got miserably cold. Luckily there was any amount of wood about, and we lit a great many fires. The men of course had an impromptu concert, various rival singers and funny men performing. Some of the groups around their fires were very good and it kept everyone's spirits up, but it was very cold all the same. About 11.30 p.m. our mess corporal and several servants very gallantly rode out from camp with food and great-coats, which was as welcome as it was unexpected. It was a slow night, and the poor Jocks were very cold.

20th - Early on, the remaining 17 wagons got across quite easily, and we waded. It was about 40 yards broad, with a 3 ft deep bank on each side. However by going slowly one kept dry enough with a kilt, but it was very cold. We got in by 11, across alternative muddy spruits and sand. Nelspruit is the usual station buildings, and boasts one store, and an old Boer Hospital building, and like the rest of the Crocodile valley is an awful fever hole.

CONSTRUCTING A BLOCKHOUSE: FILLING IN THE WALLS WITH SHINGLE.

LIFTING ON THE ROOF.

23rd - We all left Nelspruit that morning. H and half G got out at Alkmaar, ten miles up. Nearly all our men were sent off to different blockhouses on the line at the different Kilos. The Welsh Regiment have detachment at these places, but there are scarcely any of them left owing to fever, which has been very bad. Sworder and I went for a ride in the bush, we took guns but saw nothing. I shot 2 or 3 doves, but they are not much sport. There are lots of buck, but difficult to get and also partridge and koran. This is very rough hilly country; the river is lovely, very clear in parts like rivers at home, though most of the banks are covered with thick bush and trees. It runs just below here. There are plenty of fish in it and eels, though we have not yet caught any. We have out a night line for eels. Sworder and I share a tent with a floor of boards! The men are in tents and are comfortable. All these stations have their plantation of gum trees which look nice and are good against fever. 35 men are away with fever, even the Doctor is pretty bad.

25th - Unloaded some blockhouses to be erected. We have taught the Welshmen, 3 very good fellows, bridge and play every night. More men down with fever.

26th - I went by train and visited our blockhouse up the line and chose sites for two others, inspected a drift, and distributed native boys at each post to do intelligence work.

27th - I started work on the blockhouse - a round one. First a wall, over 2ft high and 3 ft thick, and on top of this a corrugated iron wall made double, so that 6" of shingle can be put in to it to make it bullet proof. I had 14 natives, and we finished the one at kilo 146, bar the roof, which is rather complicated We got back by the last train, having started at 6 a.m.

Undated - probably early June. Father to Lachlan. 40 Grosvenor Square

Last mail has brought news of 6 May to me, and of following week to Joan! We are glad to think that your sores have gone, not to return I hope. As for the scars, time will soon take them away. I fancy a good many will have them.

Joan and I go home tomorrow night. We have had a hard week of amusements, with dinners and 4 operas. Tonight she and I have dined alone here, and are just going to your Aunt Margot who has arranged a very smart dinner for Lord Milner, who is the hero of the hour, as he deserves to be, I think.

She seems to have got the most celebrated beauties in London, three or four of them, but several of her lions have failed her, such as Arthur Balfour. They are going to the Tenniel dinner. Tenniel is at last retiring from Punch. Joan may be able to tell you more of it tomorrow.

This morning we went to Lord Balfour's room at the Scottish office to see the King give away medals to 300 returned men including Buller and Roberts. I could not go until it was nearly over, but it was a fine sight. I believe the feature of the day was Sir H. Trotter moving a squad of generals who went through their drill vilely! They were a mixed lot who came up for medals, generals and bishops, doctors and volunteers, uniforms and plain clothes, tall hats and billycocks! The Queen stood the whole time and bowed to each man! I wish you had been among them. Captain Madden who was married to Miss Macpherson-

Grant last Thursday had to come back for his. Mrs Botha's arrival has set everyone speculating about a speedy peace again. I trust it may be so.

You seem to have been in a pleasanter country lately. It must have been a treat to get vegetables and oranges.

Thursday - Well, we saw Margot's band of Fair Ladies; Lady Aberdare, Lady Dunscombe, Lady Curzon and the rest. I had the honour of a chat with Milner. I did not learn any secrets! He actually remembered having met me for 10 minutes 11 years ago! It must be very useful having such a memory. Joan is sending you a proper account of the medal giving. I dare say you will never get it. Call on Hercules Tennant if you find yourself in Pretoria.

10 June 1901. Lachlan to Joan. Alkmaar

I am afraid it is some time since you have had a letter from me, as I stupidly missed the last mail, so this will arrive with one for father. We are still sitting here quietly enough, and until we go home I am quite content to stay, as we are comfortable and have not much to do and, for the winter, this is a delightful climate, never really cold nor hot, no rain, and just occasional frosts at night. It is very pretty too, ranges of broken hills on both sides of the valley with the old Crocodile running past about a hundred yards away with splendid bathing and a certain amount of game, though frightened away by the troops who have been here so long. The chief drawback is the fever which has been very bad indeed, but it is quite safe now for people who have never had it. Sworder and I have been out after buck several times. Usually we ride, which is not much use, as they stay by day in thick bush, where we cannot ride.

30 May - Sworder and I had to do a rough survey of our section of the railway, showing all the fortifications and the river. I took from here about 7 miles, towards Elandshoek. The line is marvellously curly, roughly following the river, though now and again leaving it a long way off. It was rather interesting work, the first sketching since I left Sandhurst. Luckily I managed to borrow a compass and protractor from Cobb, an R.E. chap putting up blockhouses from here. I did about 4 miles the first day and walked back after dark. The days are very short and it is dark by 5 p.m.

Col Parkes' column came in that morning, crossing the river by a drift a few miles up. It is a bad drift and several of the Royal Irish were drowned in fact. A considerable portion of the column stayed across until the following day. They had done nothing but capture a lot of families, who were promptly sent off to Middleburg.

31 May - Rode out and finished sketch. Tommy, the pony, behaved very well. I led him across all the bridges including one very slippery with new foot plates between the rails, and very high above the water. He is a fidgety little brute as a rule, but in a bad place very clever, and quite good at climbing kopjes. I dined and played bridge with Gordon, the gunner major, who was at Broochhoek with us, also Scott and Adams, all of whom were with the column.

Sunday 2 June - Macneal performed a little service in the clump of Gum trees. Spens and old Miller went through the Nek Spruit, Sworder accompanying them on his way to Barberton to buy mess stores. Next evening Murray, the last newly-joined, arrived with 12 men for H Company. He had brought out a draft of 146 men, and seemed a good chap.

The 3 gunners dined with us, so we were a tight fit in a small room. Sworder got back on 6th with plenty of stores, reporting that Barberton was a ripping place. He spent a night at Kaap Muiden and another at Nelspruit.

7th - The long-looked-for Scots Fusiliers arrived but 2 officers only, and the poor Welsh got away. They had had enough of this place, having lost 80% from fever; the rest also looked absolutely played out. They are excellent chaps. Sworder and I shifted into their room, where we each have a spring bed, and are more comfortable than we have ever been. A glass door opens onto the platform. There is also a window and it is a trifle public, but that is nothing. Spens and Miller went through from Machadodorp to Nelspruit, and brought the news that we were to go to Pretoria to rest and refit, not later than the 20th.

That afternoon I went out with Kennard to try and shoot partridges across the river, which we crossed by a rough bridge put up for sheep. He has got a good setter, but we only got one and came in to tea.

8th - Macneal, Sworder, and Kennard with 4 or 5 natives went out and got 9 birds, which is wonderfully good for this place. The natives were very useful and keen.

9th - Padre Robertson came down from Elandshoek and gave us a short service. Woodside came with him. It was a rainy sort of day. L'Estrange, the new doctor, has also got fever though not badly.

10th - The Colonel has just gone by for Elandshoek. He seems quite pleased at the idea of Pretoria, but we shall probably be picketing hills all the time, and then go off to Krugersdorp or some such place to hunt De la Rey. That was a stiff bit of fighting the other day, and a fine charge for the guns though you know a lot more about it than we do I expect.

Your last letter was when you had just got back again. You and Grandmama have had a very successful visit. Venice must be a delightful place. I hope we shall be able to see all these delightful things some day, as you said. Your foreign letters are exceedingly interesting. You certainly did not waste much time. How is the fascinating Mr Chapman?

Give my love to Grandmama and Nanny, and please thank the latter very much for the socks, which arrived from Elgin quite safe. I am afraid I forgot to do so before.

I am very sorry to be leaving this place, as it is so comfortable. We have also struck the best cook I've ever come across out here, which is a great thing, and the work is very easy and the climate delightful. Love to Father and Mildred and the kids. I expect this fearful note paper will surprise you, but it is just to show what can be grown on the veldt. This is a stupid letter, but there is little to tell you and I am feeling very stupid.

PS Many thanks for the little photo, which is excellent.

22 June 1901. Lachlan to Father. Between Belfast and Wirfontein

I am very sorry I missed writing last mail. We have been having quite a good time at Alkmaar and are now en route for Pretoria.

13th - I and Bray, my servant, started at 11 a.m. for Barberton to get some stores up. Bray distinguished himself by forgetting the box of provisions. Luckily we never wanted them, as there is a store at Kaap Muiden where one can get very good meals. We were kept 22 hours at K.M. which was annoying. Barberton is a delightful little town nestling under a range of steep hills, very fertile; splendid fruit, flowers and vegetables, with a lovely view over the plain to the hills out west. They are very well off, fairly good shops, tennis, cricket etc., and even dances. Fever and horse sickness are rather drawbacks in summer. I left at 10 a.m. and reached Alkmaar by 6 p.m., travelling with Boward, who has a furnished van in which he goes round inspecting guns and ammunition.

Next day Bruce went down by the river and put up a 10 ft crocodile sunning itself on the bank. He nearly walked on it in the long grass. The armoured train was in the station so we got dynamite and the whole camp turned out with guns and cameras, to blow it up. However the fuse went wrong and the croc had gone! Bathing was off after that.

19th - Spens and Col. Burney came in with the latter's column in the early morning, having killed 7 Boers and captured a few. We were very busy making preparations for a gymkhana that was to be held next day for the benefit of the column on our race-course. We had a splendid circular track, half a mile from the station. Mott, Sworder, Murray, Bruce and self, with our respective servants and 5 natives worked desperately hard putting up jumps. We made five. The first was a great work of art, a sort of Irish bank, built with sods and sticks to peg them together with a ditch on either side, about 3 ft high, a total width of 10 feet, flanked by bushy trees cut down for wings. Then we had a low post and rails, then a hedge. Macneal presented the 'Alkmaar Gold Cup' a white-enamelled soup tureen done up with yellow paint and a little picture of men racing on horseback, by Mott. My pony, or rather Maclaren's was not allowed to run, as it was thought that others would not have a chance against it. It was supposed to be bigger than the rest.

The race was awfully funny, many of the ponies never having jumped. There was frightful confusion at the first jump, all refusing, however they all scrambled over after a little. There were several falls. There were only two entries for the mule race, and it was a dead-heat the first time. The mules evidently thought they were being driven in harness, they could hardly be separated. We also had a flat race for ponies, and a foot race for men, altogether a very successful afternoon and a fair attendance.

Yesterday Murray and I left at 6 a.m. with 70 men, and we were all perched on trucks, and the smoke was beastly. We reached Onder in good time, but had a long wait while the one-cog engine took up one train, and then ours, each a different journey. We dined with the Liverpools and had a splendid hot bath, sleeping in a railway carriage. I am going to stay 2 days with Graham Tennant at Middleburg on leave.

3 July 1901. Lachlan to Joan. Cable Hill, Pretoria

Your last to hand from the Boltons. I suppose by now you have been at home for some time after your long round of travels and sight-seeing.

Last time I wrote was after arriving from Middleburg I think. We have not been doing anything particular I bought an excellent pony for £16, and a brand new saddle, rugs etc. for £5, not a bad bargain. The pony is worth £20 and he is a good stayer of the regular Boer type, very clever over rough ground, and has a good mouth besides being a respectable size, considerably better all round than the kind of beast dished out to the M.I. We live in tents, but there is the house of an ex-publican across the road which we commandeered and which is very comfortable There is a dining room, and we have purchased glasses, crockery etc., so that it looks most respectable. Also we have an anteroom carpeted and furnished with arm chairs, tables etc., besides a kitchen and store room.

We have our detachment cook in the mess as the proper one got drunk and fought one of the waiters. He is a very fine cook, quite a South African dream in his way. HQ arrived en bloc on the 28th; 2 colonels, 1 adjutant, 1 doctor, 1 divine, 1 quartermaster.

28th - Allen and I with half G Company were shot off here at 8 a.m. Cable Hill is one of the Mahaliesbergs and is on the west of the Pietersburg railway facing Wonderboom, another fort on the east. We are about 2 miles from Daspoort where the camp is and 5 miles from Pretoria.

There is a wire cable whereby all kit and rations are sent up. Sacks of stores are hung onto the top lift, and the weight of them descending fetches up the stuff down below. There is a steep and winding pathway up which one has to climb, and six donkeys which carry up water in curious bags slung over their backs. One however has just died and another is lame. The panorama from up here is lovely. North it is very flat with a few dotted little kopjes, and one can see for about 40 miles.

Pretoria from Cable Hill July 1901

Pretoria due south, looks lovely, nestling between the hills and half-hidden by the gum trees all over it. East and West are nothing but hills, while along the little river are fields of young corn, farms and gum woods, which gives a welcome touch of colour. The kind Government have provided one Mounted Infantry cob for the use of the officers, quite a respectable animal but a bit sick of it's life. He lives below with my pony in a shed at the base of the cable. Six ponies belonging to the ration cart, and a lot of Royal Engineers' donkeys, engaged in building a block house, also live there, so my pony gets plenty to eat which is a great relief. Also he is away from prying eyes as I believe there is an order out that all officers with horses they are not entitled to must hand them in to the Remount people. Anyhow he is not a government pony, so if he ever has to go, I hope to get £20 for him.

We have a little tin house to live in up here. It has a dining room, a sitting room and two diminutive bedrooms, and it is furnished. The men have a great blockhouse where we also go if attacked. There are also two others though one is still building. Altogether it is very comfortable, though it is a terrible climb to get back when coming from town. One of us has always to be here, so we take it in turns to go away.

30th - I visited a farm through the poort and was lucky enough to get 2 doz. eggs at 4d each, quite fresh too. I had to carry them a mile or two in a haversack and unfortunately broke three when the pony swerved and they all leaked through the bottom, however the rest were excellent, and are not yet finished.

1 July - Allen went in, so I spent rather a dull day. We inscribed our names in Kitchener's visitors' book. He lives in a gorgeous house in the town. All the bigwigs of every description have a house and do themselves A.1. I am unlucky enough to have got a veldt sore from a shaving cut, however Woodside cauterised it with Nitrate of Silver - a very good cure if the thing is young enough. I have also one on each fore-finger, which are very slow in going, but do not bother me much. They are horrid things to get free of. Ointments, I think are quite useless If you cannot cauterise them, nothing but cotton wool poultices seem to be any use. It is a slow job but they are nothing to worry about, unless really bad, though they leave huge scars.

11 July 1901. Joan to Lachlan. Drummuir Keith

I have a very delightful letter to thank you for this mail, written from Alkmaar, thank you very much for it. We were very glad for many things, especially that you were to go to Pretoria to get out of the fever district and to get your comforts and rest. But, at the same time, refitting sounds as if you were not coming home, alas.

Since I last wrote to you, we have had the hottest week I have ever remembered here. I have enjoyed it immensely. I love the warmth as long as I can be lazy and sit about, which I need hardly say I have done. The hottest it went to, was I think 82.

Miss Burnett Ramsay also arrived that evening and stayed till Tuesday. We all like her immensely. You will be amused and surprised to hear that she brought me a present from you! A packet of compressed tea which you had once given her. It was very dear of her to think of it, and it is delightful to think that it was yours, and that you touched it and carried it. It will be kept as a precious relic! She was very sweet to me about you. She came and sat in the schoolroom and told me everything she could think of, and I showed her all your photographs and anything that had to do with you. She was very interesting too about all her experiences. What an interesting time she had, and how deeply desperately do I envy her. She had two books of photographs; so many of graves and cemeteries, so terribly sad. It made me realise how tremendously deeply thankful I must be that you have been spared, my dearest.

Yesterday evening I went for a ride and got caught in very heavy rain though it was rather nice and refreshing. The thunder growled around but did not come near. The roads are as hard as iron, so I went very slowly. It rained steadily for about an hour and must have done a lot of good, but instead of the thunder having cleared the air I think it is hotter than ever today.

Mildred has got a young jackdaw (the older one came to a violent end while we were away). He is a very fascinating person and looks unutterably wicked. It is great fun stuffing food down his throat and, though he can feed himself now, he is too lazy to do so. He is not of a clean nature and absolutely refuses to get into his bath and pretends he is going to die when he has been dipped.

11 July 1901. Lachlan to Joan. Cable Hill, Pretoria

I don't think it is your turn for a letter but I can't quite remember, and I have an envelope addressed to you, which is too valuable to be wasted, and rather old to wait. Your last letter from London ended in an abrupt and undignified manner, with something illegible scrawled at the end. I imagine Father was yelling at you not to miss the train; do not let it occur again! The medal distribution must have been very funny to watch, but an awful ordeal to undergo. I think I would prefer it by post, or in some such easy way. Poor old Bobs I hear was turned back by a policeman when trying to escape by a private exit, and every one else had to follow him back by another way.

I have a great admiration for him as a general, but I think he is more responsible than anyone else for the continuation of this war, owing to the idiotic way he treated the people, making them take an oath, and then be free to do as they jolly well pleased when we were out of sight. It is of course easy to be wise afterwards, but he must have been warned by tons of colonials all along, who were always saying it was not the way to treat the Boer, and they were quite right. The only advantage is that there will be fewer left to look after at the end than if it had ended much earlier. And we are helping to rid the world of a lot of promiscuous ruffians. Lyttelton, talking about the end coming this month, was talking bosh - unless a miracle takes place in the next 3 weeks. It may happen gradually in another year. I shall always expect to have another year to do, till we get on board ship, to avoid false hopes, and even then I have heard of people who were hauled ashore at the last moment and kept here.

However, to return to the daily round etc.; last Friday, after getting some eggs and having a gallop on the white pony who is a clinker - I can't get a name for it - Allan went in. I was then much disturbed by a long and ominous heliogram from Gordon, wanting a certificate that I had drawn a horse from the remounts, and harness from the Ordinance. Also, for the Colonel's benefit and by 10 a.m., a written statement giving authority for my having done so, and what the very deuce I meant by doing what I did, and why the blazing Dickens I didn't do what I didn't - or words to that effect. As there happened to be an order out against people having horses, my conscience smote me, though there was something wrong, as I never drew anything from nowhere.

Then Allan came back with terrific accounts of the Colonel's wrath and Macnab's indignation and everyone else's dismay, because none of the horses were handed in. I would be lucky to escape with a slanging and the confiscation of the horse and any other property they might fancy.

We spent the evening trying to write out something that would appease everybody, inventing all sorts of excuses (more or less leaky) and bearing in mind that a soft answer sometimes, though rarely, turns away a Colonel's wrath. So next morning I went in with my precious document in fear and trembling, fully expecting to be torn from the horse and in bits, when 'mirabile dictu' every one was happy and in smiles from the Colonel downwards. The horse was left and I still have him and everyone else kept theirs.

The reason for the previous flumbustio and subsequent relenting was that poor I was supposed to have drawn all these things on the plea that I was a C.O. or something. Then the Colonel very nobly determined to risk censure and allow us all to keep our ponies, so every one is happy.

Lumsden and I watched our Mounted Infantry doing their first mounted drill. It was as good as a circus, though no one came off. In the afternoon some of us went to the Yeomanry hospital and had tea and listened to our band giving their first public appearance for over a year. They were not bad, and the sisters charming but limited. Dingwall arrived back from Capetown quite sober, but without the lion, Cecil Rhodes having refused him one.

Sunday - I sat here...

Monday - I went in and lunched with Charlie Russell, who seems quite well. He is paymaster of his Regiment, and expects to be made captain in consequence He is very busy all day at his office in the National Bank Buildings. I then called on Hercules Tennant, having plucked up courage to enter the law courts or rather Government buildings, a huge and very fine looking structure bequeathed to us by dear old Kroo before his departure. They were never opened, and only just finished, and cost about half a million. I found him in a very fine office, very busy. He was very pleased to see me, so he said, and having arranged to lunch one day at the club, I went off

Charlie Russell near Pretoria

I went to our egg farm at dusk and heard a fearful row through the poort. About 200 baboons had come and were very noisy. I also met an iguana, a lizard, about 4 ft long, who lives in river banks. He has a yellow stomach, and is said to be very poisonous I don't believe he is, but don't intend to experiment The natives use them as charms.

I keep the pony up here at night as there are so many horse stealing Bojas [sic]. It is not safe below, as he would probably be shot. They took some government sick horses from our egg farm the other night and incidentally shot two natives.

CHAPTER FOURTEEN

Pretoria 1901

11 July 1901. Lachlan to Mildred. Cable Hill, Pretoria

Just a note to thank you for the ginger cake, which as usual is excellent, and particularly useful just now, as we are only two on picket together, so it does us for many days. Tell Mrs McW she will be immortalised. We are on a most beastly hill, by far the worst in the place, and as there are no others here we can only get away every other day, and the other spends a solitary existence on a crag. Allan and I get on a bit better than formerly, though we do not always hit it off exceptionally well. When we have our tête-a-tête meals it brings home to me how awful it must be to be married if one of the parties turned out to be a bore. I shall have to be very careful.

We are the only picket that cannot be driven to, and where there is no proper place for horses. It is a very stiff and annoying climb to get up there in the dark, though there is a good but stony path. It takes about half an hour to do it comfortably from the bottom.

Anyhow I think it is no worse than being at Daspoort with Headquarters. There are very few of them, and they have a lot to do in the way of boards, court-martials etc. as well as constant orderly officer, escort duties etc. All the other forts around us have electric lights and telephones, which is another grievance we possess. We are so hopelessly inaccessible too that no one thinks of visiting us if he can possibly help it! Charlie Russell funked it the other day most disgracefully. He and Hercules Tennant are both very busy, and never get out of their offices all day, except for meals. Rather a beastly existence. Love to the kids.

By the way, this is my last bit of lovely pink paper, you ought to feel very honoured that your unworthy self should be the be the unworthy recipient. It is not to be met with every day.

18 July 1901. Lachlan to Father. Cable Hill Pretoria

Things are going on as usual. Yesterday a summary for July up to date came in announcing 72 killed, 60 wounded, 161 prisoners and 480 surrendered; 8800 horses and 22,800 rounds captured. This kind of thing is bound to tell on them in time. I wonder what the 8000 horses are - mostly mares and foals with those that have fallen out I suppose.

We get no news to speak of. I suppose you are the same, judging by the home papers. The weather is dry and very windy at night. This place is not nearly as cold as Johannesburg or Krugersdorp, where we were last year. The middle of the day is just right and, as we are not trekking, the nights do not much matter. Last Sunday I lunched with Hercules Tennant and afterwards we strolled to the Burghers' Park and listened to the band of the Fifth Fusiliers. It is quite a nice place, shady with a big fountain in the middle and walks all around. There are chairs and tables about with tea under the trees, quite like Europe for once in a way. A good many civilians of sorts turned up with the occasional top hat and black coat, and of course plenty of soldiers. Yesterday I lunched at Proclamation Hill, and it is a very uninteresting, bleak spot.

We are doing a lot more work than we ought. In camp we are always on Court Martials, Boards, etc.; they even fetch us down from these hills to do likewise. The men have a worse time, what with train escorts all over the country, guards, pickets and fatigues. We were told we came to Pretoria for a rest, but the work is double what it was at Alkmaar and those places. It is very useful having a pony here, as places are all so far apart.

Its always a very bad thing to be near a General Headquarters when one is supposed to be resting; though there are a few perks, such as seeing and talking to the opposite sex. But then the brave local staff officers, who have never heard a shot fired in anger, are usually well dug in, and the battle worn warrior has little chance with the girls. He's probably forgotten how to talk nice anyway!

25 July 1901. Lachlan to Joan. Cable Hill, Pretoria

Another week gone, and as far as we know nothing seems to be forrarder. This place is full of unsubstantiated rumours. The other day it was Botha killed, and as a matter of fact I believe a Botha was killed, but not the B. Also a convoy was captured near the Swazi border, and the Seaforth and Argylls lost pretty heavily, but we hear no more than that. Now everyone is wondering if it is true if M battery, RHA, was captured with its escort near Norval's

Port, and also if there was heavy fighting near Vereeniging and a train and 150 men were captured, and if De la Rey has taken the Knock. All this combined with the authenticated story of Steyn's narrow escape is rather depressing, though very vague; unfortunately rumours of bad news usually turn out to be true.

I also went to a tea-fight at No 7 General Hospital, the Colonel and a few others of our chaps went. The 5th Fusilier band were there, very poor. I knew nobody and it was exceedingly dull.

Sunday - Charlie Russell and a friend turned up here at 8 a.m. We were both in bed. They stayed to breakfast and I rode in with them; we had great fun at the Mounted Infantry jumps. They have put up 10 of all kinds. My pony was very good, so was his. I lunched with them and afterwards attended Mrs Kruger's funeral. Poor old lady, she has not been well treated by Oom Paul. The whole place turned out, or rather the civilians, and I never saw such a collection of Boers and Boeresses, many awful old scoundrels, very typically dirty and unshorn, everyone almost wearing deep mourning She was buried in the big cemetery. There was a service in Kruger's chapel, which is a curious and fantastic redbrick building opposite his house. It reminds me of the pictures on boxes of red and white bricks given to children. The service took so long we did not wait for the procession. There were cameras on every available roof in the neighbourhood, and many people brought Kodaks. There were very few soldiers.

In the afternoon I called on a Mrs Biccard with a friend. She is an educated Boeress, and talks English and she knows most of the Boer Generals and told us stories of De Wet. She was rather amusing, but refused to offer us tea, which annoyed us.

This morning I went in early and breakfasted with Charlie. Piet the pony came head over heels over a little sort of stream about 6 ft wide that we always have to jump going in. He was extremely careless, and we were both a bit shaken, but otherwise unhurt. I borrowed a nice pony of Charlie's and visited Dingwall at Shanzkop fort. He thinks he is very busy and scarcely ever comes in. I lunched at the Headquarters' mess and went afterwards to play tennis at the Pretoria Hospital, used for I.M.R. patients. They have one beautiful tennis court. There were a good many people, all very pleasant, and it was rather fun, a good many nurses and Doctors of course. I am so out of practice, I did not enjoy playing much, especially as some of them were very good. There was one quite pretty girl, the first I've seen almost, but I don't know her name!

All the between days I sit up here and there is not very much to do. I have taken up signalling in a mild way again, and get a little Helio practice by working up one of the many stations. I am no good at all yet. We can signal from here to Pienaar River on clear days, about 40 miles and also to all the intermediate stations, and it shows how flat it is beyond here. I am getting Maclaren's gun out as there are a lot of partridges on this hill and also some bucks.

Macneal is going to get some ponies down from Pietersburg from Hunter Blair, who will teach us polo. It will be great fun if it can be managed.

Father was asking what I wanted sent out. I was thinking that a good Kodak would be very useful; lots of people have them. So far I have held out, but my fall is only a matter of time, so I think it is an excellent idea. A motor car, speed 60 miles an hour also, though perhaps that cannot be managed so easily. It would do to hunt De Wet and Steyn. Thanks for letters, Love to all.

Gordon Highlanders signalling at West fort, Pretoria.
Photographed by A. T. Gordon.

The blockhouse programme intensified as the South African winter deepened. Successful as it was to prove to be, it did not entirely curtail the freedom of movement of the Boers.

Cable Hill must have seemed luxurious after 18 months of trekking and fighting and took some getting used to. The British were at last learning some of the tricks of the Veldt war and, as can be seen from Lachlan's letters from this time, there was growing confidence proportionate to the increasing demoralisation of the Boers.

On the 10 May 1901 there was a conference held to discuss the possibility of an armistice with the British Government. None present was keen to be thought of as an advocate of surrender and any decision was postponed until the intended Joint Council meeting to be held at Standerton in the Eastern Transvaal in June. Organising any conference was a difficult business, and Kitchener was determined to prevent this council taking place. Drives into the northern part of the country were stepped up, with a view to rounding up as many Boers as possible to dampen their fighting spirits further.

But, though they were as heartily sick of Kitchener as he was of them, the Boer leadership refused to give in. To quote Rayne Kruger;

"Against this continuous pattern of activity, and often entangled in it, the outstanding events of the winter of 1901 took place. Above was the winter sky, unflecked blue by day, a black, jewelled brilliance by night. On the yellow-brown veldt below were endless mounted columns, infantry trudging with mule or ox-wagon convoys or patrolling between blockhouses strung along shimmering railway lines, the untold miles of ravaged fields and smouldering farm houses, while weaving among all this rode keen-eyed and resolute men. In particular, the efforts of the Boer leaders to meet for their proposed conference spun a thread by which the developments of early winter may be traced".

So, these brave, determined men set out on their dangerous journey from all parts of the country. De la Rey and President Steyn went through the western Transvaal hunted by various columns, but managed to elude capture. At Vlakfontein, one of their party, Kemp, set the veldt alight by a trail of gunpowder, charging through the smoke, firing from the saddle.

In the Orange Free State there was another great drive of seven columns between Bloemfontein and Kimberly. This was simultaneous with another sweep between the Central Railway and Natal. Despite this frenetic activity they managed to slip through Kitchener's nets. He was particularly keen to capture the

Boer Administration - known these days because of its very unsettled existence as the Cape Cart Government - and he sent no less than 11 columns in what was a vain pursuit of the nomads.

On 12 June 1901 General Muller surprised 350 Australians at Wilmansrust on the Middleburg-Ermilo road and looted the camp, leaving the prisoners behind. What might have been only an embarrassing incident turned, however, into something nastier. The Australians were attached to a column commanded by a Cavalry General who did not like the Australians and who levelled accusations of cowardice at the men, calling them 'dogs'. The Australians mutinied and sparked off a military and political furore.

This and other successes for the Boers raised their morale and on 20 June at the Standerton Conference they unanimously decided to fight on with General Smuts appointed to lead an invasion of the Cape.

A conference of influential Boer leaders was something that the British could not afford to ignore and after the conference several attempts were made to detain these remarkable men as they returned to their homes But luck was with them and most managed to get away. One of the most dramatic of escapes is that mentioned by Lachlan in his letter. President Steyn and his presidential party planned to spend the night of 10 July at the town of Reitz, which had just been resettled by the Boers following a British evacuation. Recapturing towns was a typical Boer manoeuvre and, anticipating this, British forces returned under the cover of night to find the President and his entourage asleep and vulnerable.

All were captured, except for the President himself who, roused by his cook, jumped onto his pony and galloped away to freedom dressed only in his night shirt and cap, and with only a halter for a bridle. He left behind state papers and £11,500 in banknotes. De Wet was not caught as he was at a farm some miles off.

Smuts, who also escaped unharmed and unhindered, led a September expedition into the Cape, thereby creating a good deal of havoc and instability.

Kitchener was exasperated by the stubbornness of the Boers and his solutions for dealing with them became more menacing. He suggested such measures as resettling half the Boer population somewhere outside South Africa, shooting all rebels, and advocating a perpetual exile for all the leaders. In August he issued a proclamation which threatened just such retribution if the Boers did not surrender by 15 September.

PRETORIA 1901

To create a safe area and preserve some form of stable civilian life around Johannesburg and Pretoria, a line of blockhouses was built, starting at Mahaliesburg. Running thence, across the Vaal, it ended north of the railway at Kroonstadt, a distance of 150 miles. Though the blockhouses were 'mass-produced' the whole exercise must still have been a costly one. By the time the war ended, there were 8000 blockhouses standing. Meanwhile, the 15th came and went and Kitchener's threats of banishment and punishment were ignored.

The war was not over yet and there would be still a few surprises in store for both sides. The British had the upper hand, but the guerrilla war waged by the Boer was prolonging the conflict and costing the British taxpayer about £1 million a week. Predictably perhaps, the political parties were divided, but more importantly, the public at large was sick of it all.

1 August 1901. Lachlan to Joan. The Magazine, Pretoria

Here is August around again. The moors out here are in good condition; the heather, to be sure is rather backward, and birds scarce, but hawks are very strong on the wing, stones very plentiful, and most of the grass burnt, the weather of course being all that can be desired. I wonder what sort of 12th we shall have this year? Last year we spent it at Banks railway station as far as I remember, where the sport was rather poor.

We have left Cable Hill you see, after one month of that desirable and salubrious spot. Otherwise things go on as before. Allan went into breakfast with a friend, and I went out at noon when he returned. I borrowed Charlie's horse which dashed up and down various streets with his native, who was taking it to the hospital for me. When we got there I took Sister Alexander out for a ride on Piet, she of course providing a side-saddle. She was very keen on riding, but absolutely hopeless. If we went beyond the slowest canter she looked very funny, and her head looked as though it would be shaken off. She nearly had an accident as she rather lost her head once, and pulled hard at the wrong rein thereby nearly dashing into a row of gum trees. Luckily I was on that side and shoved Jack, a beast of ample proportions, and barged her off by superior weight, so after that I thought it as well to be very cautious. Jack could only trot or canter at a very rapid pace, and having no mouth nearly tore my arms out, so I was not sorry to get back to tea. We are not likely to ride again!

This place, as its name implies contains vast quantities of ammunition of all sorts, which I hope will not go bust before we go. It is a sort of little fort built by the Boers on the north side of the hills just south of Pretoria, near the artillery barracks. Allan and I live in one large room and we have made a low partition at one end where we sleep, and are going to divide the other half off by a curtain hung on a string from wall to wall for a living room. There is a great iron curtain which helps. Allan did a tremendous lot of shopping, buying plates, carpets, curtains, etc. and stores. The furniture we will sell to the people relieving us, as we did at Cable Hill. There was a sofa and a patchy looking table, much too small, and we bought a few chairs, so it is pretty comfortable.

I did a trek round some of our posts which occupy commanding positions on various kopjes in the S.W. neighbourhood overlooking some of the bleakest and most desolate country imaginable. We walked about 6 miles, then had lunch, and this afternoon visited the remainder on Piet, some 4 or 5 miles more. It is awfully warm here compared to our last place.

8 August 1901. Lachlan to Father. The Magazine, Pretoria

Only three days from the 12th and two to your birthday; I wonder if we shall be home for the next. This place is a great improvement on Cable Hill, and we are having a very good time indeed. One advantage is that we can both be out during the afternoon. One can dine out and we are comparatively close to everywhere. The weather is delightfully warm this last week, quite hot in the middle of the day and very fine.

On Saturday I had to attend a Court Martial at Proclamation Hill. After lunch drove out in a Tonga with the Colonel to hear our band at the I.V. hospital. The drive was like being at sea in a small boat, the roads are vile and the springs powerful. The hospital is very prettily situated out of the town in Arcadia. A lot of people turned up, and it is very nice sitting in the shade.

In the afternoon I went to tea and tennis at the Pretoria hospital, quite close. I got a lift into Proclamation and attended our weekly ‘at home’ with a band, tea, and many fair ladies who were rather fun. Allan and I were driven back by the Pretoria Hospital people, so we were lucky.

Wednesday morning I rode round all our blockhouses which takes a good time and in the afternoon played in a left-handed cricket match with pick-handles against No 7 General Hospital. It was very hot. The Col was skipper and we won.

Tea and Tennis at Pretoria Hospital

Lockley took me to tea with the Solomons, they have a splendid house. Mrs Solomon is a fine woman, and has a rather pretty and fast daughter; they hail from India. Mr Solomon is a judge, but did not appear. They do not look like Jews.

Yesterday, Adams the gunner and I took out two sisters of the I.V. Hospital for a ride. We went through Eloiffsdal, a fine gum wood. The trees are planted in very symmetrical rows, whichever way you look. We had tea with Holdsworth, who looks after the Birdcage where the Boer prisoners are; it was built by them for us, and is a long white-washed kind of shed, very bare and no floor, but quite comfortable and clean. There were a good many prisoners, who were all setting out for Bermuda the next day; the usual medley of old men and boys of all sorts and descriptions. They are visited by their friends, and do not seem unhappy, as they get plenty to eat and smoke, though I think they are kept considerably cleaner than they like. I am going with Maclaren to a picnic with No 7 General Hospital. It seems rather absurd wanting to picnic, after so often eating one's food off the veldt. You see we are having a fearful outburst of festivities.

16 August 1901. Lachlan to Joan. The Magazine, Pretoria

I got a fine long letter of yours from Inverness the other day, and a very disturbed note from Mildred, assuming that you had told me about some tremendous fire that spread into the Auchluncart woods, and seemed to be going strong still, wherever Broadwood is. I hope there is not very much harm done, though from her account it sounded very bad indeed. The weather seems to have been hot, and every thing must be very dry.

Here we continue as before. I do not think much of authoritative rumours and I imagine Kitchener from all accounts does not intend to send anyone home for a while if he can help it, and I think he is perfectly right. The Boers really seem to be losing heart a bit, and the very thing to buck them up would be to see a lot of troops clearing out of the country. They would at once conclude that the Russians or Turks were occupying London and De Wet had captured Capetown and was shelling the fleet.

Also the infantry are not much good to trek with just now; they are doing a lot of work holding places and communication centres, escorting trains, and convoys etc. Even in Pretoria itself there are only two regiments doing the work of three, which shows they are not too plentiful. As for withdrawing 70,000 men this Autumn, unless all the Boers surrender - which I bet they won't - it seems a preposterous idea. Personally I am having a pretty easy time and am in no hurry to go anywhere, except of course home.

That same afternoon I went to the picnic of No 7 General Hospital. Fountain Grove is a sort of pleasure-ground belonging to a derelict hotel about 2 miles down the Elandsfontein road near the railway. It is one of the prettiest spots about, being in a narrow valley, with a burn and lots of trees and shrubs and bamboos and other plants, though all very untidy now, as there is no one left to look after it. I only found it by accident, but partook of a magnificent tea. Then we went back. A lot of us rode, and many of the sisters went on in a gigantic bus, drawn by 8 mules and driven by a native, they looked very attractive with their blue and white dresses and scarlet capes. Most are pretty elderly, nearly all plain and all with any pretensions to look nice were ruthlessly sent home a long while ago, and no more came out. Very sad indeed!.

Charlie Russell, and Dickenson, his captain on the pay job, dined here with us; we played bridge. Charlie and I rooked the Captains, much to their annoyance.

Monday, we practiced knocking about at polo near the Proclamation hill mess, quite a good bit of ground. Piet ought to do well!

Tuesday, Alan and I dined with old Moulton Barrett (known as the Moulting Parrot). He and the other Ordnance Corps officers who have to do with the stores live here. They are quite close and have many fine trophies made of shells etc. It was not exciting.

Wednesday morning I attended a great hunt for three Boer spies supposed to be hiding in a certain part of the town, which was surrounded by a ring of sentries, while we proceeded with detectives and more men to systematically search every house and hut. It rather astonished the inhabitants. One of the three shot a detective a little while ago so we thought they might show fight. Of course we got nothing, except people who were not wanted.

Yesterday I rode around our blockhouses and then played a round of golf on the Yeomanry links with Boyd, one of the 53rd battalion. He is good. I was very much out of practice of course and the ground is hard and lumpy, and putting a nightmare. I have got a cold and have been a bit seedy for a few days, nothing to speak of but very annoying.

How did the 12th go off? We all would have liked a magic rug or something similar that day.

21 August 1901. Lachlan to Father. The Magazine, Pretoria

I got your letter last Sunday and was glad to hear the fire was no worse, though I suppose it will make a considerable difference to the number of birds in Towie for some time to come. It will have done a lot of good if it cleared away much of the scrub that covered so much ground.

I wonder if the 15 September will see any great change in the state of affairs. I see that some of the papers say we shall try anybody who kills soldiers for murder, like in America; quite a change for the soldier who has hitherto been killed with impunity. We shall make our motto 'nemo me impune lacessit' in future. Here, I am still in a kind of giddy society whirl. My last letter was on the 16th and that afternoon we had our first regimental game of polo. It was rather funny and slightly risky as our notions of crossing etc. were rather vague, but it was great fun. I rode Piet, the white pony; he does not think much of the game. There is too much pulling him about and the ball is rather hard on his shins; however he will not do badly I think.

Saturday - I lunched with Hercules Tennant at the club, and met Sammy Marks, one of the richest men in South Africa. He is a funny jolly looking little Jew, very ugly with a short grisly beard and he cannot read or write or sign his name, except in Hebrew. But he has a marvellous memory and is very clever. He owns the Erste Fabrieken drinks factory.

Sunday - I rode around our 6 miles of posts and lunched with Charlie. After dinner we all went to a great smoking concert given by the N.C.O.s in honour of Mackay, Hodgson and Mathers, who have got commissions, the former in the Kings Own Scottish Borderers, Hodgson in the Scots Fusiliers, and Mathers in the Royal Scots. It was great fun and the proceedings were fast and furious, beer and John Dewar whisky circulating vigorously. I was sitting between Mackay and a Sgt Farmer of the Camerons, who had just been to Maritzburg and got a VC, so I had one each side. I stayed a good while, but retired eventually somewhat overcome, and you will be shocked to hear that the remainder who stayed to the bitter end were, with a few exceptions, a great deal more overcome!. The Sgt Major finally broke the Pipe Major's head, so that the next day, the pipes were not heard at our Tuesday afternoon 'at home'. I rode home across country in the dark on a pony that did not know the way, without accident, and very rough it was.

Tuesday - I lunched with Charlie, and took him to our 'at home'. There were a tremendous number of nurses and some civilians; the band played nicely, and it was very pleasant. On the way from our entertainment Charlie and I swapped horses. His is a big raw three year old, full of beans with a snaffle on and a hard mouth. We had a gallop round the track around the race course where polo was going on. Coming to the gate in the palings, I could not pull up, and as luck would have it, two staff fellows were riding through. I just managed to stop in time to avoid cannoning them, but their horses got very excited hearing us galloping up behind, and began to fool around sideways and generally play the ass. I said I was very sorry but I could not pull the brute up, and just then one looked round with a horrible scowl, and we recognised the great K. himself. We walked off without a word. Charlie had the audacity to look around a little further on and says K. was grinning at us but it was rather embarrassing at the time.

This afternoon we had a great game of polo in camp. I can hit the ball much better, and I am beginning to grasp the rules. It was great fun, but very hard work. My legs are practically skinned and my wrist was paralysed towards the end.

22 August - This morning I tramped around our posts - we have taken over 2 more - so it is a long round. Yesterday Lockley and a party had to shoot a rebel, a very unpleasant job it must have been.

The cigars were excellent, and kept in splendid condition in spite of there being no tin. I have still a good many, but would like another 100 of the cheroots, or even 200. I think they were 14/- a box.

P. S. Hercules Tennant told me to remember him to you a long time ago but I believe I forgot.

Please tell Joan that Charlie Russell says she promised to send him out her photograph, the big one in evening dress like she sent me, but it has not come, and I said I would remind her, so tell her to buck up and send it.

30 August 1901. Lachlan to Joan. The Magazine, Pretoria

Many thanks for a fine long letter, containing the news of Alexander's arrival. That makes 5; how many more? Glad to hear Mildred is well.

I will wish you many happy returns of the day for your 20th birthday, but fear I ought to have put it in my last letter. How fearfully old we are getting. Even you are out of your teens, it does not seem at all right. Any way I wish I could be home to celebrate it, but I begin to think it will be lucky if I get home for your 21st. It sounds pessimistic, and is I hope wrong.

We were interested about the France and Turkey business. I think as far as S. Africa is concerned it is as well that nothing should have come of it, as it would have given point to some of Mr Steyn's utterances, and might have done a little damage. Kitchener's last proclamation seems to have done some good, more than is usual. We are going to advertise the farms of those in Commandos for sale after the 15 September, I believe. I think I must buy some and discover some gold mines!

I fetched up Jack, Charlie's horse. He is coming to Kroonstadt for a little, and I am taking care of him. He is a ripper, one of the finest looking in the place, and delightful to ride. He will be very fast I think, but is only three years old. He jumps like a bird, and hates traction engines!

I played tennis at the hospital, which is very close but a fearful dust storm came on in the middle which rather interfered though it was rather fun.

2 September 1901. Lachlan to Joan. The Magazine, Pretoria

I went round and visited Company Sgt Major Mackay's blockhouse, a neighbour on the Quagga section west of us. He gave me a beautiful new coat, which he insisted on my taking as it would not do for him, and no one else wanted one of the Government ones that are issued. I suppose he thought I was disreputable! He is an excellent fellow, one of the best fighters and hardest workers in the Battalion. I got your parcel of books, which were very welcome. I think your own production splendid. It is very clever and energetic of you to have done it so thoroughly. If I had realised what you were doing, I could have got you many photos quite appropriate, tho' as they are usually sent home by the takers to be developed I have not got them here. We must have a revised edition in a year or two if the war looks like ending, as there are sure to be many more names by then and I will try to get some photos of Banffshire people, and the regiment. Wednesday, our infernal old Court Martial reassembled, but we got away by 1 p.m.

Thursday, I lunched at the club, and saw old Tennant about returning his blooming pony. He was very huffy at my keeping it so long and then deciding not to buy it, but he wanted about twice its value, and anyhow he has now sold it to some one else and is quite pleased. I played some mild tennis at the Pretoria Hospital where there was a very pretty girl, a daughter of the Administrator or some big bug, which is a very unusual phenomenon.

Friday - I went into our Regimental Polo. However only four others turned up; they are rather lazy. Charlie returned from Kroonstadt and told us of a little trek they did. He said that the farms that had been burnt were roofed again, had new doors and windows and were swarming with pigs, poultry and children, so they do not starve.

CHAPTER FIFTEEN

Pretoria to Hornesnek 1901

4 September 1901. Lachlan to Mildred. The Magazine, Pretoria

It is some time since I last wrote to you. I hope you and the last of the tribe are still going on satisfactorily. I shall hope to see them someday, but Geordie will still be in time to come and hunt a stray Boer or two. The Boers intend their small children to carry things on in future years, and many of the little scoundrels show plenty of willingness judging by their behaviour and words, which would rather scandalise you I expect.

Lumsden told me he had heard that afternoon from someone who said his authority was impeccable that ten regiments are going home at the end of the month and some militia, and that we are among the ten. We don't mind being long-suffering, but it does amuse us, especially the silly reservists and militia men who occasionally display an extraordinary and fatuous desire to leave dear brother Boer to his own devices.

Our men had a lucky escape. We always furnish a train escort, but that very morning they happened to run two trains, and a party of West Ridings were going up. The major in charge tried desperately hard to go by the second train, but they had to go by the first and they got caught; ours went afterwards, thereby escaping. This occurred last Saturday morning near Waterval, in a low cutting.

Charlie took Jack, his horse, back that evening, so there is nothing but Piet left, my stud of three having dwindled. Jack is one of the best looking horses in the place; he is a colonial, but will be very fast and jumps like a deer. He is only three year's old, and a trifle lively on occasions. Yesterday I tramped around about 8 miles of out posts, pretty warm.

In the afternoon, the elderly but still youthful Miss Cross and the fat and flighty Jones honoured this establishment by coming up from the Pretoria Hospital to tea. It is about half a mile off, and they are a couple of nurses. I showed them around the ammunition. One vast room full of barrels of gunpowder and cases of cordite rather flustered them, and I had to hunt for their dog in it who was in turn hunting a cat. They seemed to think he would strike a match or something. We looked at countless shells from the 9.5 armoured-piercing shell to the pom-pom, and quantities of fuses etc. (a considerable amount being Boer stuff) by the light of dingy lanterns in the bowels of the earth.

I gave them a sumptuous tea in our gorgeous apartment and took them to the top of the hill behind here, whence a good view of Pretoria may be had, as far as Jo'berg south. They seemed to think it a great performance, as it is not high, and there is an excellent path.

Stopford (Secretary to Fiddes, the Transvaal Administrator) who looks far gone in consumption, came to dinner and we played more bridge. Our dinners are peculiar owing to the distance to the kitchen, which has to be outside for safety and the small numerical strength of the plates which want a deal of cleaning between courses, so the waits are somewhat protracted. The other night a serious thing happened. Bray evidently considered it to be genteel to give us microscopic portions of meat, and when we desired more, informed us that the cook (Green, Allan's servant) had inadvertently tipped the remainder on to the ground and both our guests with voracious appetites. Tableau!

Last night the cook forgot the lovely tinned whitebait expressly caught for the occasion, and the eggs on toast were so long in appearing we had to send and find out if he was trying to hatch them or not!

This afternoon I ambled round our posts on Piet. Spring is here at last, the air is full of moths and bugs who won't keep out of the candle as I write, and the veldt is putting forth a few shoots of grass from its murky bosom, which will soon become green. The mimosa and peach blossom is lovely, the trees are getting quite green. Please tell Joan if she is sending out any more socks to make them about 4 inches longer. I think I mentioned it before, but without result.

20 September 1901. Lachlan to Father. Skinners Court, Proclamation Hill

The wet weather arrived and the country is looking a little less dead. There will soon be respectable grazing. All the trees are in full leaf and the flowers are looking splendid.

Since I last wrote I have changed my abode, and am now in command of H Coy. Tell Joan I got her letter with a nice little bit of white heather. I wish it grew out here.

Old Bray, my servant has left me and I don't know why, as we were always the best of friends, though he has been rather short in the temper lately. He has gone to Lord K's bodyguard, 100 of the best men we could raise, so he is having a very easy time of it. I have now a man called Royston and he seems all right, though until we get to know each other's ways the change is tiresome. That afternoon we had our Puggle Gymkhana. Enclosed is a programme. We had any number of people down; one had to be nominated by a lady, and if you won she got the prize. The Band played and we had a Marquee on the polo ground and there was a fair number of entries for each event.

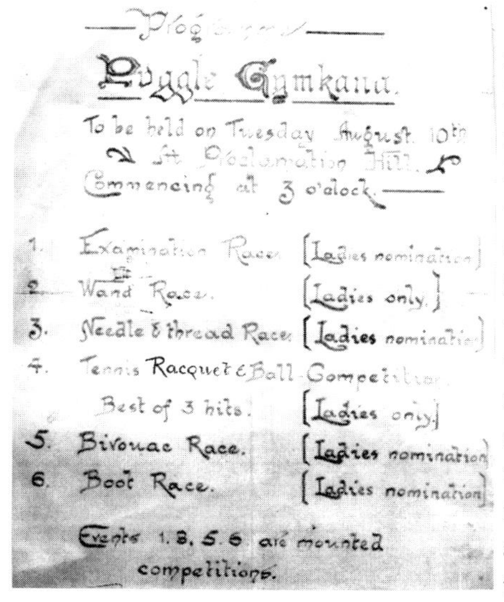

Prog[illegible]

Buggle Gymkana.

To be held on Tuesday August 10th
At Proclamation Hill.
Commencing at 3 o'clock.

1. Examination Race [Ladies nomination]
2. Wand Race. [Ladies only.]
3. Needle & thread Race. [Ladies nomination]
4. Tennis Racquet & Ball Competition
Best of 3 hits. [Ladies only.]
5. Bivouac Race. [Ladies nomination]
6. Boot Race. [Ladies nomination]

Events 1. 3. 5. 6 are mounted competitions.

I had Jack down, as Charlie Russell was off for a week to Kroonstadt, and I took him over. He was too young and headstrong, and I could never stop him. The bivouac race was fun. Everyone rode up the field at a gallop, and when the bugle sounded the halt, you got off unsaddled, tied your horse to a peg, rolled up in a blanket, went to sleep till reveille went, when you had to saddle up and get to the winning post with all your belongings. The boot race was on foot. Everyone's boots were tied up in a sack and they had to run barefoot for them. The sack was tied, and there was a fearful fight at the end with boots flying through the air. I looked in on that one, which was much the best way.

12th - There was a great hunt for Boers in the town; I was not in on it. Practically all the officers and men in the camp were paraded, and marched straight out to Daspoort, 7 officers and 30 men! We carried knobkerries and revolvers and, when there, we were brought back, as they said it was a mistake, and three officers were dismissed. I was one and very glad. They caught 3 I believe.

"A ripping little American buggy"

13th - We had a great guest night. A lot of Greys came, their regiment having come in for a little rest. Sworder and Murray were wonderfully dressed as Mr and Mrs President Steyn. We tried them by Court Martial. There was much fighting, singing and some window smashing.

I have bought a ripping little American buggy for a fiver - worth 15 - with a set of double harness. My pony and Sgt Macmillan's (who got it when he was on Smith-Dorrien's staff) and which I have taken over from him, go rippingly together, stepping out like blazes. It is very light and strong, carrying two people.

At 11.30 p.m., just as we were off to bed after playing bridge, a heavy fire broke out in our picket to the west. We stood to arms for an hour, and it gradually died down. It was pouring. About 3 a.m. I was woken by the sentry on the stoep firing two shots. My first impression was that the Boers were having pot shots at me through the window. The sentry says he saw three men trying the stable door and, as they would not answer his challenge, he fired. Anyhow they vanished utterly, and we all stood to arms again. Probably they were hoping to get some horses under cover of the dark.

There was a great dance given by a lot of chaps in a house in Sunnyside on Arcadia belonging to the De Courcy's. I was on duty that day but by getting round Gordon, he very kindly persuaded the Col to let me go. It was a fearful night of rain and lightning but everyone went in spite of it, and we stayed till the end. There was some news of two reverses, one bad in Natal. Will it ever end? Half a Battalion of Camerons were being sent off suddenly.

We get a little tennis at different hospitals sometimes. I went out with Alderson's bobbery pack on the 13th with Woodside, on Jack. We arrived ten minutes late and by the time we found them they were three miles off and going hard. We chased them to the Mahaliesberg, east of Wonderbroon, and crossed by a fearful path catching them eventually across the Ridge near Onderspoort away north. We discovered it was a dog they had been running and no buck. About 50 people were out and 4 women. There is no jumping as a rule, but one has to be careful of ant-bear holes. We got back soon after 9, having done over 20 miles with an Alpine climb in the middle, the last 6 very slow. The bobberies were mostly terriers and mongrels with 3 mangy greyhounds, who all chased birds for lack of anything better.

Today is Joan's 20th birthday, she is very old!

Of the two reverses mentioned by Lachlan, the one in Natal was at Blood River Poort on 17 September 1901 where the British had 285 casualties and lost two guns. The other was at the Frontier post of Mount Itala on the Zulu frontier which was more of a bloody draw, rather than an outright victory for the Boers, each side having heavy casualties of around 100.

22 September 1901. Lachlan to Joan. Skinners Court, Proclamation Hill

Many thanks for your Glen Letter. I heard the same day from Uncle Archie at Lossiemouth as well as from home, and am well up in everyone's goings on.

I must tell you about the great Ball last week and the bazaar. The former was got up by a lot of people, mostly staff, in Mr and Mrs De Courcy's house. Charlie and I are going to call on them some day. It is about 5 miles from here, but that is nothing. Maclaren and Lockley also went. I picked them up in town in the tonga and took them on. I raised a sporran from Carlan, the Quartermaster, which made them very jealous, and with pumps and buckles was quite respectable though, it being Wednesday, I could not get any white gloves as the shops were all shut early. A tremendous storm of thunder, hail and rain came on the way. This was unfortunate as the garden was all tricked out with lanterns and electric light, which was rendered useless. The supper marquee necessitated a run through rain and puddles which did not improve the smart dresses. Our band performed very well, and an extraordinary number of people turned up. Where they all hide themselves at other times is a mystery to me, though I am beginning to find out.

There were quite a lot of girls, excluding the ubiquitous hospital sisters. (I beg their pardon.) About half a dozen were quite pretty. Of these, five were Dutch. However they all spoke English perfectly, with that slightly foreign intonation that sounds very well. There was a Miss Raymond (Dutch), a Miss Flannigan (more Dutch!), a Miss Celliers (pronounced Seleers and also Dutch), and several others.

The Solomons did not turn up and are now giving a small rival dance. There were lots of elderly majors, mostly staff wallahs and a room full of chaperones and elderly ladies who did not dance. The rain made the crush inside pretty considerable, as otherwise people would have been sitting out in the garden. The stairs were very narrow and crowded.

I found dancing rather difficult after such a long interval - 2 years nearly - but we got on fairly well, and most of the females seemed pretty good, though my right arm did ache a bit for the next few days.

Miss Jones from the Pretoria Hospital was there, a particularly pudding-faced young lady and exceedingly nervous. When she was departing, the horses in her cart got a bit unruly and she went into hysterics. Bouliam, a staff captain, lifted her out shrieking and as she said she must get back, and nothing would persuade her to go in her own trap, he put her in our tonga, and took her home himself, so I hope she felt soothed. I called on the Raymonds in my shay. Papa was on the stoep and regarded me with much suspicion, quite unjustly.

I had an exciting hour or two at the remount place trying to get a couple of leaders for my trap. The ones that went well were usually mangy or else rather lame, and three sizes too big. The others kicked and fooled around tying every thing in knots and as the road is along the foot of a kopje and rocky we had very lively times. We raised quite a fair team, though not what might be called fault-less when closely examined Anyhow they trotted out pretty well and were fairly manageable.

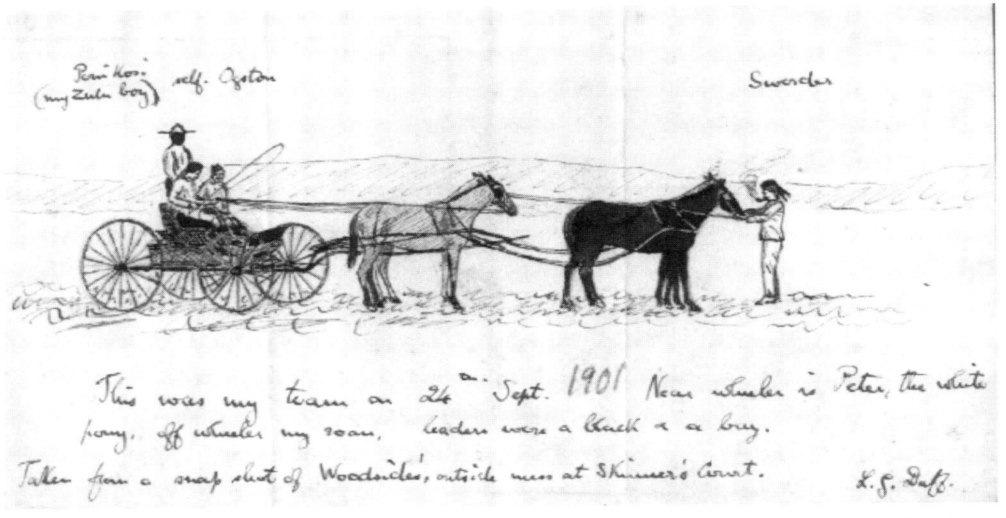

Tuesday was the great bazaar in the 'Burghers Park', for the cathedral, a barn like structure. The Park looked very pretty and green with fountains, band stand, stalls, cocoa-nut shies, 20 photos for 5/-, aerial slides etc. and also a weighing machine. My last weighing was at Belfast, and I have lost 8 lbs, being now only 9 st. 10 lbs in my clothes - so much for Pretoria's hard work and dissipation! Like all bazaars it was very expensive and money vanished like snow in summer, leaving nothing to show why or how it went. I drove Miss Celliers from the Pretoria Hospital in my four in hand, and we arrived without accident. Luckily my boy, Peri, was with us, as on the way we had a few minor casualties, such as harness coming undone etc. I got him from the Native Passport Office, and share him with Ogston. He's a nice Zulu, wears brown boots, black riding breeches, a yellow turban and a better coat than I can raise. Notwithstanding this he works well and is very intelligent, so we are quite satisfied. He feeds on scraps from the mess.

Lockley and I gave a little dinner party at The Cafe Royal. I asked the fair Miss Raymond, who was running a stall with her mama but she would not let her go. They ought to be abolished. Any way I got Miss Celliers to come. She is awfully nice and great fun. Lockley had two sisters, but they were forbidden by Sister Rose Innes, as they did not ask for leave in time. On hearing this Lockley took a cab and dashed off to interview her about this bit of tyranny, but it weren't no go!

That evening we had quite a merry party. The next table, separated by a screen, was occupied by little padre Mullineuse and his sister (who told me at the dance that she was a terrible tom-boy) and their party, who kept up a bread battle with us over the screen, and quite scandalised the rest of the room. After dinner we returned to the bazaar. It was a lovely moonlight night and we saw the entertainment at the Cafe Chantard. The Sgt Major danced, people sang, ventriloquised etc, and the band played. I captured the unfortunate Miss Raymond and took her in, in spite of Ma who was very angry because we stayed some time, so to pacify her I drove them home in the buggy, returning for Miss Celliers.

After that we dined with Alexander at the Spruyts Hotel, and went on in the tonga to Lady Solomon's dance. We started the show at 8.30. They danced in the hall, which has a splendid floor but is rather small.

There were about 35 men and 15 girls of different ages and we danced a good lot, though there was a fearful lot of red tabs. Miss Celliers is a very nice girl and was much sought after. Today I have been round posts, and am going to drive Charlie out to call on the De Courcy's as he has been told to go and see them there. All this sounds very frivolous, and so it is. I hope there will be more dances, and I think it is very patriotic of people to take the trouble and the expense of giving them out here.

I wonder if there is any chance of Botha being caught?

Charlie Russell was Lachlan's cousin, his mother, Isobel, being one of the nine daughters of Colonel Thomas Gordon, his great-grandfather.

Spring had arrived and the veldt was becoming green again and, almost as if it too were drawing strength from the signs of new life, the war was intensifying. 64 columns of troops were now deployed throughout the country, each trying to catch the slippery Boer who was still active and who showed no signs of surrendering.

Louis Botha had many narrow escapes on his way back from his incursion into Natal, which in itself was only partially successful. He got as far as Vryheid and, withdrawing to the mountains east of there, he was trapped by the British in a mountain pass with 3 Brigades of infantry at one end and a column of 3400 men at the other. Taking advantage of his knowledge of the terrain, he and his party abandoned their transport and dashed through the gorge, leaving a rear guard and getting clean away, dislocating the planned disposition of British troops for some time.

Botha regained his Headquarters near Ermilo on 11 October to find that Colonel Benson, an expert Boer hunter, and his column, had been successful in carrying out some brilliant night raids to the south near Carolina. He was so successful that the Boers never camped two nights running in the same place. Botha was nearly captured once, but escaped, leaving his hat and papers behind. In the end Benson was defeated at Bakenlaagte where the British lost 358 casualties and the Boers around 100, and where, after making a brave stand, he died of his wounds.

Kekwich had been the commander at the Siege of Kimberly in 1900 and was now in charge of a column in the Mahaliesberg mountains near Rustenberg. On 29 October he camped near Rustenberg and was attacked by the Boers under De la Rey, who failed to take the position, but inflicted 200 casualties and the loss of 600 mules.

The war was bitter, tiring and seemingly endless. During the spring campaign there were a wearying 9 major engagements, costing the British 1360 casualties, the Boers 430. The spring drives picked up 4000 prisoners.

There was a great fuss in Parliament when Winston Churchill claimed that Kitchener was tired and ought to be replaced by Lyttelton. Kitchener immediately offered to resign his command. Whatever the wisdom of it, Churchill was right when he announced that the army had been 'bucketed to pieces by constant trekking and should be rested'.

PRETORIA TO HORNESNEK1901

Chamberlain wanted larger protected resettlement areas, something that Kitchener disapproved of. The only thing that everyone was agreed upon was that the war had to end and soon. Typically no one could agree on how best to end it.

4 October 1901. Lachlan to Father. K.S.F. Office, Pretoria

Yet another week gone, with the news of a fine old English disaster, and also a few successes. Kekwich had a very poor time at Rustenberg, losing first a Yeomanry patrol, then having his picket rushed at dawn (I suppose they were sleeping) after which I imagine they tried to recapture the hill, losing two officers and 24 wounded, 31 men killed and about 160 wounded, also 400 odd horses and mules lost, but I suppose it has reached you long ago.

We have had rumours of a great Boer attack at Umtala, or somewhere in Natal, where the Boers are said to have left 100 dead behind, but I have heard no confirmation.

The weather is beginning to get hot and it is difficult to keep cool. The flies are noxious brutes and mosquitoes rather objectionable, though infinitely preferable to the former.

Monday. - The usual round of blockhouses, and some very hot tennis at the Race-course hospital, interrupted by a severe dust storm.

Tuesday.- We had our usual 'at home' to which a good few people turned up. I had to drive 3 ladies back about 5 miles in the Cape Cart.

11 October 1901. Lachlan to Joan. Skinners Court, Pretoria

A year ago today since the first shot was fired, and nearly two since our departure. What do YOU think of the aspect of things? Not wildly cheerful?

We are suffering from depression of the weather, which is marvellously gloomy and grey, and the mud horrid. It is a relief all the same after the hot weather we have been having lately, which had begun to get a little oppressive, though trifling to what Komati Poort was last year of course.

Saturday, as usual I visited blockhouses. I met major Agar R.E. who was out here a long while ago and who remembered mother and Aunt Laura at Winburghe, though he did not remember Father so well. In those days he must have been very junior. He seemed a nice chap and it was curious meeting him like that. Ask father if he remembers him.

Tuesday we had the usual "at home" and, just after commencing, a dust-storm followed by torrents of rain. The band fled and so did we. There were a good many people, mostly sisters, and we regaled them with the broken-down gramophone. The rain was terrific, however we gradually got rid of all but 4 in the Spider and Cape Cart.

Wednesday 9th was the rose show at the Zoo. We all looked in. There was a huge crowd of people, most amusing to watch and many singular indeed, and our band and pipers were playing. The roses were poor, the ones at home would easily have taken firsts, and roses out here have very little scent though of course the rain the previous night rather knocked them about. Yesterday I was again on duty and it was very wet and wretched. There is a gymkhana given by the Inniskilling Fusiliers coming off next Wednesday. We are to compete.

Tell father the cigars arrived all right.

The Spider was the name given to Lachlan's four-horse-power light buggy. It took a great deal of skill and no small amount of courage to drive, but must have been enormous fun all the same. It was the turn-of-the-century equivalent of the sports car and was a 'must' for any adventurous young man.

18 October 1901. Father to Lachlan. Drummuir, Keith

I did not write to you last week, but Mildred did. Now I have yours of 20 September and write to thank you for a fine long one. You said you had got a Company, and I suppose that is satisfactory, even if it does give you a lot of work. It is a pity you had to change servants. Was it that Mr Bray had got tired of your untidy habits? But your clothes must be few. I trust you have had another kilt sent out or the bobbery pack will be hunting you soon! It must be a nuisance if they can steal your ponies so easily. What on earth do you want a trap for, even a £5 one? I expect to hear that you are all in bits in the road some day soon.

The war news is not very good at present and I fear you are in for another summer's work. Lotter is shot, but I don't know if that will encourage the other scoundrels to give in. The Regiment seems to be quite broken up. I fear I shall hear next that you are out of your camp quarters. You seem to have a deal of fun.

Since I last wrote, I have been up at Castle Grant with the old lady, who enquires tenderly after you. By the by, there is an account coming from Camberly that you really should pay off. It is hard on these men. To Stallwood, for tennis shoes, £1.17s. Tell me if I shall pay it.

PRETORIA TO HORNESNEK1901

Lotter was a Boer leader who was captured and accused of murdering two half-cast scouts. He was found guilty by Court Martial and executed.

18 October 1901. Lachlan to Father. Hornesnek, Pretoria

This place is 10 miles from Pretoria, west of Cable Hill in the Mahaliesberg. The road runs over the Nek in a N.W. direction.

Saturday 12 - Woodside and I got up at 4 a.m. and reached the meet of the Buck hounds at Eloff's farm beyond Dass Poort at 5.30. It was a cold blowy morning, but the country was nice and soft after the rain. General Alderson's pack are no longer Bobberies. We had 6 couple of hounds out and the field was only about 25, quite small.

We did not find a buck for a long time. Eventually when it looked like a run, the beast climbed the Mahaliesberg, and we scrambled after it. We had a fearful rough bit along the top east of Wonderboom, and of course lost it, and were very thankful indeed to get down safely. It is wonderful where horses can go. I was riding Jack, Charlie's horse. I got an old pair of shafts put in my spider that morning and took up the roan animal to bring it back (I have bought him for £15, a rattling good little pony). He had never been in single harness and did not like it at first, jibbing and getting on his hind legs. With assistance from the carriage-builder however we got away and back safely. For the next few days he always jibbed at starting, but he goes splendidly, and is a fast trotter.

Sunday, I paid a visit to the dentist. A few teeth want stopping and a nerve killing. He is an army dentist and supposed to be good. Anyhow he is gratis, which is something.

I put the two ponies in as a tandem in the cart and they went wonderfully well for the first time. The grey makes a first-class leader, stepping out well, and very steady.

PROGRAMME OF INNISKILLING GYMKHANA.

EVENT 1.
POLO BALL COMPETITION.
COMPETITORS TO HIT BALL ROUND A POST, 200 OFF AND BACK.

EVENT 2.
LLOYD LINDSAY.
TEAMS OF 4 TO RIDE OVER JUMP. 2 DISMOUNT AND BOWL POLO BALL AT BOTTLE ON POST, THEN MOUNT, ALL OVER 2ND JUMP, OTHER 2 DISMOUNT AND BOWL AT BOTTLE, THEN TEAM RIDE OVER 3RD JUMP AND IN. MARKS FOR STYLE.

EVENT 3.
RIDE TO LADY PARTNER, WHO GIVES YOU A WHISKY AND SODA, LIGHTS A CIGAR FOR YOU, HANDS YOU AN UMBRELLA, WHICH YOU OPEN, THEN REMOUNT AND RIDE ROUND COURSE.

EVENT 4.
SADDLE UP AND LIFT TIN POT OFF GROUND WITH STICK, AND RIDE OVER JUMP WITHOUT TOUCHING IT.

EVENT 5.
KADIR CUP.
STICK A PIG WHEN IT APPEARS WITH CHALK MARKED LANCES. PIG WAS STUFFED AND TOWED BEHIND A HORSEMAN.

EVENT 6.
RIDE A MULE AND DRIVE 2 MULES OR PONIES ROUND POST IN FRONT OF YOU.

Wednesday was the Gymkhana day, Lloyd Lindsay. W.E. Gordon, Lockley, Sworder and myself entered. 2 of the 4 horses had never attempted it before and we found great difficulty keeping together round the course. All the jumps were very easy. I forget who won; we did not!

Event No 3 was in 3 heats. Sister Rose Innes, who is boss of No 22 General Hospital, was my partner. We came in third and so ran into the final. Event 4, I tried on Jack who strongly objected to the whole proceeding. In Event 5, there was a nasty bit of cannoning in the first heat, no serious injury. Event 6, I entered my 2 ponies, but the infernal mule would not move. You never saw such a sight, the wildest confusion. Event 7, Stewart of the 92nd, doing MI work, and

I, entered with Jack. It was not over till nearly dark, and was a great success, a huge lot of people being there.

I relieved Allan, who has been alone here for 5 weeks. He has built 4 splendid block houses holding the Nek. The whole of G Company are here. It is comfortable enough. I live by day in a tent, and sleep in a block house.

There are 2 farms about 1000 yards north, one occupied by 25 cattle-rangers, the other supplies vegetables for the troops. One can get a nice bathe in the dam.

I have brought out some paints etc. and the spider is being painted, body dark blue, wheels etc. red; it will look well I think, though the weather is against it, windy and showery. The Colonel I hear has also had to go to hospital with Rheumatism. We are unlucky, 2 colonels and Macneal all in hospital which leaves Willie Gordon in command, who of course does adjutant work as well.

25 October 1901. Father to Lachlan. Edinburgh

Last Saturday Joan got yours with your account of a ball at de Courcy's. It amazes me to think of any Dutch having the heart for that sort of thing. You seem to have had good fun at it, and perhaps it was just as well that it rained and that the seductivity of the garden was not experienced!

There has been a dearth of war news for last week. Progress is very slow. I only trust that something is hatching. Winston Churchill goes about swearing that the situation is no better than it was 2 years ago, and people are getting uneasy and not merely on account of his chatter. The government are getting it hot all round. They deserve a good deal, and now this Buller business comes and it bids fair to cause a lot of harm. They made a great mistake giving him that command and now it is doubtful if they can put him out. He has shown himself a vulgar braggart by his speech, and certainly I never met a single officer who gave him anything but abuse for his Natal work, but presumably he seems able to captivate men. The whole war has been lamentable and I wish I could see you all home!

When you get this you will have been almost two years in S. Africa. Strange that a quarter of your life should have been spent in that vile country, i.e. if we reckon your life from the time you speak of, it doesn't reckon for much before that!

With regards to Charlie Russell when you see him. I hope you don't lead him into extravagance, for he has got to be very careful.

Hercules Tennant was a member of the clan on Lachlan's mother's side. One of her forebears, Alexander, went out to South Africa towards the end of the last century, settling in Grahamstown where he married and had two sons, Hercules and David. The latter was Speaker of the Cape House of Assembly from 1874 - 1896 and married Josina du Toit. They had two sons and a daughter; the eldest son was the Hercules of these letters. Gertrude, his sister, married the Major Copland, who also crops up in the letters occasionally. Hercules' son Graham was a pal of Lachlan's. Charlie Russell, a cousin of Lachlan's on his father's side, rather neatly connects two widely separated families in Pretoria!

CHAPTER SIXTEEN

Hornesnek to Johannesburg 1901

30 October 1901. Lachlan to Joan. Hornesnek

We are having a lively time as I write; it is pitch dark, raining, thundering and lightning as it can in S. Africa when it wants to, and in a way I do not appreciate. I am glad there are no rifles in this particular tent as they are apt to be unpleasant companions in a thunderstorm. I wish you were in here for a minute to get an idea of it, a clap just went off that gave me 'frissons de coeur', though I am more or less acclimatised, and the roar of the rain on the tent makes a fitting back ground. Inside there is a sort of fine drizzle though it is not a leaky tent, except where there are air holes.

The lightning is blinding, and the uproar infernal, and it is horribly cold. Thank goodness we are not trekking now. The weather is very changeable; as summer comes on it seems to grow colder, though we occasionally get a hottish day. Yesterday was lovely and I went to bed on a glorious moonlit night, and woke up in a thick white fog, driving gale and a deluge, which lasted about 4 hours. All day it has been cold and threatening, and now has come the fulfilment. My unfortunate ponies! I'm afraid they are not enjoying themselves out in the open, though they both have a rug and waterproof sheet, which is more than the four transport crews and water-donkeys can boast of. I shall never grouse at the weather in Scotland again, that is until I get back I suppose.

This last week has been very uneventful as far as I am concerned. Hornesnek is not lively, and I see no one except the Company and cattle-rangers, and a few stray farmers near here, all very kind and obliging in the way of lending tools when required, and even books, (by the way your supply stopped very suddenly), also eggs and afternoon tea.

The carriage painting went very well, and the machine looked tremendously smart, but the rain this morning did not improve it as the paint was not dry.

Peter and the roan are both very fit, much fatter in the last fortnight as they eat a lot, grazing all day, and do very little work, just a daily run. There are a lot of cactus hedges and stone walls about which give a little variety, as they both jump well, though Peter is the best and in fact will take a 4 ft wall.

I hear the Colonel has gone with prisoners to India, for the benefit of his health. He will enjoy the trip. Yours and father's letters were very dismal last mail, but I hear the last summary is good, 70 killed and over 300 captured in the last week. I wonder who they all are. If Dutch there ought not to be any left when the war ends. I should think there must be lots of scoundrels from all over the world with them now, having a run out here for their money.

There are a lot of buck and baboons round here. My servant is a tremendous sportsman, and keeps a weird dog of sporting instincts. He trapped a hare the other day which I assisted to eat, a singularly nasty one too, or perhaps it was his cooking. He has pets, one ferocious little ant-bear; (another escaped); and two young hawks, very tame. He will probably have some more beasts shortly.

It is a fortnight tomorrow since I came here, and there is no word of anyone coming out. Allan came for a week, and stayed 5, so I don't know what to expect, unless it be 10! I have been golfing a bit every day with a driver; it helps to pass the time, but the excitement consists of losing as few balls as possible. Anyhow this kind of life and weather are conducive to a sort of 'don't care' philosophy, which is to make the best of circumstances.

They had a second Royal Gymkhana in camp last Tuesday week, quite successful I believe, though the deluge came on at 5.30 p.m. which must have soused a good many of them. I bet the ladies swore a bit!

The storm has passed only to return in its tracks, which is a habit they have. It is now only raining steadily as if it meant to continue, and the thunder is further off. Jim, my servant's dog, votes it absolutely beastly, and it does not improve his cough, contracted going into a stream some months ago. He ought to have medical advice! The weather is having a fatal effect on the Ant-bear's temper, who reviles and spits at anyone who approaches him!

Love to all the family, when you get this it will be nearly Xmas again,

Labuntur anni..... I forget the rest.

1 November 1901. Lachlan to Joan. Middelburg

I am sorry I missed writing last mail but I was very hurried and worried and omitted to do so. I left Hornesnek on the 10th, relieved by Allan. We had been having a lot of wet weather, fearful storms of thunder and rain every evening. I drove in with the tandem, 10 miles of very rough road, and arrived just in time to avoid a heavy storm. After dinner that evening we got the order to go to Middleburg on Tuesday, that being Sunday night. 400 men were wanted, which meant practically all, including Hornes and Smiths Nek and West Fort, which was relieved by the Camerons.

Monday, I was on duty and was to be left behind with details as a rest! Shortly after I was told another 50 men were urgently needed, so they were made up of men previously rejected as unfit owing to want of teeth etc. and some bandsmen, and I was to bring them here. We left after 6 p.m. in the rain for the rest camp where we stayed the night, as the train left at 4 a.m.

I spent the whole night, barring two hours, trying to arrange to get Peter taken. Eventually, at 1 a.m, I found a friend in the West Australians entraining horses for the Canadian Scouts for Middleburg, so, by bribing a shunter, we got the box to the platform and he put the pony in with his and brought it here by the next train. The other pony and trap I left in Charlie's charge, with enough food for 3 months. So if we never return he will sell them for me. He has a fine stable and every convenience, and in the meantime uses them.

We reached this place without incidents by 12 a.m. Here I found the Battalion divided into two parts. We left at 4 a.m. on the 14th, the two columns together. Ours consisted of some 700 Australians and Canadians, Mounted Infantry and 2 horse-guns and 1 pom-pom and 250 1st Gordons under Col Williams of the Buffs, a very good man I believe. The others were the same, but only 300 Australians and odds and ends of Mounted Infantry.

It was a fine morning, and we shortly walked on into the good old fog of the country for a bit. We went down the Ermelo road to a farm called Bankfontein, deserted and destroyed of course. We did 12 miles arriving at 9 a.m. I was on picket that night, and we left at 4 a.m. next day doing a very stiff 16 miles, to arrive about 10 a.m. We went very fast and not one fell out. Hardly any Boers were seen. We had an alarm at 1.30 a.m. when an Australian picket opened fire vigorously at nothing, which rather disturbed us.

This was an unfortunate day as Col Williams riding a strange horse got a bad fall. The horse reared and fell back on top of him. The doctors don't know the extent of the injury, but he has been laid up ever since, and in considerable pain. Col Leicester of the Australians took over command, under Fortescue who always accompanied us.

16th - We did 3 miles to a low round hill just above the Groot Oliphants river about 30 miles from here and 20m from Bethel. The guns had a few shots at some Boers and deluded themselves with the idea that they had hit one. A considerable lot of sheep and horses were caught. The horses as usual were unbroken, from 3 years to 3 months, and all ponies, many very small and weedy. It was an amazing sight watching the Australians selecting them out of a kraal, noosing the beast they wanted and then 3 or 4 pulling it out by main force. They fought like devils and it was wonderful to see the way these chaps went into the middle of the struggling mob and were never hurt. They don't take long subduing them.

Sunday - The mounted troops went out early, rode some miles and did nothing. We found an old Boer wagon a couple of miles up the river, which was very acceptable for fire wood. The country is a huge undulating plain, though never flat, with an occasional deserted farm miles from its nearest neighbour, and except the ones at the farm, never a tree or a bush. It is terribly monotonous, nothing but grass, vast and billowing generally, or a boggy spruit between the rises. I saw a few duck or the occasional buck, quail or hare.

We had a fearful thunderstorm Sunday night. I never saw heavier rain. The Oliphant river rose about 12 feet or perhaps a lot more before morning, and the valleys seemed to be under water. The drift which the night before was 2 ft deep was a vast muddy torrent, and one of our black scouts in trying to swim across with his horse got drowned. I suppose he got separated, and his rifle and bandolier sunk him.

Monday - We still remained. The mounted people reported Boers trekking east, but did not get in touch with them. I was on picket and it rained a little, but the mosquitoes laid low for which I was thankful.

Tuesday - The river still only to be crossed by swimming. We have an awfully nice padre, Couper is his name. He was with the Camerons, where Robertson, our old Doctor of Divinity and D.S.O. (he is always rubbing in that fact to everybody) has remained behind to look after the spiritual welfare of all Presbyterians in Pretoria and nurse his lumbago. Yesterday we started our return journey on three-quarters' ration. All we had achieved being to burn a few kraals, whose occupants with their portable belongings were brought back. We also collected some Boer women and a certain number of sheep, cattle and horses.

It was very disappointing. The mounted people were disgusted with Fortescue for doing nothing. The country was frightfully sodden, so we abandoned the roads and kept as far as possible along the tops of ridges, where the ground was firmer. We rode about 5 miles in empty wagons which came out with forage and rations and we got along fairly well, and did about 17 miles to our camp.

I skinned a heel wearing a rather new pair of ammunition shoes and did not enjoy myself. This morning we came in here leaving at 6 a.m. and arriving by 11, very fast going. I started rather a cripple, and found the 16 miles very long.

Some 40 Boers were seen overhauling our deserted camping ground. I hope the empty tins etc. pleased them. They must have been hanging round all night till we left and probably expected to find a lot of loose ammunition. In the old pouch days we lost lots, but bandoliers are much better, and we have a search before leaving to hunt for stray rounds. Williams gave out that any man dropping his ammunition was to be fined 2d a round.

We got some fine cows from a farm near here, where an old woman had evidently been entertaining two Boers as they were seen departing in the distance as we came up. Some native scouts were left secretly in case they came back, which sure enough they did when we were at a safe distance. I have not yet learned the denouement. The reason she was left with her cattle was that an intelligent staff officer gave her leave to stay as she is a German subject. He was over there this morning and there were no Boers and we had no business to bring the cattle along. The Australians are very angry. Asses like Reeves and Barton do more harm than good.

Love to Mildred and the kids, and best wishes to all for a happy Xmas.

I hope we shall all be for the next year one.

Spring 1902 had started and the blockhouse stage continued. The Boers' movements were curtailed, and they could not take their artillery with them. They had to rely on their determination and courage. It was Kitchener's attempt to tame the veldt.

Blockhouses were going up at a great rate. Soon there would be 10,000 spread along 5000 miles, including the railways; each containing seven bored men. They could be crossed by determined Boers on a dark night but it was not easy for them.

The protected area around Johannesburg was paying off and had been extended. The mines reopened, producing 53,000 ounces of gold. Uitlanders (foreign workers) were coming back. The University also re-opened. Things were definitely getting better.

There was a steady flow of reinforcements from the UK, Australia and New Zealand, bringing the strength of the British Forces up to 240,000. The tide was turning for the British and against the Boers. Many were sick of the war and wanted peace, so much so that a Corps of National Scouts was formed by an organisation called the Burghers' Peace Committee to fight side by side with the British. The idea did not catch on and only about 2000 people joined, and they were from the dreadful concentration camps, where the death rate was 344 in every 1000, but it was good propaganda for the British.

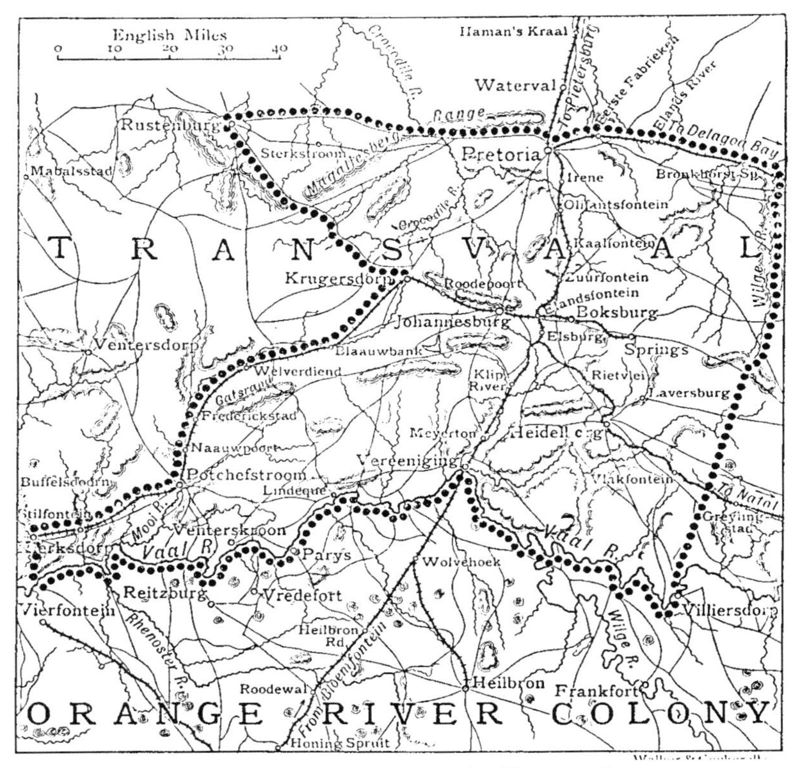

Blockhouse system in the Transvaal

Two thirds of the British casualties were due to disease.

This was the last summer of the war. Kitchener, determined to catch the three main Boer leaders, Botha, De la Rey and De Wet, using his tactics of the multi-column drives and single-column raids. By early November he had a large, well-equipped army of 300,000 men and was in a position of strength.

The blockhouses created more safe areas where the Boers could be found and caught. By the 3rd of December the line had reached Carolina and the Delagoa

Bay Railway. The much-travelled Government-on-wheels was moved north to Lydenburg, after breaking through the blockhouse line.

During the next two months there was a great deal of activity in the Ermilo-Swazi border area where the British had several successes. The Boers had a few also but had lost 700 men in the process.

On the Transvaal front Kitchener was determined to get De Wet. His plan was to sweep the area south of the Vaal and herd all the Boers into a corner and capture them. To do this he had 15,000 troops divided into fourteen columns to converge on Frankfort, which they did, but no Boers were there. Their intelligence had been too good!

De Wet fought a successful action at Groenkop on Christmas Eve inflicting 350 casualties, which was a lot when the Boers were supposed to have been defeated.

The blockhouse policy was not working as it should, so a 'new model drive' was designed.

26 November 1901. Lachlan to Joan. Middle Kraal

Thank you very much for your letter. We are back again in this salubrious spot.

We left Middleburg on the 21st at 8 a.m. and marched to Wonderfontein, 16 miles, halting 2 hours to rest the mules at midday. The wagons are all heavy on the outward journey, with rations and forage that get eaten before we return, and the mules are not fliers. I was on picket by a bog and eaten entirely by mosquitoes; they were something awful and I could hardly sleep a wink. It did no good rolling oneself in a blanket, they got in everywhere.

Next day we started at 6.30 a.m. and came here through 16 miles of hilly road, very hot, one of the most exhausting marches we've done. Many of us are very sore-footed, this being the 4th 16 mile march in succession, and all very rapid marches. I had a stiff thigh, got I suppose on picket, and found it very hard work.

We are camped on the next hill above the Groot Oliphants. The mounted people went out at midnight, coming in next morning, Sunday, they caught 6 prisoners. Yesterday was a glorious day. We sent out a wood party with an Australian escort to get fuel, which is exceedingly scarce. They went to a hill 6 or 7 miles off on the other side of which was a farm or two, burnt of course. I rode out some time after and had a look round. The 3 carts were filling up with paling posts, the only timber available, except for the trees around the farm houses, which were too green to be much use. The houses and gardens presented a mournful appearance of ruin and desolation.

It had evidently been a very prosperous place, splendidly built houses and cattle Kraals, with a nice garden all run to seed and disorder, fine trees and a pretty little glen, thick with fruit trees and lovely grass and streams about. It is impossible not to be sorrowful for the owners, however much they deserved it. We saw a few Boers miles away keeping a wary eye on our movements. Williams came with us and reassumed command yesterday, though he cannot be well yet. He tried some days ago to get up and fainted each time, but came along on a Cape cart. We are all very glad as Fortescue seems rather a rotter, and refuses to attempt anything as he is so afraid of being 'Stellenboschéd'. Now that Williams is in command everyone expects great things, as he is supposed to be full of dash.

Last night was full moon and the Sgt Major got up a concert. A wagon was a stage and the spectators and performers stood or sat all around. It was very successful; a lot of Australians performed. There were comic songs, heroic or sentimental and the Sgt Major recited the death of Montrose very well. Some of our men danced flings and sword-dances and reels - to the pipes of course.

I expect tomorrow, we shall either go to Belfast or return to Middleburg. We are discussing our St Andrew's dinner, and are going to invite all the Scotsmen we can. Our limit is about 25 including ourselves. All told with Doctor and Padre, we number about 15. There are so many candidates that it is difficult to decide. Half the Australians have names like Campbell, Macintosh, etc. and there are four Cameron MI officers. We expect to be in Middleburg, and hope to get the champagne from Pretoria by signalling to Broukhout Spruit. I will finish when I get a chance of posting.

4th - We were trekking when the mail left, so this has been delayed another week. We left Middle Kraal on the 27th. I had just come off picket and turned in when the order came very unexpectedly to march. We left at 8 a.m. and did 15 miles of pretty hilly road, the wagons being rather delayed by several muddy drifts. It was very hot and we got to camp about 3.30. Col Lassiter of the New South Wales Mounted Regiment gave us a tremendous lunch in his tent; salmon, billy tea and shallots being the principle ingredients, the latter were excellent and were collected at a farm.

8th - Off early, 12 mile trek, very hot. Guns firing at parties of Boers on right flank, rear guard sniped as usual. Our 6 Middle Kraal prisoners were made to march with us. They did hate it too. They kept on sending messages to say they could not go any further before they had done a mile. It was rather absurd, as they carried nothing and ought to have found it easier than us by a long way. Anyhow they had to do a bit but, some miles from the end, were allowed to get on a wagon. De Wet used to drive his prisoners along with a sjambok much greater distances, and did not feed them half as well.

29th - To Wonderfontein. Fortescue's lot were camped 6 miles ahead of us the night before and got in before us. We were astonished to hear we were bound for this infernal place. We halted about 8 a.m. 1 mile from the station and the men cooked their breakfasts. Gordon, Allan and I breakfasted for the second time with Lassiter and some of his people and at 10.30 we fell in, after taking a tender farewell of our many Australian friends who cheered us like mad, the whole lot turning out to see us off. They gave special cheers for the pipers, and of course we answered. I think we were all very sorry to leave the column to come and sit in a place like this.

It is a strange thing how much more friendly our men are with Australians or Canadians than any English regiments. They are great sportsmen and very good fellows, but their ranks contain some fine ruffians too who will sneak your horse and put their brand on it in the twinkling of an eye if they get the chance. Peter has always trekked with Royston and his pack of dogs, carrying my kit and two sacks slung across his back. At Wonderfontein he was nearly lost, and was tied up to a tree by an enterprising vagabond but was found just in time to get him on the train. We relieved the blockhouses on the line half way from Wonderfontein to half way to Dalmanutha. Just before leaving Wonderfontein, I made Fortescue's acquaintance, as he accidentally heard my name, and I found he was Aunt Frances' brother. He is short and not like her except in his way of speaking, where the resemblance is great. We had a short talk and were then off. He is a very nice chap and much liked by everyone. Being in Williams' lot I did not meet him before.

This place is very strongly held with a line of blockhouses round the town, where there is a large refugee camp. The 30th was our third St Andrew's in South Africa. We had rather a dull dinner. There are several of the Shropshires with us and a stray doctor and a parson or so. Luckily the doctor played the piano beautifully for hours and he is a great addition.

Sunday - A black day for me, as Piet strayed away while grazing and absolutely vanished. It is incomprehensible and we scoured the surrounding country, but not a trace was to be seen. I thought it was a clever robbery. He was grazing with the mules in the charge of the natives and they said he came into camp. Anyhow that night he was reported by an intelligent boy at Van Wytes Vli, 15 miles off. I have offered a reward to any boy who brings him in. I'm afraid the chances are infinitesimal and some beastly Dutchman has him. It is sickening luck; he was a delightful pony, and it is impossible to get another like him. I still think a native or someone rode him out and left him, as he could not have strayed like that when grazing.

Monday night the Boers tried to cross the line about 4 miles east of this. They were more or less expected, and a good bit of shooting took place. Yesterday, the 4th, Fortescue's column, came into Wonderfontein. They are now on the Carolina trek, backwards and forwards with stores. I rode over with Bruce, a Victorian here and a very good chap, to see if Peter was among them. I saw Fortescue and had a talk with him and he told me how the Canadians the other day drove off his horse, saddle and all at a halt. It had rather short-cropped ears, so to fake it up they lengthened them with a bit of blanket neatly frayed at the edge, so that he was lucky to get it back. There ain't no flies on them, you bet!

This morning we were engaged in catching some wild horses. They were no good barring 2 or 3. This letter should tell you about Xmas and New Year. There are no cards to be had, no presents. Many thanks for the books which are most acceptable. I suppose the parcels will come, though neither the cheroots nor cigars Father ordered from Sinclair have come, which is strange. I wonder if you will get any skating this winter. This is a ridiculously long letter written at different periods, about nothing in particular.

Love to Grandmama and Nanny and any other relatives up for Xmas and all the family, and may it be a much more cheerful one than the last year or two. I hope you will have a Xmas tree this year. Give my best wishes to everyone round the place, particularly Mrs Macwilliam to whom I am writing. Let us hope that by Xmas 1902 we may be home.

13 December 1901. Lachlan to Father. Belfast

Another uneventful week. We have not had our mail yet, as apparently the ship broke down. I expect two lots will come together. We have been having hot weather for Belfast and the occasional sea fog.

A nasty thing happened last Saturday, 3 men of the Shropshires were on a look out post near Monument hill, about 1200 yards only from a blockhouse. They were watching several Boers who were knocking about, and thought they had better get back to the sangar. They ran across and about 20 yards off were fired on by some Boers concealed in it who had managed to sneak round unobserved while the ones in front were being watched. 2 of the men were killed, the third was missed. They stripped all 3 and got away. We are having blockhouses built round this station instead of the old earth works, so the garrison will be reduced.

25 December 1901. Lachlan to Father. Belfast.

I was very sorry to hear you have all been having the 'flu again. It is a very old fashioned complaint, but apparently you all recovered pretty quick.

I got a wire from Aunt Charty in Capetown and applied for leave, but it was refused by the G.O.C. - friend Barton - who does not approve of Capetown. This morning, curiously enough, I got a wire from W.E. Gordon saying he was trying to get me detailed to take the mails to Capetown this week and as this is Wednesday I shall have to start tomorrow if I am to go. The beauty of the arrangement being that Aunt Charty leaves Capetown tomorrow for Pretoria according to her letter, so I shall miss her, and should not be surprised if I missed them altogether, that being the usual thing. Unfortunately being Xmas day I cannot get a wire off. Gordon's arrived late last night and I only got it this morning. This has arisen through Gordon, in the kindness of his heart, getting me leave indirectly by sending me down with K's mails.

I tried that dodge before, but as Aunt Charty only gave me about 6 days' notice it could not be done, and as I got her letter some days after saying they were coming to Pretoria on the 26th I took no more steps in the matter. However as it is probably arranged I will go. I may not get another chance and travelling expenses are paid together with a daily allowance which is something. I will look up Sir David Gill, the astronomer.

We all leave here on the 27th for Pretoria anyhow. I expect Pretoria will not be much catch, infernally hot, and full of horse-sickness. I hear our camp has been moved from Skinners Court to Johnson's Redoubt, about the same distance east of the town. It is a higher and healthier place but we shall lose our mess houses.

Xmas is a melancholy occasion somehow and seems a farce with no humour in it. I have been suffering from a skinned nose which is once more presentable. I was riding a pony of Brace's, the Victorian, and we were jumping it, but unfortunately it did not rise once, and we came head over heels, a tremendous crack and both our faces suffered. There is a fellow called Dwyer in the Leicesters who used to know us at Davos. He is a subaltern and cannot be more than 30. He went out on subsequent occasions for the tobogganing races, and I believe won once. He also knew Aunt Margot at St Moritz. He looks old, and is a nice chap.

I just got a message from Hilliarn, O.C. Canadian Scouts saying he had just got me a pony instead of Peter. It is very good of them to do it. I hope they will get me to Wonderfontein tomorrow.

Love to Joan and every one

Wishing you a very merry Xmas and New Year (how funny it sounds).

1902

2 January 1902. Joan to Lachlan. Drummuir, Keith

Thank you very much indeed for your splendid letters of 20 November and 4 December. I am so sorry about Piet; I do hope you have got him back, though I am afraid it is very unlikely. It is bad luck, and a severe financial loss too. How strange you should be back at your old Belfast. I wonder if you are still there or moved on again.

The news has not been good the last week. The Tweefontein defeat has made everyone rather despondent, but I suppose really it cannot make much difference. Kitchener's weekly summary of prisoners never varies, it is always between 350 and 400, since May. The papers put out rumours of more cavalry and more infantry to be sent out, but it is probably not beyond the usual drafts. How strange to take so many men from you to go to India; have you got any from the 92nd?

I have sent the part of your letter about Col Fortescue to Aunt Frances, NOT the part where you called him a rotter, that would hardly please her. She has sent me his letter and he says you are a very good man on a horse. I know this will please you so I cannot help repeating it. He praises the Gordons tremendously and says he was very sorry to lose them. He wrote from Wonderfontein.

There is little to tell you here; it thaws one day and freezes the next. I have never seen anything so changeable; the consequence is the snow goes very slowly and the roads are ice.

They have had two days curling, neither very good. Yesterday the loch would have been beautiful for skating, but of course father was out all day. I happened to walk down in the afternoon and saw it ;but it had rained hard all night so it will be spoilt again.

Yesterday they had a roe hunt on Bellahack, but they found the snow so much deeper than they expected that they were worn out by 2 p.m. and went and curled. They got 2 roes and 17 hares. Father says the snow would bear him for three steps then down he would go up to his thighs. They said George and Davidson floundering about in it were very funny.

The children have all been having colds, as usual; and now the baby is rather ill, but they are now so far recovered that father and Mildred are going to Hatton for 2 nights for a shoot tomorrow.

Davidson, the keeper, had a son born to him yesterday, his first. Mildred and I went up and saw it and drank its health. It is fearful how the population of the parish increases; they have a bad example here. There are about 60 children for the Xmas tree this year, more than ever.

I dreamt the other night that the old ruin in the church yard had been cleared away, trees and all, and I cried and thought it was quite natural when they had already made the present church so new and horrid.

I have been working very hard at my Soldiers and Sailors Association accounts. At present I am 1/11 wrong somewhere. I ought to be working like a native now to find out the mistake! I am afraid my special talent is not book-keeping !

Granpapa Tennant sent you nice messages the other day, and said he would be very glad to see you back at the Glen again. He did not send me a Xmas present, the first time he has ever omitted it! Father is going there on Saturday.

Nanny sends you her Love

3 January 1902. Lachlan to Joan. The Convent, Newcastle

I am at last away. I have 10 days, and left Pretoria yesterday morning at 5.30. We left Belfast on 27th. A fine foggy morning, but it soon got hot, and we travelled the whole way in a truck, most uncomfortable, as it was very crowded. I wonder if I shall ever see Belfast again?

Lady Ribblesdale, 'Aunty Charty'.

Lord Ribblesdale, 'Uncle Tommy'.

28th - We relieved a party of the 92nd, extending from the Birdcage (the building where prisoners of war are temporarily housed) along a line of little kopjes. It is in some way an excellent place, being central and near the town. And we can get away a lot. Pretoria is hot now, it fairly licks creation. I never stop perspiring, to put it politely, and the mosquitoes are in great form. After Belfast it was like being in an oven.

That night I gave a little dinner at Spruyts Hotel for Dingwall and two of the prettiest in Pretoria, one a Miss Cellier, and the other Miss Schultz, both dance acquaintances. We were going to a concert afterwards, but they thought it was sacred as it was in St Andrew's Hall which is sometimes used as a church, so we played ping-pong and had some music at the latter's house. Old Dingwall was rather astonished as he did not expect anyone else. I told him I would bring a party, but he did not take it seriously. They are very nice girls, and I think you would like them, especially the first. They are not like the ordinary colonial girl in the least.

I got here by 5.30 a.m. and was met by one of General Lyttelton's staff and had a wash at his house. Aunt Charty and all the party arrived at 9 a.m. I met them, and we all went up to breakfast. The general and his wife seemed awfully nice. Aunt Charty seemed very well. Uncle Tommy is seedy, having had a slight touch of the sun, and looked rather ill. They have just come from Durban. They are staying at the Convent where the nuns run a sort of hotel and where all the fashionable people stay. There is no room for me, so I sleep at the Salisbury quite close.

It is very hot. They do not know whether they are going on to Jo'burg or back by sea. Its just dinner time and we are off to the General's. I will tell you the rest next time.

Many thanks for the parcels from Grandmama, and cigars from father, others not arrived. Love to all. Your moist and mosquito-eaten brother Lachlan.

9 January 1902. Aunt Charty to Joan. Heaths Hotel, Johannesburg

I meant to have written to you last mail, but when one's right arm has only been mended 6 weeks and it is 97° in the shade as it was last week when we were at Newcastle, it makes it more difficult than ever to write.

It was a heavenly moment when we met Lachlan on the platform at Newcastle. He is looking so well, brown and delicious, and is a greater darling than ever, and so manly and sweet and thoughtful to me and everybody. He has such quantities of thrilling experiences and thrilling things to tell one. I long to write them down but there is no time though I must try and write a few down. I never saw him looking so well and he seems to have grown. However he flatly denies this, so it may be my imagination.

He has got a little moustache, which he says he must dye as it is too fair. He thinks perhaps it would be better if it matched his nice trousers! He is always in his kilt with a khaki coat and apron which is so comic. He has evidently done splendidly and often lets out his doings without any kind of self consciousness which shows how brave morally and physically he has been.

We have great fun together and I shall miss him horribly when he has to return to Pretoria the day after tomorrow. He will have been 10 days with us, and I hope he has been happy. He is naturally such a happy creature that I think he has been. We had three nights at Newcastle where we spent nearly all our time with General and Mrs Lyttelton. But for their delightful society Newcastle had few attractions and we exhausted its resources in 3 days, so we came on here, a 13 hour journey in which Lachlan was a glorious Cicerone for he explained all the military defences such as blockhouses etc. He enjoyed seeing all the beautiful country of saddest history in Northern Natal, Majuba, Laingsnek etc. as much as we did. The Transvaal which we traversed is the most unattractive dreary country, oceans of brown veldt and nothing but ruined farms, burnt black and roofless. It is very sad. In fact all South Africa is sad now. As for Ladysmith, where we stayed 2 nights with the Lyttletons before meeting Lachlan, I shall be a sadder woman always for having seen it.

Luckily the soldiers themselves seem the least sad of anybody and Lachlan is in splendid spirits.

I kept wishing that you could be with us. We took Lachlan to dine with Lord Milner, which he liked, and they had a long tete a tete together. Lachlan is never shy now and it was most amusing to see him with General Lyttelton whom he treated as any other equal. They were like two boys together. The General was delighted with him and I am sure everybody is.

We all went down a gold mine yesterday, Agnes included (whom I sent for when I broke my arm which was cruel luck and wasted 5 weeks of my time here). Lachlan was presented with a tiny scrap of gold and so was I. It was an alarming experience to slide down into the bowels of the earth. The most interesting process was the cooking at the end where they poured the molten gold into an iron box from a saucepan and made an bar worth 3500. Lachlan and I wandered about trying to find something nice to bring you, but this is a hopeless place to get anything, for there is literally nothing to be had which does not come from England.

We wanted to get him a pony so much while he was here but all animals are sick or lame, so we have been unable to find a mount for him, much to our sorrow. I rode for the first time since I broke my arm yesterday. I felt nervous as my arm is very weak. We leave probably on the 22nd. We hoped to have a peep of Tommy but his colonel can't spare him. Lachlan returns to Pretoria.

I shall miss him sadly.

Aunt Charty was the second eldest daughter of Sir Charles Tennant and was married to Lord Ribblesdale. She had two sons. Tommy was in the 10th Hussars, and was later killed in action in Somalia in 1904; he was a great friend of Lachlan's. Charles, the other son was killed in France in 1916. There were also three daughters: Barbara, a great friend of Joan's, married Sir M. Wilson; Laura, married Lord Lovat, and Diana married, in succession, Percy Wyndham, Arthur Capel and Lord Westmorland.

CHAPTER SEVENTEEN

Pretoria to Silverton 1902

24 January 1902. Lachlan to Joan. Pretoria.

Many thanks for your letter last week. I left off in my last letter to father when we were still in Johannesburg. On Wednesday the 8th, Aunt Charty having returned from her second inspection of the refugee camp and all its attendant horrors, we set off in two cabs to do a personally conducted managerial tour of Robins Deep Gold Mine.

The mine was wonderful. All the crushing machinery and chemical processes were quite elaborate. We descended in a little car 600 feet down into the bowels of the earth. It was rather an eerie sort of place and all the time you expected to feel your head knocked off by the roof. However, no one lost his or hers, and we alighted three stories from the bottom and walked round some passages with tallow candles. After coming up and seeing more machinery and processes we were allowed to inspect a gold block 70 lbs in weight and value £3700. I would have liked to steal it but the difficulties were too great! We were allowed microscopic chips of gold for keepsakes and the manager gave us tea in his house before we returned.

We had to dine early that evening as Milner was to make a great speech to all the influential people of Johannesburg and Pretoria; Heath Hotel was the only suitable place. We listened at convenient doors and heard the whole thing. It was a great speech, admirably given, and if you have not read it you ought to.

Next day I took Aunt Charty for a stroll in the afternoon. She was keen on curios and photos but we saw none worth the taking. We dined at Lord Chesham's; a pleasant dinner. There were a fair number of people there including Colonel Girouard and the Marquis and Lady Tullibardine. They seemed a particularly nice couple.

Friday we started at 8 a.m. in a landau for the Modderfontein Dynamite factory. It is a great undertaking, as the expense of getting the raw materials to such a spot is terrific making the dynamite very expensive. Of course, in the old monopoly days it was all right, but I do not know if it will be able to compete in the market in future. It was the Boers' principle arsenal during the war, supplying them with quantities of powder and ammunition, a lot of the expanding stuff too.

Aunt Charty and I dined at the Tullibardines that evening. Lady T. is a splendid musician and composed a pipe tune called The Scottish Horse; our pipers often play it. She played it to us after dinner, also some Wagner, and then sang some children's songs, words by Robert Louis Stevenson.

On Saturday the 11th I had to return and Aunt Charty wanted to see Pretoria, so we travelled up together. There we drove to the Law Courts and were shown over by Hercules Tennant, and then on to the Raad Zaal where we sat in Kruger's chair. The Zaal is weirdly ugly but rather impressive. After that we went over Kruger's house. The ornaments and furniture are like a third rate mediaeval boarding house in appearance. We were taken round it by an S.A.C. man. They use it as their headquarters now and scarcely anything is changed. The chapel opposite has a clock with no hands. A pair of solid gold ones were once given to Kruger but he had them melted down.

The following week I was on duty and did a lot of blockhouse visiting which is tedious work. One of our two government ponies died of horse sickness very suddenly, and only that morning I had ridden him about 8 miles.

The end of last week we had a lot of rain. Saturday last it never stopped! Monday I took Miss Celliers, a very jolly Dutch girl, out for a drive in the spider. We went through Wonderboom Poort, completing about 18 miles of very rough ground. The roan is a splendid goer. He will take on any horse in the place in a trap, and I have had several offers of 25 for him though he only cost me 15.

Monday I borrowed Jack who is in tremendous spirits, and he nearly bolted with me in the town. I was to spend the night with Payne-Smith at Hornesnek. He is an ex-Yeoman who now runs a Government Farm. He has to do almost everything himself there. The house is an old Boer one with mud floor and cane ceilings with more mud on the roof, but the rooms are fair-sized, cool and comfortable.

Next morning I rode with McDowell, an Australian ex-cattle ranger from a neighbouring farm and was in on an RCM at Johnstons Redoubt. Brace had just left and I had his grey pony to look after. He has worked it to death; it was badly shod, had corns and bad teeth, and would hardly eat, so I am having it seen to and rested. He is a good little beast when fit

The Marquis of Tullibardine was heir to the Duke of Atholl, head of the Clan Murray. The family home is Blair Castle in Dunkeld. The Marquis was killed in France in the Great War.

18 January 1902. Lachlan to Father. Prisoner of War Camp, Pretoria

I am sorry I did not write last week from Jo'burg, but Aunt Charty wrote Joan a long letter so I did not.

On my last day at Newcastle the general took Uncle Tommy and me for a ride up Signal Hill, whence we had a splendid view of the surrounding country; the Biggarsberg, Drakensberg, Pogwana, Majuba, and many other historic places. We could see Botha's Pass where Buller went through, and Laingsnek.

6 February 1902. Father to Lachlan. Drummuir, Keith

We had a letter from Aunt Charty from Johannesburg which described you as 'most blooming' and fit to collogue with generals and High Commissioners. You were in luck to have dined with Lord Milner. I hope you told him a thing or two, to stiffen him into dealing with the Boers. It must have been interesting to see Johannesburg again with some life in it. I hope to see Aunt Charty next week and hear more of you.

I wonder if she stopped at 'Maryburg' and looked at our old quarters. I am wondering too what you wore in civilised society! I hope you have had a new kilt sent out within the last 12 months, otherwise you must be like a high pheasant at a dinner table, only appreciated by those with vitiated tastes. However, Aunt Charty did not draw my attention to scents amongst your other charms.

Yesterday we had a good haul of prisoners; it is more cheerful reading.

Last week we had a very hard frost and we got work to make rinks for the Bonspiel on Monday. Of course the thaw set in on Saturday night and lasted until Tuesday, but they played anyway in awful slush. Poor old Cheyne died that day. I did not think he would live when I saw him the week before. He was buried yesterday and a grandson in the Seaforths was there; he had been wounded in August. Cheyne's eldest son told me that he had another two sons out there; one in your Battalion, another in the Black Watch. I think you did mention the fellow once.

The children are now quite well but have to take great care lest this vile tonsillitis comes back.

'Maryburg' was the house Tom rented when he and Posie were in South Africa for her health, and where Lachlan and Joan had lived as children.

15 February 1902. Lachlan to Joan. Prisoner of War Camp, Pretoria

I feel most horribly sleepy and lazy. This is a funny sort of place; all the inhabitants go to bed every afternoon after lunch until 4 or 4.30. We scoff at the habit but I occasionally succumb and I daresay that if we lived here we should all do the same.

There have been some good captures recently. If Kitchener had strengthened the blockhouses round Rimington's driving moves I believe a lot might have been caught. I hope they get most of the rest this time.

Wednesday, A.F. Gordon and I played polo. We had some good chukkas. Brace's little grey is pretty good but the roan really wants a lot more schooling. The Colonel has gone to Pietersburg on the great murder court martial, so Neish has gone up to Headquarters to take his place, leaving Gordon in command.

Today there was a sale of poor Ogilvie's kit by auction at Johnsons Redoubt. It made £45 and I bought a few things such as his bed, lunch bucket, 2 horse blankets etc. Altogether things fetched very good prices.

Captain JCH Ogilvie was killed whilst serving with the South African Constabulary. He had recently transferred to the Gordons from the Canadian Army.

The blockhouses were effective but the drives were not as successful as it was first hoped they would be. The gaps between the advancing columns enabled the Boers to slip through them at night. Kitchener devised his 'new model drive' and the first of them took place in February. 9,000 men were drawn up into a continuous line fifty four miles long between the northern and southern blockhouse lines which ran from Frankfort to west of Hebron. There was one man to every twelve yards. The line was to move some 20 miles a day, preceded by an unbroken line of scouts a mile ahead of the main body. The column was to arrive at the Central Railway line in two days and three nights.

At the same time 8,000 men were waiting along the blockhouse line and railway, with seven armoured trains patrolling at regular intervals. It sounds an impossible manoeuvre but it was surprisingly successful. However, as the means to capture De Wet it failed, but only because of the lack of vigilance of some of the men in the blockhouse garrisons. De Wet, aided by a large herd of cattle driven through the line of defence, slipped through. One commando made the crossing, though badly mauled in the process and another failed completely to cross and lost 300 men.

Kitchener rested his troops and then began another drive, this time eastward between the Northern line and the Natal Railway, with a second cordon approaching from Kronstadt to catch the driven Boers. De Wet knew that he had to break free in order to save as many of his people as possible and chose to make his move at Landverwagt, twenty miles north of Vrede.

1,200 men, women and children, a thousand cattle with their native drivers, a straggling chain some six miles long, forced a gap in the line and escaped under cover of pitch black darkness. In the chaos Boer casualties numbered 800, a huge proportion for such a small force. De Wet fled westwards across the River Wilge where the mountainous terrain created natural and indefensible gaps in the line.

There is little doubt the enterprise was a success and Kitchener needed to exploit it all he could. The Boers were in poor shape and were forced to rethink their campaign. It was decided that Botha should leave the high veldt of the eastern Transvaal and, with De Wet - who had moved from the Orange Free State - should concentrate their reserves and energies in the Western Transvaal. Meanwhile Smuts and De la Rey threatened Cape Colony to the south, forcing Kitchener to keep troops in the area that could have been better deployed on the drives.

21 February 1902. Father to Lachlan. Drummuir, Keith

No letter from you this week and your last was so short and unfinished. I fear the delights of the Birdcage have been too many! However, you may have been hard-worked.

I trust it is a little cooler - Pretoria must be an awful place for heat, though from the sketch that you sent me it is not so shut in by the hills as I thought. Your works of art give a very good idea of the places and I am amazed by your portraits. You seem to have a great facility for them. You may make a living from Art when the revolution comes here!

In the meantime it is my pleasant duty to tell you that my father has made further provision for you and Joan, and will give you 100 a year more at once with a large surplus accumulating until you are thirty, with a view to helping cover death duties. Jack and Frank and Archie are trustees. You now have four hundred a year and your army pay, and I believe you have not spent all your income so far.

Aunt Charlotte told me more about you. She said that your trap was going to fall to pieces at any moment and was scarcely worth the paint, but that maybe is what keeps it together. She seemed to think that the Dutch females, high or low, were a vile lot. My own recollections of 20 years ago agree with hers - and I had more experience of them.

I found snow here and frost and thick, rough ice. However a thaw set in and the snow is slowly going.

PS. I should have mentioned how greatly Aunt C expressed herself pleased by your attention to her

Good news that Sir Charles Tennant decided to give his grandchildren, Lachlan and Joan, a further allowance of £100 per annum with the prospect of accumulated capital when they reached thirty - but not until then. What generosity from one of the richest men in the United Kingdom; he could have made it a thousand and not noticed!

Lachlan's father's letters show a strange mix of affection masked by sarcasm. He must have been very fond and proud of Lachlan but terrified of showing it. In those days, and indeed when I was brought up between the two wars, to show affection openly was not the done thing, unless over sporting prowess - especially cricket!

Aunt Charty had said many nice things about Lachlan in her letter to Father, but these were only acknowledged in a p.s. at the end.

There seems to have been a great flap about the idea that Lachlan should marry a Dutch girl; "vile Dutch females"! That would have upset the apple cart! He was at least entitled to some female company, however vile, after two years in the veldt and marching all those hundreds of miles.

20 February 1902. Joan to Lachlan. Braemoriston, Elgin

Thank you a thousand times for the "sjambok", it is such a nice one, and I shall indeed be a proud woman when I go out riding with it.

Thank you for the most interesting packet of drawings; some of them are splendid. Father and Grandmama were quite amazed and said they had no idea you had such talent; I knew you had the talent but had never seen you put it to such good purpose.

The portraits really are quite brilliant. Lockley sleeping is beautifully done and the head of Woodside looking down is very clever, as it is such a difficult position; and I am sure the one of Captain Allan is a most excellent likeness.

Your little diary was also deeply interesting; you saying in it that you had a cold, and felt seedy, which you never mentioned in your letter, I suppose thinking it would worry us. Dearest old thing, there is no one like you in the world.

The poem was a delight. May I send it to the "Banffshire Journal" signed a "Banffshire officer" or "soldier"? It is ever so much better than the ridiculous poems they generally have.

I wonder if Father is telling you this mail about our fortunes; it really is too wonderful, I can scarcely believe, far less realise, what I am to have now, besides my own shares; what on earth shall I do with it all? It is too glorious to be rich, never to have to worry about saving and hoarding. And I am so thankful that Grandpapa is giving Father the use of the money now. He wants it much more then we do, as he has been so worried about money lately. Oh! it is too wonderful. I shall imitate you and get a trap and an animal to drive in it, and a groom who will also ride the animal with me when I ride. I mean to be a real spendthrift; you mustn't be.

But the last few years I have had a pretty good training in economy. Of course, you will not talk about this money to any one, as it would do no good, and I don't know what Father has told you.

Monday afternoon I walked down to see poor old Mrs Cheyne; she is a pathetic poor old thing. Her daughter was with her, and as soon as the 'storm' is over she is going to live with her son at Blackhills, near here.

Monday evening old Sheriff Crawford came to stay. He made me tell him a lot about you. If you will give your oath of secrecy, I will tell you that he is very devoted to me, and told me that he only came to Drummuir to see me! He is an old dear I think and can be very amusing. That night before he had told me this, Mildred said to me "I am afraid he will be broken hearted when you are gone" and I said laughing; "He won't stay long". On Tuesday morning he and I walked up past the keepers, and down past the manse, where we met father and Mildred and all went on to the shop, and looked into the garden on our way back, and as it was a lovely day with delicious hot sun we sat on the seat for a bit, and then the Sheriff told Mildred that he would have to go that afternoon at 4.39 as he was not strong enough after his cold to go the whole way to Edinburgh in one day. He was not looking at us, and I could not resist looking at Mildred with a grin. She nearly burst and only just controlled herself. It really was rather funny. Mildred says "old fool" but, of course, she thinks anyone a fool to like me, who has not got any ties or connections.

He is a real old flirt anyhow. Now be sure and not say any thing about this! If you write, send it here and put strictly private on the letter. And what about your flirtations, you naughty person? "Sybil is a dear girl" indeed! But why should she be Sybil, and the other one Miss Shultz?

Is the drawing (which I did not show to Grandmama) of the two ladies in their stays playing billiards, drawn from the life from Miss Shultz and Sybil!!!?

Beware of the wiles of the fair Boer ladies. Is she Miss Celliers? I was amused to see that you had Rachel Geddes' address in your book. Do you write to her or did that forward minx write to you? How was it that Aunt Charty did not see Sybil? Do tell me some more about her ... but I don't think I am much alarmed. I must stop.

PS. Do you think the men have got plenty of warm things for this winter or should I collect some to send out to the Gordons?

Mildred was not nice to her step-children. And, according to Aunt Frances, there was little love lost between Grandmama and Mildred, whose gaudy way of dressing annoyed her. There was one frequently worn skirt, described as Duff Tartan, about which Grandmama was heard to remark; "Mildred, I would like to buy that skirt from you. I would like to give it to the blind to be worn among the blind"!

21 February 1902. Lachlan to Father. Prisoner of War Camp Pretoria

I got yours of 26 January some days ago. You said snow was falling, and in yesterday's summary it said the weather was very cold at home, and skating general, so you will be all sitting around fires and wrapping up. Here the heat has been very great. Even a thin Khaki coat is intolerably hot by day and we would gladly swap temperatures for a bit. I have been on duty this week, but have not had a bad time. Monday I played polo, 2 chukkas on Brace's little grey pony. It is a very good one, wonderfully handy; I always play him in a snaffle and though very small he is faster than a good few others that play. It is great fun and I am getting more used to it. At first there were so many good players one felt very much at sea but it is much the best way to learn. The roan I am still schooling. He is gradually improving, and I intend to play him in one chukka tomorrow. He has become an excellent tandem leader and goes as steady as a rock.

On Tuesday I got Kerr to do my duty and went to a quail shoot of Maclaren's. We started at 7 a.m. Neish and Maclaren drove, taking the guns, cartridges and scoff, and a servant. I joined at the Wonderboom Examining Guard and we went straight ahead to Ondertpoort, which is 10 or 11 miles due north on the P.P. railway. We were caught up by Mackenzie, an ex-burgher and a very nice chap. He came out 16 years ago for his health and has been farming. His father was a British colonel and he has several brothers in the army.

We were met by Ogston at the other end. He and Alexander live out there on a kopje, with K Company, occupying 4 blockhouses, not a very lively occupation. They spend most of the time playing cricket, having a tin net as a pitch on top of the hill. Poor Sandy was rather bad with a touch of fever. He and Jim Gordon get it periodically, so we did not see him. We had a lot of small natives as retrievers, cartridge carriers and beaters, who swarmed out of the Kraal, also 2 pointer dogs, one enormously fat, and the other a sort of living skeleton. The latter was the most useful, as he did occasionally find a dead bird, but they could not be persuaded to work as they ought. There were plenty of birds about, mostly in long grass between patches of mealies. The worst of it was the difficulty in picking up your bird. About 2 out of 5 shot must have been lost I think. We made it a rule that if you had a bird down you were never to fire at another however tempting the shot. So you glued your eyes to the blade of grass where it fell and went straight for it. The piccaninnies were fairly good retrievers, but often in the long grass they were impossible to see and occasionally it was over our heads.

It was really one of the hottest days we have had and from about 11 we could not flush a bird and went in after 12 and had an excellent lunch under a thorn tree with quite a gathering of natives and their wives assisting, rapidly polishing off the surplus food. I never enjoyed a bottle of beer so much. Our total bag was only 32 quail, but certainly 10 to 20 were snaffled by our youthful beaters. One was caught marching off with 3 or 4 and we hauled him back and extracted them out of the capacious pockets of his coat, his only garment, and about 100 sizes too big. After lunch we went further up the Poort where I was very lucky and got a lot of shooting. They were just like little partridges, getting up sometimes in coveys, often in 2s and 3s.

Ogston had to go away for some field firing from blockhouses, but I don't think it made much difference as he was shooting most harmlessly. We had tea in a Government farm run by a fellow called Simpson, with unlimited peaches and tomatoes, and stopped till about 6 o'c. Our total pick-up was 64 quail and 1 pigeon. I saw no hares or buck. Mackenzie and I rode straight home getting in about dark. It was hard work, though if we'd had a good retriever we should have had a lot more birds as it would have saved much valuable time. It was very rough walking occasionally, and is very pretty country out that way. Macnab is at Waterval, 5 miles north again. I believe there are lots of birds out there and they move very quickly, being migratory. Wednesday more polo, and still scorching. Sworder is back to duty, his back is still rather sore occasionally, but got well wonderfully quick. They thought at first it might take five or six weeks instead of one.

Yesterday was again suffocating. Sworder and I were invited to a moonlight picnic at 6 Fountain Grove! We were both to bring a machine. I took the Spider with Sarah, the mule, in the shafts, and the roan leading. We met at the Pretoria Hospital at 6 p.m. Miss Celliers, one of the nurses, was hostess. The weather looked very threatening, heavy clouds having gathered. Also we numbered 13, several people having failed. However nothing daunted we all set forth in the gathering gloom and reached the Grove safely. (It is about 3 miles down the Irene road from the station). Luckily there is a hotel there so we had just time to outspan and stable our animals in inky darkness, when down came the deluge, accompanied by the usual South African thunder and lightning. Luckily it was warm and there was a splendid big stoep where we had an excellent dinner. It does not sound a very pleasant sort of amusement but our spirits kept up wonderfully considering, and we played games such as 'IT' and Dumb Crambo with great success, but the storm abated no whit and we had to return like drowned rats. Luckily we had plenty of coats and umbrellas.

The road is very hilly and twisty with plenty of drifts etc. which came down in a spate. We are going to pick a fine night for our next attempt! The wind here was terrific, several sheds and things were clean blown over even though they were fairly solid. Sworder's tent collapsed ignominiously; mine stood fast.

This afternoon Alistair Gordon and I have been schooling our ponies on the only level bit of ground in the neighbourhood. Tomorrow morning I start at 4.30 a.m. on a mule. I've just elected to do what is known as a night visit around the blockhouses. Sarah goes out to the tent in the veldt with Kerr, and I am not anxious for another ride on the buck jumper - it is too hard. We take the mules, as in the early morning there is a great danger from horse sickness owing to the dew, and mules are not our private property, and the ponies are wanted for polo!

You asked me after Charlie Russell. He is very well and has just taken a new house in Arcadia. He and a fellow called Duncan, also in the Pay Department of the KFS, run it and there are always one or two others of them turning up for different reasons, so they have a little mess of their own and are very comfortable. Charlie frequently runs down to Heilbron or where ever his regiment is to pay out etc. I suppose you know he is a Captain. When the war ends I imagine his job does.

Jim Gordon is at Headquarters. He is getting a great piper, and thinks of nothing but cows, pipers and cricket! Picton Warlow I have never seen or heard of. He is I believe with the M.I. Several fellows have been sent out to the M.I. and never seen the regiment. I hope the children are better at last. It is funny how the fever seems to be about. There is another rumour that De Wet has been caught, with the usual details. I wonder if the last drive will be successful? The Boers came in here the other day and tried to take mules from the sanitary farm, but the natives fired at them and cleared them off. They came in and out of the S.W. blockhouse line undetected somehow. The government farms in the neighbourhood are constantly being raided.

By the way do you remember sending out some Indian Cheroots? You said they left, but they never arrived. I wonder whether Sinclair ever sent them?

21 February 1902. Uncle Jack to Lachlan. 33 Bruton Street

I have been on the point of writing several times and have always been prevented. I did in fact write about New Year from Glen, but I think I put you in the 2nd Battalion so I doubt if you can have got the letter. We are all agog over the political situation, which really has been rather interesting. I think I told you in one letter that I dashed off to Chesterfield in the middle of December to hear Rosebery speak. The whole political world after that speech seemed to vie with each other in claiming to agree with everything he had said. A.J. Balfour was as strong as Campbell Bannerman on the "I told you so" track. Then Rosebery was off to Liverpool and made a big speech and about 7 little ones in the course of which he chucked Home Rule.

This was too much for Campbell Bannerman who had to speak at Leicester on Wednesday. He had previously and quite out of the blue, renewed his adherence to Home Rule in the debate on the address. So, much to the annoyance of his intimates, whom we call the "Central Party", he goes for poor Rosebery and asks him whether he speaks from inside the Tabernacle or from some outside vantage ground, to which Rosebery replied in a letter in the Times today definitely separating himself from C.B. So the fat is in the fire and the real struggle begins. We are all to work in real earnest, organising, speaking and giving dinners. Rosebery is coming to dine here on 11 March and we shall have, I hope, a great function which ought to be rather fun.

Joan is coming here in about 10 days. Your father was up last week about settlements which I am glad to say are flourishing, both for you and him. He has come in for something useful from the Bart, which should help him. You know Aunt Marion is dead. The Bart got about 33,000 from her estate, not bad. I have taken the Laithers fishing on the Deveron from 25 March to 28 May. I have also bought a motor car, a little steam Dog-cart, and we have taken the Blackhouse shooting for 7 years at an exorbitant rental. It is past 1 o'clock a.m. and I must to bed, Goodbye,

Uncle Jack was a Liberal member of Parliament and at one time became a minister. He was Pauline's youngest brother and was doubly connected with the family in that he married Great Aunt Helen, who had the most gorgeous red hair. She died of TB shortly after the birth of her daughter Mary, who died of the same affliction. Campbell-Bannerman was leader of the Liberal Party at the time. A J. Balfour was another powerful Conservative intellectual and a friend of Margot and Laura Tennant. Aunt Marion was Sir Charles' younger sister married to the Reverend Wallace.

27 February 1902. Joan to Lachlan. Braemoriston. Paardeburg surrender day

Thank you a thousand times for your delightful letter. It was delayed somewhere and only arrived with the one to Mildred. I am so glad you are having such a good time and have so many interests.

This morning I have received from Louisa Appleby a charming photograph done by a Doctor Goodwin at one of the hospitals, in which you figure looking quite blasé and very wicked. Dr Goodwin has many naughty tales of your improper behaviour. I really am shocked to think of it! However the only thing that Louisa tells us is that Dr Goodwin knows you very well and you spend a great deal of time at their hospital and that you were very kind (!?!) to the nurses, taking them out driving often, and that you were a general favourite, which she says is an old story. Some of the nurses in the photo look very nice. I am not sure I would not prefer them to Miss Cellier for you to flirt with but you must send me the latter lady's photo. I am sure my Kodak has often been turned upon her.

I have got less than ever to tell you today. The week has gone very quickly; at first it was deliciously soft warm weather, but today was horrid with a tearing bitter east wind, and is cold and dark, though I am thankful to say the wind has died down. My great excitement has been a visit to the dentist. The poor little man was very ill in winter, almost died, and he has got to go to Edinburgh to be operated on soon, so he is frightfully busy. As usual he kept me waiting for ages, nearly an hour, and we had two Miss Baird's coming to lunch, so I told him I must be home in time, and he said he couldn't give me another appointment so he hurried tremendously and stopped 3 holes in 3 quarters of an hour. I feel rather nervous about their being well done with such lightning rapidity, and he didn't hurt me either. While he was mixing the amalgam we had as usual a lot of conversation. He takes a great interest in your career. It was just 5 minutes to lunch time when I got away and ran home.

The Miss Baird's are quite nice. One of them has got such beautiful red gold hair and she is tall and graceful, but not pretty. We go to lunch with them today. I went to church twice on Sunday, wasn't it virtuous? But I walked out before the sermon in the evening. Apparently no one else dares to do this, and they looked at me with surprise and envy. There always seems to be something to be done in Elgin, wild shopping, letters to be posted, books to change, or messages to give, or pay calls, (feeling very pleased when people are out) or visits in the village. I play the piano a good deal, and read Dr Johnson, which is a very long book.

Grandmama has not been able to read much out aloud, her cough was too troublesome. I have only got one week more before I go south. I go home on Wednesday for one night and south on Thursday. I shall look forward to seeing Capt. Dingwall, he sounds most interesting. I wish I could manage to see him in London, but I don't quite know how to arrange anything, and of course he may never be in London at all. As for being eccentric, really delightful people always are a little; either Irish or slightly cracked or original in some way or other, which makes their charm, don't you agree? An example is Capt. Campbell, who you must admit is eccentric, but charming. You will see him with a broad grin in the scrap of photos I enclose. It is part of a group Mildred did in November, and I have cut out Nora Martin's head, as it was so pretty of her. Father is kneeling in adoration of her. Behind him is Col. Morrison with a bottle of rum shrub, and the Comte de St Ferriol sitting on the fence; and part of me with a marvellous pale blue head-piece which Mildred made for me.

Do send me some of your photographical productions. I am sending this week's Banffshire Journal and a French paper which Frauline sent me and two books. I don't suppose you have ever read any of Meredith's. They are rather difficult at first, his style is so involved, but they are so clever and amusing. I have not read

Diana, but it is supposed to be one of the best. I am afraid the print is rather small, so don't read it at night.

It is a wonder that Lachlan sent his risqué painting of two girls, playing billiards in their underwear, back home to his sister. Fortunately she did not show it to Grandmama, who would have consigned it to hell fire! Joan, on the other hand, was highly intrigued that it might be a décolleté preview of the Misses Sybil and Schultz! Joan was on dangerous ground to be critical of her brother's amorous adventures, considering her country walks with an elderly Sheriff and his admission that he had come especially to see her and not her parents.

Joan loved going to London and staying with the Tennant relations, swapping the cold and discomfort of Drummuir for the intellectual delights of her Aunts. Returning home must have been rather dismal when her brother was not there.

The Misses Baird came from Byth House near Turriff, quite some distance from Drummuir.

28 February 1902. Lachlan to Grandmama. Prisoner of War Camp, Pretoria

It is about 4 months since I wrote to you from Hornesnek. The time seems to have slipped away pretty rapidly during the interval, for here is March in the offing, the third and I hope the last in South Africa during this particular war. There seems to have been some great captures lately. We had 250-odd sent in here a few days ago, of whom 201 are off today to Bombay, and we have just heard of 600 being taken in the last drive in the Free State, but to set against all this we have taken a very heavy knock in the west from De la Rey and Kemp.

Fearful stories follow each other. Apparently there were 140 casualties and 500 taken prisoner besides 100 wagons taken with their mules, as well as several guns and pom-poms, which means large supplies of ammunition and rifles for the Boers. Here in Pretoria we are half in peace, and yet the war is ever present at our doors so to speak and one is always meeting people from the different scenes of operations. I should have liked to have been present at Rimington's drive around Heilbron. It must have been very interesting. Our experience of small columns supposedly working together has generally been that we could not keep in touch or at any rate did not, and no one knew what anyone else was to do, so the value of combined operations was greatly diminished.

Boer prisoners off to Bombay.

Here the weather has been quite home-like, so very nasty and unsettled, though considerably hotter. We have a good bit of rain, very heavy storms coming up suddenly, always at the most inconvenient moments, and when you feel it is going to rain, it usually doesn't. We get Polo 3 times a week from here which is great fun. Up at Headquarters they do nothing but drill like slaves, and play cricket. They get so much of the latter that I think they are pretty sick of it; it amounts to almost a craze, which I think will wear them down in time. Sworder, who is also here, and I, gave a moonlight picnic of our own last Tuesday, having been so much struck by the beauties of the one we went to before, when it rained cats and dogs the whole time. We spent a very anxious day watching the weather which had been very bad, also making arrangements, which was no simple matter as we had to provide everything necessary for about 15 people including transport.

All our guests turned up except 2 unimportant ones and we drove out in great style, and had a most amusing time. There were 7 ladies, 4 nurses, the beautiful Dutch girl I think I mentioned to you, I drove her, a sister of hers, and a Mrs Dubuisson, a Scottish lady, very nice, who acts as chaperone to the party. I took Charlie's trap and horse with my roan pony as leader and had a lovely turn out; they are nailers to go. We came back hilariously by the light of the moon, being in by 11 or soon after. Ever since, Sworder and I have been trying to collect the remains of our feast. We have somehow lost 10 shillings worth of hired crockery, 3 bottles of whisky and 1 of brandy, none of which were used, also 5 bottles of hock, and some soda. Sworder was mess president and greatly over-estimated the needs of the party. We had 5 traps of different sorts out and, before coming back, everything was bundled in anywhere by anybody, this being the result, so we will be more careful next time. I had a good day's quail shooting not long ago and hope for another soon.

PS. Thanks for 2 pairs of socks, which arrived 3 days ago.

Rimington was one of the most successful leaders of the war. He commanded his own regiment, the Rimington Scouts. A unit as flexible and mobile as those of the Boers often beating them at their own game. David Stirling, who founded the Long Range Desert Group had the same ideas in the second world war in North Africa.

16 February 1902. Lachlan to Father. Prisoner of War Camp Pretoria

Thank you for your letter of the 10 January. I am awfully sorry about poor little Alexander's death; it is very sad. It seems rather hard to realise that he should have been born and died in such a short time, and that I have had and lost a brother whom I have never seen. Poor Mildred, it must be much harder for her than anyone else. I hope Geordie has got well again, and all the rest. You must have had an awfully anxious time.

I am looking out for your next letters. If the mail is early they arrive on Friday which will be tomorrow, though we often do not get our letters till Sunday. I thought I explained why we were sent to Belfast. The reason was that the 92nd were off to India, and we were to arrange an exchange of men, all their reservists and newly time-expired men coming to us, and our men with a year or more after 1 October 1901, going to them. As we were trekking at the time we could not be taken from our columns without being replaced, and Belfast happened to be the most convenient place to send us to, half a Battalion of Shropshires being withdrawn from there and the neighbouring station east, to go in our place.

Normally I believe we still counted as being in Pretoria, as our Headquarters were still there, so as soon as all arrangements were completed, and some other people scraped together to take our places along the Eastern line, we came back here. The garrisons all along there have been greatly reduced by the blockhouse system so it was more easily managed. Tytler was commanding us out there and when he went away Alistair Gordon was in command. Before we returned the Col. came back from his trip to India and he seemed in better health, but has been suffering a lot from rheumatism ever since. Neish, whose place as adjutant of the London Scottish Tytler went home to take, was here and is now 2nd in command. Col. Burney is D.A.A.G. Cape Colony, a very good job I believe.

You also ask why Dingwall got a DSO. I am sure I cannot say, but I suppose for all round meritorious service. He is very hard working and conscientious and never spares himself, or for that matter anyone else! He certainly did well at our convoy fight at Paardeburg, Houtnek, and everywhere else I think, though nothing very brilliant in particular. He also did a good job on the Compensation Committee, of which he was a member for about 3 months. He was excellent and painstaking.

The weather has turned very hot lately though it will begin to cool down by next month. The following Saturday after I wrote to you I went and saw Woodside at No 22 General Hospital. He is convalescing after enteric and has a nasty beard on, but is quite cheerful. I also saw Stewart the vet, who broke his leg and he is doing well. I have just cured 2 veldt sores; one is on my foot, the other on my hand. My previous experiences of them proved useful, and they did not give much trouble. Sunday I paid a last visit to the dentist, and had two teeth stopped, which completes the list. It is a great thing getting them done free! Payne-Smith came over from Hornesnek, and stopped the night; we dined alone as everyone else was out.

Tuesday - Ben Viljoen arrived with his ADC or second in command. He was ordered to be treated with every consideration, so the two of them had a tent pitched in the cage. I went into see them in the evening taking a bottle of whiskey from Houldsworth, and introduced myself as an old friend. We had a long talk about everything, and of course had plenty of mutual acquaintances and otherwise. He is a nice looking man with a little imperial, and talks excellent English. You will remember how he was caught. He showed me his coat where a bullet went right across the breast and through a notebook in his pocket. He had seven bullets in his horse and the other man seven, a third man was killed. He did not like the National Scouts, and seemed to have no more idea as to the possible duration of the war than we have. He has since been to see K. and is now out on parole. I took several photos of him with the camera Joan gave me, and I hope they will be successful.

Yesterday I went down with Neish and Sworder to the polo ground, and played 2 chukkas on Braces little grey pony, it is not quite fast enough, but quite handy at training though it takes some time to get into it. Next week I intend to play the roan. He is a good pony, but needs practice knocking the ball about, and is too hot-headed at present. We practice on a fairly good bit of ground near here. Sworder and Neish have been out once or twice after quail, there are any amount of them and 4 guns got 56 brace one afternoon and lost a good many more through being unable to pick them up. I must borrow a gun and go out one of these days. I am glad I am not at headquarters as they give the subalterns a lot of drill and work there, which is no fun in this sort of weather. Horse sickness is still very bad, we have lost another mule this week.

There were two Boer Generals called Viljoen, Piet and Ben, the latter being Lachlan's guest at the Bird Cage. His capture was not so important as it might have been earlier in the war, when he had been an able and energetic commander. By now he was war-weary, physically and emotionally tired of fighting and, at this stage in the war, he had more or less resigned from the conflict, taking up his Headquarters at the village of Pilgrim's Rest, east of Lydenburg. There, he and 1,000 burgers were practically ignored by Kitchener, who was concentrating on the capture of De Wet and Botha in the Transvaal.

14 March 1902. Joan to Lachlan. 33 Bruton Street

Thank you very much for your dear letter enclosing the two photos and the drawing. I wish you would send me a photo of Sybil, as I am afraid the drawing is done by a partial hand. You have made her look very old, however!

I came up on Saturday night. On Saturday morning Father and I drove up to see the old house of Drummuir, which they are altering to make into the Farmhouse. It will make a very nice house indeed. I had a comfy journey. Here I found Jack and May were away, the latter recovering from influenza. They returned on Tuesday. In the meantime I had my meals with Aunt Charty and heard a lot more about you and S. Africa in general which was most interesting. K of K has sent her a glorious Boer flag. She was looking very ill but has got better the last day or two. Barbara appeared on Monday, looking very well and handsome. On Monday Ettie Mannering (sic) had tea with me.

Uncle Jack now keeps a motor car, and no horses. It is a very jolly little steam one, quite silent and smooth and the motion is lovely, just like a sleigh. But what is rather a bore is that it is open, and yet they use it at night, which is chilly and disturbing to the hair! On Wednesday afternoon I went up to St John's Wood, which is miles off, to see Cousin Annie's picture by H. Rivere.

We had great difficulty in finding it but at last arrived. The picture is very pretty and to my great surprise really very like, though of course not beautiful. I then walked a good way back to Regents Park Road to tea with Ettie. She was out at first and I found it rather difficult to talk with the old Aunt who does not attract me much.

Ettie had not been well, but is looking forward very much to going to Cannes next week. I stayed some time with her, then took a bus home. I dined that evening at Grosvenor Square. Marguerite had just had her tonsils out and was in bed, but Grandpapa and Nelly and Emma Hill were there. Nelly is a very charming person. We went up and sat with and talked to Marguerite. Then Jack and May fetched me and we went to Lady Haytor's Liberal party. It was not very amusing. The most dull dowdy looking set of people you ever saw, but one or two things interested me. The first person we saw was Campbell-Bannerman, then Mr Herbert Gladstone and his wife who was our old friend Dolly Paget. She looked rather pretty with a queer blue enamel wreath or tiara in her hair. She recognised me which I thought was rather surprising. The only other people I knew were Sir Algy West and Mr Rees who I dislike. I was very tired and glad to come away.

Yesterday I shopped with Barbara and could not get anything I wanted, and felt miserable and tired. In the afternoon we went to the House of Lords which interested me very much. The debate was on public laundries and common laundries, and that they had to be inspected. Lord Lytton, who has a beautiful face like a young poet's, spoke very well and the Bishop of Winchester also spoke in favour of it and the bill passed its third stage; it still has two more. We saw and talked to Edith Davidson and Mrs Chapman. We live in an atmosphere of factories here at the moment.

This afternoon I am going with Captain Campbell to the Polo Pony Show.

Herbert Gladstone was the Liberal party chief whip, descendant of the great W.E. Gladstone.

22 March 1902. Lachlan to Joan. Silverton

I am horribly bored by a thing called a telephone! Luckily it breaks down now and again. We are playing a game of general post, which is anything but amusing. I came here a few days ago, and am now O.C. Silverton, a much more trying position than Wonderboom as everything is topsy-turvy, and a chronic state of chaos prevails.

Rations are partly supplied by the Middleburg people, partly by Pretoria with the result that they don't come up or go away, and there is endless fuss. This place is about 8 miles from Pretoria and 5 from Erste Fabrieken, and consists of blockhouses, one each end of the railway bridge over the river, with several block houses along the railway that we run. I last wrote from Wonderboom on Saturday, where I thought I was settled for at least a month. On Monday I played polo from there and I sent my 3 ponies on by Whitton (my groom, and my first servant in the Regiment) through Dasspoort and past the cemetery to the race course. Luckily I gave them 2 hours to do the 5 miles, as of course they went as roundabout away as possible getting bogged and generally into difficulties but arriving all right.

The Col I heard that day, had gone to C.C. to try Kritzinger, and D'Arcy Alexander has been shot off to Kroonstadt to join the 6th M.I.

I don't think he was at all keen on it. They are all around Klerksdorp way now. Tuesday, I rode into Headquarters to draw the Coy's pay and have a game of tennis, when I was informed we were to be relieved by the Leinsters, and I had to scoot off to the top of my mountain once more. The Leinsters were supposed to be up by 4 p.m., but never arrived till 7.30 so we played ping-pong, and we are great performers! A Major Evans-Lombe relieved me but he had only one cart so before all my detachment were into Johnson's Redoubt it was 3 a.m. The Leinsters are from Jamaica and Trinidad and such places and have only been 3 months in the country and have been more or less Stellenbosched I believe. They are full of buck about their doings.

Wednesday morning at 8 a.m. B, C, and F entrained for the east; B for here, C from here to Erste Fabriken, and G having since gone there, being relieved from Waterval. Murray, my own subaltern, is here and Victor Gordon was too, but old Barton did not at all approve of more than 1 officer here, so Gordon had to go to E and F and Murray was nearly taken. We relieved the Argylls who are off on trek and the confusion is great.

There are 3 new blockhouses barely finished and devoid of the multitudinous articles supposed to be in them, such as ammunition, reserve food, rockets, picks and shovels, etc. Half the existing rations were bad, and the bread never arrived. It is hurled out of a passing train every day in a rain of loaves. The meat arrives in a similar manner, but from the east, the sentry on the bridge being greeted by several legs of mutton hurled at his head by a passing train. Hunting for these and loaves in the long grass down the embankment side is quite a job. If they are not found someone goes hungry.

The first thing that happened was a visit of a dear old native chief "Mabele" of the Mapoch tribe who brought me a present of 16 eggs and several passes for members of his family to go to different parts of the Transvaal, one to bring his five wives back - the good ladies apparently strayed - and another to collect some of the clan from somewhere else. With the assistance of an English speaking boy, I made them out several so they went away quite pleased. Murray gave the old chief a large glass of hock, as we had no whisky in the place. He did not seem to relish it at all, but drank it out of politeness, and after a prolonged hand-shaking, we parted with mutual expressions of esteem. I have not seen him since, but I get occasional telegrams from ferocious officials in different parts wanting to know why I made out passes to natives. Apparently I have no right to, and there are several Army orders to that effect, and no natives are allowed to trek round the country, however I treat them with contempt.

Every one not in a blockhouse lived comfortably in tents. However, Barton has decreed that no tents are to be permitted, except for the officer, and the officer must not mask his fire from the blockhouse, or give away its position. The latter is absurd as the blockhouse can be seen for miles around. So our half dozen tents have been pulled down and everyone we are unable to stuff into the block-house is trying to make himself a bit of shelter with old bits of tin etc. I hope the weather will keep dry.

We have a second telephone to Erste Fabriken and have to transmit endless messages for them. I am being driven mad! When trying to hear something on one, the other rings up, and you stand with a receiver at each ear trying to pacify people miles apart at the same time. They are rotten telephones too and are responsible for much waste of time and loss of temper. I think they are the Devil's invention.

Yesterday I went in to polo; it is rather a long ride, but we go in quietly in the morning and come back in the afternoon, lunching at Johnson's Redoubt or Charlie's house. I am an honorary member of his mess so can make free use of it with an easy conscience. I dined at Johnson's. Friday is a guest night, so we had the band and pipes which is always nice, also a considerably better dinner than Murray and I indulge in out here, though Bray is an excellent amateur cook. This afternoon Charlie and Castera drove out and had tea here. It is a nice drive from Pretoria and a great place for picnics.

General Kritzinger, a Cape rebel who operated with Smuts in the Cape and East Midlands, was wounded and captured in November of 1901. He was tried by court martial on charges for "offences against the laws of war" but was honourably acquitted.

CHAPTER EIGHTEEN

Silverton 1902

27 March 1902. Lachlan to Father. Silverton

It is a very hot day for the time of year and the flies are most annoying. Things are progressing much as usual; the detachment is much troubled by streams of orders from Barton on every conceivable subject, most of which upset the existing arrangements which have worked smoothly for over a year. Also our strength is such that we have only enough troops to do the ordinary routine of such a place, and they only get every other night off guard so that it is impossible to get men for fatigue to dig the shell-proof trenches and alter the wire entanglements and generally play the ass required by Barton. However we are gradually settling down. All the morning I have been doing musketry at the far away blockhouses of my section, firing through the loop holes at targets we stuck up. It is done once a week by all blockhouses and is rather tedious when you have to superintend it all.

The post-cart comes in at 10.30 daily and always brings masses of correspondence in blue envelopes for O.C. Silverton, a lot of which requires answering, together with a bunch of orders, Army, Cape Command, Middleburg and Pretoria District, and Regimental, as well as tons of special instructions and confidential memos. We have at last got all the equipment required for the section out from Pretoria, after a lot of bother and writing. The cold storage agent at Erste Fabrieken always sends our meat short, sometimes a lot, and looks upon it as rather a joke. We report it regularly to the supply depot but it has no effect. We have to send in for everything but rations by bullock or cape cart to Pretoria, about 8 miles, so our transport is pretty hard worked. Quantities of engineering stuff such as iron posts for wire fences, big hammers, wire cutters etc. and tanks for water at blockhouses also have to be sent for. Hardly any of these were here on our arrival.

Last Monday I went in to polo on the little grey mare. The roan unfortunately ran a nail into one of his feet when grazing, so has been laid up for some days. It is a horrid place to go wrong as apparently it often takes months to recover. We have poulticed it diligently however and it seems all right and today he is going sound enough though I am not working him yet. He is improving at polo steadily, and is fast and very hard and strong, so I miss him much.

Barton wanted to cut some nice trees of Sammy Mark's, but Sammy kicked up an awful fuss and wired to Milner about it (so the story goes), with the result that they are to be left. Sammy's house was looted by a party of Boers the other night for about the third or fourth time and they took all his boots and clothes etc. everything of real value having been previously taken. He has thousands of pounds worth of undiluted spirits on the place ready to be made into 'Old Highland', fine champagne or any thing else. I believe he imports corks for his bottles, and charges according to the brand on them! He has any amount of lovely fruit out there and I am going over there one day to sample it.

Twelve Boers went to raid a government farm in Dutch Poort, 5 miles north of us that night. The two fellows there had been raided before, so they hid their rifles in the garden at night. The Boers took the only horse in the place and loaded whatever took their fancy onto it and went. As soon as they were gone these chaps got their rifles and started for a place where they though they might cut the Boers off, and sure enough they came past by moonlight, and on being fired on, galloped off in confusion leaving the horse and their booty behind. Since then however the two farmers come in every night and sleep in Koodoospoort station, which is empty and just by one of our blockhouses. I think they are wise.

When you get this it will be Spring again with you, and the beginning of another Winter here. I wonder if we shall complete 3 years or not.

4 April 1902. Lachlan to Joan. Silverton

Many thanks for your letter from Bruton St. I hope you have been amusing yourself in London and not got mixed hopelessly in politics. Laundries and factories do not sound very interesting! I suppose because I know so little of them. Ask Uncle Jack to present a Bill to prevent holes being worn in one's shirts and everything lost in the wash.

We have had a short spell of pretty hot weather, but it has changed for the better after several cloudy days and a little rain, and is now perfect, and looks as though there might be a frost before long. The stars were fine. I happened to notice the old Great Bear upside down and Orion and Scorpio all to be seen at one and the same time, which is rare in many parts of the world I should think. There are also many other familiar groups with names unknown to me.

Monday, I again played polo on the other two ponies and came out in the dusk and a drizzle, very unpleasant. Wednesday, I went by our cape cart, exchanged my wretched mule for a good one and returned next morning. Yesterday morning at 7 a.m. Bray rushed into our tent with the news that General Barton was getting off the train, so I tumbled into some clothes and rushed out to meet him. The old horror was accompanied by his poodle and Cols. Maxwell and Mansard, R.E. s. He was in a peevish humour having got up at 5 a.m., and found fault with everything. The cook house was not where it should be, our mess shanty must be moved, our tent was masking the field of fire, why was not everyone sleeping in the blockhouse? (the said B.H. holding 10 men tightly packed and 20 men living here besides Murray and self). What was this? Who slept here? etc, etc. Then he fussed around other blockhouses and groused and whined away.

He kicked up an awful shindy, gave us a lot of work to do and said he was going to reduce our numbers .He also said we all seemed to live as if we were on a big picnic party. Murray and I are to be deprived of our tent; anything for us to crawl into at night 'would do' was his expression. Next he went and saw Neish about it all, expressing his dissatisfaction, with the result that he and W. Gordon rode out this morning to inquire into the matter and they both agreed that he is most objectionable and a fussy old fool, which is the opinion of every one who has ever had any thing to do with him, and they then considerably modified his decrees for our benefit.

One rather funny incident was when Barton and Co. and myself called in at Mr Munetts' farm yesterday and questioned him about his natives. Munett said he had 20, but since the British came they said they were the white man's brother and refused to do any more work, and being old he could not make them, the result being that they lived on his land and stole his stuff and had high old times. So much for the good effect of British occupation. I expect there will be plenty much trouble with the natives before long, they are frightfully above themselves and think themselves better than you, if not very strictly looked after. They get such enormous wages from the Government for doing nothing, which also cannot last. I have authority to commandeer Munetts' boys and make them work, but at present most were taken to Erste Fabrieken to work two days ago. I must get a good sjambok ready; it is a fine persuader.

The A and B exam comes off the day after tomorrow. I wish I knew more about it, but time for work out here is very limited, something is always cropping up to interrupt.

MAJOR-GENERAL BARTON, C.B.

Photo Debenham & Smith Southampton

It now seemed as if the war would never end, and the depressing feeling that it could last for at least another year was creeping in. There was also the very real fear of a native uprising against the Boers in retaliation for all their ill treatment. But there was a movement towards peace taking place behind the scenes.

Cecil Rhodes died on 26 March 1902 and his remains were carried up to the Mottoppos near Bulawayo in a luxury train that he had designed himself. It was an impressive and dramatic final journey for one of the creators of modern South Africa. The funeral cortege swept through the countryside, heralded by an armoured train with flashing searchlights. Sentries presented arms as it passed by.

12 April 1902. Lachlan to Mildred. Silverton

Many thanks for your letters There is some little excitement here as Steyn, and I believe De Wet, De la Rey, Botha and many others, nearly 50 I hear, are in Pretoria today, and the betting in Jo-berg is 6 to 4 on peace, though personally I should put it against. I wonder what they are doing. Reitz, I believe is very much against it and I suppose De Wet, unless the latter is sick of drives. I expect they won't care about being turned adrift on the veldt again after a few days' good feeding.

I am very sad, as the poor roan pony had to be shot last Wednesday, his foot got much worse very rapidly and absolutely rotted away. I could not have believed it was possible in so short a time. The vet was out twice, and the second time said it was hopeless, as indeed it seemed. He said in a few days the whole foot would come off, and it looked like it.

On 11 April 1902, the day the Boer delegation met Kitchener at Pretoria, General Hamilton decisively defeated Kemp at Roodewal, the Red Valley, near the Great Hart valley 200 miles to the west. It was a timely victory, for it gave Kitchener an advantage in the negotiations that followed and served as further notice to the Boers that the superior numbers of the British forces could not be withstood for long.

The Pretoria conference eventually broke up on 18 April having failed to convince Kitchener to accept their terms. They returned to their own people to consult and, after much wrangling, they came back to the Council Chambers at Vereeniging and 15 May with their revised proposals.

The native uprising, so long feared, was beginning to gain impetus and on 6 May a force of Zulus murdered 57 Boers, men and women, at Vryheid. It was a settling of old scores, an added threat to the Boer nation.

Despite the ongoing peace talks Kitchener's 'drives' continued until the 10 May, applying constant pressure. Technically the Boers were not defeated and they detested the word 'surrender'. They had the determination and the inclination to fight on, but food was scarce, horses thin, and the women and children starving. What Boer troops remained were demoralised and in poor fighting shape. Any massed uprising of the natives would be an additional drain on their already depleted resources, and it was doubly worrying that the previously friendly Basutos were becoming hostile.

The Boer leadership was divided. De la Rey, Louis Botha and Smuts were for continuing the peace talks to their inevitable conclusion; De Wet, President Steyn, who was in poor health, and Kemp, fresh from his defeat at Roodewal were all in favour of fighting or at least hanging on for renegotiated terms.

As a final crushing blow to the Boer fighting spirit, there were the growing numbers of what were called "Hands Uppers", those war-weary Boers who were joining the British and who, despised by their fighting fellows, brought the unthinkable threat of the possibility of civil war.

19 April 1902. Lachlan to Joan. Silverton

We are in the throes of a Boer drive. Most of the Battalion are out somewhere sitting about in uncomfortable kopjes. Thank goodness Murray and I and B Company are left comparatively alone as our little section of the railway is acting as one of the guns, and the beaters are supposed to be working the birds up to us from the south, if they have not already flown. Anyhow I do not think it likely that they will try to break through here as there are so many hills and blockhouses, but we are to be strengthened this afternoon all the same, and may be spending the next few nights in the railway ditch, or some equally jolly place, though not if I can avoid it.

The Boers are more likely to remain further east I think, the other side of Erste Fabrieken. I have been playing polo whenever possible and am getting very keen. The exams took place last Monday week. We all passed but two; yours humbly squeaking through very neatly. We had to get 75%, so it was rather tough, especially for me who was on detachment the whole time. It has involved a lot of work, and when not working I would play polo. The subjects were Musketry, Interior Economy, Discipline, Duties etc. Those who failed and the others not present all have to pass on some future occasion, so it is well to have done with it.

You will be pleased to hear that I have disposed of my poor old Spider for £9 (first it was only to be £8) to the Doctor man at Erste Fabrieken, however the bill after the 2nd moonlight picnic came to £4.5s. and when he came over to pay I was out, and Murray very nobly and entirely on his own, stuck up the price and actually squeezed another £1 out of him.

The next thing was to get the machine out here for him. It was standing in Charlie's backyard and of course as ill-luck would have it, when Herman the doctor went to enquire after it, it was attending a marriage. Next morning when they told the boy to inspan he put Jack into the Spider instead of the right cart, and bringing it around Jack bolted down the road for no apparent reason. The boy who is not a great driver tried to turn him and upset the whole show. Luckily the horse parted with the cart, so the damage done is not as great as might have been, and it will be complete again on Monday. It is annoying and Herman is rather sick. We tell him he ought to be grateful as he will get an almost new cart, and say we will put the price up again!

We are still very busy finishing up the wiring and blockhouse building and general alterations to the section, and shall some day get comparatively ship shape. The next little job I have on is the making of an absolutely unnecessary drift in an impossible place in a ridiculous manner across the Hartebeestspruit with some natives.

All the figs and other fruit are over and eggs and vegetables are getting scarce. Steyn is nearly blind and dying of paralysis. De Wet, Botha, (Botha says of De Wet "That man irritates me"), De la Rey, Shalk, Burger (Vice President of the Transvaal) and others were in Pretoria for some days pow-wowing, and I believe have gone out to their commandos again. I wonder what the result will be? The betting was 5-1 on peace the other day, but I feel doubtful. The fault of the Dutch is he gives you too little and asks too much. We have been going on steadily catching more of them lately so it may come to something.

I have told Sybil to look you up in London if you are there, I do not know where she will be so cannot let you know. You seemed so curious I thought it might amuse you to see a Huguenot Dutch Boer. If you are in town drop a line to her c/o Transvaal National bank, 75 Cornhill, London, EC. and be kind to the poor exile who is perfectly respectable and nice.

Love to everybody. Mildred is wonderfully good at starting a letter just as the post is leaving.

26 April 1902. Lachlan to Father. Silverton

Another week gone and still nothing new. Brace was very pleased to see his grey pony had not yet come to grief. He is an awfully good chap. I drove his pony out here that night in the old Spider, which after many adventures ceases to be mine for £9. The carriage maker I think will give £10 for my Scotch cart, so they were not such bad investments, though the spider cost me about £9 in repairs while I had it, so I will be quits, as far as expenses goes.

Tuesday night there was a total eclipse of a full moon It was beautifully clear and an interesting sight; the moon was covered by about 7.45 p.m. and started to appear again about 8.50. It was always faintly visible beneath the shadows, but it was quite dark during the period of eclipse; it was rather uncanny. That afternoon a distressed R.E. appeared leaving a motorcar. He had run out of petrol.

CHAPTER NINETEEN

Silverton to Pretoria 1902

3 May 1902. Lachlan to Joan. Silverton

The pack is going to be started again here very shortly, though only five of the original stag hounds survive, and a few puppies. It is sad the way they all died, ordinary dogs seem to thrive exceedingly, so why should not they?

People still talk of peace and going home. About the former we ought to know in 10 days time or so. There is considerable difference of opinion, but the balance is strongly in favour of peace. As to going home I have no confidence in the rumours going about. Lots of people think we are going, some even think we are to be at the Coronation. One of my sergeants here has a brother, a clerk at the War Office, and he is firmly persuaded that we start shortly for Capetown, peace or no peace. However the best plan is not to worry about it. There are lots of other things to bother about without looking so far ahead. "Sufficient unto the day are the evils..." which never come singly! I am getting pretty sick of this place, so is Murray, though it is much more peaceful than headquarters, where the air is full of 'knocks' as they are vulgarly termed and where the wretched subalterns are being awfully bullied by the Adjutant.

Murray and I have lately arrived at the conclusion that soldiering of this sort is no game for a gentleman, and the times to come when we get home, if this sort of thing continues, will be wicked. Murray is a very keen and good soldier, though he has been unfortunate in having no fighting in the year he has been out. He is a very nice chap. There is an end to every descent however, so let's hope we are near it.

Since I last wrote we have not done much. I played polo that day. The two grey ponies are very fit and they live in town in Charlie's stable.

Mabele has at last, through our combined exertions, got his 'cattles' up and is very grateful, and I no longer badger the Provost Marchal by telephone about them, but they are always wanting passes to go somewhere or do something, and there is sometimes need of some discrimination as to what course to pursue. I am the Big Baas of this little neighbourhood, but am constantly compelled to refer to bigger ones! Then they bribe me with eggs and I feel I must do the best for them.

A few days ago there was a case of attempted murder by stabbing. It was of course brought in here, for my benefit. The sufferer was accompanied by his elderly pa. His wife and piccanins and a very voluble interpreter all came to tell about it. The interpreter was greatly excited and spoke so fast and incoherently that it was only by cunning cross- and leading-questions that I extracted any truth at all. I suggested to him that it would have been much simpler if the intended victim had gone and done likewise, but they wanted JUSTICE, so I had to send out some of my eight scouts to arrest the assassin which was done, and he and the victim, with a hole in his shirt and a scratched chest were taken into town and there the defendant was awarded 2 months, which does not mean much, for what they really fear is the sjambok.

Murray and I sold £2. 8s. worth of cast off clothing to the chief's boys the other day and we have bought a football etc. for the Company with the proceeds, and also eggs.

I wonder where you have been, and if you ever saw Sybil, give her my love if you do!

4 May 1902 . Lachlan to Father. 19th General Hospital, Pretoria

I am sorry I missed last mail, but I was very lazy and rather seedy. As you see I am in Hospital for the first and I hope the last time, a very mild concussion of the brain being the formidable name of my complaint. As a matter of fact it was merely a case of being stunned rather severely, and it has taken a few days to get completely over it. I am still kept in bed, but hope to be out of hospital in a few days. My sight was upset, and one pupil bigger than the other, and there was considerable headache but the sight is now all right, the pupils nearly the same, and the headache nearly gone. I have been up before but it did not seem to improve things and the Doctor said complete quiet was best till it went away.

It is very dull here, but comfortable and the feeding good. There was a poor man next door crushed by a train who made a great noise. They said he was unconscious but it did not sound like it and he has since died. There is a terrible sister in charge. I call her rude and objectionable and she certainly is not popular, but I may be prejudiced as she does not view me with favour, chiefly through my having got up one morning without being told to, which was a frightful crime.

18 May 1902. Lachlan to Father. No 22 General Hospital

Since I last wrote on the 3rd before my accident I had a day's shooting. Hudson (APM) and some friends of his had a Guinea fowl shoot 2 Sundays ago at a farm called 'The Willows', not far from Silverton, where there are big plantations of young Gum trees near some kopjes. I was to drive out and join them there in the early morning, but arrived rather late as a boy I took to show me the place (there are several farms dotted about and he did not know which it was) took me to Sammy Marks' place at Schwartz Kopjes. S.M is the local millionaire, and has a gorgeous country house where he keeps his family, near Erste Fabrieken. It is surrounded by woods.

I met Sammy by his house and he gave me the right directions. Eventually we found the Willows in some thick woods, a fine old Dutch farm. We walked about a good bit but had little sport, 6 or 7 came flopping over like great turkeys, but I missed them in great style. After an excellent lunch at the farm we did some severe kopje climbing. I went to Polo that afternoon and in the first chukka Maple the little grey mare crossed her legs and somehow I got a severe blow on the left side of my head, which stunned me completely. I was driven by Stanley to no 19 Hospital where I recovered consciousness. It was very unlucky, the pony is all right. I don't know how she did it, she is usually very neat at turning, being quick on her feet and quite fast at galloping.

One advantage of No 19 Hospital is that it is in the town, and lots of friends come and see me. If they walked in it was all right, but if Sister Beckett caught them she was usually very uncivil to them and kicked them out, and it was only afterwards when they came successfully that I knew anything of it. I eventually found out that she seemed to think I had too many friends coming in and it was too exciting for me! So I was packed off on the 16th up here, though not till I had caught a bad cold, chiefly from the general draughtiness and neglect of the other hospital.

This used to be the Yeomanry hospital and is far nicer in every way. It is out of the town near Johnsons' Redoubt, a very breezy healthy spot with a lovely view. The officers' part is a magnificent house. Sister Rose Innes runs the show, she is very nice and is an old friend, the other sisters are also quite different and take a lot of trouble in making one comfortable and it is as pleasant a place all round as the other is the reverse. I have been in bed and still am with this cold, slightly on the chest. My head seems all right though the pupils vary a little.

Lady Hely Hutchison and Fiona Poore, wife of the great cricketer, our Provost Marshall, visited No 19. I was introduced to them in bed. Lady H.H. was quite effusive, as some one or other who was or had been related to her had been in the Regiment on some previous occasion. She is quite nice looking. Lady F.P. said she was not surprised I was there, as she had often seen me at polo! She seemed rather pleased at the verification of her dismal predictions, though why she should have had any I don't know.

We have no news of peace. A big draft of 240 men arrived the other day. I hope my next letter will not be from hospital.

23 May 1902. Father to Lachlan. Brooks' Club, St James Street

We had two letters this week and last week to Joan. You seem to be enduring blockhouse life in spite of General Barton's irritability and the fact that the birds do not come over your head. I trust they will not come over anyone's head any more. Though it would be hard to say it is peace, it really looks like it. The cabinet met today but no news has yet come out. I fancy they will keep it until the house meets on Monday.

By the way you never answered my repeated questions as to the statement of my account with you! I hope you get your account from Holts and look at it sometimes!

You said you had seen Ernest Russell. I may tell you he is the most heartless, ungrateful fellow I have ever come across. He has treated his mother and sisters abominably. I do not even think him honest. Charlie is quite different and I trust will remain so, though he may be rough.

24 May 1902. Lachlan to Joan. 22nd General Hospital, Pretoria

I am still kept a prisoner in this confounded hospital, and don't know what to do with myself. The worst of it is that I am feeling perfectly well in every way and want to get back to duty and polo. In future I shall play in a helmet, so I shall be safe. I am no longer an absolute prisoner, as I can go for a drive in the afternoon or a mild walk. The pupils of my eyes are still a trifle unequal, I suppose it is merely a matter of time, but it is trying to the temper and the infernal doctor won't answer questions. I feel it is a horrid waste of time, which hangs pretty heavy in the meantime; it is nearly three weeks since I've been in hospital.

On Wednesday last I was permitted to have my grub downstairs. They feed in the conservatory, a long icy place, at least in the present state of the weather, at other times it is like a blooming incubator. The patients are all labelled and sit in their proper places like good boys. Stanmere, the doctor, presides and does school master! He's really a good chap but is apt to get above himself, and is sat upon accordingly; Macnab is quite good at it. I am still absolutely teetotal, so stand a good chance of getting typhoid!

That day sister Williams, boss of No 7 General, came over to see me and Macnab. She has a brother in the Canadian Scouts who I have sometimes mentioned. She has a little Red Indian blood in her I think and she is very sporting and is known familiarly as 'Horsey Bill'! I have undertaken to train one of her ponies to polo for her and she has 3 for sale from £150 downwards, but I am not taking any.

As soon as she departed, Polly, Ernest and Charlie drove up in Charlie's new Shay, a magnificent turn out, four yellow wheels, a black body with a hood, holding two inside and one on a little seat behind. He sold one of his old ones and got this. Polly was looking tremendously fit and blooming and it did one good to look at her. She had been out a few days and was staying in Charlie's house, and has since gone to Jo-berg. Peace was said to be certain that night having been dead off just before. It is off again now and will be certainly directly on again.

Tuesday afternoon Sister Rose Innes took me for a drive in her little pony cart. She has a nice white pony we caught on trek last November, that goes awfully well. We then went to call on the Celliers but Sister Rose Innes did not know them. Evelyn was in and played to us; she is a beautiful musician and plays by heart in an extraordinary way. She plays some of the Chopin you used to, but by heart. We only stayed a short time as I had to be in, being such an invalid.

All my Pretoria friends heard a rumour that I was off home, it is wonderful how they start, and were nearly as surprised to see me as if I had been a ghost! We drove round by Eloff's wood and picked up a sister belonging to No 19 General Hospital pursuing her horse on foot. She is the one I call the prize-fighter, she has a face just like one though I don't know her name. Luckily her esquire, a doctor man, returned with the errant steed. I hope you enjoy the ball, and will have some more. I suppose you will see the coronation.

The Peace Conference reconvened on 15 May at Vereeniging, each country in its own tent, with a large marquee for plenary sessions. There were 60 delegates representing the various Boer States.

Every one wanted peace, both British and Boer, and after a fortnight of hard bargaining and discussion a treaty agreeable to both sides, the treaty of Vereeniging, was signed at Pretoria on 31 May 1902 at 5 minutes to midnight after 2 years 8 months of war. The terms were similar to those rejected at Middleburg a year before; the main ones being ;

1. The Boers to lay down their arms.
2. All prisoners and internees to be released.
3. Surrendering burghers to keep their liberty and property.
4. Dutch to be taught in the schools if parents wished, and to be used in the law courts.
5. Self Government as soon as circumstances permit.
6. Native franchise not to be granted before self government.
7. A gift of 3 million pounds towards rehabilitation from the British Government.

The British had lost 22,000 men in the war, two thirds of them from disease. The Boers had 24,000 casualties, many were women who had died in the camps, far from the field of battle.

The War Office had thought initially that the war would probably be over in three months and that 75,000 men would be sufficient. In fact the real number required was 450,000 and the war lasted just under three years. The original estimate of the cost of the war was £10,000,000, the actual cost was £200,000,000. Nearly 400,000 horses had to be sent as remounts to South Africa from all over the world.

1 June 1902. Lachlan to Father. No 22 General Hospital, Pretoria

PEACE was brought off last night at 11 p.m., at least that's what they say this morning. The town was singing and kicking up an awful row till 2 a.m. this morning, so I hope it is true. Old Grumming, Principle Medical Officer of this hospital told us an hour ago, and says the Boers were 53 to 3 about peace and signed the agreement, whatever that may be. Everyone takes it quite quietly, and we have been waiting so long that it falls rather flat. A lot of people are rather sorry, as they think that if we had gone on a little and wiped them out thoroughly there would be much less trouble thereafter, but I think they will think twice before they try on any more games.

I wonder if we are likely to go home very soon? Personally I think it most improbable, but some people seem to think we will, however time will show. First of all the commanders must come in, and I imagine the Guards and all sorts of other people will go before we do.

I am going back on duty tomorrow, and feel as fit as ever. This week I have been out a good bit, riding around and doing a little exercise. I am glad Joan is getting a good season. Love to all.

The arrival of peace at last after so long was greeted phlegmatically, almost with disbelief. The shooting had stopped, the men would be returning home soon.

5 June 1902. Joan to Lachlan. 32 Green Street, Park Lane

No words can describe the intense relief and the wonderful joys of peace after 2 years and 7 months. Dearest brother, how can I ever thank God enough for his mercy and goodness? Of course we had been expecting peace for some days, but one always felt here might be a hitch at the last moment. Uncle Tommy and Aunt Charty were in the country, and Barbara and I and Belle and Mlle Bigot were sitting at dinner that evening, when Reggie Lister arrived from Paris and told us. I couldn't speak or eat, it seemed so incredibly glorious that it was all over, all our anxiety and sorrow.

After dinner we took Hansoms and Mlle. Bigot and I drove down to the War Office to make sure; the streets seemed ridiculously quiet, but of course it was Sunday. There was a small crowd outside the W.O. and we shouted 'Hurray' rather mildly, then I went to see Grandmama at her Hotel. I longed to shout and dance, but everyone had made so sure of peace for days that they took it very quietly. Then I wanted to telegraph home and to you and I drove up Vere Street, but the office was shut, so I thought I would leave that till morning, but my nice cabbie said he was going home past the General Post Office, so I gave him my telegram to send home and sent mine to you the next morning.

The verse in Galatians kept running in my head 'The fruits of the Spirit are Love, Joy, Peace etc' and I felt the long suffering was over. Barbara was sharp enough to drive down to the city where she said the crowd was wonderfully enthusiastic. I could hardly sleep for excitement and wondering when you would get home. Not for months yet I suppose, but how different it is now.

The next day everyone put out flags. I wanted dreadfully to hear Lord K's despatch read in Parliament but Margot failed to get me into the H. of C. and the house of Lords was crammed too, however it was not as interesting as it might have been. Lord Salisbury hates emotion and display and simply read out the terms, and no good speeches were made. That night we thought we would be patriotic and go along to a music hall. We suggested to Grandmama that she should come too, and to our astonishment she said she would like to, however when she realised what it was she refused.

A very nice friend of Barbara's, Mr Lindley dined with us and then we started; Aunt Charty with Lady Cranbourne and Barbara and me in one hansom and Uncle Tommy and Mr Lindley in another. The drive down the Strand was wonderful, thick, thick crowds, very orderly and quiet, walking along, a few with flags and penny trumpets, and other unmusical instruments, and others with paper rattles and peacock feathers. It was rather frightening as they all crept under the horses and one felt there must be accidents.

Barbara didn't like it a bit, as there were a few drunk people and they tried to tickle us with their feathers. However at last we arrived and after one short struggle with the human mass on the pavement, got in. It is not a pretty thing an English crowd, their clothes are so hideous and they can't sing, and their shouts and noises are dreadful too, but I love their enthusiasm. The Tivoli was not as amusing as it might have been. We sang 'God Save the King' and wished it was still the old Queen, and we cheered a little and a man sang a stupid ode to Peace. May Tennant and Uncle Archie were there and they took me home in the motor. We went along the embankment which was a desert. Uncle Tommy and Aunt Charty had to walk the whole way down the Strand, so they really mafficked, and arrived home in the small hours in a dilapidated condition.

Tuesday I spent mostly with Fraulein and Grandmama, who were both on the point of leaving London.

Wednesday 4 June was a horrid wet day, and all I did in the morning was to go round to see Miss Celliers and ask her to go to the Military Tournament with me. They have got very dark rooms near Baker Street. I thought they were so rich, so I was surprised. I saw Mrs C for a moment. She is incidentally very delicate so it must be dreary for Sybil. We went to the Tournament and enjoyed it very much. It is a delightful show and I wish I had gone more than once. The musical rides were so pretty, and artillery driving alarmingly wonderful, and there was a lot of regular circus driving which was great fun.

Sybil recognised a Mr Kearns, one of the riding masters, who also won the officers tent-pegging in very good style and as we went out we ran against him in the passage and she spoke to him. He was amazed at seeing her and he gave us tea in the officer's place, and got us a cab. He was rather amusing and chaffed Sybil about being a wicked little Boer !I found afterwards he was an A.S.C. man. He had seen you but evidently did not know you very well.

I think Miss Celliers is very nice and I expect you had great fun with her. She is prettier than the Geddes girls, but not so amusing.

25 May 1902. Lachlan to Joan. Kloppers Court, Pretoria

What do you all think of Peace now that it is here? It has come sooner than I thought it would, and I would much like to know what the terms are. I hope we have not caved in and done anything magnanimous; the Boers will say it is weakness if so. I think (in fact we all do) that it would have been better to hammer them a bit more and bring them thoroughly to their knees before stopping, unless it is really unconditional surrender, time enough to make promises after that. There is a rumour that we have given them pretty soft terms, and also that Chamberlain has resigned in consequence, but nothing official is out.

I came out of hospital yesterday, and am once more at large, and perfectly fit again. I was to have stayed in headquarters, but an order came at 2 p.m. that 1 officer and 10 men were to start at once for the Coronation. Lumsden went and I am glad he was chosen, as he has been all through and never missed a day, and is an excellent and hard working chap. He was at Silverton and came straight in and up to the station that night. He had hardly any decent clothes and borrowed a coat, and was very busy packing and getting things together. His servant unfortunately got drunk at the last minute, how I know not, and Bray and I had to assist. Lumsden and the lucky 10 were seen off by the band and everyone who was in Headquarters and are now on their way to Capetown.

I suppose we shall follow in due course though it seems impossible to believe, we have been here so long. In spite of everything, it will be with a feeling of regret that I will leave the Sunny South, strange as that may seem; but of course that feeling will be far outweighed by joy at leaving for home.

9 June 1902. Ex-Gordon Highlander A. Bowie to Father. Unionist Club, Falkirk

Mr Gordon Duff, I have just thought of answering your letter about the peace terms accepted by the Boers, now that the war is at an end. There will be a great many homes rejoicing through the land. We first received the news last Sunday night from the Provost of Falkirk to the public from the club windows. Hoping the Gordons won't be long till they are home and also hoping that your son is in the best of health, as there is not much fear of being shot now, for he was a young brave officer, I found him so, as did all the Company. I have not got much news from the front for over a year so I don't know how my gallant regiment is going on, when you rite him you mite let him know I was asking for him and about the Company, as I like to hear about them. Dingwall is home, he was the Capt. of B Coy. This is all the news I have at the moment, Sir. Hoping you are in the best of health.

CHAPTER TWENTY

Pretoria to Aberdeen 1902

2 June 1902. Lachlan to Father. Johnson's Redoubt, Pretoria

I did not write last week as Polly Russell volunteered to, and I was rather lazy, also I thought none of you had written but I was mistaken as my letters were sent to No 22 General Hospital and lay there several days.

Thanksgiving service for peace. W.E.Gordon receiving V.C. from Kitchener. Pretoria, 8 June 1902

So peace really has descended on the land, and the burghers are coming in pretty well. What a lot more there were than any one suspected! I have seen a few surrenders come in. They looked very fit and had serviceable though patchy clothes; some were riding mules and some donkeys even, though most had ordinary veldt ponies that appeared wonderfully fit considering all things, and a lot of them said they would have gone on fighting for another 5 years, probably bravado. I hear that Botha, De Wet and De la Rey are to be made C.Bs.

The weather is horribly cold, bitter gales and dust all day, and hard frost at night - it is impossible to keep warm. I came out of hospital on the 2nd and Lumsden and 10 NCOs and men started for the Coronation that night. He was at Silverton and only got the order at 2.30 p.m. so it was quick work. If he had not wished to go I should have.

They have started pulling down some of the blockhouses today.

The 3rd, I went off to Klapper Kop and took over G Company from Tim Gordon. It is a big Boer fort, just like Wonderboom and very comfortable with electric light etc. Milner rode up that afternoon, and walked down. It was pretty late and he only stayed a minute and looked at the view which is a regular panorama. I did not see him as I was some way off, and he went at once, but he sent me his remembrances.

I was relieved on the 5th at 6.30 p.m., and we walked into Johnson's Redoubt in an hour or so, pretty good in the dark. I found them collecting every man in the camp for the Peace ceremonial on Sunday and drilling them. We had a great guest-night with boxing etc. after dinner - which was rather trying. Lockley got his hand cut open playing a game called "Broken Bottles".

Sunday morning at 5.30 a.m. reveille, very chilly, marched away at 7.15, reached the Church Square at 8.30 and took our place. There were some 6,000 troops brought into Pretoria for the occasion and the place was packed. A platform draped with red was built in front of the Government buildings, where K. and his staff were with all the big bugs, and the people going to get decorations, and a lot of nursing sisters and spectators, and all "Hallo Australia" juveniles in a row. I recognised Polly in a window above the platform, and she waved vigorously at Charlie and me who happened to be next door.

The balconies of the Grand Hotel were packed with people and cameras. There were 13 bands performing, and the conductor stood in a thing like a Punch and Judy show box draped in a Royal Standard.

First the Bishop of Zululand made an inaudible address, then K. presented decorations. Gordon got his V.C. and Sister Becher (my friend of No 19) got a R.R.C. and there were a few others. Then we had a sermon from the Archbishop of Capetown, also inaudible, and Kipling's thing, 'Lest we forget' sung to the tune of the hymn 'For those in peril of the sea'. It was wonderfully impressive, the choir and clergy and band marching slowly across the square.

Thorneycroft was stage man, and everything went off swimmingly. It was a glorious day, and luckily they watered the ground till it was all mud and puddles, as the dust would have would have been awful. We saw a good many old acquaintances come up from all parts of the country to take part. They were nearly all camped up near us, and are now mostly gone again to their units. We got down at 8.30 a.m. and stood till 11, when we marched up with band and pipes.

I dined at Charlie's house and after dinner we had a little dance in the drawing room. There were only a few people, but it was rather fun. Jack White is up here but off tomorrow; it is like old days seeing him again and he looked very fit.

Our M.I. are at Kroonstad just now. Last night a good many of us went to see the Juveniles perform. 'The Barmaid' was the piece. They were marvellous, and danced very splendidly and the acting was very comic. They are all quite kids.

14th - The weather is still miserably cold; it is strange how one feels it. The mail train was delayed by snow at Nieupoort, and I hear 3 or 4 men died of cold coming up by it; it is an unusually severe winter. They say the Boers were considerably influenced in their surrender by the signs of a particularly severe winter so they must be good weather prophets. I can understand their fear of this sort of thing out in the veldt with no shelter or warm clothing. Neish has just returned from receiving the surrender in the Pietersburg and Nylstroom districts. He got over 300.

The Volunteers are going home very soon and I believe the reservists will not be long. I hope there is a chance of some of us going with them, in which case I should probably be one. I am sick to death of this sort of life. If we don't go with them they might open leave as they say the regiment is not going before Xmas. So if I did manage to get home I would probably have to come out again and join them here. I have a liver you will be surprised to hear. I discovered it was that when in hospital! I think a change would be a good thing, and I long for a sight of the sea.

Last night I went to a subscription dance. Hercules was one of the committee running it. It was at the Hotel Cecil. The room was very good, and the music not bad, but it was very badly done. Hercules dances hard and seems to be thoroughly enjoying himself. I do not like that man. There were a lot of people there I did not know and I was very bored indeed. We had a terribly cold 3 mile drive back in a Cape cart. Got to bed by 2 a.m., no more of these sorts of dances for me.

We have a large crowd of recently joined subalterns, most of them very big chaps. I have considerable difficulty in feeding my ponies up here, and cannot get a native to look after them; the little mare has had a bit of fever, and is very much out of condition. I wish I could get rid of both of them and clear out of Africa but that seems impossible. I feel what is commonly called 'fed up with everything' including myself.

Lyttelton has arrived and is going to take over command from K. I must go and call on him, as he is a dear old boy.

This was the last of Lachlan's letters from South Africa; rather sad for me in a way. I've enjoyed getting to know him through them and following all his ups and downs. He was a lovely man and I'm proud to share his genes and hope to meet him again.

16 June 1902: Lachlan's wish to leave South Africa was granted that morning. He would be leaving for home two days later.

The following is a summary of Lachlan's journey home taken from his diaries.

Wednesday 18 June.

The home repatriation party consisting of 3 officers and 150 other ranks paraded at 10.30. The Colonel made a little speech and they marched to the station, followed by large crowds to see them off. The ponies were sent to Charlie. It was a long journey to Capetown, 1040 miles. Taking five days, it must have been boring, cold and uncomfortable. Meals were the outstanding events of the day, as recorded in his diary. But they were going home!

Thursday 19 June.

Breakfast at Kroonstad; dinner at Bloomfontein, where they went for a walk in the town in the bitter cold

Friday 20 June.

In the train. Breakfast at Norwalsport; lunch at Naaupoort; dinner at De Aar. There was a lot of snow on the ground and in the ditches and hollows. Seven men got left behind! (Presumably they did not want to go home or just got drunk and disappeared).

Saturday 21 June.

In the train. Breakfast at Beaufort West where the train divided at Fraserburgh Road and continued with the North Lancs Volunteers in the guards van. Dinner at Grootfontein. This was the coldest night of the journey, men were taken ill.

Sunday 22 June.

It was warmer at last after the bitter cold of the last few days. Breakfast was at Worcester. They arrived in Capetown at 5 p.m. when they went straight on board the S.S. Orotava. Lockley and Lachlan were given a wretched little cabin which they managed to change later. Ogston was going home with them and they all dined together. What a wonderful feeling to get up that gang-way onto the ship and to know one is going home!

Monday 23 June.

Lachlan and Lockley with MacDonald, his servant had a final shopping expedition, and lunched on board. Lachlan described Capetown as 'a horrid place' and thought it 'too full of generals and staff officers'.

The ship was due to sail that day at 3.30 p.m. At 3 p.m. the generals arrived; Kitchener, Hamilton, French, Rawlinson - quite a formidable collection to have on board. On the quayside was a sea of red tabs and their ladies. There was meant to have been a Guard of Honour from the Camerons and Suffolks which failed to turn up, but nobody seemed to mind and they sailed as scheduled. It was a lovely day. Lachlan and Lockley changed their cabin to a better one on the outside, and settled down to a relaxed time for the next two weeks.

The voyage lasted from 22 June to 12 July when they docked at Southampton 6000 miles away, but was not without incident. The Coronation had been due to take place on 26 June but on Friday 4 July The Ortova received a signal from a passing ship that the King was 'out of danger'! People were worried as no one on board knew that he had been ill!

Sunday 6 July.

There was a scheduled stop at Las Palmas, where they heard that the Coronation had been cancelled because of the King's illness.

Tuesday 8 July.

The ship's engines broke down at 6 p.m. Luckily the sea was calm and they drifted about all night. Typically, no one knew what was wrong, or would not say. Lachlan spent some of the time fishing and caught nothing, which added to his frustration. Freddy Gordon was discovered to have contracted smallpox and was isolated to a ship's boat aft. Then all were vaccinated at 3.00 p.m.

Wednesday 9 July.

The engines started up at 5 a.m. and broke down at 5 p.m. It was getting colder. The King was better.

Saturday 12 July.

Arrived at Southampton. Kitchener got off to cheers and enthusiasm. Uncle Archie and Joan were there to meet Lachlan but were not allowed on board, Archie and Joan had to lunch at a hotel. By pure chance, Sybil and her mother were sailing to Capetown that day and were at the docks. Sybil was looking sad and rather pretty.

The troop train to Aberdeen, 500 miles distant, left at 6 p.m. Joan travelled on it with Lachlan. It was quite dashing in those days for ladies to travel on troop trains. What a joyful journey it must have been!

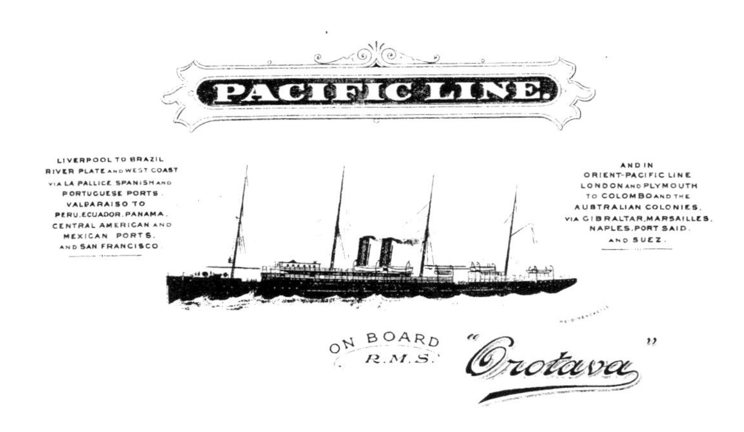

THE PACIFIC STEAM NAVIGATION Co's. S. S. "OROTAVA."
TRANSPORT No. 91.

Sailed from Cape Town, Monday, 23rd June, 1902.

Commander—HENRY COLLINS

G. H. Bindley, R.N.R., Chief Officer
J. H. Jenkins, Second Officer
J. J. Hayes, Third Officer
P. A. G. Kell, R.N.R., Fourth Officer
H. D. Morgan, Purser
T. P. McKell, Surgeon
J. Mitchell, Chief Engineer
J. Scott, Second Engineer
J. H. Potter, Chief Steward

LIST OF PASSENGERS.

General Viscount Kitchener, G.C.B., G.C.M.G., Commander-in-Chief
Lieut-General Sir I. S. M. Hamilton, K.C.B., D.S.O.
Lieut-Colonel W. R. Birdwood
Lieut-Colonel W. N. Congreve, V.C.
Capt. F. A. Maxwell, V.C., D.S.O.
Capt V. R. Brooke, D.S.O.
Capt. E. Gibb
Civil Surgeon E. L. Hunt

Lieut-General Sir J. D. P. French, K.C.B.
Capt. Hon. R. Ward
Capt. S. L. Barry, D.S.O.

Lieut-Colonel Sir H. S. Rawlinson, C.B.
Lieut-Colonel Hon. F. Gordon, D.S.O.
Lieut-Colonel A. W. Money
Capt. H. J. Macandrew, D.S.O.
Capt. H. L. Pritchard, D.S.O.

Major F. J. Heyworth, D.S.O., 1st Scots Guards, Commanding Troops
Capt. C. Ogston, 1st Gordon Highlanders, Acting Adjutant
Lieut. R. E. H. Lockley, 1st Gordon Highlanders, Acting Quarter-Master

Lieut. Hon. R. Coke, 1st Scots Gds.
,, Hon. J. J. Dalrymple ,,
Major G. P. Stewart, 1st Inniskilling Fus
Capt. J. N. Crawford ,,
Lieut. R. C. Smythe ,,
Capt. A. C. Richards, 2nd Hants
Lieut. H. F. Ashby ,,
2nd Lieut. F. W. Earle, 2nd Hants
Major C. B. Moreland, 1st Welsh
Lieut. W. H. Ferrar ,,
,, F. H. Romilly ,,
Lieut L. Gordon-Duff, 1st Gordons
Civil Surgeon Bywater
,, Wilkinson

CHAPTER TWENTY ONE

Peacetime. The years in between. 1902 - 1914.

The war was over and the fighting man was home. There were three lost years to be made up.

Reunited with Joan at Drummuir.
Stepbrothers and Sisters.

Driving with Joan and Mamie Lindsay

With the British Army in Ireland 1904-1908

British Army near Cork

Mr. R. Hall and the Glanmire Harriers

Fred Sworder and Archie Craufurd
Field Training at Cork

Lachlan Gordon-Duff on Juanita
after winning the military race.

1902-04

After Lachlan's return the Regiment followed and was stationed at Glasgow until April 1904 when they were posted to Ireland. It was a land of beautiful girls, horses, racing, yachting, rain, and a social life of a kind that disappeared 12 years later in the mud of Flanders. They were based in Cork, a plum station for all sports.

1905-06

Lachlan started keeping his diary again. He had lost the previous one in South Africa. In its brief entries it painted a picture of an intense sporting and social life. It catalogued all the sporting fixtures and society engagements of which there were many. It depicted the life of a popular young bachelor and a dashing horseman. In it were the names of numerous young women including that of my mother, the beautiful Miss Pike. But in this methodically kept diary which listed his expenditure and days hunting and racing, there was no mention of any romantic feelings towards any lady. He seemed fonder of his horses. During the hunting season of 1904/05 he was out 55 days and rode in five races, coming second once and fourth twice. In 1906/07 he hunted 70 days, rode in eleven races, winning three and coming second six times. He owned three horses, Juanita, Penelope and Kitten. This was surely a remarkable record of equestrian achievement even in horse-mad Ireland.

1907

In the meantime Lachlan was not idle in his pursuit of Miss Lydia Pike, the auburn-haired daughter of the Cork shipping magnate, Joseph Pike. She was a brilliant rider, and they hunted and rode together. In contrast to the excitement of hunting and riding there were many invitations to Dunsland, the Pikes house. It was beautifully situated overlooking the River Lee near Glanmire outside Cork. The first recorded visit for tea was on 30 January 1907. It was to be the beginning of a lasting relationship. On Sunday 21 July 1907 Lachlan went to morning service at Glanmire with Lydia. Afterwards they walked in the oak wood and read together Lubbocks "The Pleasures of Life". Suddenly the diary somewhat cryptically records "And we will henceforth be as one. All very wonderful and unexpected". They were engaged to be married. Reading this diary 80 years later, the strange thought occurred to me that these two young things were to become my parents. 1907 was a good year for Lachlan, he had become engaged to Lydia Pike and also won the Army Lightweight Steeplechase on his Juanita. Juanita

Dunsland House County Cork.

Waiting to play

Fair ladies of Cork

Lydia washing her dog

Mr. and Mrs. Joseph Pike
with steam launch
on the river Lee

died that winter, it was a terrible blow, he really loved that horse who had served him so well. He was very upset but now he had another love called Lydia.

1908

The 22 April 1908 was a fine day. Lachlan and his best man drove to Glanmire Church in their full dress uniforms arriving twenty minutes early. Lydia was fifteen minutes late with a retinue of ten bridesmaids. The Bishop of Cork, assisted by Canon Archdall and Mr Purcell conducted the service. After the ceremony there was a large reception in a tent on the lawn at

22 April 1908

Dunsland. There were toasts, speeches, telegrams, photographs and all the paraphernalia of a society wedding. The happy couple escaped by car amid a storm of rice at 5.30 arriving at Coolekelure at 7.45. It was very cold.

The rest of the honeymoon was spent in Venice and at Riva and the Italian lakes. They then moved into their new home, Llanturk Lodge, Aldershot, where the regiment had moved from Cork. This was a change of scene, but the same hectic social life went on including Ascot and numerous trips to London visiting Tennant relations. There was hardly a dull moment. In July, Lachlan's leave was spent mostly in the North of Scotland, showing

At Riva

Llanturk Lodge

Gordon Highlanders at Aldershot

LGD

September 1908. Celebrations at Drummuir Castle

Lydia off to all the relations, an ordeal for her no doubt. There was much fishing and golf. They were guests of honour at a party given for the combined tenantry of Park and Drummuir Estates to celebrate, belatedly, Lachlan's 21st birthday and safe return home from the War, and of course to meet Lydia, his lovely bride. The holiday over it was back to work but

House party of Duffs, Pikes and Gordon-Duffs

Lachlan at Dunsland
with Pauline. March 1909

Lachlan and Lydia out with the V.W.H.

Maxwell [illegible] Hardie Munro.

THESSALY
LODGE

Sydney Montagu John [illegible]

Wharton Duff.

[illegible]

Polo at Cirencester.

not for long, they both got some form of infection and were very ill for most of August. Lachlan got sick leave until mid November. The first part was spent at Dunsland the second at Drummuir learning about the family estates he was to inherit and how they were managed. After Lachlan was passed fit by a Medical Board in Edinburgh they returned to Aldershot. Xmas was spent at Dunsland.

1909

As a result of his recent stay at Drummuir and his inspection of the property Lachlan realised he knew very little about modern estate management and decided to leave the Army and go to Cirencester Royal Agricultural College to study there. The technology of farming and agriculture was changing rapidly with the arrival of the petrol engine and cheap imported food. Lachlan left the Regiment on 9 January and was gazetted into the Reserve of Officers of the Gordon Highlanders. It was a difficult decision to make, but obviously correct. He must have been sad leaving so many proven friends. A few days later Lachlan and Lydia left their Aldershot home Llanturk Lodge for Dunsland accompanied by Scott, the cat, four horses, one maid, two grooms and a lot of luggage. Two months later, my sister Pauline was born. There was great joy slightly tinged with disappointment that she was of the wrong gender. To ensure the continuity of the family the first born should always be male. During the season 1908/09 Lachlan hunted 30 days. To comply with Society protocol of the times, newly married women were presented to the monarch, this was usually done by the bride's mother. In Lydia's case her mother was still in mourning for her son Cecil, so she could not do so. She was presented at Court by Aunt Margot Asquith, the Prime Minister's wife. A suitable and lively substitute.

Lachlan's first term at the Agricultural College started in the Autumn and they got busy house hunting, deciding to live at Thessaly Lodge near the College. It would have to have large stables. While the house was being decorated in August they went North for the Inverness Ball and the Grouse shooting, meaning to stay only a day or two with Grandmama on the way. But Lydia developed Scarlet Fever and could not be moved. What a catastrophe. All their plans had to be cancelled and poor Grandmama had Lydia for several weeks. She returned to Cirencester on 22 October. The college term had started on 5 October.

United once more, Lachlan and Lydia settled down to an intense social life and plenty of hunting, which was fitted in somehow with the college curriculum. Christmas was at Dunsland and again they did not travel light, taking four horses, Maxim, Pluto, Kitten and the Impulse, two grooms and Scott the cat.

Maxim taking a wall

Schooling Maxim

1910

The Christmas holiday was very sociable with hunting and numerous balls. The final one at Castle Martyr was described by Lachlan, as "a good dance, rowdy Lancers, some danger, lively people, home at 4.58 am". He had to be back for the College term starting on 25 January. Lydia followed two days later with the baggage train of horses, grooms and the cat, plus Posie the baby and Nana. From then onwards it was all go, hunting, schooling horses and taking Posie for a walk. Occasionally Lachlan attended a lecture at the College. In February the Royal Agricultural College Point to Point Races took place. Lachlan rode in one and came second. It was a very successful meeting with 70 entries. On 6 April he went to Blumsden for Butt Millers Point to Point, riding Maxim, who fell at the last fence. Ten days later he ended his point to point season by coming second in the Ladies Plate in the Vale of the White Horse Races at Oaksey on Maxim. Lachlan's sister Joan and her husband Jamie Lindsay came with them. This was the smartest meeting of the season, it was fashionable. During the 1909/10 hunting season Lachlan was out 99 days. After a brief Easter break at Drummuir, it was back to studies at the college. He started to play polo again, a game he had played often in South Africa. According to his records, he played 136 chukkas during that summer. His other interest was the internal combustion engine of which he acquired quite a knowledge. He was always messing about with the machine when not engaged with horses. Two contrasting methods of transport.

The summer holiday was spent at Drummuir grouse shooting with relations. He stayed with Uncle Jack Tennant at his estate The Glen in Aberdeenshire. Amongst the other guests was the Prime Minister, Herbert Asquith. They shot over 300 head that day.

In September Lachlan had to do his three weeks Annual Reserve Training with the Regiment at Aldershot. He enjoyed this and saw all his old friends. Taking the part in the manoeuvres was one of the first military aeroplanes. The college term started on 12 October. It was back to the usual winter routine of hunting, attending lectures at the college, going flat out all the time. Lachlan went to the motor show in London and was interested in a Crossley. He could have the body of his choice.

Xmas was again spent at Dunsland with the same number of livestock and human beings shuttling across to Ireland once more.

1911

The winter holiday at Dunsland was very much the same as others. It was extremely sociable with some form of entertainment nearly every day or night. It was mostly involved with horses and hunting and with numerous dances and dinner parties. To know how to play Bridge was most important, especially for young bachelors hoping to be asked out to dinner parties. Strangely "Racing Demon", which was not considered a socially correct card game, was often played as well as Bridge. Lachlan described it "as a game very trying on the temper". The mind boggles 85 years later, trying to imagine this hedonistic life style enjoyed by so few. They were mainly from the Irish Ascendancy and the Officer Corps of the Army in Ireland. It is hard not to sympathise with the genuine Irish people, who so far have not been mentioned in the diaries and to whom the country belonged.

27 January. The College term began and Lydia followed two days later with the Baggage Train. Hunting started in earnest again. The College point to point was held on 18 March and Lachlan won the Students Challenge Cup, riding Pluto. Lydia did some form of Red Cross training between social engagements and hunting. The Motor car was becoming more and more efficient and had obviously come to stay. It had the same fascination

for Lachlan as his beloved horses. He wanted a good make of car and was interested in two, the Armstrong Whitworth and the Crossley. In those days cars were custom built, mass production was a long way off. The procedure for a purchaser was first of all to try out the chassis which included the engine of the car of his choice. If he liked it he decided on the type of body he wanted. Lachlan decided to purchase a Crossley after testing it out on the test hill at Brooklands. It was loaded with three people. "It did a great pace in second speed" according to the Diary. He bought it and had driving lessons then and there. The car was to have been ready by 4 April and Lachlan

Lachlan and Lydia in the Crossley

went up to London to take possession of the new toy but could not do so. The spare wheel had vanished, believed stolen. It had in fact gone to the wrong address. The hood was too low for Lydia when she was wearing her best hat. This made getting into the car difficult and undignified. All this had to be sorted out. Thursday, 6 April was a bitterly cold snowy day, when Lachlan took possession of his precious brand new 12.14 Crossley car. It had a Windham detachable body and was painted grey with red leather upholstery. All very exciting. He took five hours to travel the 100 miles from London to Thessally Lodge, including stopping times.

During the College Easter holiday, Lachlan went North to Montrose to do his annual Reserve training with the 3rd Battalion Gordon Highlanders from 19 April to 14 May. Lydia remained at Drummuir while this was going on. She was accompanied by the usual camp-followers, Posie, Nana,, Scott and a new comer, George the dog. There is no record of how she got on with Mildred.

Aunt Charty died on 2 May and was buried at Gisburn. She had always been very fond of Lachlan and reminded him of his mother. Her only son Tommy, had been killed in action in Somalia in 1902. He was a great friend of Lachlan's. She sounds a lovely person, caring about people, particularly the displaced blacks in S. Africa. An unusual interest for the aristocracy of those days. After the death of Lord Ribblesdale the title became extinct.

On 22 June, Lachlan went up to London for the Coronation of George V and Queen Mary. When it was over he met many old friends. Could there have been a slight touch of nostalgia for the old carefree bachelor days and male camaraderie? During that summer, Polo was again the main form of entertainment. Lachlan played the astronomical number of 188 chukkas as well as finding time to shoot grouse and visit his relations in Banffshire and attend lectures at the College.

Lydia was expecting her second baby in October, so they returned to Thessaly Lodge early in September and then went on to Dunsland where the baby, a boy, Thomas Robert, was born on 5 October. An heir at last to the acres of Drummuir and Park. A great fuss was made. Even I, who came three years later can remember my mother talking about 'womans great work', meaning the production of male heirs. She obviously felt that she had slipped up by having a daughter as her first born, but all was well now. To make certain that woman's great work had been properly completed, a second son, a sort of 'fail-safe', had to be born, just in case anything awful should happen to the heir. That 'fail-safe' was to be me, arriving on 23 November 1914. Potentially important. As it turned out my brother and I were both involved in World War II. He was in the Rifle Brigade and was captured at Calais in 1940 and was a POW for 4 years. I was in the Gordon Highlanders, Lachlan's Regiment. My mother was convinced that one of us would be killed, luckily she was wrong. There are quite a few references in the diary to the new arrival, Thomas Robert, but they gradually diminish, the focus returning to the beloved horses. During the hunting season 1909/1911 Lachlan was out 99 times. At the end of October they went on an extended tour of relations in Scotland starting with Lydia's mothers family in Dumfriesshire, the Critchleys who lived at Stapleton Towers, Annan.

They stayed a week filling in the time at shooting parties. Next week they were at Hatton Castle in Aberdeenshire doing the same thing, then for a fortnight at Drummuir and finally spent a long week end at Beaufort Castle, Beauly, Inverness, with the Lovats. Lady Lovat was Aunt Charty's daughter and Lachlan's first cousin. After this bout of shooting and visiting relations, they dashed back to Thessally Lodge and presumably the neglected college. Lachlan, leaving Lydia and the children, went on to Colchester to celebrate St Andrew's night with the Regiment. It was quite a party. After that it was back to hunting, going to lectures at the College and the usual round of dinner parties. Xmas that year was at Thessaly Lodge, a family affair attended by Lydia's parents. There were lots of presents for the children and a supper party for the staff, while the family fed in the nursery with the children. On Boxing day the Xmas spirit seemed to have waned as the diary

Lydia. Red Cross training.

records cryptically, "Row in the stables" . Two days later it records "Peace in the stables pro tem." One wonders what all that was about?

1912

The status quo in the stables having returned to normal, hunting continued several days a week. The population of foxes in Gloucestershire must have been very high, it's a wonder there were any left the way they were harried all season. Lachlan attended the college from time to time and Lydia was examined at the end of her Red Cross course in "the manoeuvring of casualties on horseback" which would have been frightening for the casualties. She passed, and with some of her colleagues and did a further days drill at Bingham Court in "the technology and use of mounted stretchers". By the end of the hunting season Lachlan had seven horses who between them were out 105 days.

Lachlan became interested in politics and spoke at a Conservative party Rally at Cheltenham.

August 1912 Park House, Cornhill, Banffshire.

15 April. Lachlan went to Montrose for his annual Army Reserve training and Lydia took the children and attendants to Dunsland. News had just come in about the sinking of the Titanic. Everybody was very shocked. After the camp, at which Lachlan's company won the musketry competition, they were reunited at Thessaly and polo was resumed. In June, Uncle Jack Tennant was promoted to Under Secretary for War by his brother-in-law, Herbert Asquith, the Prime Minister. Lachlan's last term at the Royal Agricultural College, Cirencester, ended on 9 August 1912. It was goodbye to Thessally Lodge after three wonderfully happy years.

They moved up North to their future home, Park House, Cornhill, Banffshire, in time for the Grouse shooting and the Highland Balls. The furniture had to be moved to Park and the house got ready. There was a lot to be done. While all this was going on the children, their attendants, horses, grooms, cats etc. stayed at Dunsland until sent for.

Lachlan and Lydia decided to drive North to Park in the Crossley. It was a journey of about 700 miles which was quite an adventure in those days. The roads were not all that good, and hotels could be variable, not being used to "travelling motorists". Cars could break down and did, mainly due to punctures and the radiator over heating on steep hills. They left Thessaly Lodge at 3.30 p.m. on 19 August and stayed the first night at Coventry. They travelled via Stow in the Wold, Broadway, Stratford on Avon and Warwick. They arrived at The Kings Head, Coventry at 7.30 p.m., which they described as "big, dirty and very noisy". Distance covered 64 miles.

20 August. They left at 9.45 am travelling via Derby, Buxton, Glossop, Huddersfield and Skipton, stopping the night at The Black Bear, Hellifield, which they reached at 7.50 p.m.. It was small and comfortable, but not used to "touring visitors". Dinner consisted of toast, chops and tea. The distance covered for that day was 162 miles. It was a beautiful drive and the road was reasonable except around Huddersfield and Halifax where it was ugly and there were miles and miles of tramways.

21 August. This time they had a definite destination to get to, to stay with the Lauderdale Duncans for the weekend and to play golf. They left Hellifield at 9.30 am and journeyed North via Settle, Kendal, Carlisle, Langholm, Hawick, Stow and Pathead and arrived at North Berwick at 6 p.m. after a drive of 191 miles. They were very tired. That day's drive had not been without incident. All went well on the climb up Shap Fell, the car behaved beautifully but the radiator boiled over and had to be refilled going up Soutra hill near Pathead.

Revived by a weekend of golf, they continued their journey North to Stonehaven via Edinburgh, Queensferry, Newport, Dundee and Montrose and arrived at the Mill Inn Hotel, Stonehaven at 3 p.m. Mileage that day, 130.

28 August saw the final leg of the journey to Braemoriston. They left at 10 am arriving at 3 p.m., a journey of 107 miles. The route was via Banchory, Kincardine O'Neil, Bridge of Alford and Huntly. The total mileage from

Thessaly Lodge to Braemoriston was 638 miles with no mechanical trouble. Lachlan had chosen an excellent car.

The next thing Lachlan, now a fully qualified agricultural graduate, had to do, was to take over his inheritance. It was a small estate for those parts, consisting of 4000 acres, all rented farms, except for the Home Farm of 300 acres which he kept in hand. Nearby was the ancient mansion Park House in which Lydia, Lachlan and family were to make their home. Like so many large houses in North East Scotland it was very cold. There was no central

The drawing room at Park.

heating or electric light. Candles and oil lamps were the only form of illumination. But not for long; Lachlan got busy and a firm came from Glasgow to put in central heating. The next step towards civilised living at Park, was to install an Acetylene Gas Lighting Plant to provide gas for the fifty lights in the house. The total cost was £135, including carriage from Glasgow. A new era of comfort had arrived in the cold North East of Scotland. This miniature gas plant consisted of a small gasometer in its own shed, known as the "The Gas House". It was a very important place, feeding acetylene gas down a pipe to the mansion. It illuminated the rooms with a lovely soft light. The gas made a slight hissing noise and a wonderful pop when being lit. Dod Barry, the head forester and not over bright, had now become senior gas technocrat. He was the Gas Man, his domain the Gas House. Of course it was off limits to small boys, but one of my earliest memories is of a time whenNana's surveillance was lifted and I managed to get into this technological palace. I watched spellbound as Dod, the High Priest, went about his rituals, shovelling white carbide powder into mysterious receptacles and pouring water into them, thus creating light in the Big House.

September was the last month of the Scottish Season, the culminating fixture being the two Northern Meeting balls in Inverness, to which Lachlan and Lydia went. It was a great social event, especially for ambitious mothers of debutantes looking for suitable sons-in- law. It was very exclusive. Tickets were limited and could only be got through members of the Ball Committee. It was always held at the end of September, when the Navy, based at Invergordon, had finished its exercises in the Moray Firth. It was a large Navy in those days and there were lots of young naval officers available. The army was in the same position with its visiting regiments and their young officers. There was no shortage of eligible young men. The dress regulations were very strict, all gentlemen who could, had to wear either the kilt or uniform. If not in possession of either, a tailcoat with coloured facings had to be worn. The ladies wore long ball dresses with their tartan sashes pinned on with the clan broach. There were two nights of revelry and a strong constitution was required. Mrs Logan's Scottish country dance band, the best in the North at that time, played for all dances except for the reels. The music for these was provided by the Regimental Pipers from Fort George. A Reel danced properly is a most colourful scene. The red jackets and kilts of the Army, the blue of the Navy, mixed with all the colours of the various tartans. The girls billowing dresses formed a brilliant back drop as they danced to the magical rhythm of the music. Every one knew the steps and danced them in a dignified manner. It was a joy to watch. Lydia and Lachlan got to bed at 3.30 am after the first ball and at 4.30 am after the second.

Their extraordinary pattern of life could not go on for ever. They were all living in a pleasure seeking time-capsule, far away from reality. Two years later the First World War broke out and things were never the same again.

The capsule was shattered and everything changed. Many young men never came home. Lachlan was one of them. In November Park was closed down for the winter and the family moved to Dunsland. The hunting season had

Posie and Robin in the Garden at Dunsland.

started and the horses were already there. Xmas was as usual with masses of presents for Posie and Robert.

1913

The Point to Point season started in March. Lachlan rode in three races. He won one, was second in an other and fell in a third. He had 62 days hunting and Lydia 46. They returned to Park in April. Lachlan went to

Montrose for his annual Reserve training while Lydia supervised the decoration of the house. There was also great activity planting shrubs in the grounds as well. In June they went to London to buy carpets, kitchen equipment and so on. It was very expensive but must have been great fun. Lachlan

Left to right. Back row. Margaret, Geordie, Constantia, Mildred, Randall, Thomas, Archie, Jane and Francis.
Centre row. David, John and Helen
Front row. Lachlan, Lydia with Robin and Posie, Joan (Lindsay) with Harry and Michael

Last Gordon-Duff family group at Drummuir. Summer 1914

was worried about his hair falling out and went to see a Dr Walsh, a specialist in curing baldness. History does not relate what the result of the consultation was, it would certainly have been expensive. Park was being reborn with new carpets, lighting, a kitchen range and new paint everywhere. Outside there was a new hard tennis court. The farm was stocked and new implements, including a Reaper Binder, were bought. Darling Park was throbbing with life and enthusiasm. Eighty years later I witnessed its death, from sheer stupidity. It was mutilated by bad architectural advice, change of ownership and lack of love. In December the family went back to Dunsland for Xmas and the hunting.

1914

In March all hunting and racing was stopped because of an outbreak of Foot and Mouth disease. The only way to prevent it spreading was to stop all movement of animals. It was extremely infectious. There was no more hunting and all Point-to-Point races were cancelled. What an awful blow to the hunting set to be deprived of their recreation. What could they do instead? Lachlan took the opportunity to go to Park for a few days to see what was going on there. Due to the weather not much farming could be done but plenty of trees had been planted. He was now part of the Local Government machine, a County Councillor and member of the School Board. After a few days he went back to Dunsland to pick up Lydia and drive her back to Park. The children and Nana would follow in due course. (What any of us would have done without her it is impossible to say).

2 April. The journey was not without incident. On arrival at the Broomilaw, Glasgow, there was no docking space available for the boat to tie up to unload the car. They waited in the Central Hotel, very cross and could not leave for the North until 4.30 p.m.. Their route was via Stirling, Doune and Dunblane. They finally arrived at Drummond Arms,Crieff at 8 p.m., where they spent the night. The distance covered was 65 miles.

3 April. They travelled to Drummuir via Rumbling Bridge, Dunkeld, Pitlochry, Kingussie, Black Pots Bridge, Aberlour and arrived at Drummuir at 7.30, a journey of 135 miles.

4 April. They arrived at Park and found all well. The car had been misbehaving and had to be left in Elgin for several days to be repaired. This meant using the railway which was not at all convenient. They had been over to Braemoriston for lunch with Grandmama and to shop. They came back by train laden with parcels filling the carriage and the corridor. Lydia took so long to unload that the train moved on to the next station while she was hurling the parcels out of the window. Cousin Ernest Russell, from South Africa turned up to stay.

15 April. Lachlan went to Fort George to do his annual three weeks Army Reserve training. After that, in early June, they went down to London, Lachlan for his regimental dinner and Lydia to meet her mother, who had come over from Ireland for a shopping spree. Lachlan met numerous

Tennant relations and visited the House of Commons. He also met cousin Dolly Duff and congratulated her on being engaged to Commander James RN, the original of "Bubbles" in the Pears' Soap advertisement.

17 June. They went down to Worcestershire to stay with Uncle Archie at the Red House, Overbury, for two nights, then on to Stratton House near Tidworth to stay with the Haslams, friends of Lydia's for an army review. It must have been a fine sight, several batteries of Artillery, three regiments of cavalry and nine of Infantry. The most impressive sight of all was the fly past of twelve aeroplanes, as they dipped their wings over the saluting base. They were all going to be needed very soon.

18 June. Lachlan and Lydia returned to Park and the children. The weather was lovely, fine and warm. They had had an idyllic time and really settled into Park and taken part in all the community activities. Lachlan was especially keen on the Boy Scout movement and Lydia on the Red Cross. They were both well liked by all.

CHAPTER TWENTY TWO

1914. At War Again.

Wednesday 29 July. War was declared between Austria and Serbia. That day they had picked 120 lbs of blackcurrants for a green grocer in Banff at 3 pence a pound. An aeroplane was flown from Cruden Bay, near Peterhead to Norway in five hours - the shape of things to come. There was much talk of the imminence of war and how the whole of Europe would be involved. There was a truce in troubled Ireland.

Saturday 1 August. Germany declared war on Russia and invaded France. The British navy was mobilised. Lachlan expected to be called up at any time. He and Lydia went for a drive with the children in the pony trap. They probably appeared to be completely calm, carrying on as usual. Inwardly they must have been worrying though not fully realising the seriousness of the situation.

> 2 August 1914. Anxious day, expecting to be off to war, preparing kit

He had received a travel warrant to Aberdeen and been told to await further orders.

4 August. Britain declared on Germany. Lachlan practised revolver shooting in the sand pit behind the house. He was ordered to report to Aberdeen on the 7th. The situation for both of them as for so many others was tragic. To be separated at a moment's notice after only six years of marriage was the cruellest of fates. They had worked so hard to activate Park House, its garden and farm. In some ways it was harder for Lydia, a comparative stranger, hundreds of miles away from her relations in Cork. She had two toddlers to care for with another baby on the way, due at the end of November. Now, suddenly, she had to run the estate as well as the family, with her husband liable to go overseas. Lachlan had survived the war in South Africa. He had been lucky. To take part in another one was to tempt providence.

[No. 703, December 16, 1914]

ONOUR—AND OFFICERS OF TWO FA

have Given their Lives or are Giving their Servi

THE OFFICERS OF THE 1ST BATTALION GORDON HIGHLANDERS

From left to right are: Back row—Lieutenant and Quartermaster J. Macdonald, Lieutenant J. K. Trotter, Lieutenant H. M. Sprot, Lieutenant G. T. Burney, Lieutenant W. A. F. Sandeman, Lieutenant G. R. V. Hume-Gore, Lieutenant Hon. A. A. Fraser, Master of Saltoun, Lieutenant A. S. B. Graham, Lieutenant M. V. Hay; middle row—Lieutenant Johnson Watson, Captain and Quartermaster J. Maclennan, Captain J. K. Dick-Cunyngham, D.S.O., Major C. J. Simpson, Captain G. N. McLean, Lieutenant C. G. D. Huggins, Captain H. A. Ross, Captain C. R. Lumsden, Captain S. R. McClintock, Lieutenant Ritchie, Captain Alexander, Lieutenant James Hunter; front row—Lieutenant A. P. F. Lyon, Captain L. Gordon Duff, Captain J. U. M. Ingilby, Captain C. A. S. Maitland, Lieut.-Colonel F. H. Neish, Colonel Hon. F. Gordon, D.S.O., Lieut.-Colonel H. P. Uniacke (2nd Battalion), Captain P. W. Brown, Captain T. M. Booth, Captain W. B. J. Mitford

This picture was taken before the regiment went to the front

1914. AT WAR AGAIN.

Life in Aberdeen was chaotic, the place was awash with troops coming and going. There were the usual shortages of equipment and accommodation which the British Army always has when it goes to war. Most troops were billeted in schools and the officers in hotels and clubs.

Joan and her family went to Park to keep Lydia company for a bit. Uncle Jamie, her husband, was in the London Scottish and had been called up. Lachlan's first letter from Aberdeen, dated 8 August, is full of optimism. He said "I think the German attack will falter before long, they appear to have had another big reverse at Mulhouse. Good bye my precious, take care of yourself, it does not look like your poor Lachlan will be going across the seas to rout the Kaiser".

15 August. To Lydia. Aberdeen.

I think the Kaiser has got near the end of his tether, even without the Russians who will be soon felt. Germany is in a bad way and will be short of food in not many months.

Meanwhile Lachlan and Lydia corresponded with each other, mainly about the children, the farm and all the everyday things of their lives. Lydia had trouble with the car. Toby Roche, the Irish groom, would drive it too fast. She had to engage estate staff and so on. She was very competent.

23 August 1914. To Lydia.

It was ripping seeing you today and I feel greatly bucked up and look forward to your arrival next Saturday. I hope you were not frightfully tired but you had a long day, I fear. I hope we are wrong about the war going on so long, but if God wills it, we can but say Amen and trust to his mercy. I think He will be kind and bring us all safely through and back to each other, how lovely that will be. Good Bye, my Angel, and God be with us both and keep us, I pray for you constantly, and feel you are always near, whatever happens. I hope the chicks like the drum and gun. I will get the flags on Monday.

Love to you all, especially your Dear Self, Ever Yours, Lachlan

The war was not going well for the allies.

21 August. The Belgian army retired to Antwerp and the Germans occupied Brussels.

25 August. The Germans captured the strategic fortress town of Namur. The British Expeditionary Force was engaged near Mons. There were many casualties. It was rumoured that Russian reinforcements from Archangel had landed, but no one knew where. Someone, somewhere had seen a lot of men in strange uniforms getting into a train. They had snow on their boots and people thought they must have been Russians. Lydia came for the weekend driven over from Park by Toby Roche, slowly. She stayed at the Grand Hotel to meet her mother who had come over from Dunsland. They optimistically ordered some furniture for Park. The British casualties in France were heavy, 6,000, in a very short time. They had to be replaced from the various regimental depots, including the Gordon Highlanders at Aberdeen. The more casualties there were the sooner Lachlan would go. He knew he would have to go some time, but when? It was like being on a knife edge. Lydia spent as much time as she could with Lachlan. She was torn between Aberdeen and the children at Park. It was very difficult for both of them but better than nothing. Lachlan was trying to find lodgings, without success.

25 August. 1914. To Lydia.

What a nice visit you paid me, but it went too fast. It's a pity you are not here today as we are busy cleaning up this place. I have an afternoon with nothing to do and could have driven you out. Instead I am writing letters. It has been a lovely day again. I wonder if you are at the seaside. I hope you are not too tired after such a long day.

Au revoir, cherie. Love to the children and your mother. Your Loving Lachlan."

The war news was mixed, the Russians had had a victory over the Austrians. The Allies had retired to Compiègne which was depressing. The Regiment had suffered heavy casualties at Charleroi and Mons including Lachlan's friend Neish of South African days. The first tragic list of casualties appeared in the papers. They would continue until the war ended in 1918. On a lighter note Lachlan dined with an old Boer War friend, Granny Duncan. They played Racing Demon. He had a cheery evening.

1914. AT WAR AGAIN.

8 August. 1914. To Lydia. Aberdeen

Yesterday 10 officers left for the front. Its a big clearing out and leaves John Ingleby and then me next on the list of Captains for the 3rd Battalion. They all went off to Southampton by the night train. We all went down to see them off and give them a cheer. I am disappointed that you cannot spend next week here, but I quite understand how the land lies. The trouble is that I have no idea when I may be ordered to France. By the time we get there this continued retirement will have ended. It is annoying that the car is misbehaving. I feel sure that if I were there it would be right enough. I think you must go to Ireland, poor old girl, I am awfully sorry for you, but I do not think I shall be here much longer. I shall be happier to think that you are in your parents care in your coming ordeal. What a glorious reunion we shall look forward to. Could you not come, mother and all, as I may be off at any time? There is never more than a few hours notice. You had better drive over if the car is right, if not come by train. Toby will bring the car. Good Bye, my angel, cheer up, and with Gods help all will be well.Your Loving Husband Lachlan.

On 13 September 1914, Lydia drove out and stayed the night at the Palace Hotel, Aberdeen. Next day they moved into the lodgings Lachlan had found in 38 Bonaccord Street. It was complete with cook and maid. They spent as much time together as possible. Lydia watched his parades on the Links. She, braving the cold, sat on a bench on the sea front. They shopped and went to their solicitor and signed their wills. But time was running out. The war was not going well. A big battle was raging on the river Aisne near Paris with many casualties. Many officers were killed.

The last entry in the diary.

Saturday 3 October 1914 Bought Robert a present, read to Lydia

They only had one more day together. The next communication from Lachlan is dated 7 October. Lachlan was in charge of a draft of 350 men and 4 officers. On 7 October they left Aberdeen at 4.30 am going to Southampton. They got breakfast at Carlisle at 11 am. The meal before that was at 3 am. They must have been hungry. He wrote cheerfully,

About 9 p.m. Basingstoke. It is a tedious journey and one fair damsel gave me a box of matches. I found some blankets on an empty bed and slept for three hours and incidentally was annexed by two fleas. One I caught in the train, the other I viewed but it escaped. I hope you did all you wanted to and got home safely and found all well. I expect we shall spend 24 hours at a rest camp before going up country. I will write before leaving the ship. Good Bye, Dear Angel, be brave and do not fret about me, and be careful of yourself, and don't get too tired. Give the children a hug from their unnatural parent. I shall see a lot of change in them I expect when I get back, but lets hope they won't have time to quite alter. God bless you and them and be with us, and bring us through all dangers and difficulties to a happy reunion."

Saying "Good Bye" in war time is heart rending. For Lachlan and Lydia just his going to nearby Aberdeen for a while would have been bad enough, but later when he was to go overseas for an unknown length of time, as I remember from my own experience, it was so much worse. There is so much to say and so little time to say it. Beyond saying how much you love each other and talking about the children, conversation dries up. A sort of helplessness comes over you, with the fear that you may never see each other again. If the stiff upper lip attitude is adopted "don't worry, see you soon, all will be well" etc., that's just as bad because it cannot and does not ring true.

They arrived at Southampton early amidst chaos. The men were to be kitted out with greatcoats. There were none left so, they got flimsy mackintoshes instead. There were 2000 men aboard the ship from 20 different units. There was great confusion. He writes

8 October 9 p.m. 1914. To Lydia. At sea.

Luckily we have had a perfect trip, quite calm and warm. I have found a berth in a second class cabin. We are bound for St Nazaire and have no idea what will happen tomorrow. I believe we get in at noon. I have not seen hot water since I left. I am sending home my sword and spare kilt, as the former is an impediment and the latter has small prospects of ever being seen again. It is quite a relief not seeing a daily paper. There are a lot of rumours about the fall of Antwerp. I have had little sleep since I left and am very weary so am off to bed. I hope you are well, good bye, old girl. Keep your pecker up.

Lots and Lots of Love from Lachlan.

1914. AT WAR AGAIN.

11 October 1914. Sunday. Camp St Nazaire

Dearest One,

I have scarcely had a moment to do anything since landing. We got ashore at 11 am and marched to this camp. There are thousands of troops waiting until wanted. It is an awfully pretty place if only we had time to go about it. We found no accommodation and it was very hard to get anything to eat. All our rations were left on board the ship, which was stupid. This is a most wonderful climate. We have been most amazingly lucky so far. I would like a few more days here to get things straight. I am worried by countless returns, rolls and indents and papers of all sorts. Always trying to get things which you can't have. It is a never ending rush and complete uncertainty, just like Aberdeen. Good Bye Darling, I hope you are well and will have a comfy journey over. Do be careful so as to be fit when I return, tho I cannot yet fix a date. Give my love to the children and tell Robert I have not seen the enemy yet. Also to everybody else at home you may see. Ever your most affectionate, Lachlan

The Regiment had been involved in the retreat from Mons and had suffered many casualties. It was occupying a position between Bethune and La Bassée.

16 October 1914. To Lydia .Camp St. Nazaire.

Darling, I brought up nearly 1500 officers and men from St Nazaire, and had a beastly time. Lots were getting drink from the populace and lived in cattle trucks. They got fed at irregular intervals, as we never knew when or how long we would stop. Of course we crawled and we lost several stragglers. A big lot of Irishmen were troublesome and ill disciplined. By all officers doing policeman and putting out guards at all stations to watch exits and keep people from bringing wine etc., we did better than some trains. We got straight up to the regiment and found them having a bad time in which we have shared for two days. We seldom sleep or wash and hardly ever see our kits and get frightfully tired. People are wonderfully cheerful and the men as jolly as any thing. I have a company of my Aberdeen draft and the same officers as I brought out. We went straight up to the fighting just in time for some very heavy night shooting. I lost my cap comforter in the excitement, but it turned up covered in mud. Since then we have had a fairly important little fight in which my lads led an advance by striking a blind ditch, worked in quite close near to the enemy. We had a lively day and were unsupported but had good cover. We held them off until reinforcements and more ammunition arrived. The Germans got more than they liked. We had a nasty time under shrapnel fire and were fired on by our own side due to faulty intelligence. The gun fire was tremendous and set several houses occupied by the enemy on fire. Towards dark they cleared out and we occupied the position without opposition. The Brigadier and the Colonel were delighted with us and said we did grand work so we are very bucked. We only lost three slightly wounded. I did not sleep until 4 am as we were on outpost. At 5 am, after one hours sleep in a cow byre with straw instead of a great coat I was up again. Last night I had two hours dozing in a wet hole. I was very tired. We are having a rest today and are billeted in an abandoned farm. We have plenty to eat and a wash. It is sad to see the crowds of homeless people. Every house and farm damaged by shell fire and looted. Everything turned inside out and in the devil of a mess, abandoned in panic and terror. The havoc and destruction of life is appalling.

17 October. On the march. I was too lazy to finish. Thanks for yours, just received. Glad all well. Please send me a cap comforter in one letter. I have lost my woollen gloves. Please send me a pair and a box of 25 cigars. Love to all. I am very fit. A padre is posting this. Glad all is well. Ever your loving husband, Lachlan.

18 October 1914. Field Post Card to Lydia

Am very well and command a company of Special Reserve who are doing A1. There has been much fighting of late and we have had our share too, much trying work and often scarcely any sleep, Nights are very cold. We are billeted in farms where possible and straw is plentiful. The people are kind but many are homeless and the destruction is dreadful. Much caused by gunfire and much wanton damage on part of the Germans. We seldom see our valises and the dirt is beastly, after wet trenches and lying on the ground. There has been a good deal of rain and I never knew such greasy and sticky mud. Trying to cross fallow ground under fire with a lot to carry is exhausting work. Natural cover is often plentiful, to which I attribute the small losses of my Coy, incurred a few days back in our first real engagement. The battalion has suffered a lot but we continue to advance and get fed, except in the trenches and can burrow like rabbits. Give my love to all. I will write again. Letters are very welcome here. People are kind but nearly all are homeless.

19 October 1914. To Lydia.In the front line

All goes well . We have had 3 pretty quiet days in reserve in billets, sudden calls always to be expected. Artillery is usually to be heard , often very heavy. We have spent the night in a huge farm and its cottages. The Germans had only just gone and have taken everything eatable and otherwise. An old peasant and his wife did compulsory host to us. They were alarmed at first, but soon got alright and made us quite comfortable. They produced some home made bread and even beer. I actually slept in a bed. It is a fine day and we have been hanging about listening to the guns and usually pretty busy. There are masses of returns and things to be made out and organisation of all sorts and we have cleaned up a bit. We are hoping to continue our advance but can't yet. We get no news, you get it all instead. Higgins (batman) is quite at home cooking etc., trying to understand and talk French with our voluble dame. She has three grandchildren."

20 October 1914. To Lydia. Somewhere in France.

Darling One, Thank you for your two letters. I hope you are all safely over and feel quite well and that the great event will pass off easily and successfully. We have been sitting still for a while as the battle rages on all sides. We had some shells surprise us on Sunday in our billet, which was most disconcerting. Two poor lads of my company were done for but by great good luck nothing else was damaged. We all cleared out to a field nearby, out of the line of fire. The church had a shell or two into it and more all round. A cottage and the curé's kitchen wrecked. The old people and three small children luckily escaped, but next morning, on our advice, they took themselves to relations in a safer place. We are a bit too near the fight as shells are nasty visitors. We spend a lot of time in the open, my men now burrow like rabbits right into the ground and survive. We manage to live pretty well. A lot of most welcome gifts for the troops have been distributed. We got our valises up and got some clean clothes out of them. We are expecting to move momentarily, and shall have our turn for the next few days. Darling I also pray God will be with us, and bring you and me together in his good time. I like to think of you as my Guardian Angel. Please send me another pair of woollen gloves, mine are lost. At present I have plenty of things and am very fit and the men are quite cheerful. We have no news of what is going on in our immediate neighbourhood, but the noise is tremendous. Ever, my angel, your own husband, Lachlan.

That was the last letter he was to write.

RENDEZVOUS

by Alan Seeger

I have a rendezvous with Death,
At some disputed barricade,
It may be he shall take my hand
And lead me into his dark land
And close my eyes and quench my breath.
It may be I shall pass him still.
I have a rendez vous with Death
On some scarred slope of battered hill.

God knows 'twere better to be deep
pillowed in silk and scented down,
Where love throbs out in blissful sleep,
Pulse to pulse, and breath to breath,
Where hushed awakenings are dear.
But I've a rendezvous with Death
At midnight in some flaming town,
When Spring trips North and again this year.
And I to my pledged word am true,
I shall not fail that rendezvous.

)NDAY, NOVEMBER 2, 1914.

THE ROLL OF HONOUR.

FURTHER HEAVY LISTS OF CASUALTIES.

General Headquarters, October 26th :—

Killed.

AINSLIE, Lieut. D. A. L., Devonshire Regt.
ANTROBUS, Lieut. E.; COLBY, Major L. R. V.; SOMERSET, 2nd Lieut. N. A. H.; WALTER, 2nd Lieut. S., Grenadier Guards.
BRANSBURY, Lieut. V. D. B., Lincolnshire Regt.
COWAN, Lieut. C. J. A., Royal Scots Regt.
DEANE, 2nd Lieut. D., Royal Warwickshire Regt.
DENNIS, Lieut. J. O. C.; NIXON, Lieut. G. F.; FOLLAND, Lieut. G. B., R.F.A.
DUNLOP, Capt. J. S. S., South Staffordshire Regt.
GORDON DUFF, Capt. L., Gordon Highlanders.
HOPE JOHNSTONE, Lieut. W. G. T.; WALLER, Capt. Sir F. E., Bt., Royal Fusiliers.
KELLY, Capt. H. H.; SMEATHAM, Lieut. J. M., R.E.
SMITH, 2nd Lieut. C. S., Dorsetshire Regt.
WILLIS, 2nd Lieut. R., York and Lancaster Regt.
WRIGHT, 2nd Lieut. G. D. C., Bedfordshire Regt.

28 October . OHMS, War Office, London. To: Mrs Gordon Duff, Dunsland, Glanmire, Co Cork

Deeply regret to announce Lachlan reported killed on 24th. Tennant.

28 October . OHMS, War Office, London.. To: Mrs Gordon Duff, Dunsland, Glanmire, Co Cork

Deeply regret to inform you that Capt. L Gordon Duff, Gordon Highlanders was killed in action 24 October. No further details received. Lord Kitchener expresses his sympathy. Secretary War Office.

30 October. Buckingham Palace.To: Mrs Gordon Duff, Dunsland, Glanmire, Co Cork.

The King and Queen deeply regret the loss you and the Army have sustained by the death of your husband in the service of his country. Their Majesties truly sympathise with you in your sorrow. Private Secretary

Col Greenhill Gardyne, Lachlan's commanding officer, gave the main facts of his death.

On 24 October about dark, a German attack on our line had been brought to a standstill. We believed it was over. I sent Lachlan to make contact with the Regiment on our left. On his return to his Coy, which was in reserve, not long after dark, there was a sudden attack on our centre. The enemy had charged and broken the line. Being in reserve Lachlan's Coy counter-charged ending up in a farm yard full of hay stacks and Germans. Lachlan shouted at them to put up their hands and surrender which they refused to do. Somehow or other, according to eye witnesses the battle moved to a nearby wood in which both sides got mixed up, trying to reorganise. Lachlan was next seen talking to a German officer who was ordering him to surrender which he refused to do. The German suddenly drew his revolver and shot Lachlan dead. One of Lachlan's sergeants killed the German immediately".

Next morning the reserve Battalion came up and reoccupied the trenches. Lying there, amongst 40 to 50 bodies of British and German soldiers was Lachlan. He was shot in the chest facing the enemy. Dead. He was buried next day in an orchard in the small village of Fauguissant on the road to Levantie. Some of his soldiers planted snowdrop bulbs on the grave. They were very upset at his death. They loved him because he cared for them. He was a good leader.

After the war was over Lachlan was reinterred in the Rue du Bois military cemetery between Bethune and Fleubaix, where he now lies. It is a small cemetery, with only about 200 people in it. They had come from all over the British Empire to fight for their mother land. But not all were British. Three graves which faced the rest were occupied by Bavarians. There is a farm nearby and a garage. Inside the cemetery there is peace and much sadness. One cannot fail to be moved. On each headstone is carved the man's name, Regimental badge and a quotation from the bible. My mother, Lydia was a very brave woman. She was seven months pregnant when she received the official telegram announcing Lachlan's death. She was a person who did not show her emotions but her strongly held Christian beliefs will have been a great support to her in this terrible situation. I was born six weeks later. She returned to Park in early 1915 and started to run the estate. Doing this research I have learnt a lot about her which I never knew and which has increased my admiration and respect for her. She was a great lady.

There were many letters of condolence from which I have selected some. The first is from Kenneth Dingwall, Lachlan's company commander from South Africa days.

6 November 1914. Kenneth Dingwall to Lydia.

Dear Mrs Duff, I wrote to your father-in-law, but lest you should think me remiss, the reason I did not write to you before was that feeling the loss so much myself, I hardly dared to think what it must be to you. Cubby was one of the most loveable characters I have ever met. His few weaknesses were of the nature of virtues, such as rather too great a disregard of his own personal safety, a boyishness in regarding risks light-heartedly. They only endeared him the more to those who knew him. Occasionally he would exhibit a canniness and caution about some triviality, in marked contrast to the risks which gave anxiety to friends, lest accidents should befall him. I hope your children may be a comfort to you and as they grow up you may see in them much to cherish which will remind you of the mate who sought you out. At least his has been a happy, useful life, unclouded by anything which could sully it. In my presence I never heard him utter a word his wife or mother could not have listened to complacently. Even when things went wrong, I never once recollect his rendering the feeling of hurt or injustice in more than regret, that he had not been able to please. Men seldom speak their feelings towards each other. I esteemed Cubby sufficiently to wish that I was more like him. I loved him sufficiently, not to resent that he showed me so often my own imperfections. Of this he was quite unconscious. I am glad, at least, that I had the wit to recognise the goodness in him and to seek to bring it out while the character was still in the mould.

With great sympathy, from Kenneth Dingwall.

The second letter is from one of the soldiers who fought with him.

15 January 1915.To. Mrs Captain Duff .From No 1297 Private A.Collier, 1st Gordons, 60 Baker Street, Aberdeen.

.

Dear Madam,

I have just heard that you have been wanting information regarding your husbands death. I left Aberdeen and went straight to the front under your husband and was proud to be under such a hero for there was one night when we were attacked and Captain Duff gave the order to fix bayonets and charge and many brave lives were lost that night but Captain Duff fell gallantly leading his company and we buried him in the morning. He was shot in two places in the chest and through the back but we were all very sad for we lost 50 that fateful night. I can't say too much. I am only telling you what I saw myself and was proud that I fought under such an officer. I have been invalided home but am going back to the front on the 11th. I am sorry I can't give you any more information for this is a terrible war and we have to give our lives for our king and country.Yours Respectfully.Private A. Collier.

23 November 1914. (The day I was born). Rev Andrew Currie to Lydia.

Dear Mrs Duff,

How glad we were to have the telegram today. We do rejoice with you in this your great joy. We hope your son will be spared to be an ever new comfort to you, a constant reminder of him whom we all mourn. We hope you are feeling well, and that we shall hear from yourself soon. Everybody here will share in your joy and wish you every happiness in your children, and them in you. With our warmest regards and heartiest good wishes. I am, Yours Truly, Andrew Currie.

The author, born on 23 November 1914
with his aunt, Joan Lindsay.

APPENDIX

Officers who Served with Lt. L. Gordon-Duff in South Africa

1. Embarked at Liverpool in S. S. Cheshire. November 1899

Lt. Colonels

G. Downman - Commanding Officer - killed at the Battle of Modder River - 13 November 1899.
Forbes Macbean.

Majors

W. Campbell.
H. Carlaw - Quartermaster.

Captains

E. Towse - V.C. at Hout Nek. Blinded in both eyes. 30 April 1900.
F. W. Kerr.
Greenhill Gardyne.
R. A. N. Tytler.
E. R. Macnab.
A. S. Wingate. Killed at Modder River - 12 December 1899.
K. Dingwall. Lachlan's Company Commander.
G. S. Crauford.
W. E. Gordon. Adjutant.

Lieutenants

D. R. Younger. Killed Krugersdorp - 11 July 1900.
J. D. Dalrymple-Hay. Died of disease - 26 May 1900.
J. Ingleby.
J. M. Ogston.
J. Maclaren.
J. R. White.

2nd Lieutenants

J. Campbell. Killed Modder River - 12 December 1899.
C. R. Lumsden.
L. Gordon-Duff.
J. R. Lockley.
A. Cameron. Killed - 6 June 1901.
W. B. Mitford.
S. V. B. Clowes. Killed - 30 January 1901.

2. Arrived Later. April 1900.

Lt. Col. H. H. Burney.

<u>Captains</u>

F. H. Neish.
G. S. Allan.
J. W. Buchanan (Volunteer)
A. P. Murray.
H. C. Meyrick. Killed - 29 May 1900.

<u>Lieutenants</u>

D. Alexander.
F. R. Swarder.

<u>RAMC</u>

Captain Woodside.

Bibliography

Abdy & Gere.	The Souls. Sidgwick & Jackson 1984
Belfield. Enersley	The Boer War. Leo Cooper 1993
Bennett. Daphne	Margot. Gollancz Arena 1986
Blow. Simon	Broken Blood. Faber & Faber 1987
Bulloch. M. A.	The House Of Gordon. 3 Vols. Aberdeen 1903
Churchill. Winston	The Boer War. Mandarin 1990
Doyle. Conan	The Great Boer War. 1900-2.
Fuller. J. F. C.	The Last of the 'Gentleman's Wars'. 1937
Gardyne. Greenhil l	The Life of a Regiment. Leo Cooper 1972
Kruger. Rayne	Goodbye Dolly Gray. Pan Books 1983
Lambert. Angela	Unquiet Souls. Macmillan 1984
Pakenham. Thomas	The Boer War. Weidenfeld & Nicholson 1979
Smith. Dorrien. H.	Memories of 48 Years Service. 1925
Taylor. A & H.	The Book of the Duffs. 2 vols. Constable 1914
Tennant. H. J.	Sir Charles Tennant.
Wavell. A. P.	Other Men's Flowers. Cape 1958
Wilson. H. W.	With the Flag to Pretoria. 2 vols., After Pretoria. 2 vols.

Index

Page numbers in italics denote illustrations.

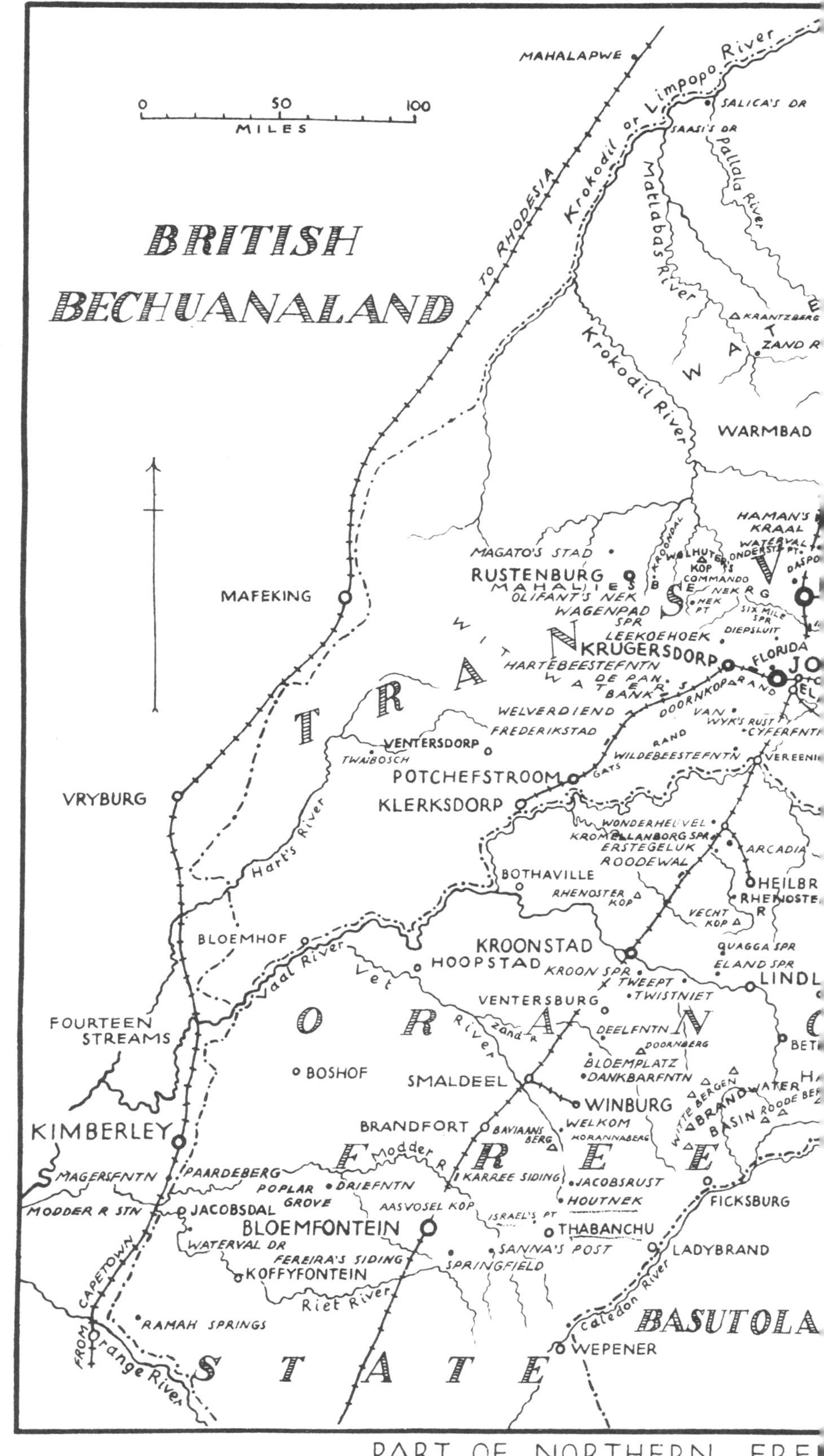

PART OF NORTHERN FRE